AF621389

THE EMOTIONAL BRAIN AND THE GUILTY MIND

This book seeks to reframe the normative narrative of the 'culpable person' in American criminal law through a more humanising lens. It embraces such a reframed narrative to revise the criteria of the current voluntarist architecture of culpability and to advance a paradigm of punishment that positions social rehabilitation as its core principle.

The book constructs this narrative by considering behavioural and neuroscientific insights into the functions of emotions, and socio-environmental factors within moral behaviour in social settings. Hence, it suggests culpability notions that reflect a more contextualised view of human conduct, and argues that such revised notions are better suited to the principle of personal guilt. Furthermore, it suggests a model of 'punishment' that values the dynamic power of change of individuals, and acknowledges the importance of social relationships and positive environments to foster patterns of social (re) integration.

Ultimately, this book argues that the potential adoption of the proposed models of culpability and punishment, which view people through a more comprehensive lens, may be a key factor for turning criminal justice into a less punitive, more inclusionary and non-stigmatising system.

The Emotional Brain and the Guilty Mind

Novel Paradigms of Culpability and Punishment

Federica Coppola

•HART•

OXFORD • LONDON • NEW YORK • NEW DELHI • SYDNEY

HART PUBLISHING

Bloomsbury Publishing Plc

Kemp House, Chawley Park, Cumnor Hill, Oxford, OX2 9PH, UK

1385 Broadway, New York, NY 10018, USA

29 Earlsfort Terrace, Dublin 2, Ireland

HART PUBLISHING, the Hart/Stag logo, BLOOMSBURY and the Diana logo are trademarks of Bloomsbury Publishing Plc

First published in Great Britain 2021

Copyright © Federica Coppola, 2021

Federica Coppola has asserted her right under the Copyright, Designs and Patents Act 1988 to be identified as Author of this work.

All rights reserved. No part of this publication may be reproduced or transmitted in any form or by any means, electronic or mechanical, including photocopying, recording, or any information storage or retrieval system, without prior permission in writing from the publishers.

While every care has been taken to ensure the accuracy of this work, no responsibility for loss or damage occasioned to any person acting or refraining from action as a result of any statement in it can be accepted by the authors, editors or publishers.

All UK Government legislation and other public sector information used in the work is Crown Copyright ©. All House of Lords and House of Commons information used in the work is Parliamentary Copyright ©. This information is reused under the terms of the Open Government Licence v3.0 (http://www.nationalarchives.gov.uk/doc/open-government-licence/version/3) except where otherwise stated.

All Eur-lex material used in the work is © European Union, http://eur-lex.europa.eu/, 1998–2021.

A catalogue record for this book is available from the British Library.

Library of Congress Cataloging-in-Publication data

Names: Coppola, Federica, author.

Title: The emotional brain and the guilty mind : novel paradigms of culpability and punishment / Federica Coppola.

Description: Oxford, UK ; New York, NY : Hart Publishing, an imprint of Bloomsbury Publishing, 2021. | Includes bibliographical references and index.

Identifiers: LCCN 2020043776 (print) | LCCN 2020043777 (ebook) | ISBN 9781509934294 (hardback) | ISBN 9781509944569 (paperback) | ISBN 9781509934317 (epdf) | ISBN 9781509934300 (Epub)

Subjects: LCSH: Guilt (Law) | Punishment. | Criminal liability. | Criminal law. | Emotions—Psychological aspects.

Classification: LCC K5065 .C67 2020 (print) | LCC K5065 (ebook) | DDC 345/.04—dc23

LC record available at https://lccn.loc.gov/2020043776

LC ebook record available at https://lccn.loc.gov/2020043777

ISBN: HB: 978-1-50993-429-4
ePDF: 978-1-50993-431-7
ePub: 978-1-50993-430-0

Typeset by Compuscript Ltd, Shannon

To find out more about our authors and books visit www.hartpublishing.co.uk. Here you will find extracts, author information, details of forthcoming events and the option to sign up for our newsletters.

[L]aws and institutions must go hand in hand with the progress of the human mind. As that becomes more developed, more enlightened, as new discoveries are made, new truths disclosed, and manners and opinions change with the change of circumstances, institutions must advance also, and keep pace with the times.

Thomas Jefferson
12 July 1816

ACKNOWLEDGEMENTS

This book is the result of many years of hard work, intense study and passionate research in criminal law and justice, including the connections of these legal fields with brain and behavioural sciences. Over the years, I have enriched my background, developed new ideas, drawn nuances, and changed my mind. I have read a lot; I have studied a lot. I have interacted and worked with a broad range of interdisciplinary scholars, including scientists, philosophers, historians, and students and researchers who have been impacted by the criminal justice system. I have listened to their perspectives, trying to grasp their different standpoints on common themes, and sought to make the best out of those conversations to shape and refine my arguments.

Many people, either knowingly or unknowingly, have contributed to this book. I thank each of them, and in particular:

I thank Dennis Patterson, to whom I owe my entrance in academia, for having encouraged me to write this book.

I thank my mentors at Columbia University: Jeffrey Fagan, for pushing me to critically think about my arguments from different perspectives; Paul Appelbaum, for always finding the right answer to my many questions; Geraldine Downey, for opening my eyes on the real potential of my work.

I thank the Presidential Scholars in Society and Neuroscience programme at Columbia University for giving me a unique opportunity to continue my research in criminal law, justice, and neuroscience.

I thank my friends and colleagues of the Social Relations Lab and the Center for Justice at Columbia University for welcoming me since the beginning and for having me become a part of an incredible project. I notably thank them for their critical support and feedback on my work, which has helped me see beyond my 'normative' horizons and feel that I was doing the right thing. But above all, I want to thank them for teaching me the fundamental lesson that a new life is always possible.

TABLE OF CONTENTS

TABLE OF CASES

US Case Law

UK Case Law

ECtHR Case Law

TABLE OF STATUTES

US Federal Statutes and Acts

US State Statutes

Other Sources

International Documents

Foreign Laws

Prologue

On 18 October 2019, I walked to Edgecombe Facility in Manhattan for the first time to teach my first class of the Inside Criminal Justice[1] course. I had just finished a lecture to some university faculty members. In that lecture, I talked about topics I had worked on for a while, such as the importance of emotions in criminal law, the potential of restorative justice, and the value of social relationships in punishment. The lecture left me with a profound feeling of self-doubt. The sceptical expressions of some participants when I was illustrating those concepts and ideas were sculpted in my mind. It was not the first time that I had been confronted with some scepticism regarding my views. Once I was even told, 'Criminal law is meant to punish criminals, not to treat them nicely!'

I was walking to Edgecombe with these thoughts on my mind, unsure of what to expect over the next two hours. The course I was about to start involved the participation of assistant district attorneys (ADAs) and incarcerated women, who would sit together around the table every Tuesday for six weeks to dialogue and confront each other on topics related to criminal justice, restorative justice, and social psychology. The immediate aim of the course was to have the students explore these themes, sharing their perspectives based on their experience, and to work together on policy proposals to suggest changes to the criminal justice system. The ultimate aim of the course, as I understood it, was to have the two groups confront each other, listen to each other, learn from each other, and understand each other's perspective. In short, to humanise each other. Over the past years, I have often heard the words 'humanisation' and 'dehumanisation'. But what does humanising really mean? What does humanisation entail in practice? Could the criminal law be ever meant to be humane? Would it be fairer? If there is so much reluctance to even imagine a more humane law and justice system, is it not the case that the criminal law is simply not designed for this? I walked up the street blocks asking myself these very questions.

When I arrived at Edgecombe and managed to get inside, I found a class of smiling women with their notebooks open on the desks. I do not think I ever felt so comfortable entering a new class and meeting new students. While waiting for

[1] *Inside Criminal Justice* is a prison education programme launched by the Director of the Institute for Innovation in Prosecution at John Jay College of Criminal Justice, Lucy Lang, and the Director of the Center for Justice at Columbia University, Professor Geraldine Downey. I thank Luis Morales and Aimee Baker for sharing with me this wonderful teaching experience. For an intense glimpse of the programme, see J Daniels, *What Prosecutors and Incarcerated People Can Learn from Each Other*, TED Talk, available at www.youtube.com/watch?v=jATCr-gQvPA.

the group of ADAs students – who were stuck in the subway traffic during a typical rush hour in New York – I introduced the course to the Edgecombe students and began an informal discussion about criminal justice to start grasping their standpoints. To stimulate the discussion, I asked the students to think about key words that were suggestive of the main gaps of the justice system based on their views. After a (long) couple of minutes of silence, M timidly raised her hand and said: Empathy.

In less than a second, I forgot about the earlier lecture and remembered again why I was there.

When the ADAs students arrived, what happened next was striking. I expected long moments of silence and embarrassment that I would try to interrupt somehow, but it did not happen. The class came together with great enthusiasm, curious to meet each other and learn more about one another and about the course.

During the following weeks, the lessons covered many justice-related topics, some of which invited difficult class discussions. I heard many stories, often containing traumas, injustices, missed opportunities, and lacked opportunities, but filled with a strong willingness to get life back on track and do better. In one class after another, I was very impressed to see the growing mutual sensitivity between the two groups, an increased willingness to understand, mutual support to change things, and strong respect. I remember being full of amazement as I observed the classes. The two groups left their 'social roles' outside the classroom and became one large and cohesive group of classmates who shared their ideas, their stories, their emotions.

At the end of each class, on my way home, my mind was struck by always the same thoughts and questions: judges, prosecutors, and even legal scholars are not trained to gather knowledge about how trauma impacts people's lives and behaviour; they are not supposed to learn about the importance of social relationships; they are not supposed to learn about the effect of incarceration on the life of an individual; they are not supposed to place an individual's actions in context; they are not trained to care as to why people break the law. It is well known that criminal law operates through strategies of depersonalisation: it functions to depersonalise legal controversies for the decisionmaker, to depersonalise procedures, to depersonalise legal actors. Notably, the human dimension of justice-involved people is ignored and largely disregarded in legal inquiry. Instead, facts matter. What a person was thinking at the time of the crime matters. Whether he or she could control his or her impulses matters. Whether he or she acted premeditatively matters. Punishment, control and separation matter.

Yet this principled commitment to rigorous parameters of individual responsibility and punishment curbs when legal actors confront the vast majority of justice-involved people. When the 'law-abiding' public encounter people impacted by criminal justice and realise that they look or sound like themselves or tell their stories with echoes in the listeners' lives, perspectives on responsibility and punishment begin to shift. Although the idea of holding someone accountable for a crime or that crime entails a state response is not questioned, perspectives shift regarding the criteria for ascribing criminal responsibility as well as the idea of punishment itself. Most notably, perspectives shift as regards the fairness of inflicting severe and exclusionary penalties, which too often entail (unintended yet foreseeable) collateral consequences in terms of stigma, inequality and discrimination.

What if, then, the criminal law itself was more humane to the people who do wrong without abdicating its foundational functions of behavioural guidance and protection of the public? How would the law adjudicate these people? How would legal actors behave if they were confronted with a criminal law that, other than being meant to respond to crime, also valued people and their social identities, their past, their future? What opportunities could justice-involved people such as my Edgecombe students have?

These are some of the questions that animate my research and have accompanied the writing of this book.

This book is premised on the assumption that Anglo-American criminal law relies upon a rationalist and individualist view of the culpable person. Central to dominant penal discourse is the idea of the individual as a rational and autonomous agent who consciously chooses to engage in offending behaviour based on instrumental practical reasoning about which action he or she can or cannot perform in light of normative parameters of right and wrong. This idea lies at the core of culpability ascriptions, and is also foundational to ideas of punishment. In fact, the moralistic narrative that cuts across the justifications for punishment aligns with the idea of the individual as a rational and autonomous being: the state inflicts harm and deprivation upon and excludes a person who chose to do wrong because he or she deserves it as well as because, through such harm, deprivation, and exclusion, this person will understand the negative consequences of his or her misbehaviour and refrain from re-offending in the future.

In my and other scholars' view, this rationalist and individualist model of the criminal law's person, coupled with the language of blame and punishment, has contributed to generating a pejorative image of justice-involved people and fuelled the maintenance of punitive attitudes to crime. In a society obsessed with fear of crime, the rhetoric of individual choice, blame and retribution, and control has implicitly supported public and political urges for harsher penalties for a wide range of criminal offences. The narrative of individual responsibility and (harsh) punishment of people who do wrong for the harm inflicted to victims and society is sculpted in the collective imagery. The outcome of such a narrative has been a system that decontextualises people and their actions, turns a blind eye to the profound social injustice that is inextricably bound to criminal offending, hides itself behind rhetorical concepts of neutrality, equality, and dignity, and redistributes crime rather than solving it. It is a system that has 'given up on rehabilitation, education, and services for the imprisoned because providing assistance to the incarcerated is apparently too kind and compassionate'.[2] It is a system that has

[2] B Stevenson, *Just Mercy: A Story of Justice and Redemption* (New York, Spiegel & Grau, 2015) 15.

'institutionalized policies that reduce people to their worst acts and permanently label 'criminal', 'murderer', 'rapist' … 'felon' – identities that cannot change regardless of the circumstances of their crimes or any improvements they might make in their lives'.[3]

Against this backdrop, this book seeks to reframe the normative narrative of the 'culpable person' in American criminal law through a more humanising lens. It embraces such a reframed narrative to revise the criteria of the current architecture of culpability and advance a paradigm of punishment that positions social rehabilitation as its core principle. The book constructs this narrative by considering behavioural and neuroscientific insights into the functions of emotions, and socio-environmental factors within moral behaviour in social settings.

This book does not seek to dismiss or reject the foundations of criminal law with empirical knowledge. Rather, it uses empirical knowledge to suggest culpability notions that reflect a more contextualised view of human conduct, and argues that such revised notions are better suited to the principle of personal guilt. Furthermore, it suggests a model of 'punishment' that values the dynamic power of change of individuals, and acknowledges the importance of social relationships and positive environments to foster patterns of social (re)integration. Ultimately, this book argues that the potential adoption of the proposed models of culpability and punishment, which view people through a more comprehensive lens, may be a key factor for turning criminal justice into a less punitive, more inclusionary, and non-stigmatising system.

Before I introduce the reader to an overview of the structure and contents of this book, some preliminary caveats are worth making. This book does not intend to propose another legal-philosophical theory of criminal law nor to advance philosophically appealing accounts of culpability and punishment. Although legal-philosophical accounts of culpability and punishment represent an important and integral part of my analysis, this book does not seek to meet standards of academic legal philosophy in the rigour of competing argumentation and consideration of rival perspectives. This book is intended for criminal law scholars, legal professionals as well as for a general audience of those interested in the connection between criminal law, (neuro)science and justice. The narrative hereby proposed invites the readers to rethink critically fundamental pillars of criminal law by viewing the people who are involved in the criminal justice system through a more humanising lens.

Furthermore, this book does not analyse every single corollary that may follow through the potential implementation of such re-thought paradigms of culpability and punishment, as space does not allow me to do it. The analysis of the implications of revised models of culpability and punishment I propose is limited to selected doctrines and selected areas of criminal justice. I am well aware that other issues deserve to be analysed, and that several aspects of my arguments may need

[3] Ibid.

further refinement. I hope I will be able to address in future works what my present argument omits.

A final caveat on terminology: criminal law is about *people*, and language creates perceptions and images. Thus, throughout the book I deliberately refer to 'culpable person/agent', 'justice-involved people', 'people facing conviction', 'people facing punishment', 'people in prison', 'incarcerated people', 'people who are incarcerated', and 'people impacted by criminal justice'. Unless I need to report the language of one of my sources, I eschew clinical and moralistic terms such as 'offender', 'criminal', 'inmate', and 'prisoner' – which are regrettably still frequent in legal literature. These labels are being increasingly stigmatised as dehumanising. I believe that criminal law scholarship should reconsider its language too, in view of its influence on legal policy and, indirectly, public opinion.

Federica Coppola
New York City, 3 May 2020

Overview of the Book

The book contains six chapters. The chapters include three levels of analysis: descriptive, empirical, and normative. The descriptive section comprises the first three chapters and details dominant paradigms of culpability and punishment from theoretical, doctrinal, statutory, historical, and jurisprudential angles. The empirical section comprises chapter four and consists of a review of the wide body of behavioural and neuroscientific knowledge about the role of emotions and socio-environmental factors within moral and social behaviour. The normative section comprises chapters five and six. Both chapters advance normative proposals to revise the paradigms of culpability and punishment in view of the analysed empirical knowledge.

Chapter one traces the paradigm of the 'culpable person' through a normative analysis of criminal culpability. The chapter begins with an analysis of the concepts of rationality and autonomy *quo* fundamental features of the 'culpable person'. It then moves into canvassing the theory of voluntarism (also called as choice/capacity/opportunity theory) as the major theory of culpability in legal scholarship, and how voluntarism is reflected in culpability-related doctrines such as *mens rea*, legal insanity, and duress, including their statutory definitions and jurisprudential interpretations. The chapter then discusses the weight of emotions and social factors within the voluntarist model of culpability, and in legal doctrine accordingly, as well as how these factors are considered at sentencing. The central claim that emerges from this chapter is that the dominant model of culpability, in all these dimensions, largely builds on a rationalist view of personhood and human agency, one that is strongly embedded in the cognitive capacities of the individual and largely overlooks the participation of emotions in and the influence of contextual factors on human choice and behaviour.

Chapter two canvasses how the narrative of the culpable person has shifted through different understandings of human behaviour, crime, and punishment. The approach followed in this chapter is primarily historical, and it contextualises the evolution of culpability and punishment, starting from Enlightenment philosophy and moving to the affirmation of voluntarism and retribution as the most supported theories of culpability and punishment within a variety of contexts, including statutes, legal and penal policy, and courts. The analysis continues with a description of the backlashes of the voluntarist rhetoric of retribution and its tenets on real-life criminal justice. It notably highlights that the rationalist and individualist rhetoric of this scholarship has yielded the (probably unintended) consequence of fuelling the increasingly punitive nature of the justice system by offering a moral cover for legitimising harsh, exclusionary and stigmatising punitive practices.

Chapter three and chapter four set the stage for the normative arguments I put forward in chapters five and six. Chapter three reports scholarly criticisms of the rationalist and individualist model of the criminal law's person that underpins the dominant paradigms of culpability and punishment. The analysis highlights four main critiques: the first critique focuses on the criminal law's mistaken understanding of emotions as mere disturbing factors of thought and behaviour that the individual is required to control thanks to his or her reasoning and control powers. The second critique concerns the exclusion of social factors from legal inquiries of responsibility and the substantial disregard of such factors at sentencing. Part of this critique even views the exclusion of social factors from legal inquiry as a political strategy to ignore the objective link between certain situations of social disadvantage and crime and redistribute crime to the most disadvantaged people. The third critique concerns the irrelevance of the capacity for change in punishment theories and determinations, which promotes a view of the culpable person as irredeemable. The fourth and final critique suggests that the rationalist language of choice, blame, and retribution generates a dehumanised image of the people who break the law. The central theme that links these critiques is that the normative depiction of the culpable person in rationalist and individualist terms is a factor that either incites or contributes to fuelling punitive instances.

Against this background, chapter four reviews the body of empirical knowledge emanating from social psychology, as well as social, moral and affective neuroscience, concerning the role that emotions and socio-environmental factors play within moral and social behaviour. The analysis highlights four key insights that contradict dominant views in criminal law and assume relevance for the purposes of the book: first, emotions are not disturbing factors for moral choices and behaviours, but are inescapable components of them both consciously and subconsciously. Notably, moral decisions and behaviour appear to be largely mediated by the experience and regulation of certain social/moral emotions – notably certain self-conscious or self-reflective emotions – as well as emotion-related faculties, including empathy. The second key insight is that the experience and regulation of emotions within moral decision-making and behaviour are largely determined by contextual factors, including the features of the current situation and, more broadly, the ongoing socio-environmental context of the individual. Regarding the latter factor, the analysis highlights that problematic socio-environmental factors, such as the chronic exposure to traumatising and adverse social experiences, may alter brain pathways that govern socio-emotional skills, with negative implications for prosocial behaviour. The third critical insight concerns the relationship between brain plasticity, emotions, and the social environment. The analysis highlights that the human brain has a unique ability to re-organise itself and to adapt to changing environments and behavioural interactions throughout life. In view of this ability of the brain, individuals can learn from new experiences, create memories, rewire their emotions and emotional reactions, and adjust their behaviour accordingly. Crucially, healthy environments and social connections, including meaningful social relationships, stable social bonds, social inclusion, and perceived belongingness, foster positive changes in the brain regions that support the emotional processes that are involved in morality and prosocial behaviour. Furthermore, social exclusion can either precipitate or aggravate problematic neurobiological patterns in the same brain regions, which has dramatic implications for psychological well-being, mental health, and prosociality.

Drawing connections between this body of empirical insights and the scholarly critiques illustrated in chapter three, chapters five and six are dedicated to proposing paradigms of culpability and punishment that (re)consider the importance of emotions and social factors in human (moral) agency and personhood.

Chapter five proposes changes within the articulation of the current voluntarist paradigm of culpability to requalify the normative relevance of emotions and social factors within its notions. To this aim, the chapter focuses on the revision of the current model of culpability, which is based on a holistic and situated view of human behaviour. The proposed normative model draws on David Brink and Dana Nelkin's conception of the architecture of culpability and expands it to give more prominence to emotional and social factors in its criteria. The chapter subsequently examines the potential implications that such a re-thought theoretical model of culpability can have for legal doctrines. This part of the analysis initially focuses on the potential revision of the criteria of legal insanity and then underscores the potential provision of a 'generic partial excuse' – following Stephen Morse's lead – the normative excusing condition of which lies in a person's non-culpable limited choice to do otherwise. In the final section, the chapter discusses the personal guilt principle to support the normative relevance of a culpability model that embraces a holistic and situated view of human behaviour.

Chapter six discusses punishment and proposes a paradigm shift. The chapter draws upon the body of empirical knowledge about brain plasticity, emotions, and the social environment to develop an argument championing the greater rationality, humanity, and efficacy of a model of punishment that espouses a dynamic view of the person and challenges wrongdoing through an empowerment and inclusionary approach aimed at encouraging self-change and ensuring social (re)integration. Considering that different (however similar) labels have been used to describe this approach in the literature, I refer to it as *social* rehabilitation. Drawing connections between (neuro)scientific knowledge, views in the literature, and domestic and international jurisprudence, the chapter advances a paradigm of punishment that positions social rehabilitation as its overarching principle. The chapter begins by tracing the penological aspects of social rehabilitation, including its features, its normative justification, and its relationship with retribution, incapacitation, and special deterrence. It continues with an analysis of the practical corollaries that may follow from the hypothetical implementation of the paradigm of punishment I propose. Because the implications of a social rehabilitation-oriented model of justice potentially involve most or all domains of criminal justice, the analysis is limited to selected criminal justice areas, including sentencing, mandatory life imprisonment without the possibility of parole, incarceration, and solitary confinement.

This chapter concludes the book. It is followed by a short epilogue with some remarks about the arguments developed in the book, including the indirect contribution of (neuro)science for humanising criminal law and justice.

1

The Rationalist Soul of Culpability: An Analysis of the Guilty Mind

I. Introduction

Criminal law is obsessed with the human mind. No doctrine, theory, or debate is immune to a minimal consideration of the psychology of the accused. Scholarly discussions, criminal trials, and lay conversations of crime always and inevitably revolve around questions such as the following: What was the defendant thinking at the time of the crime? Did the defendant suffer from a mental disorder? Did he or she act purposefully? Did he or she know what he or she was doing? Is it fair to punish this person considering his or her mental conditions? Has this person's mind changed after serving his or her sentence? The human mind – with its multiple facets, profound nuances, and articulated dynamics – is probably the characterising feature of the high complexity and timeless fascination of criminal law.

The most exalted expression of the connection between criminal law and the human mind is (criminal) culpability. The ancient maxim *actus no facit reum nisi mens rea*, which is commonly attributed to the seventeenth century jurist Edward Coke, states the fundamental principle that an act does not make a person guilty of a crime unless his or her mind is also guilty. Over the years, the word 'guilty' has come to encompass a twofold meaning: according to the first, a person is guilty when he or she has materially committed a given crime (ie, he or she is the material author of the offence); based on the second, a person is guilty when he or she has committed the crime in a given mental state (ie, he or she is the mental author of the offence). The latter meaning of guilt posits that no person should be punished unless he or she had some intent in carrying out the crime. Through such a dual meaning, guilt is assessed (and punishment is administered) when a person not only performed a wrongful act but also committed that act with a culpable mind.

The central importance of culpability within guilt assessments finds support in the fundamental notion that guilt is *personal*.[1]

[1] See eg *United States v Scales*, 367 U.S. 203, 224–5 (1959) ('In our jurisprudence guilt is personal, and when the imposition of punishment on a status or on conduct can only be justified by reference to the relationship of that status or conduct to other concededly criminal activity … that relationship must be sufficiently substantial to satisfy the concept of personal guilt in order to withstand attack under the Due Process Clause of the Fifth Amendment'); *United States v Dotterweich*, 320 U.S. 277,

The personality principle mandates that culpability must be attributed to the material perpetrator of a given wrongdoing; more broadly, it also requires an individual's actual mental participation in the commission of an offence.[2] In a slightly different formulation, a guilty act must belong to the mental domain of a person in such a way that it expresses his or her disregard for the interests of other individuals that are protected by the law. This personal guilt principle entails that culpability embraces certain mental features and states that an individual must possess and act upon in order to be susceptible to blame and punishment. It namely concerns attributing a normative significance to certain aspects of the human mind in virtue of which a person is expected to (or *ought* to) comply with the social and moral values that are enshrined in criminal law's dictates and, when he or she fails to do so, be held liable and punished.

From this perspective, culpability represents a normative paradigm of the human mind. It reflects the faculties that allow individuals to live together and, more generally, to comply with public rules and standards that preserve social life in a given community under threat of sanction. Yet which mental faculties are normatively presupposed for grasping such rules of conduct and sanctions? Which mental faculties are necessary to enable criminal law to provide effective guidance for social behaviour? In other words, *who is the culpable person*?

In this chapter, I first explore these questions through a descriptive analysis of the architecture of the dominant paradigm of culpability in both criminal theory and doctrine. This analysis – together with the one I carry out in the next chapter – is the fundamental premise underlying the core arguments of this book.

II. The 'Broad' Nature of Culpability

An analysis of the dominant paradigm of the culpable agent requires a brief preliminary discussion about the nature of culpability in the criminal law. The question 'who is the culpable person?' needs to be preceded by the inquiry 'what does being culpable mean?'. Considering the complexity and the controversies that surround the exact significance of this doctrine, I find it necessary to introduce the understanding of culpability I consider and explore in my analysis.

286 (1943) (Stewart, J, dissenting) ('It is a fundamental principle of Anglo-Saxon jurisprudence that guilt is personal and that it ought not lightly to be imputed to a citizen who … has no evil intention or consciousness of wrongdoing'). But see P Arenella, 'Convicting the Morally Blameless: Reassessing the Relationship Between Legal and Moral Accountability' (1992) 39 *UCLA Law Review* 1511, 1622 ('The United States Constitution generally does not require the legislature to incorporate moral culpability principles into its definitions of crimes').

[2] The rationale of the personal guilt principle cites the strict relationship between criminal responsibility and the definition of punishment. See HLA Hart, *Punishment and Responsibility: Essays in the Philosophy of Law* (Oxford, Oxford University Press, 1968) 4–5 (arguing that two of the five essential features of punishment are the infliction of 'pain or other consequences normally considered unpleasant' and that punishment 'must be of an actual … offender for his offence').

Culpability is a multifaceted concept in the criminal law. It is generally distinguished into two main kinds, which play different (yet complementary)[3] roles in criminal jurisprudence: narrow culpability and broad culpability.[4] Narrow culpability describes elemental *mens rea*,[5] namely the state(s) of mind that, together with the relevant material conduct, the criminal law identifies to define an offence. In more technical language, culpability as elemental *mens rea* consists of those elements of the offence definition that describe the required mental state in terms of purpose, knowledge, recklessness, and negligence (using the language of the Model Penal Code [MPC]),[6] of the defendant at the time of the offence. Thus, narrow culpability is the subjective element in wrongdoing insofar as elemental *mens rea* is a constituent of the offence itself. As such, narrow culpability encloses only a factual and time-specific psychological relationship between the criminal act (the *actus reus*) and its perpetrator. Its scope nevertheless omits excuse defences as well as any other doctrines that are not included in the offence definition.[7] Thereby, excuses such as insanity or duress constitute 'a "new matter" proposed by a person in an effort to escape punishment'[8] but are not a part of guilt assessments. Altogether, being culpable under narrow culpability means having committed a wrongdoing with a specific state of mind that is described in the relevant offence definition.

By contrast, broad culpability is synonymous with a person's blameworthiness[9] – or, more precisely, with 'those conditions that make a person's violation sufficiently blameworthy to merit the condemnation of criminal conviction'[10] and the application of sanctions. Broad culpability is, therefore, 'the responsibility condition in virtue of which the agent's wrongdoing is blameworthy and without which she would be excused'.[11] Accordingly, broad culpability goes beyond elemental *mens rea* and qualifies excuses such as insanity, immaturity, and duress as *central* (negative) components of guilt assessments. In such cases, the individual does not deny any element of wrongdoing, including elemental *mens rea*, but alleges an excuse based on mental incapacity or extreme coercion. A finding of any of such excusing conditions 'eliminates' an agent's responsibility for a given wrong. As a consequence, he or she cannot be fairly blamed and punished for his or her crime.[12] Altogether, being culpable under broad culpability means satisfying certain conditions that are necessary for being held responsible and punished.

[3] See D Brink, 'The Nature and Significance of Criminal Culpability' (2019) 13 *Criminal Law and Philosophy* 347.

[4] J Dressler, *Understanding Criminal Law*, 4th edn (New York, LexisNexis, 2006) 126–8.

[5] ibid.

[6] American Law Institute, Model Penal Code § 2.02 (1962).

[7] See eg, G Williams, *Criminal Law: The General Part*, 2nd edn (London, Stevens & Sons, Ltd., 1961) 102–3.

[8] G Fletcher, *Rethinking Criminal Law* (New York, Oxford University Press, 2000) 540.

[9] Dressler (n 4) 126.

[10] P Robinson, 'Mens Rea' in J Dressler (ed), *Encyclopedia of Crime and Justice*, Vol. 2 (New York, Macmillan Reference, 2002) 995, 995.

[11] Brink (n 3) 349.

[12] ibid.

Broad culpability aligns with culpability conceptualisations in positive criminal law as well as with the deeply established jurisprudence of finding a person not guilty when he or she successfully pleas an excuse. Broad culpability has also attracted significant support in legal scholarship. Such scholarship has generated a massive body of literature to describe the prototypical conditions that a person needs to meet in order to qualify as culpable under this broad account. How are these requisites framed, and which mental faculties support them? Alternatively, who is the paradigm agent that lies behind this kind of culpability? And what aspects of this agent's mind render him or her susceptible to responsibility and punishment? The analysis in the first part of this book explores these very questions.

III. Autonomy and Rationality: Framing the Model of the 'Person' in Criminal Law

Contemporary culpability debates have been dominated by legal/moral philosophical analyses of the foundations of criminal law. The search for the ideal culpable person in philosophical investigations has led to substantial literature over the past 60 years. These analyses have fundamentally contributed to a deeper understanding of culpability (alongside that of punishment) to such an extent that they have ultimately informed the current meaning, narrative, structure, and interpretive contours of this doctrine. Because of space limitations, I cannot delve into each account in detail; thus, my discussion will focus on the views that have dominated contemporary criminal law theory debates and whose interpretations of legal doctrine – as it exists in positive rules and standards – have gathered a robust consensus over the years.

To begin with, the dominant position in criminal theory is that criminal law adopts a compatibilist perspective of personhood in evaluating culpability.[13] Although compatibilist accounts of culpability assume several forms, most versions of compatibilism that criminal theorists have articulated fundamentally reject the originationist view[14] that free will is a prerequisite for culpability.[15] Rather, this

[13] See eg M Moore, 'Stephen Morse on the Fundamental Psycho-Legal Error' (2016) 10 *Criminal Law and Philosophy* 45, 69–70 (describing classical compatibilism in Humean terms: '[w]e are at liberty – free – whenever our choices (or intentions) cause the actions chosen (intended). We have the power needed for responsibility, the ability, the free will, whenever our choices cause what we choose them to cause because we made those choices. This is a compatibilist sense of these terms, because the causation of actions by our choices to do those very actions is quite compatible with such choices themselves being caused by factors outside our control. On this version of compatibilism, being a causer in no way requires that one be an uncaused causer').

[14] On this account, an agent is in a strict and literal sense an originator of her free decisions, an uncaused cause of them. See eg R Clarke and J Capes, 'Incompatibilist (Nondeterministic) Theories of Free Will' in E Zalda (ed), *The Stanford Encyclopedia of Philosophy* (2017) available at plato.stanford.edu/entries/incompatibilism-theories/; D Pereboom, *Living Without Free Will* (Cambridge, Cambridge University Press, 2001) 4; M Corrado, 'Automatism and the Theory of Action' (1990) 39 *Emory Journal of Law* 1191, 1192, 1212.

[15] For discussions on the compatibilist essence of criminal law, see eg SJ Morse, 'Avoiding Irrational Neurolaw Exuberance: A Plea for Neuromodesty' (2011) 62 *Mercer Law Review* 837, 845; SJ Morse, 'The

position holds that a person is culpable for his or her act even if it was caused by forces beyond his or her control. In other words, the fact that factors outside a person's control influence his or her actions is *compatible* with the idea that *the person* is the ultimate causer of his or her actions. Thus, the person is culpable (ie, responsible) for the actions that *he or she* causes, even if external factors contribute to the production of such actions.

From this perspective, even if criminal law acknowledges that certain circumstances (eg, one's genes and environment) do influence and, in a sense, cause human behaviour, it still presupposes that human beings have a margin of freedom that allows them to act in a non-compelled way. Many compatibilist accounts of criminal culpability situate this margin of freedom in two essential features of personhood: individual autonomy and rationality.[16] Culpability attributions ultimately build on and derive justification from these two fundamental features.

Ashworth[17] has identified two elements of individual autonomy: factual and normative. The factual element of individual autonomy perceives that individuals have both the capacity and sufficient will to make meaningful choices. An autonomous person has the ability to choose, formulate, and carry out his or her plans as well as the ability to govern personal conduct by rules and values. Thus, individual autonomy is understood as the individual capacity of self-governance, which allows him or her to master his or her own thoughts and actions in order to achieve his or her aims, despite external influences or circumstances. People are capable of making choices about how to live and are entitled to pursue their own interests however they wish. In short, individual autonomy is the overall 'causal power of persons'.[18]

The second, normative element of individual autonomy dictates that individuals should be respected and treated as agents who are capable of choosing their actions. Without accepting such independence of actions, it is hardly possible to regard individuals as persons. The respect of an individual as an autonomous being involves taking into account that he or she is self-determining and self-governing as well as capable of acting autonomously.[19] On this basis, the autonomy principle allows individuals to be held responsible and punished if their actions are harmful to others.

Non-problem of Free Will in Forensic Psychiatry and Psychology' (2007) 25 *Behavioral Sciences & the Law* 203; SJ Morse, 'Determinism and the Death of Folk Psychology: Two Challenges to Responsibility from Neuroscience' (2008) 9 *Minnesota Journal of Law Science & Technology* 1.

[16] See eg M Moore, 'The Relevance of Philosophy to Law and Psychiatry' (1983) 6 *International Journal of Law and Psychiatry* 177, 179 ('The law presupposes a view of man [sic] that allows us to view his behavior as the rational product of his autonomous choices').

[17] A Ashworth, *Principles of Criminal Law*, 3rd edn (New York, Oxford University Press, 1999) 27.

[18] M Moore, *Placing Blame: A Theory of the Criminal Law* (Oxford, Oxford University Press, 1997) 611.

[19] Ashworth (n 17) 29.

Individual autonomy intertwines with (minimal) rationality.[20] According to many legal-philosophical accounts, the statement that a person is (minimally) rational conveys that he or she is a practical reasoner, that is, he or she has the ability to respond to and act for reasons.[21] Thus, an agent is rational as long as his or her behaviour stems from elements of his or her psychological constitution that, to some degree, permit him or her to conform with or respond to the vagaries of reasons for action.

The concept of 'reasons for actions' can be descriptive or normative; both senses are supposedly embodied by the notion of rationality that pertains to culpability. In a descriptive sense, 'reasons for actions' refer to a person's mental states, including his or her desires, factual beliefs, and intentions,[22] all of which motivate, causally explain, and rationalise his or her action.[23] The establishment of 'belief/desire/intentions sets' gives rise to practical syllogisms that lead to practical conclusions about how to proceed. Actions that are carried out accordingly are both exhibited as instrumentally rational and explained as a consequence of a process of individual practical reasoning.[24]

In normative terms, 'reasons for actions' are 'facts in virtue of which the action is good, and these facts need not be limited to the desirability of the goals that are achieved through action but may concern intrinsic properties of the action itself'.[25] In the context of criminal law, the meaning of *good* reasons for actions embraces the prescriptive and proscriptive contents of criminal law rules and standards. Such contents provide the *good reasons* that a person is supposed to internalise and be motivated by when determining his or her behaviour.

Stephen Morse has suggested that the normative view of the individual as a practical reasoner derives from the nature of (criminal) law itself. The primary function of the law – and of criminal law in particular – is to guide human behaviour through the provision of rules of conduct and sanctions for violating them.

[20] There is a wide range of usages of the word 'rationality' across contexts, areas, and disciplines. Here, I only consider the particular usage of 'rationality' that is central to criminal culpability.

[21] See J Fischer and M Ravizza, *Responsibility and Control: A Theory of Moral Responsibility* (New York, Cambridge University Press, 1998).

[22] The descriptive account of reasons for actions fits the criminal law's folk psychological understanding of human behaviour. Criminal law accepts commonsense-based causal explanations of human behaviour. Lay people account for the actions of others, and explain their own, through the language of individual mental states including beliefs, desires, and intentions. Although intuitive and commonsense-based explanations are not genuine causal explanations of behaviour, these are nonetheless the types of explanations that fit the criminal law's folk-psychological narrative of human thought and behaviour. See generally Morse (n 15).

[23] See D Davidson, 'Actions, Reasons, and Causes' (1963) 60 *The Journal of Philosophy* 685. *cf* R Audi, 'Acting for Reasons' (1986) 95 *Philosophical Review* 511.

[24] See SJ Morse, 'Excusing the Crazy: The Insanity Defense Reconsidered' (1985) 58 *Southern California Law Review* 777, 783 ('It is easier to assess the rationality of the means an actor chooses to achieve goals because this assessment involves factual beliefs about the world or logical relationships. The inquiry becomes whether instrumental behavior is rationally connected to achieving identified goals. In Aristotelian terms, is the actor a good "practical reasoner"?').

[25] C Korsgaard, *The Constitution of Agency. Essays on Practical Reason and Moral Psychology* (New York, Oxford University Press, 2008) 212.

Accordingly, its recipients are presumed to be able to understand the prescriptive and proscriptive contents of its rules and standards and to use such rules and standards as premises in the practical reasoning that guides their actions *vis-á-vis* their inner mental states.[26] Thus, a person is susceptible to culpability when, despite possessing these understanding and practical reasoning abilities, he or she chooses not to conform his or her behaviour to the law and acts *contra ius* accordingly.

In partial contrast with Morse, Herbert Fingarette has maintained that being rational under criminal law does not simply or necessarily require the ability to act for (descriptive) reasons.[27] Instead, it more fundamentally requires the ability to respond to the '*essential* relevance' of a given situation. Responsiveness to 'essential relevance' builds on the apprehension of certain physical aspects of a given action in the relevant situation (the physical nature of the action) as well as of the material and normative implications of such action in that situation (eg, the potential harm inflicted by that action and the wrongness or criminality of the action). The ability to apprehend the physical and normative dimensions of a certain action in a given situation is the *sine qua non* condition to respond appropriately and adaptively to that situation. Inversely, an inability to apprehend the essential relevance of a given action in the relevant situation, including its physical and normative dimensions, impairs an individual's 'response-ability' to that situation. When this 'response-ability' is impaired, the individual is incapable of acting rationally.[28]

Legal-philosophical literature has frequently associated the term rationality with that of Reason. It has depicted rationality – and its predicate, rational – as a *distinctively human feature that derives from the use of Reason*, that is, that is made, conveyed by, or consistent with Reason.[29] Reason, on the other hand, has been described as the active power of the mind[30] that enables humans to think abstractly, judge critically, comprehend rules of conduct, and orient their behaviour accordingly.[31] In short, Reason is the faculty of the mind that makes an individual a rational being.[32]

Throughout the evolution of criminal law and its notions, the concept of Reason has tendentially been equated with cognition[33] or intellect.[34] The latter is generally understood as comprehensive of those mental processes that enable

[26] See Morse (n 24) 783.

[27] H Fingarette, *The Meaning of Legal Insanity* (London, University of California Press, 1972) 185 (suggesting that 'action for no reason at all still permits the ascription of rationality').

[28] ibid, 179–94. *cf* SJ Morse, 'Rationality and Responsibility' (2002) 74 *Southern California Law Review* 251, 255.

[29] Morse (n 28) 252.

[30] C Korsgaard, 'The Activity of Reason' (2009) 83 *Proceedings and Addresses of the APA* 23, 30.

[31] *Rex v Arnold* [1724] 16 How. St. Tr. 695, 764 ('If a man is deprived of his reason, and consequently of his intention, he cannot be guilty').

[32] Fingarette (n 27) 181–82 (describing Reason as 'that guiding or directing faculty of the mind by virtue of which man has traditionally been said to be a rational being').

[33] Etymologically speaking, the word cognition comes from the ancient Greek verb *γιγνώσκω* ('gignosko'; verb-stem *γνω* ['gno']) and from its Latin version *cognosco*, the traces of which can be found in numerous words of Western languages, including the English verb 'to know'.

[34] See eg *Sinclair v State*, 132 So. 581, 583 (Miss. 1931) (Ethridge, J, concurring) ('The "common law" proceeds upon the idea that before there can be a crime there must be an *intelligence* capable of comprehending the act prohibited, and the probable consequences of the act, and that the act is wrong').

knowledge, including abstract thinking, judgement, reasoning, observation, and understanding. Most discussions of rationality and culpability literature have referred to such cognitive abilities to describe the meaning of being a rational agent. Notably, legally relevant rationality has often been identified with two main cognitive abilities: understanding and instrumental practical reasoning. First, a person is assumed to possess the ability to understand information that is relevant to the decision to engage in given behaviour, including information about the physical (factual nature) and normative (rightness or wrongness) significance of one's conduct. Second, a person is assumed to be able to use such information to orient his or her practical reasoning about whether or not to engage in that behaviour; thereby, he or she is able to logically and instrumentally apply known information to guide his or her behaviour in order to achieve his or her identified goals.

From this perspective, culpable agents are framed as 'beings whose rational choice powers [ie understanding and instrumental reasoning abilities] explain why their acts can be fairly attributed to them'.[35] Accordingly, cognition is conceived of as the fundamental mental source of individuals' rationality and the ultimate function of the mind that guides individuals' decisions about what they should and should not do in light of normative standards of right and wrong.

In summary, the notion of culpability is founded on a view of the person as an autonomous practical reasoner who is able to grasp the prescriptive and proscriptive force of norms of conduct and then employ such norms as good reasons to act or refrain from acting. In this regard, he or she is expected to take precautions and reflect on the impact of his or her conduct on others. Farmer[36] has explained that this view of culpable agency presupposes a continuous form of behavioural control. In fact, it operates even in the absence of direct compulsion or punishment, as individuals are expected to conduct themselves in a certain way.[37] Thus, the subject of culpability is a being with a stable, unified interior life as well as a continuous sovereignty over the self, thoughts, decisions.

The view that autonomy and rationality are the essential features of the culpable agent has found considerable traction in philosophical and legal literature as well as in courts and legislations. As chapter two illustrates, these notions have been critical to reaffirm the centrality of the *person* in criminal responsibility and punishment attributions. Notably, they have been key to the rise of retribution as the overarching justification for punishment – the only one that demonstrates respect for people who break the law by treating them as moral equals who are aware of the nature and consequences of their actions and nonetheless freely choose the fate of their behaviour and, more broadly, of their life.

[35] P Arenella, 'Character, Choice and Moral Agency: The Relevance of Character to Our Moral Culpability Judgments' (1990) 7 *Social Philosophy & Policy* 59.

[36] L Farmer, *Making the Modern Criminal Law: Criminalization and Civil Order* (Oxford, Oxford University Press, 2016) 193.

[37] ibid, 194 (suggesting that the model of the culpable agent manifests a 'generalized expectation of proper conduct for individuals in modern society').

IV. The Voluntarist Architecture of Culpability: Choice, Capacity, and Fair Opportunity

The human features of individual autonomy and practical rationality are at the core of the legal-philosophical theory of culpability that is known as 'voluntarism' or 'choice/capacity' theory. Voluntarist accounts imply the strong assumption that we are not culpable for who we are or for our social status. Rather, we are culpable for the acts that *we choose* to do or, in exceptional circumstances, refrain from doing.

Voluntarism is founded on exquisite philosophical grounds. The theory, which is inspired by the Kantian views of the 'will' as the locus of moral worth and moral appraisal,[38] dictates that a person is justly held responsible and punished only if he or she broke the law through an action that was an outcome of his or her choice. Consistent with the principle that guilt is personal, voluntarists maintain that only actions that result from a person's choice can be ascribed to him or her, the domain of his or her mind, and his or her control power. An action that goes beyond the person's choice cannot be said to belong to him or her; it can be causally attributed to the individual, but 'it cannot be ascribed to him [or her] as its responsible agent'.[39]

The leading voluntarist scholar HLA Hart has proposed that one should understand the function of choice in culpability by 'consider[ing] the law … as what might be termed a choosing system'.[40] With this understanding, (criminal) law should be viewed as a system that 'guide[s] individuals' choices as to behaviour by presenting them with reasons for exercising choice in the direction of obedience, but leaving them to choose'.[41] Considering its 'choosing' nature, criminal law perceives individual human beings not as mere sites for utility or as automatons to be controlled by incentives but rather as purposive, choosing agents. Consequently, criminal law is not merely a means of social control but instead a system of rules that imposes itself to human beings and gives them reasons for the choices that they make.

Furthermore, the importance of anchoring culpability to choice is intrinsically connected with the liberal notion that each individual person must be protected from arbitrary inflictions of state punishment upon them. Hart has argued that the state must have a 'moral licence' to intervene by punishing a person. This moral licence is required 'in the form of proof that the person punished broke the law by an action which was the outcome of her free choice'.[42] From this perspective,

[38] I Kant, *Groundwork of the Metaphysics of Morals* (1785) A Wood (ed and transl) (New York, Yale University Press, 2002).

[39] RA Duff, 'Choice, Character, and Criminal Liability' (1993) 12 *Law and Philosophy* 345, 347.

[40] Hart (n 2) 44.

[41] ibid.

[42] ibid, 22.

free choice is vital to limiting inflictions of punishment upon individuals to only certain cases, which, according to Hart, is a 'requirement of Justice'.[43]

Commentators have recognised that a choosing agent is eligible to culpability when two conditions are met: the first is that the agent possesses sufficient mental capacity (or normative competence) to behave in accordance with the law and the second is that the agent finds himself or herself in a situation that affords him or her a fair opportunity to avoid wrongdoing.[44] Under the mainstream voluntarist model, an agent's culpability is assessed separately in each area. We decide whether the agent had the relevant mental capacity, and then we determine whether he or she had a fair opportunity to do otherwise. If both conditions are satisfied, then the agent is culpable.

As regards mental capacity, most voluntarist criminal theories frame it in terms of (higher) cognitive and control capacities. In legal jargon, (higher) cognitive capacity generally include knowledge, comprehension, abstract thinking, and instrumental reasoning. On the other hand, control capacity[45] generally refers to the capacity to exert control over alternative courses of actions and conform behaviour to the law. Thus, control capacity reflects the agent's ability to govern his

[43] ibid.

[44] ibid, 152; see also M Moore, 'Choice, Character, and Excuse' in EF Paul, FD Miller Jr and J Paul (eds), *Crime, Culpability and Remedy* (Oxford, Basil Blackwell, 1990) 29 ('we are responsible for wrongs we freely choose to do, and not responsible for wrongs we lacked the freedom [capacity and opportunity] to avoid doing.').

[45] A terminological caveat is needed. The concept of control is often associated with the philosophical notion of volition – especially as regards excuse doctrines. Different theories of volition have proliferated in philosophy of mind and philosophy of action, and philosophers are still debating about it. Some accounts hold that volitions are acts of the will. Other accounts treat volition as a species of intention that execute 'our more general intentions and … the background states of desire and belief that those more general intentions themselves execute'. See M Moore, *Act and Crime: The Philosophy of Action and Its Implications for Criminal Law* (New York, Oxford University Press, 1993) 121. On this account, volition is a functional, or executory, mental state that translates desires, beliefs, and more general intentions into 'basic' actions, including by resolving conflicts between intentions. Following the latter account, Michael Moore has remarkably developed a folk-psychological and metaphysical model of volitional capacity and excuse (see M Moore, 'The Neuroscience of Volitional Excuse' in D Patterson (ed), *Law and Neuroscience: State of the Art* (New York, Oxford University Press, 2016). Moore's characterisation of cases requiring a control excuse are those in which the agent did not do 'what he [or she] most wants to do', either because he or she was unable to form the 'right intention' or because he or she is able to form the 'right' intention, but is unable to execute it. This account of volition does not fully correspond to the excusing rationale of control excuses like insanity. As Morse has noted, in such excusing conditions, volitions successfully execute the defendant's motivating intentions. That is, the plea of insanity admits that the defendant intended to and did cause harm. Thus, lack of control cannot be plausibly grounded in defective volition. Moreover, Morse argues, Moore begins his analysis of the folk psychology of loss of control with a number of stipulations about 'desire, strongest desire, and intention'. Even conceding the plausibility of Moore's stipulations about conflicting mental states, asks Morse, 'what is a poor country lawyer-scholar to do if others contest them?'. See S Morse, 'Legal Insanity in the Age of Neuroscience' in D Patterson and S Moratti (eds), *Legal Insanity and the Brain* (Oxford, Hart Publishing, 2014) 260. Against this backdrop, I eschew the word 'volition', considering the complexities that surround its meaning as the numerous philosophical theories of volition emphasise. Since this book does not purport to provide a philosophical analysis of criminal law notions, I avoid engaging with hardcore philosophical terms and discussions that fall beyond its scope.

or her impulses to act and refrain from engaging in criminal behaviour under the circumstances.[46]

These two capacities are framed as the essential mental ingredients of culpability precisely because of, once again, the guiding function of criminal law. As Hart has noted, the institution of law depends on the capability of people to understand legal rules and make decisions that abide by those rules. Therefore, capacities for understanding legal rules and conforming one's behaviour to them are essential to enable criminal law to influence and guide human behaviour. As a consequence, if a person cannot comprehend legal norms or conform his or her behaviour to them, then the law cannot influence his or her behaviour. Moreover, punishing him or her would lack any moral and practical justification.

The relationship between cognitive and control capacities has been heavily debated in scholarly discussions. Much of this dispute concerns whether these capacities should be viewed as mutually independent or if control capacity should be grafted onto cognitive capacity. Notably, the cognition/control dispute approaches one fundamental question: is it plausible to think that a person who knows or understands (both factually and legally/morally) what he or she is doing can nonetheless be unable to control his or her behaviour? Some commentators have responded affirmatively. However, a more sustained group has subscribed to the view that cognitive capacity (which defines rationality) is rather *functional* to control capacity. Thus, control capacity is fundamentally a matter of rationality (ie, cognitive capacity). First, these authors maintain that, with few notable exceptions (eg, rare cases in which a person with schizophrenia commits a crime because he or she is obeying a commanding voice), a person with sound cognitive capacities will most likely be able to control his or her behaviour as well. Moreover, these authors have emphasised heterogeneous definitions of control across the literature, which range from the capacity to resist an impulse or the capacity to inhibit reactions to the capacity to act in conformity with one's appreciation or the capacity to conform to the law, among other interpretations. Amid such conceptual confusion and the weak practical consistency of these definitions, these authors have called for a solid conceptual and operational account of control that is also susceptible to reliable verification. Until such account is achieved, the issue of control should still be conceived of as one of rationality (ie, a question of cognitive capacity). That is, control capacity (in any meaning) should be viewed as parasitic of cognitive capacities of knowledge, understanding, reasoning, and so forth.

Beyond sound mental capacity, culpability presupposes a fair opportunity to do otherwise. Hart identified the fair opportunity element with the possibility to

[46] Cognition and control figure prominently across accounts of responsibility. See Hart (n 2) 227; J Raz, *Engaging Reason: On the Theory of Value and Action* (Oxford, Oxford University Press, 1999) 68; Duff (n 39); RA Duff, 'Who is Responsible, For What, To Whom?' (2005) 2 *Ohio State Journal of Criminal Law* 441, 456; D Brink and D Nelkin, 'Fairness and the Architecture of Responsibility' in D Shoemaker (ed), *Oxford Studies in Agency and Responsibility, Vol. 1* (New York, Oxford University Press, 2013) 284.

exert (legally relevant) mental capacities.[47] In another, more situational conception that has been endorsed by commentators such as Moore and Morse,[48] fair opportunity and capacity are distinct factors that entail two separate evaluations. In partial contrast with Hart, these scholars assert that the fair opportunity to do otherwise does not necessarily relate with one's mental capacity. There are cases in which a person is entirely mentally competent, yet external factors render his or her choice genuinely hard. Hence, a fair opportunity to do otherwise rests on the situation in which the agent finds himself or herself acting. Such situation must present the agent with a fair chance to choose differently besides his or her cognitive or control competence to do so. Under this account, an individual who lacks a fair opportunity to do otherwise keeps his or her status as a culpable agent. However, he or she is not culpable (ie, he or she is not responsible) for his or her wrongdoing because external circumstances unfairly constrain his or her choice to do otherwise.

In either account, the fair opportunity inquiry captures a person's physical and mental freedom to effect practical choice and act appropriately in a given situation. Such inquiry is narrowly focused on whether the actor, through no fault of his or her own, acts free of immediate, intense, transitory, and unfair coercion or threat. The notion of *fairness* translates, therefore, to a judgement of the actor's immediate situation, which must grant him or her with the physical and mental possibility to behave differently.

To summarise thus far, voluntarist criminal law automatically perceives people as (morally) rational and autonomous persons who enjoy the freedom to choose how to behave with reference to the law. To be culpable, such persons need to possess specific mental capacities (ie, higher cognition and control) and must find themselves acting in a situation that affords them a fair opportunity to avoid wrongdoing. It logically follows that culpability might be displaced in certain extreme circumstances such as severe mental impairments or unusual situational factors.

V. Voluntarism and Legal Doctrine

The voluntarist model of (broad) culpability – including its tendential devotion to cognition – is largely mapped in criminal law doctrine onto excuse defences.[49] A *prima facie* culpable actor is excused when unusual and exceptional circumstances, such as severe mental impairments or extreme threat, either compromise

[47] See Hart (n 2) 152.

[48] See Moore (n 18); SJ Morse, 'Culpability and Control' (1998) 142 *University of Pennsylvania Law Review* 1587.

[49] D Brink, 'Situationism, Responsibility, and Fair Opportunity' (2013) 30 *Social Philosophy & Policy* 121, 131 ('excuse is the flipside of culpability … conceptions of culpability and excuses should have corresponding structure').

his or her mental capacity or deny him or her a fair opportunity to do otherwise. The latter cases are emblematically represented by the doctrines of legal insanity and duress.

A. Mental Capacity and Excuses: Legal Insanity

Legal insanity is the paradigm doctrine that exemplifies the (lack of) mental capacity criterion of the voluntarist model of culpability.[50] In a doctrinal sense, the excuse of insanity negates the actor's culpability on the grounds that, at the time of the crime, an *endogenous* pathological mental condition deprived him or her of the relevant mental capacities that are necessary to be held guilty. The theoretical rationale of such excuse is that a mental impairment deprived the actor of legally relevant mental capacities that are necessary for culpability.

As a caveat, legal insanity is a normative concept rather than a clinical one. While a pathological mental condition in the clinical sense generally constitutes the 'but for' condition of legal insanity, such condition must ultimately satisfy predetermined legal criteria to obtain the status of insanity. While there must certainly be a mental condition, there is always a second requirement, namely that the condition be of such form or degree that it meets certain criteria that are established in the relevant insanity standard. In sum, it is not a mental condition *per se* that provides grounds for excuse by legal insanity; rather, the insanity determination depends on whether, at the time of the crime, the mental condition compromised the person's cognitive or (where provided) control capacities as defined in the relevant insanity standard.

Legal insanity is commonly called a 'rationality test'. Notably, it measures whether the actor's endogenous feature of his or her mental makeup led him or her to act irrationally (in a legally meaningful way) at the time of the crime. Such interpretation of legal insanity is consistent with the cognition-based formulation (and subsequent adaptations) of the M'Naghten rule.[51] The well-known test within this rule attaches a finding of legal insanity to the condition that the accused's 'defect of reason' from a 'disease of the mind' led him or her 'not to know the nature and quality of the act she was doing or that it was wrong'. [52]

Few legal scholars – and even fewer courts – have fully explored the concept of 'reason' in the formulation of the M'Naghten rule, and its meaning remains unclear.[53] According to Fingarette, the expression 'defect of reason' as it is used

[50] See D Husak, 'Broad Culpability and the Retributivist Dream' (2012) 9 *Ohio State Journal of Criminal Law* 449, 465 (noting that in common law systems 'insanity, along with infancy, provide the context in which commentators have thought most deeply about the capacities needed for criminal responsibility').

[51] See *Clark v Arizona* 548 U.S. 735, 750 n.12 (2006) (listing state statutes).

[52] *R v M'Naghten* [1843] 8 Eng. Rep. 718.

[53] See W Sinnott-Armstrong and K Levy, 'Insanity Defenses' in J Deigh and D Dolinko (eds), *The Oxford Handbook of Philosophy of Criminal Law* (New York, Oxford University Press, 2011) 299, 306.

in the M'Naghten rule clearly refers to a defect in the capacity for (moral) rationality.[54] He has argued that the concept of rationality has been largely disregarded in debates about the insanity defence since the M'Naghten test's 'defect of reason' phrase 'has not been understood'.[55] Fingarette has posited that this disregard is a 'profound mistake [because] the defect-of-reason clause tells us that "know the nature and quality of the act" and "know that is wrong" must be taken to apply with reference to the person's … capacity for rational conduct'.[56]

If one accepts this interpretation of 'defect of reason' as a 'defect of the capacity for rationality,' then the cognitivist substance of this clause primarily emerges from the knowledge requirement. The verb 'to know' is admittedly pivotal, as it 'circumscribes the entire test by singling out one aspect of a human being's total personality, the cognitive one'.[57] However, there has been controversy over how broadly this knowledge requirement should be understood. Some authors have proposed that it is limited to the actor's awareness of the factual and normative nature of his or her wrongdoing as if it would be manifested by a verbal acknowledgment or purely intellectual assent to a normative proposition.[58] Meanwhile, other authors have maintained that the verb 'to know' should be more broadly interpreted as an appreciation of 'the significance of cognitive observation, that is, whether the defendant is able to relate what is known to the situation at hand and to govern conduct accordingly.'[59] In this sense, the verb 'to know' indicates one's capacity to be aware of and correctly understand certain objective physical and normative features of behaviour with reference to both the law and commonly accepted social standards of morality. In actual practice, courts tend not to define the verb 'to know,' so its interpretation is largely dependent on the discretionary common sense of juries.[60]

The knowledge test includes two mutually exclusive branches. The first involves a factual knowledge test (or *cognitive capacity* test). This test probes the agent's awareness (or understanding) of the factual dimension of his or her act; thus, it evaluates whether the agent has a normal capacity for understanding the principal characteristics and consequences of his or her behaviour.[61] The second branch of

[54] Fingarette (n 27) 198 ('I believe that "a defect of reason" from "disease of the mind" is to be read in paraphrase: "substantial defect in capacity for rational conduct" as "an endogenous (pathological) condition of mind"').

[55] ibid.

[56] ibid.

[57] A Morris, 'Criminal Insanity' (1968) 43 *Washington Law Review* 583, 605.

[58] RJ Gerber, 'Is the Insanity Test Insane?' (1975) 20 *American Journal of Jurisprudence* 111, 120.

[59] R Bonnie et al, *A Case Study in the Insanity Defense: The Trial of John Hinckley, Jr.*, 3rd edn (New York, Foundation Press, 2008) 12; see also A Goldstein, *The Insanity Defense* (London, Yale University Press, 1967) 49–50.

[60] L Raider, 'Toward a New Test for Insanity Defense: Incorporating the Discoveries of Neuroscience into Moral and Legal Theories' (1998) 46 *UCLA Law Review* 289, 306; see also JRP Ogloff, 'A Comparison of Insanity Defense Standards on Juror Decision Making' (1991) 15 *Law & Human Behavior* 509, 526; N Finkel, *Commonsense Justice: Jurors' Notions of Law* (Cambridge, MA, Harvard University Press, 1995).

[61] J Hall, 'Responsibility and Law. In Defense of the McNaghten Rules' (1956) 42 *American Bar Association Journal* 917, 917.

the test evaluates whether the agent knows that his or her act is *wrong*. The original wording of the M'Naghten rule suggests that this branch consists of a *moral capacity* test and determines whether the person was able to distinguish between good and evil, regardless of whether he or she knew what he or she was doing. Over the years, states have adopted different variants of the M'Naghten rule.[62] Some have utilised an insanity test that focuses solely on moral incapacity, while others have applied one that examines only cognitive capacity. In addition, more than 10 states have reoriented the test to concentrate on the defendant's understanding that his or her act was 'illegal' rather than 'morally wrong'. Thereby, in these states, the ranks of the insane exclude those who know an act is illegal but still believe it to be morally right.

The knowledge requirement circumscribes the meaning of the 'disease of the mind' clause to encompass only cognitive diseases. As has been observed, courts vary on how they define 'disease of [the] mind'.[63] Hence, a finding of such disease 'follows almost automatically'[64] when it is found that a defendant was in such a state that he or she did not know the factual and moral implications of his or her conduct.[65] However, an explicit interpretation of the substance of the 'disease of the mind' requirement can be found in *R v Kemp*,[66] a case that was heard at the Bristol Assizes in 1957. Commenting on the relationship between the 'defect of reason' and 'disease of the mind' requirements, Justice Devlin wrote that '[t]he law is not concerned with the brain but with the mind, *in the sense that "mind" is ordinarily used, the mental faculties of reason, memory and understanding*'.[67] This interpretation of the 'disease of mind' requirement is pivotal because it emphasises the M'Naghten test's reliance upon cognitive faculties.[68]

Criticism of the excessive narrowness of the M'Naghten test over the years[69] prompted the American Law Institute (ALI) to introduce a new insanity standard in the MPC in 1962.[70] The MPC's formulation is based on the assumption

[62] These variants have passed the Supreme Court's due process scrutiny. See *Clark* (n 51); *Kahler v Kansas* 589 U.S. (2020).

[63] J Parry, *Criminal Mental Health and Disability Law, Evidence, and Testimony* (Chicago, ABA Publishing, 2009) 36 ('Under *M'Naghten*, there must be a "disease of the mind". This term has been interpreted very differently over the years. In its broadest meaning, "any diagnosable mental disorder" is sufficient, while under the more narrow interpretation a "severe impairment, usually in the form of psychosis", is required').

[64] R Kuh, 'The Insanity Defense – An Effort to Combine Law and Reason' (1962) 110 *University of Pennsylvania Law Review* 771, 785.

[65] ibid.

[66] 1 QB 399 [1957]. For a comment, see JE Hall Williams, 'Defect of Reason from Disease of the Mind' (1957) 20 *Modern Law Review* 55, 56.

[67] *R v Kemp* (n 66).

[68] But see Fingarette (n 27) 182 (suggesting that the cognition-based interpretation of the M'Naghten Rule is mistaken).

[69] See eg J Hall, 'Responsibility and Law: In Defense of the McNaghten Rules' (1956) 42 *ABA Journal* 917; SE Sobeloff, 'Insanity and the Criminal Law: From M'Naghten to Durham, and Beyond' (1955) 41 *ABA Journal* 793, 877 (1955); Kuh (n 64) 782.

[70] American Law Institute, Model Penal Code § 4.01 (1962) ('A person is not responsible for criminal conduct if at the time of such conduct as a result of mental disease or defect he lacks substantial capacity either to appreciate the criminality of his conduct or to conform his conduct to the requirements of law.').

that insanity should be grounded in a broader understanding of cognition, and a reference to (substantial) control incapacity should be included explicitly in the formulation of the defence.[71] The expansion of the cognitive prong of legal insanity resulted in the dismissal of the verb 'to know' and the simultaneous adoption of the broader verb 'to appreciate'.[72] The drafters of the MPC purposefully incorporated the term 'to appreciate' in order to account for people who suffer from emotional abnormalities that prevent their 'detached or abstract awareness' of the wrongfulness of their conduct from 'penetrat[ing] to the affective level'.[73] Moreover, the Explanatory Notes to the MPC identify the failure to appreciate the criminality (wrongfulness) of one's conduct with a 'lack of awareness' of one's action or 'a misapprehension of either the material circumstances' or 'the significance of one's action in some deeper sense'.[74] As we will see later on in the chapter, despite the drafters' expansive interpretation of concept of appreciation, the appreciation prong of the MPC insanity test has nevertheless been taken as a cognitive test.

The other relevant feature of the ALI standard concerns the provision for a control prong in addition to (and independent from) the cognitive one. Such provision was introduced to respond to the inadequacy of the 'tacit assumption' of the M'Naghten test that 'if an individual "knows" right from wrong, his or her rational powers are intact and that he or she is, therefore, capable of governing his or her conduct'.[75] The ALI standard defines control incapacity as 'the [substantial] incapacity to conform behaviour to the requirements of the law'.[76] Neither the code nor its Commentaries and Explanatory Notes offer detailed guidelines for interpreting this part of the standard, which seems to extend beyond cases of irresistible impulses to more broadly address the defendant's control capacity, regardless of whether he or she is able to know or understand the significance of his or her behaviour.

Despite its initial popularity, the vagueness of the MPC formulation of the control tests – in combination with (in)famous acquittals[77] that generated significant public outrage[78] – led to a gradual abandonment of the MPC control test[79] and the passage of subsequent legislation that narrowed the insanity defence by removing the control defence theory. In 1983, the American Psychiatric Association

[71] See American Law Institute, Model Penal Code and Commentaries. Part I. General Provisions (1985), 164.

[72] ibid.

[73] ibid, 166.

[74] American Law Institute, Model Penal Code Official Draft and Explanatory Notes, Part I. General Provisions (1985) 62.

[75] R Gerber, *The Insanity Defense* (Port Washington, Associated Faculty Press, 1984) 30.

[76] Model Penal Code (n 70).

[77] *United States v Hinckley*, 525 F. Supp. 1342 (D.C. Cir. 1981).

[78] The Associated Press, 'Hinckley Acquittal Brings Moves to Change Insanity Defense' *The New York Times* (24 June 1982) D21.

[79] See American Academy of Psychiatry and Law, 'AAPL Practice Guideline for Forensic Psychiatric Evaluation of Defendants Raising the Insanity Defense' (2014) 42 *Journal of American Academy of Psychiatry and Law* S3, S66.

released a statement (retired in 2008)[80] that control tests may be unnecessary given that defendants who meet the exculpatory criteria of control tests usually fulfil the exculpatory criteria of cognitive impairment tests as well.[81] In view of that statement, in 1984, the ALI test was largely discarded in favour of the Insanity Defense Reform Act (IDRA).[82] This Act was the first federal codification of the insanity defence and was introduced for the explicit purpose of removing the control component from the ALI standard.

Today, a minor number of US jurisdictions employ the 'control' test.[83] The majority of jurisdictions still maintain the view that the only viable basis for a plea of insanity is a mental disease or disorder that has led to a cognitive impairment that, in turn, has resulted in an incapacity to know, understand, or appreciate the factual, moral, and/or legal significance of one's conduct.[84] A lack of control is assessed indirectly as a possible further consequence of cognitive defects.[85] Therefore, if a person is cognitively able to differentiate or understand right from wrong, and his or her rational powers are intact, then he or she are presumed to be able to control his or her own conduct and, altogether, does not meet the eligibility criteria for legal insanity.

B. Fair Opportunity and Excuses: Duress

The situational component of the voluntarist model of culpability is most glaring in the duress excuse. Duress occurs where a person is forced by an imminent threat and overwhelming pressure of another person to commit the crime.[86] In such situations, though the agent is generally mentally competent, external factors deprive him or her of a fair opportunity to avoid wrongdoing. Thus, duress does not compromise the person's *status* as a rational, culpable agent because it does not challenge his or her mental competence. However, it does challenge whether the person is culpable (ie, responsible) for his or her wrongdoing as he or she is a non-culpable victim of a wrongfully imposed hard choice, and we cannot fairly

[80] See D Norris, 'Reports to the Membership' (2008) 165 *American Journal of Psychiatry* 1214, 1214 ('The sixth position statement, Insanity Defense, replaced the statement approved in 1982 and updated it with a more concise and up-to-date formulation. This more concise position statement is aimed at underscoring APA support for a meaningful insanity defense without endorsing any particular standard').

[81] American Psychiatric Association, 'Statement on Insanity Defense' (1983) 140 *American Journal of Psychiatry* 681, 685.

[82] 18 U.S.C. § 17 (1984); see SJ Morse, 'Insanity Defense Reform Act (IDRA)' in B Cutler (ed), *Encyclopedia of Psychology and Law* 373 (Thousand Oaks, SAGE Publications, 2008).

[83] See PH Robinson and T Scott Williams, 'Mapping American Criminal Law: Variations Across the 50 States – Ch. 14 Insanity Defense' (2017) *University of Pennsylvania Faculty Scholarship* 1718, available at scholarship.law.upenn.edu/faculty_scholarship/1718/.

[84] ibid.

[85] *See Yates v State*, 171 S.W.3d 215 (Tex. App. 2005); for comments on the *Yates* case and the relationship between cognitive and control prongs, see generally B Shannon, 'The Time is Right to Revise the Texas Insanity Defense: An Essay' (2006) 39 *Texas Tech. Law Review* 67.

[86] See eg *United States v Bailey*, 444 U.S. 394 (1980).

expect him or her not to yield and behave otherwise. Metaphorically speaking, he or she has 'no' choice.[87]

Scholars are nonetheless divided in regard to the normative excusing rationale for duress, namely whether it should be defective control capacity or a diminished (or absent) opportunity to do otherwise in view of the extreme threat. One account proposes that the rationale for duress is control incapacity.[88] Such account suggests that the coerced agent wants to avoid breaking the law but is unable to bring his or her will in harmony with that desire out of fear that is caused by a threat. The threat must therefore be present in the sense that it is effective to neutralise the will of the individual at that time the offence is committed. From this perspective, the fear that is elicited by the threat must operate on the mind of the actor at the time of the criminal act. Thus, intense fear exculpates because it impairs a person's capacity to comply with the law. Altogether, the normative essence of this excuse supposedly lies in the agent's control incapacity due to extreme fear that is provoked by threatening circumstances.

Other authors have firmly rejected this interpretation and argued that agents who act under duress are generally perfectly capable of controlling their behaviour. Rather, duress qualifies as a *situational* excuse, the core of which is the objective situation (ie, the extreme threat of harm that leads the agent to yield to unlawful behaviour). In this account, the agent who acts under a serious threat is excused regardless of whether his or her control capacity was (un)diminished. In fact, the agent is excused because we could not *fairly* expect someone in his or her position to refrain from violating the law; hence, we are in no moral position to blame and punish him or her for his or her conduct.

Although this situational understanding of duress has fuelled scholarly disagreement about its nature as either a justification or an excuse,[89] it appears to be more consistent with positive formulations of this doctrine. Indeed, the law limits situations of duress to those cases in which the threat is death, serious bodily injury, or, in the language of the MPC, one that 'a person of reasonable firmness in the actor's situation would have been unable to resist'.[90] In the latter case, the force threatened must go beyond what an individual of reasonable firmness in the defendant's situation would be able to resist. The level of resistance exerted also must meet community standards of reasonableness. The meaning of 'reasonable

[87] See SJ Morse, 'Deprivation and Desert' in WC Heffernan and J Kleinig (eds), *From Social Justice to Criminal Justice: Poverty and the Administration of Criminal Law* (New York, Oxford University Press, 2000) 114, 137 (arguing that, literally, a person acting under duress has and makes a choice. Indeed, he or she might refuse to do harm, despite the awfulness of the threat).

[88] See eg P Robinson, 'Criminal Law Defenses: A Systematic Analysis' (1982) 82 *Columbia Law Review* 199, 213–14.

[89] Scholars are divided on the doctrinal nature of duress, namely, whether it should count as either an excuse or a justification.

[90] American Law Institute, Model Penal Code § 2.09 (1962). But see J Dressler, 'Exegesis of the Law of Duress: Justifying the Excuse and Searching for Its Proper Limits' (1989) 62 *Southern California Law Review* 1331, 1367, fn 195 ('The MPC language is that the Code seems to treat duress as an incapacity-oriented excuse: Was the person of reasonable firmness *unable* to resist?').

firmness' is not clarified and is largely subject to the discretion and common knowledge of the juries, who must make not only a factual determination but also a normative judgement of the degree of 'firmness' that can be expected of a person in the actor's circumstances. A number of factors help decide the reasonableness of the defendant's actions. They include the seriousness of the threat, the imminence and nature of the harm faced, and the opportunity for escape.

Morse[91] holds that duress is based on a normative conception of what we can reasonably require of persons. The reasonable firmness standard assumes that most ordinary people have a general capacity to resist threats. Accordingly, a person with less than average firmness is still held to this standard if he or she is generally capable to comply with it. On the other hand, Dressler holds (more strictly) that for duress to be a feasible excuse, the claim that 'the defendant acted like most other humans would have acted in the same situation'[92] is not sufficient. Duress being a normative defence, the actor is expected to attain and manifest a certain degree of moral fortitude. Thus, the doctrine requires jurors to compare the relevant individual to an imaginary person who encompasses the moral strength that we expect as a society.

Commentaries on the MPC state that the actor's 'situation' includes certain circumstances, such as '[s]tark, tangible factors that differentiate the actor from another, like his size, strength, age or health'. However, 'matters of temperament' would not be considered in the exculpatory judgement.[93] With these objective criteria, the Code appears to prohibit a duress excuse for having insufficient capacity for control. It rather allows it as the person's choices were unfairly constrained or made hard by a coercing agent. It is objective threat – rather than the person's fear itself – that justifies this type of excuse.

VI. Voluntarism, Emotions, and Socio-Environmental Factors

The analysis of the architecture of culpability that has been conducted thus far has omitted two aspects: emotions and the social context. Whereas predominant discourses on culpability mostly concern the language of rationality, choice, capacity, and cognition, an exhaustive examination of culpability – especially for the purposes of this book – must also examine how criminal law theory and doctrine take account of these two other dimensions of people, their minds, and their behaviours. To this end, such examination must address the following questions: How are these dimensions conceived of within the current structure of culpability? In which doctrines do they 'live', and how? Is the ideal culpable agent supposed to

[91] Morse (n 87) 124.
[92] Dressler (n 90) 1344.
[93] American Law Institute, Model Penal Code and Commentaries (1985) 374.

be also emotionally capable? Is the social environment of a person afforded any meaningful weight within culpability assessments?

A. A Mechanistic Conception of Emotions

Seminal works in philosophy of mind have thoroughly explored the rationality of emotions in morality.[94] Many of these accounts have critically suggested that emotions are key drivers of moral judgements, and they are essential – or even the ultimate – sources of moral behaviour. The richness of philosophical elaborations of emotions, rationality, and moral behaviour has nonetheless found inconsistent and fragmentary traction in criminal law.

While recent years have witnessed increasing scholarly acknowledgment of emotions in legal domains, the relevance of emotional factors to address culpability matters remains altogether marginal and overshadowed by prevailing rationalist tendencies in criminal law. In fact, both mainstream voluntarist accounts of culpability and the substantive side of criminal law still position emotions at the margins of culpability ascriptions and remain eventually anchored to cognitive models of human behaviour.[95]

In traditional legal (and common-sense-based) thought, emotions are perceived as *a-rational*[96] mental states that are not part of – but potentially disruptive of – practical reasoning and control. In this view, emotions are forces that cause action without the mediation of choice and judgement.[97] On the other hand, criminal law presumes (*rectius*: it normatively expects) that human beings are typically capable of resisting the intrusive influence of emotions on their deliberations and actions. Under this approach, the suppression or restraint of emotions requires one to exert his or her intellectual powers of reason and control. Hence, whereas 'emotions are thought to be irrational, involuntary, and animal-like … intellect is rational, voluntary, and distinctly human'.[98]

[94] The relationship between emotions, rationality and moral responsibility has been thoroughly investigated in the field of philosophy. For the purposes of this book, I shall limit my analysis to how emotions are predominantly conceived of in criminal law theory and doctrine.

[95] See N Finkel and G Parrot, *Emotions and Culpability: How the Law Is at Odds with Psychology, Jurors, and Itself* (American Psychological Association Press, 2006) 48 ('[t]he folk category of emotion can appear to threaten the orderly rule of law, for it carries with it the irrationality of primate impulses and the indeterminacy of subjective states. These perceived threats account for why the Law omits emotion in favor of more cognitive criteria').

[96] A Duff, 'Criminal Responsibility and the Emotions: If Fear and Anger Can Exculpate, Why Not Compassion?' (2015) 58 *Inquiry* 189, 193.

[97] ibid, 193 ('[s]ome see emotions as enemies of rational, responsible agency: they are essentially a-rational forces by which we are passively affected, or afflicted; they are prone to hinder that clear-eyed understanding of the world, and of the reasons for action by which we should guide ourselves, that rational agency requires. To achieve rational agency, we must quell or restrain the emotions and resist their intrusive influence on our deliberations and actions').

[98] Finkel and Parrot (n 95) 53.

Kahan and Nussbaum have famously labelled this conception of emotions as a 'mechanistic conception'.[99] Such conception dictates that emotions are 'forces that do not contain or respond to thought'.[100] As such, 'they are impulses or surges that lead the person to action without embodying beliefs, or any way of seeing the world that can be assessed as correct or incorrect, appropriate or inappropriate'.[101]

As the authors explain,[102] the mechanistic conception of emotions originates from the rationalist assumption that reason and will need to persistently oppose deep-rooted instincts or impulses in human nature that can never be internally enlightened or educated. In the past century, this conception enjoyed immense prominence owing to the influence of both these philosophical views and several forms of psychological theory. Until more recently, cognitive psychologists under the influence of behaviourism maintained that emotions could be understood as impulses or bodily forces that do not contain thoughts or evaluations.

According to Kahan and Nussbaum, 'although voluntarism is not committed analytically to any theory of emotion, it has strong links … with the mechanistic conception'.[103] As illustrated above, voluntarist conceptions of culpability predominantly appeal to the language of cognition, as they mostly structure culpability ascriptions along the agent's cognitive states and capacities. Within this framework, voluntarism also tends to conceive of emotions as 'forces that either do or do not limit an offender's choices'.[104] As such, emotions can bear on criminal responsibility only as factors that diminish practical reasoning and control.

Admittedly, voluntarism does not negate that criminal law presupposes emotionality as a fundamental feature of persons in addition to – though separate from – rationality and autonomy. Criminal law does suppose that people have emotions, but it also considers them to have the power to suppress or control their own emotions through their rationality and self-mastery or autonomy – which explains why acting under the presence of emotions is usually not excused in actual practice.[105] Although people are normally and normatively expected to be able to resist their own emotions and act as the law requires, voluntarism nonetheless accepts that an emotion can occasionally be so overwhelming that it is impossible (or unduly difficult) for the agent to resist it, and it would be unjust to fully condemn him or her for failing to resist such a powerful force. In these cases, the potential mitigating value of (certain) *strong* emotions stems from their nature as alien and external forces that overturn rational choice to the point of invalidating it entirely.

[99] D Kahan and M Nussbaum, 'Two Conceptions of Emotions in Criminal Law' (1996) 96 *Columbia Law Review* 269, 278.

[100] ibid, 273.

[101] ibid, 278.

[102] ibid, 302.

[103] ibid.

[104] ibid.

[105] See M Moore, *Law and Psychiatry: Rethinking the Relationship* (New York, Cambridge University Press, 1984) 108 ('[p]ersons are able to reason practically, and to act on the dictates of those practical reasonings, despite most (but not all) disturbances in their emotional life').

The mechanistic view of emotions that has been endorsed by traditional theoretical discourses is also manifest in positive formulations and practical applications of the doctrine of culpability. In this regard, two areas of substantive criminal law are particularly representative. The first area is the law of homicide and, specifically, the definitional and distinguishing criteria for murder and voluntary manslaughter, as they are depicted by premeditation, heat of passion, and extreme mental and emotional disturbance (EMED) doctrines. The second area concerns the irrelevance of emotional capacity as a precondition of culpability. Such irrelevance is manifest in mental-disorder-based defences, such as that of legal insanity.

i. Emotions and the Law of Homicide

In criminal law, the mechanistic view of emotions is strongly evident in the law of homicide and particularly in the definitional criteria for premeditation and manslaughter that is committed while in an overwhelming emotional state. The latter type of homicide includes killings that occur in the 'heat of passion' (ie, in response to 'adequate provocation') or, in the MPC version, under 'extreme mental and emotional disturbance'.[106] Both 'heat of passion' and EMED doctrines constitute specific forms of diminished capacity[107] that reduce murder to voluntary manslaughter and yield substantially lower penalties. Notably, these mitigations apply only to homicides.

The normative criteria for defining and differentiating between these two macro-categories of homicide are clearly rationalist. Indeed, the primary distinction between premeditated homicide and homicide that is committed in an overwhelming emotional state builds on the idea that strong emotions can mitigate culpability because strong emotion precludes an opportunity for deliberation. In such cases, the law grants mitigation by recognising that people who kill while in a state of extremely heightened emotion – with or without prior provocation, depending on the standard – are less than fully rational or in control of their actions.

Premeditation entails the most severely punished type of homicide.[108] The rationale is based on the dispassionate state of mind of the actor, who planned and perpetrated the killing after conscious reflection and deliberation, or, as one court famously wrote, 'in a cold and calculated manner'.[109] Although courts have

[106] *See* American Law Institute, Model Penal Code § 210.3(1)(b) (1962).

[107] See SJ Morse, 'Undiminished Confusion in Diminished Capacity' (1984) 75 *The Journal of Criminal Law and Criminology* 1; SJ Morse, 'Diminished Capacity' *Encyclopedia of Crime and Justice* (New York, McMillan Reference USA, 2002). *cf* P Robinson, 'Abnormal Mental State Mitigations of Murder – The U.S. Perspective' in A Reed and M Bohlander (eds), *Loss of Control and Diminished Responsibility: Domestic, Comparative and International Perspectives* (New York, Routledge, 2011) 291.

[108] Note that, following the lead of the Model Penal Code, many states have abandoned the premeditation doctrine altogether. See American Law Institute, Model Penal Code and Commentaries, Comment to § 210.6 (1980) 127–28.

[109] *State v Anderson*, 70 Cal. 2d 15, 447 P2 942 (1968).

increasingly recognised that 'no time is too short' for the necessary premeditation to occur, the principle of premeditation is as follows: when there is more careful consideration of the choice to do wrong, the person commits more actively to carrying out the killing act, and the wrongdoing therefore reveals a stronger disregard for the value of human life. When a person kills after contemplating his or her intent to kill, he or she is not only more blameworthy but also deemed less capable of reformation compared to someone who kills on a sudden impulse. Importantly, premeditation analysis does not afford any relevant weight to the type of motive that moved the defendant to deliberately commit the killing.[110] The only significant matter for the purposes of premeditation is that the defendant planned and carefully deliberated the killing.

The common law 'heat of passion'[111] doctrine permits the reduction of murder to voluntary manslaughter if the defendant was moved to act by an uncontrollable emotion in the face of a provocation.[112] Although the criteria for heat of passion vary by jurisdiction, the defendant typically must demonstrate four elements: first, he or she was adequately provoked; second, as a direct result of said provocation, he or she became emotionally charged to an extent that he or she lost control; third, not enough time elapsed between the provocation and the killing to allow him or her to 'cool off'; finally, he or she did not 'cool off' prior to killing the victim(s).[113]

The core of the heat of passion doctrine is the *suddenness* of the emotional reaction when confronting a given adequate provocation. Specifically, no or only a short period of time had to have passed between the provocation and the emotional reaction that led to the killing.[114] Second, the doctrine conditions the mitigation on the existence of an *adequate* provocation.[115] Although 'adequacy' in this context is largely established on a case-by-case basis according to a variety of factors, it is generally considered to entail 'provocation by the victim that would be sufficient to significantly undermine the rationality of a reasonable person'.[116] Thus, the provocation must be sufficient to incite a strong emotion and loss of

[110] See S Pillsbury, *Judging Evil: Rethinking the Law of Murder and Manslaughter* (New York, NYU Press, 1998) 104–6.

[111] eg California Penal Code Section 192 (a)(f) [West 1970]; Nebraska Revised Statutes 28–305 (1979); Idaho Code Ann § 18-4006 (1) (Michie 2002) ('Manslaughter is the unlawful killing of a human being including … upon a sudden quarrel or heat of passion'); New Jersey Statute Ann 2C:11–4 (West 1978) ('committed in the heat of passion resulting from a reasonable provocation'); Louisiana Revised Statutes 14:31 [2007] ('Manslaughter is: A homicide which would be murder … but the offense is committed in sudden passion or heat of blood immediately caused by provocation sufficient to deprive an average person of his self-control and cool reflection'). See also *Cox v State* 534 A 2d 1333, 1335 [1988]; *State v Ligon* 420 SE 2d 136, 146 (NC 1992); *State v Wilford* 307 NW 2d 277, 283 (Wis 1981).

[112] Although anger is the usual emotion alleged in provocation cases, some courts have enlarged the doctrine to include any '[v]iolent, intense, high-wrought, or enthusiastic emotion'. See eg *State v Jones*, 185 Kan. 235, 341 P.2d 1042 (1959).

[113] See R Griffith Fontaine, 'Adequate (Non)provocation and Heat of Passion as Excuse, Not Justification' (2009) 43 *University of Michigan Journal of Law Reform* 27, 29–30.

[114] *State v Gounagias*, 153 P.9 (Wash. 1914).

[115] eg *High v United States* 972 A2d 829, 833 (DC 2009).

[116] Griffith Fontaine (n 113) 30.

self-control in a reasonable (ordinary) person,[117] and the actor must not have had a reasonable amount of time to 'cool off'.[118]

Under dominant interpretations, the excusing rationale of heat of passion (which distinguishes it from murder) is that a strong and sudden emotion (or passion) impaired the defendant's rationality and control. The absence of deliberation coupled with an impaired mental capacity renders the defendant not only less blameworthy but also deserving of less harsh punishment. It is important to note that killing in a heat of passion does not necessitate that

> reason be entirely dethroned, or overpowered by passion so as to destroy intelligent volition … On principle … the extent to which the passions are required to be aroused and reason obscured must be considerably short of this, and never beyond that degree within which ordinary men have the power, and are therefore morally as well as legally bound to restrain their passions.[119]

Even if this doctrine accepts that strong emotion can either 'sway'[120] or overwhelm a person's reason and control, it does not assume that a person who acts on a strong emotion *lacks* the capacity for rationality and control. It simply recognises the reasonableness of a temporary and sudden loss of control in response to certain provocative circumstances.

In 1962, the drafters of the Model Penal Code provided the EMED defence as a new and significantly broader version of the heat of passion defence.[121] The MPC's EMED defence mitigates murder to voluntary manslaughter when the killing is committed 'under the influence of an extreme emotional *disturbance* for which there is a reasonable explanation and excuse'. The EMED defence foremost expands the scope of the heat of passion doctrine beyond provocation. Therefore, 'any affective experience sufficient to disable a person's "usual intellectual controls" or scrambles "normal rational thinking" counts as an extreme emotional disturbance.'[122]

Whereas 'suddenness' is the key word for understanding the heat of passion doctrine, 'intensity'[123] is the central term in EMED. Unlike in heat of passion, EMED does not limit mitigation to killings that were committed due to a sudden emotional impulse. Rather, it extends it to cases in which the emotional reaction is so intense that it amounts to a disturbance that can compromise a person's

[117] eg *State v McGuy*, 841 A2d 1109, 1113 (RI 2003).

[118] eg *State v Frederick*, 579 P2d 390, 394 (Wash Ct App 1978); *State v King* 897 A2d 534, 548 (Vt 2006).

[119] *Maher v People*, 10 Mich. 212 (1862) (citations omitted).

[120] *State v Knoten*, 555 SE 2d 391, 394–5 (SC 2001).

[121] Of the 34 states that adopted modern codes inspired to the Model Penal Code, only 11 of those codes adopt the MPC's EED formulation. eg Arkansas Code Ann §5–10–104 (2002); New York Penal Law § 125.22 (McKinney2009); Utah Code Ann §76-5-205.5 (1)(b) (2008). The remaining 23 MPC jurisdictions retain their previously existing common law heat of passion/provocation formulation or some variations of it.

[122] *See Patterson v New York*, 432 U.S. 197, 206 (1977); *People v Casassa*, 404 N.E. 2d 1310 (N.Y. 1980); *State v Elliott*, 411 A.2d 3, 7, 8 (1979).

[123] See American Law Institute, Model Penal Code and Commentaries, Comment to § 210.3(b) (1985) 55–6.

control.[124] As of *Patterson*, courts have noted that advances in psychology have increased public willingness to reduce responsibility for 'those whose capacity has been diminished by mental trauma'.[125] According to the court in *Patterson*, a mental trauma qualifies for an EMED defence as long as it developed 'for a substantial period of time, simmering in the unknowing subconscious and then inexplicably coming to the fore'. This passage implies an acceptance that, unlike in the heat of passion, an actor's emotional disturbance does not necessarily decrease over time but can in fact intensify.

The Code also indicates that there must be 'a reasonable explanation or excuse' for the defendant's emotional disturbance. The reasonableness assessment entails that the jury considers the defendant's emotional disturbance from a viewpoint of the actor's situation under the circumstances as he or she believes them to be.[126] The 'situational' element characterises the defence as partially individualised. It asks jurors to assume the perspective of the defendant 'by viewing the subjective, internal situation in which the defendant found himself [or herself] and the external circumstances as he [or she] perceived them at the time, however inaccurate that perception may have been'.[127] This subjective evaluation is followed by an objective evaluation, which enquires 'from [the subjective] standpoint' the reasonableness of the defendant's disturbed emotional reaction to the situation.[128] Neither the code nor the courts have specified how to understand 'reasonableness' in this context. Thus, its meaning is largely dependent on the interpretation of the jury on a case-by-case basis that takes into account a wide array of indicators, such as the person's temperament, character traits, or 'personal handicaps', which can include 'blindness, shock from traumatic injury, and extreme grief' but not 'idiosyncratic moral values'.[129] Although the code's formulation heavily emphasises the defendant's situation, courts nevertheless appear to grant this mitigation when there is proof that the defendant acted in a sufficiently intense emotional state, regardless of the appropriateness of the emotional reaction to the situation.[130]

Essentially, the EMED defence is founded on control impairment due to an emotional pathology that is just short of insanity. While the code accepts that extreme emotions may overturn reason and control, if a defendant acts under strong emotional influence – however pathological and enduring in nature – this condition is usually not treated as the kind of mental *incapacity* (the defence is

[124] See *State v Elliott* (n 122) (stating that the EED defence does not require that 'the homicidal act occurs immediately after the cause of the extreme emotional disturbance … An homicidal influenced by an extreme emotional disturbance is not one which is necessarily committed in the "hot blood" stage, but rather one that was brought about by a significant mental trauma that caused the defendant to brood for a long period of time and to react violently …').

[125] *Patterson v New York* (n 122).

[126] American Law Institute, Model Penal Code and Commentaries, Comment to § 210.3 (1985) 62–63.

[127] *People v Casassa* (n 122).

[128] ibid.

[129] American Law Institute (n 126) 62.

[130] See eg *People v McKenzie*, 19 NY3d 463, 467 (2012); *People v Israel*, 26 NY3d 236, 239 (2015).

uncoincidentally called *disturbance*) that might exculpate him or her. A person can be excused for losing his or her control capacity only when his or her cognitive faculties were impaired. It follows that a lack of proof of a cognitive (ie, knowledge, understanding, reasoning) defect permits no space for a control excuse on the basis of emotional impairment alone. In the absence of a cognitive or intellectual defect, emotional impairment is simply insufficient to fully satisfy the law.

ii. Emotional Incapacity and Legal Insanity

While criminal law presupposes emotionality as an additional feature of the subject of culpability (ie, it presupposes persons to have potentially incapacitating emotions that they supposedly can and should control), it does not afford weight to a pathological 'lack' of emotional capacities. Few criminal law voluntarists have admittedly wondered whether certain emotional capacities – most commonly those for empathy and other reflective emotions, such as guilt or remorse – should figure into the voluntarist model of culpability in its mental capacity component.[131] Doctrinally, however, emotional (in)capacity is not contemplated in culpability determinations.

Such exclusion is most evident in either the formulations or practical applications of the paradigm capacity-based excuse, namely legal insanity. While standards such as the M'Naghten rule or the IDRA do not consider emotional capacity at all,[132] the MPC seems to assign some relevance to a lack of emotional capacity. As discussed above, the verb 'to appreciate' was introduced with the explicit aim of expanding 'technical knowledge or detached awareness' to an actual understanding of the legal and moral significance of one's conduct. However, the flexibility of the verb 'to appreciate' has generated some interpretive confusion because the breadth of its scope is unclear.[133] A broad interpretation of the expression 'to appreciate criminality (wrongfulness)' appears to include the capacity to emotionally perceive and appreciate the wrongfulness of one's conduct.[134] With this understanding, the cognitive prong of the ALI test would also extend to cases

[131] For instance, Morse has conceded that people should also be capable of empathy and other reflective emotions like guilt, remorse, and regret. See Morse (n 87) 115. Moore has likewise recognised the importance of emotional capacities that allow people to care about morality; however, he correctly observed that criminal law in action does not presuppose such emotional capacities in persons, and left open the question of whether the law should more accurately take account of them. See Moore (n 18) 614–15.

[132] See Lord Devlin, 'Mental Abnormality and the Criminal Law' in R MacDonald (ed) *Changing Legal Objectives* (Toronto, University of Toronto Press, 1963) 71, 85 (explaining that '[i]t is reason which makes a man responsible to the law .... It is what distinguishes him from the animals, which emotional disorder does not; it is what makes him man .... So it is fitting that nothing other than a defect of reason should give him complete absolution').

[133] See Kuh (n 64) 797–98 (asserting that the words 'substantial' and 'appreciate' 'were intentionally chosen for their imprecision').

[134] RJ Simon and DE Aaronson, *The Insanity Defense: A Critical Assessment of Law and Policy in the Post-Hinckley Era* (New York, Praeger Publishers, 1988) 37–39.

in which the person is able to cognitively comprehend that his or her behaviour is wrong but, due to emotional abnormalities, is unable to 'feel' the normative significance of his or her behaviour.

However, several authors have observed that this extension is merely ostensible, as the verb 'to appreciate' is limited to a purely cognitive understanding of the normative significance of one's conduct.[135] This interpretation has been supported by numerous court opinions[136] that have made and endorsed an objectivist interpretation of the cognitive prong of the ALI test. In fact, with the exception of only a few cases,[137] courts have generally interpreted 'to appreciate the criminality [wrongfulness]' as a clause that refers to legal and social (rather than personal) standards of right and wrong. In other words, for a defendant to qualify as legally insane under the cognitive prong of the ALI test, he or she must be unable to appreciate that his or her conduct violates both law and community views of morality, regardless of his or her subjective moral beliefs and feelings. Therefore, a defendant who appreciates *both* the illegality and the societal immorality of his or her actions cannot be found legally insane in view of his or her purely personal (though however delusional) moral code.

This interpretation of the cognitive prong of the ALI standard is further confirmed by the so-called 'caveat paragraph' of the test, which explicitly rules out 'any abnormality manifested only by repeated criminal or otherwise antisocial conduct from the notion of mental disease or defect'.[138] This provision was introduced for the explicit purpose of excluding defendants with a psychopathic disorder from the range of eligible candidates for the insanity defence.[139] Descriptions of psychopathy emphasise that people with such a disorder are sufficiently intelligent to know the facts, have no misperception of reality, and understand that there are rules and consequences for violating them. They 'simply' lack empathy, regret, guilt, or, more generally, prosocial emotions and feelings. Such emotional deficiencies prevent this category of people from perceiving the interpersonal significance of harmful acts or emotionally responding to the interpersonal implications (eg, the suffering of the victims) of their behaviour in an adaptive way. Even when people with psychopathy display such significant emotional abnormalities, they are never legally excused for their criminal actions. Rather, their impaired emotional faculties (eg, poor empathy, callousness) are considered symptomatic of particularly dangerous personalities that imply a high probability of repeatedly harming society. Thus, their condition is likely to lead to harsher sentences in order to safeguard public safety needs.[140]

[135] See Goldstein (n 59) 88; Parry (n 63) 311.

[136] See, eg, *State v Wilson* 242 Conn. 605, 700 A.2d 633, 640–41 (Conn. 1997); *People v Serravo* 823 P.2d 128, 138 (Colo. 1992); *State v Worlock* 117 N.J. 596, 605–6 (N.J. 1990).

[137] *United States v Segna*, 555 F.2d 226 (9th Cir. 1977).

[138] American Law Institute § 4.01(2) (1962).

[139] See R Slovenko, *Psychiatry in Law/Law in Psychiatry*, 2nd edn (New York, Routledge, 2009) 197.

[140] eg R Schopp, *Automatism, Insanity, and the Psychology of Criminal Responsibility: A Philosophical Inquiry* (New York, Cambridge University Press, 1991) 33.

Psychopathy is a uniquely controversial and extreme diagnostic category. However, other (less challenging) types of pathological conditions, such as frontotemporal dementia or psychosis, may entail pathological emotional deficits that can result in a lack of perception of the interpersonal significance of one's conduct. Under current criminal law, such emotional dysfunctions – and the ways in which they may affect behaviour – are not considered among the host of relevant capacities that a person must possess to be legally culpable, regardless of the relevant diagnosis. As long as people possess intact intellectual faculties of understanding and substantive instrumental reasoning with reference to normative standards of right and wrong, a deficiency in emotional faculties does not affect their culpability.

B. The Irrelevance of the Social Environment

While mainstream theoretical discourses of culpability and legal doctrine afford some (not fundamental) weight to emotions in the architecture of culpability and its determinations, they entirely factor out socio-environmental factors, such as the social background and living social environment of the person. Consideration of such factors within culpability has fuelled heated debate among criminal theorists over the years, and such disputes are ongoing.

In view of the strong statistical links between poverty and other forms of socio-environmental deprivation and crime, arguments favouring the inclusion of socio-environmental factors in culpability determinations have generally focused on the potentially excusing role of particularly difficult or adverse socio-environmental backgrounds and living conditions of perpetrators. Several proposals have been advanced to afford excusing weight to such conditions. Many of these proposals, which are classed under the rubric of 'rotten social background' or 'socio-environmental deprivation' defence, maintain that adverse social conditions that influence (or even motivate) criminal behaviour should provide an excuse that is akin to that of diminished capacity or legal insanity, as living in conditions of social deprivation could feasibly impair a person's capacity for internalising mainstream social values and behaving in conformity to the law.[141]

These proposals have been vigorously rejected for numerous reasons. Most notably, recommendations to introduce a socio-environmental deprivation defence pose the dangerous risk of pathologising poverty and other adverse

[141] See D Bazelon, 'The Morality of Criminal Law: A Rejoinder to Professor Morse' (1976) 49 *California Law Review* 1269; R Delgado, '"Rotten Social Background": Should the Criminal Law Recognize a Defense of Severe Environmental Deprivation?' (1985) 3 *Law & Inequality* 9; ME Gilman, 'The Poverty Defense' (2013) 47 *University of Richmond Law Review* 495. For a list of further proposals, see A Kaye, 'The Secret Politics of Compatibilist Criminal Law' (2007) 55 *Kansas Law Review* 365, 422 (mentioning 'urban psychosis', 'black rage', 'involuntary rage' triggered by hard social conditions and 'cultural isolation').

social conditions. Such pathologising could cause socially disadvantaged people to become victims of further stigma and discrimination. Indeed, claiming that people who live under difficult social conditions lack the capacity to conform their behaviour to mainstream social values and the law, could suggest a dangerous link between social disadvantage and mental incapacity.[142] This scenario is profoundly in contrast with the egalitarian spirit of criminal law, which aims to treat and respect its recipients as equal, rational creatures who are capable of grasping its dictates and behaving accordingly.

From a purely theoretical perspective, voluntarism does not deny that socio-environmental factors have a causal role in human behaviour. Even so, it does not perceive such factors as necessary or sufficient conditions to excuse behaviour. First, adverse socio-environmental factors play a *probabilistic* causal role in that they just increase the chances that a person may engage in criminal behaviour.[143] Second, although cultural and social mechanisms certainly shape and explain behaviour, criminal law still considers human action to be governed by reason and views people as the ultimate locus of responsibility for their choices. Third, culpability is personal: it can only and exclusively be ascribed to a person in view of his or her choice. Thus, acknowledgment that external socio-environmental factors impact behaviour is compatible with the assumption that the actor is nonetheless able to effectuate rational choice and is responsible for such choice. Fourth, socio-environmental deprivation is irrelevant to both the mental capacity and fair opportunity components of the architecture of culpability.

Andrew Kaye has clearly illustrated the latter point in explaining that challenging social conditions are 'beside the point' of mental capacity inquiries, which focus solely on the state of a person's mental composition (in terms of cognitive and, possibly, control capacities) at the time of the crime. In other words, such inquiries are only concerned with whether the actor possesses a given mental capacity or if his or her mental capacity is sound enough to consider him or her capable of effecting rational choice and conforming his or her behaviour to the law. Although difficult social conditions 'can have a formative influence'[144] on such capacities, they are nevertheless irrelevant for the purpose of assessing whether the defendant *possesses* sound mental capacity. Moreover, as Kaye has noted, it is implausible that any but the most catastrophically difficult social conditions would

[142] S Kadish, 'Excusing Crime' (1987) 75 *California Law Review* 257, 284–85 ('The reason [social deprivation] fails to make out a moral excuse, as insanity does, is that it fails to establish the breakdown of rationality and judgment that is incompatible with moral agency. It may be conceded that cultural deprivation contributed to making the defendant what he is [though, of course, only some people so brought up end up committing crimes]. But what is he? He is a person with wrong values and inclinations, not a human being whose powers of judgment and rational action have been so destroyed that he must be dealt with like an infant, a machine, or an animal. Those who propose this defense are plainly moved by compassion for the downtrodden, to whom, however, it is nonetheless an insult').

[143] SJ Morse, 'Severe Environmental Deprivation (AKA RSB): A Tragedy, Not a Defense' (2011) 2 *Alabama Civil Rights & Civil Liberties Law Review* 147.

[144] Kaye (n 141) 384.

be able to disrupt the mental capacities that are relevant in the voluntarist model of culpability. In fact, it is hardly possible for challenging social conditions (eg, childhood deprivation) to disrupt a person's cognitive or intellectual *capacities* of knowledge and practical reasoning.

Socio-environmental deprivation is also irrelevant to fair opportunity inquiries. As indicated above, the fair opportunity inquiry revolves around the actor's actual situation in terms of the objective circumstances that were present at the time of the crime. It regards whether the actor received a fair opportunity to behave differently under those particular circumstances. Because it focuses on such a short timeframe, the fair opportunity inquiry 'is not interested in the sort of longitudinally measured "opportunities" such as personal development, upbringing, living conditions, education, or employment'.[145] Such conditions can be difficult and unfair or even cause the actor to feel 'anguish, resentment, and anger'[146] or experience chronic stress; nevertheless, they do not pose the kind of immediate, intense, transitory lack of choice that deprives a person of a fair opportunity to behave differently at the precise time of the criminal act.

The irrelevance of socio-environmental factors within culpability is strongly evident in positive law, wherein no socio-environmental excuse or defence exists, and legal doctrines are mostly insensitive to social factors for culpability determinations. In actual practice, adverse social conditions or backgrounds may have an evidentiary value at most insofar as they can offer insight into facts that are determinative of the existence of a given (usually legal insanity) excuse. Still, the evidentiary value of socio-environmental factors is mostly indirect and secondary to prove (or disprove) the relevant excuse. Altogether, criminal law directs scarce attention to the social dimension of the person.

VII. Emotions and Socio-environmental Factors in Sentencing

Although emotions and socio-environmental factors are not essential to culpability ascriptions, they may be granted some value at sentencing. Specifically, the emotional and social dimensions of an individual (most commonly in capital cases) *may* gain circumstantial weight – either mitigating or aggravating – to modulate penalty determinations.

Despite different sentencing systems existing at both the US federal[147] and state levels, emotional and social factors that may affect sentencing generally

[145] ibid.

[146] ibid. 385.

[147] United States Code Title 18 § 3553 (1984); United States Sentencing Commission, Guidelines Manual (2016) (hereinafter Federal Sentencing Guidelines). See also *United States v Booker* 543 U.S. 220 (2005) (stating that Federal Sentencing Guidelines are advisory only).

comprise three broad categories. The first category encompasses endogenous impairments or deficiencies in the person's mental capacity that affected his or her choice to engage in criminal activity. Such incapacity or diminished capacity may be due to mental illness or mental retardation, as well as extreme emotional distress.[148]

The second category of sentencing mitigation consists of evidence that the criminal act was out of the person's character. A reduced sentence might result, therefore, from the following circumstances: the crime was a first offence; the person tried to mitigate the harm; the person has a history of steady employment, fulfilment of family obligations, and good citizenship; or, more generally, the criminal act was aberrant in light of the person's established character traits and respect for the law's values.[149] Likewise, expressions of specific emotions, such as remorse or regret for the crime, *may* be considered as symptomatic of good character and possibly lead to lower penalties.[150] In contrast, when the person on trial displays emotional absence (eg, a lack of remorse, callousness, general blunted affect), it is usually viewed as an indicator of greater dangerousness. Accordingly, it will likely be considered as an aggravating factor and inform a harsher punitive outcome.[151]

The third, and most challenging, category includes evidence of the person's past emotional traumas[152] such as a history of abuse and neglect[153] that may connect to the crime that was committed. There is admittedly no consistent approach to the manner in which trauma is treated by sentencing systems in the US, especially in non-capital cases.[154] Federal courts generally provide no discount for trauma.[155]

[148] See eg *United States v Cantu*, 12 F.3d 1506, 1516 (9th Cir. 1993) (PTSD qualified as an appropriate basis for downward departure under 5K2.13 of the Federal Sentencing Guidelines). But see B J. Grey, 'Neuroscience, PTSD, and Sentencing Mitigation' (2012) 34 *Cardozo Law Review* 53, 65 (discussing inconsistency in federal sentencing's treatment of various mental health conditions).

[149] Federal Sentencing Guidelines (n 147) §5K2.20.

[150] eg Federal Sentencing Guidelines (n 147) 3E1.1(2); See also S Bandes, 'Remorse and Criminal Justice' (2016) 8 *Emotion Review* 14; S Pillsbury, 'Emotions and Criminal Punishment in Theory and Practice' (2016), available at emotionresearcher.com/emotion-and-criminal-punishment-in-principle-and-in-practice/.

[151] See eg K Wayland, 'The Importance of Recognizing Trauma Throughout Capital Mitigation Investigations and Presentations', (2008) 36 *Hofstra Law Review* 923, 947; BH Ward, 'Sentencing Without Remorse' (2006) 38 *Loyola University Chicago Law Journal* 131.

[152] Federal Sentencing Guidelines (n 147) §5H1.3.

[153] eg *Penry v Lynaugh*, 492 U.S. 302, 319 [1989] ('[E]vidence about [a] defendant's background and character is relevant' to the sentencing decision, 'because of the belief, long held by this society, that defendants who commit criminal acts that are attributable to a disadvantaged background, or to emotional and mental problems, may be less culpable than defendants who have no such excuse').

[154] See M Bagaric et al, 'Trauma and Sentencing: The Case for Mitigating Penalty for Childhood Physical and Sexual Abuse' (2019) 30 *Stanford Law & Policy Review* 1, 12–23 (analysing the inconsistent approach to childhood trauma in four state sentencing systems including California, Texas, New York and Florida and evidencing that 'no statutory provisions in these jurisdictions embody such mitigating factors').

[155] For a federal case law analysis, see M Gohara, 'In Defense of the Injured: How Trauma-Informed Criminal Defense Can Reform Sentencing' (2018) 45 *American Journal of Criminal Law* 1, 25–32.

On the other hand, some states[156] are more prone to confer a penalty discount on the basis of it; however, case law analyses have suggested that courts rarely afford a mitigating weight to the traumas that a person suffered – no matter how severe they are – but tend to privilege other sentencing goals, notably public safety. On average, people with serious histories of trauma rarely obtain a penalty discount in both federal and state sentencing systems. According to Bagaric et al, '[a] possible reason for this is that no clear and persuasive rationale has been developed for mitigating the penalty of offenders who were subjected to childhood abuse'[157] or other severely traumatic experiences.

From another perspective, there is not always a logical and rational scheme that underlies the evaluation of emotional and social factors to effectuate appropriate punishment. Several authors have argued that the evaluation of emotional and social factors in sentencing is influenced by – and therefore expresses – the sentencer's personal biases and emotional attitudes[158] toward the person on trial, which are based on characteristics such as his or her social background, education, employment, or race. Some authors have described this attitude as 'mercy discrimination',[159] whereas others have accounted for it in terms of out-group dehumanisation.[160] Numerous empirical studies[161] have crucially integrated and supported these accounts in demonstrating that courts tend to impose harsher sentences on less educated, poor, and unemployed people who belong to minority groups.

VIII. Conclusion

The paradigm of the culpable person that emerges from voluntarist theory and legal doctrine is profoundly rationalist. This model depicts persons as autonomous and rational beings who act upon choices, they are endowed with a sound mental (cognitive and control) capacity and receive a fair opportunity to avoid

[156] eg New York State. See Bagaric et al (n 154).

[157] Bagaric et al (n 154) 58.

[158] eg S Bandes 'The Heart has Its Reasons: Examining the Strange Persistence of American Death Penalty' in P Robinson, S Garvey and K Ferzan (eds), *Criminal Law Conversations* (New York, Oxford University Press, 2009) 635; Ward (n 151).

[159] eg Pillsbury (n 150).

[160] See M Vasiljevic and G Tendayi Viki, 'Dehumanization, Moral Disengagement, and Public Attitudes to Crime and Punishment' in PG Bain, J Vaes and JP Leyens (eds), *Humanness and Dehumanization* (New York, Psychology Press, 2014) 129.

[161] See eg, D Mustard, 'Racial, Ethnic, and Gender Disparities in Sentencing: Evidence from the U.S. Federal Courts' (2001) 44 *The Journal of Law and Economics* 285; C Betsey, 'Income and Wealth Transfer Effects of Discrimination in Sentencing' (2005) 32 *The Review of Black Political Economy* 111; The Sentencing Project, 'Report of The Sentencing Project to the United Nations Special Rapporteur on Contemporary Forms of Racism, Racial Discrimination, Xenophobia, and Related Intolerance Regarding Racial Disparities in the United States Criminal Justice System' (March 2018) available at www.sentencingproject.org/publications/un-report-on-racial-disparities/.

wrongdoing. This normative model of personhood encapsulates an overall devotion to the cognitive dimension of the mind. Culpability ascriptions are fundamentally based on the assumption that cognitive powers of reason and control allow people to grasp the guiding force of legal norms and conform their behaviour to them. Ultimately, culpability ascriptions revolve around an evaluation of cognitive states and capacities of the actor under the circumstances that were present at the time of the crime.

A further confirmation of the rationalist approach to culpable agency in criminal law emerges from the marginal role that legal inquiry affords to emotions and socio-environmental factors. While the latter are simply excluded from culpability determinations, certain strong emotions are taken into account insofar as they overwhelm reason and control to possibly ground a diminished capacity plea in homicide cases. Overall, culpability operates through a compartmentalised view of persons and their minds that focuses almost entirely on the soundness of the person's knowledge, understanding, and instrumental reasoning abilities under the relevant circumstances.

In the next chapter, I continue my analysis of the 'culpable' person by contextualising culpability within the historical, social, and political dimensions of punishment. My aim is to highlight how the criminal law has come to embrace this model of personhood as well as how such model underpins and supports retribution as the predominant goal of punishment. Furthermore, I illustrate the effects of the rhetoric of retribution, and its underlying narrative of the person, on the actual practice and reality of criminal justice. In addition to *rationalism*, *individualism* is the next key word of my analysis.

2

From the Guilty Mind to the Punished Person: Criminal Culpability through the 'Evolution' of Punishment

I. Introduction

In the preceding pages, I have traced the paradigm of the culpable agent and his or her mind through a normative analysis of broad culpability as it is reflected in both dominant scholarly accounts and codified doctrines. The aspects that have emerged in that analysis may sound familiar to anyone who has approached criminal law. From law students to navigated legal scholars, jurists are acquainted with the dogmatic notions that culpability revolves around the choice of the person, cognition and control are the two mental capacities that are necessary to be criminally culpable, and cognition is the quintessential element of most culpability-related doctrines.

However essential, examining culpability through normative/philosophical lenses does not provide a holistic understanding of it. Like all criminal law doctrines, culpability does not exist in a vacuum, and it cannot be confined to solely philosophical and doctrinal considerations of which aspects of the mind are legally relevant. There are also contextual dimensions to the relationship between culpability and the conception of human nature that it embodies.[1]

Thus, an exhaustive discussion of the criminal law's person requires an analysis beyond the realms of legal theory to delve into the history of culpability theory

[1] In her illuminating work, Nicola Lacey likewise suggests that exhaustive analyses of the responsible subject go beyond philosophy and must also take into account the historical, cultural and institutional dimensions of the criminal law. See N Lacey, *In Search of the Criminal Responsibility: Ideas, Interests, and Institutions* (Oxford, Oxford University Press, 2016). See also A Duff, 'Theories of Criminal Law' in E Zalta (ed), *Stanford Encyclopedia of Philosophy* (Spring 2009), available at stanford.library.sydney.edu.au/archives/spr2009/entries/criminal-law/#DifKin. ('Philosophical theories of criminal law, whether analytical or normative, cannot subsist in isolation. They must have some regard to the empirical actualities of that which they theorise: to the histories of the different systems of criminal law, and to sociological inquiries into their actual operations. Some critical theorists believe that such historical or sociological inquiries will undercut the pretensions of philosophical theorising: that what needs analysing is not the superstructure or superficial self-presentation of the criminal law, on which philosophers tend to concentrate, but the social, political and economic realities lying beneath that surface; and that given the oppressive or conflictual nature of those realities, philosophical theories cannot amount to anything more than doomed attempts to rationalise what is inherently irrational or a-rational').

in relation to the evolution of punishment theory and the reality of punishment practice.[2]

The idea that persons are held responsible and punished for their free and rational choice to engage in criminal conduct is fundamentally rooted in the Western liberal notion of *individualism*.[3] Among the different versions of individualism, the common theme is that the causes of behaviour are located within the person, and persons are personally responsible for their own actions. The solution to individual problems, such as criminal behaviour, entails addressing the person himself or herself but not the social structures in which he or she lives. Overall, individualist ideology in relation to criminal matters can be summarised by three basic assumptions about problematic human behaviour: first, people are the causal locus of behaviour; second, socially problematic and illegal behaviour arises from the individual person who performs it; and third, such behaviour can be eliminated or changed only by either punishing or treating that person.

Over the years, these assumptions have shaped the narrative of culpability and punishment in criminal law theory, legal doctrine, and criminal justice policies. This narrative has notably shifted through two main forms of individualism: libertarian (and subsequently compatibilist) individualism and scientific individualism. Libertarian/compatibilist individualism hinges on self-determination and self-mastery powers of the individual. It promotes the image of the person as an autonomous and rational subject whose choices are the ultimate source of his or her responsibility. Such ideology of individualism characterises the voluntarist paradigm of criminal culpability and, in relation to it, the predominant retributivist understanding of punishment. On the other hand, scientific individualism situates the locus of criminal behaviour in the person's character traits, personality predispositions, and attitudes. This type of individualism predominantly features the narrative of individual criminal dangerousness, which frames crime as a phenomenon that arises from an intrinsic deviancy of the person. Scientific individualism is more prominent in incapacitation-based sentencing criteria, penal policy, and the prison system.

In the following analysis, I highlight that although dominant paradigms of culpability and punishment are more consistent with libertarian/compatibilist individualism than scientific individualism, these two forms of individualism – and the images of the person that they respectively promote – have largely merged in actual practice. Such a merger has ultimately prompted a narrative of the

[2] This analysis does not have the ambition to canvass legal history in exacting detail, but to only capture the most important shifts in normative conceptualisations of human behaviour that underpinned evolving paradigms of culpability and punishment. While legal historians may admittedly find this analysis simplistic, non-historians may appreciate how certain historical passages have shaped today's understandings of culpability and punishment, and the effects of these on the justice system.

[3] See R Pound, 'Do We Need a Philosophy of Law?' (1905) 5 *Columbia Law Review* 339, 346 ('Men have changed their views as to the relative importance of the individual and of society; but the common law has not. Indeed, the common law knows individuals only .... And this compels a narrow and one-sided view').

criminal law's person that conveys wickedness, differentness, exclusion, and stigmatisation and has contributed overall to an increase in the punitiveness of the criminal justice system. In its turn, punitiveness has been found not only to have the paradoxical effect of incrementing criminality but also to severely violate the fundamental right to human dignity among those who are involved in criminal justice.

II. Rational Individualism and the Enlightenment

Although the origins of Anglo-American law date back to more ancient times, contemporary criminal law has largely come to re-embrace notions that emerged from the historical conception of legal and liberal individualism that took place during the Enlightenment, which is also known as the Age of Reason. Through the works of timeless thinkers such as Jean-Jacques Rousseau, John Locke, Jean-Louis Montesquieu, Cesare Beccaria, Jeremy Bentham, and Adam Smith, Enlightenment philosophy revolutionised the relationship between the individual citizen and the state and profoundly reformed the goals and methods of criminal justice.

The core conception of Enlightenment rationalist philosophy is that the civilised society is founded on individual freedom and pure reason.

It dictates that society has to be based on humanity, equity, and individual rights, and government intervention should be limited and performed in a non-discretionary manner.[4] Furthermore, all human beings who live in a law-governed and civilised society are equal, autonomous, and rational creatures whose 'reason' endows them with the powers of understanding and control. Reason also allows them to grasp the meaning of the rules of social conduct that are enshrined in legal norms and to act in conformity with them.[5]

The process of rationalisation and secularisation of the relationship between individual citizens and the state also implied a novel way to conceive of crime and punishment. The religious image of perpetrators as sinners who deserved to suffer the pains of torture to achieve redemption, which was in vogue during the *ancient regime* in Europe, waned,[6] and crime came to be viewed as a public wrong

[4] See M Foucault, *Discipline and Punish: The Birth of the Prison* (A Sheridan transl) (New York, Vintage Book, 2012) 82 (emphasising the hypocrisy of contractarians narratives of liberty and autonomy at the heart of the eighteenth century reform movement and suggesting that such narratives mask a 'new strategy for the exercise of the power to punish' … to make of the punishment and repression of illegalities a regular function, coextensive with society; not to punish less, but to punish better; to punish with an attenuated severity perhaps, but in order to punish with more universality and necessity; to insert the power to punish more deeply into the social body').

[5] For a criticism of the relationship between freedom and Reason, sustained by social contract theorists, see I Berlin, *Four Essays on Liberty* (Oxford, Oxford University Press, 1969) 118.

[6] See eg H Kramers and J Sprenger, *The Malleus Maleficarum* (*transl: The Hammer of the Witches*) (1486) M Summers (transl) (New York, Dover Publications, 1971).

against the state. People who broke the law were perceived as equal and rational agents who could understand norms of conduct, control their instincts,[7] and act in accordance with norms of conduct. Accordingly, breaking the law entailed an instrumental choice to violate socially protected values in the interest of personal gain.

The perspective of law-breakers as fundamentally rationally selfish people became the benchmark for utilitarian approaches to punishment, which also marked the birth of the modern prison system. The common idea among Enlightenment thinkers was that punishment had to guarantee individual justice and effective deterrence in order to benefit the wider society. Cesare Beccaria justified punishment as a response to a breach of the social contract by a free person[8] and argued that only a system of punishments respecting the person could effectively deter crime. In opposition to the brutal system of the *ancient regime*, which could deliver maximum and harsh punishment for the smallest crime, Beccaria advocated for a system of proportionality between crime and punishment.[9]

In Britain, the utilitarian reformer Jeremy Bentham[10] insisted that punishment was a form of pain or a cost, and its infliction could only be justified by its potential to deter the evil of crime. Such a pure utilitarian perspective defines the individual as a rational and calculating being who weighs the benefits of engaging in crime against the disadvantages of punishment. Thus, the ultimate function of (criminal) law was to guide, manipulate, and dissuade rational beings from choosing to engage in criminal behaviour by communicating rules of conduct and sanctions for their breach. Consequently, punishment (and prison in particular) was intended to communicate the painful consequences of violating the law that citizens had to consider when deciding whether to break the law. If the expected pain of punishment was heavier than the anticipated pleasure of it, then the individual would be deterred from breaking the law. Ultimately, more severe punishment is more likely to discourage a rationally calculating individual from partaking in criminal acts.

Rights and respect for the individual and public utility were equally (however through a different lens) present in the retributive philosophy of punishment in

[7] M O'Hare, *The History of the Pleas to the Crow, Vol.1* (In the Savoy, 1736) 14-15. ('Man is naturally endowed with two great faculties, understanding and liberty of will [...] the liberty or choice of the will presupposeth an act of the understanding to know the thing or action chosen by the will ....').

[8] C Beccaria, *An Essay on Crimes and Punishment. By Marquis Beccaria of Milan. With A Commentary by M. de Voltaire. A New Edition Corrected* (Albany: WC Little and Co, 1872) 19 ('Thus, it was necessity that forced men to give up a part of their liberty. It is certain then, that every individual would choose to put into the public stock the smallest portion possible ... The aggregate of these, the smallest portion possible, forms of the right of punishing').

[9] M De Caro, 'Utilitarianism and Retributivism in Beccaria' (2016) 2 *The Italian Law Journal* 1 (suggesting that Beccaria combined proto-utilitiarian views and some elements of negative retributivism including penal proportionality).

[10] See J Bentham, *An Introduction to the Principles of Morals and Legislation* (1780) (Kitchener, Batoche Books, 2000).

Germany. Kant and Hegel[11] shared the opinion that punishment was a matter of the right of and respect for individuals as rational beings. Consequently, not punishing people who break the law wrongs them. In their philosophically pure, deontological thought, retributive punishment must be based on the individual guilt and, above all, equal to the harm caused by the crime.

Enlightenment thinkers' views of crime and punishment are echoed in William Blackstone's *Commentaries* – the first common law treaty of criminal law – which heavily impacted the foundations of American criminal law. In seeking to educate the English ruling class on a rational approach to the substantive law, Blackstone reached the conclusion of Beccaria, 'an ingenious writer, who seems to have well studied the springs of human action, that crimes are more effectually prevented by the *certainty* than by the *severity* of punishment'.[12] Blackstone adopted the Enlightenment conception of crime as a public wrong and endorsed the idea that criminal liability and punishment are fundamentally concerned with the unlawful act that is perpetrated against the state.[13] Since criminal liability and punishment ultimately centred on the harm that is associated with the criminal offence, the legal inquiry into culpability was limited to assessing the 'vicious [unlawful] will'[14] of the actor. Although inspections of the moral wickedness of the individual's mind were unnecessary, Blackstone's reference to 'vicious will' reveals that an individual's choice to commit an unlawful act was ineradicable to a finding of criminal liability.[15]

Ideas of individual autonomy and rationality of perpetrators alongside a public view of crime and the preventative (rather than retributive) function of punishment and prison that Enlightenment thinkers endorsed strongly impacted the basis of criminal law and justice in the US[16] and continued throughout the nineteenth century.[17] However, the rational and libertarian individualism of the

[11] I Kant, *The Metaphysics of Morals: Metaphysical Elements of Justice* (1797) (J Ladd transl) (Indianapolis, Bobbs-Merrill, 1965); GWF Hegel, *Elements of the Philosophy of Right, Abstract Right* (1821) A Wood (ed), (Cambridge, Cambridge University Press, 1991).

[12] W Blackstone, *Commentaries on the Laws of England: In Four Books; With an Analysis of the Work, Vol. 2* (New York, William Dean Publisher, 1853) 12.

[13] See G Leonard, 'Towards a Legal History of American Criminal Theory: Culture and Doctrine from Blackstone to the Model Penal Code' (2003) *Buffalo Criminal Law Review* 691, 713.

[14] ibid, 713-14.

[15] R Pound, *Introduction to Sayre's Cases on Criminal Law* (Eagan, MN: Lawyers Co-operative, 1927) 8-9 ('Historically, substantive criminal law is based upon a theory of punishing the vicious will. It postulates a free agent confronted with a choice between doing right and doing wrong and choosing freely to do wrong'). See also *Morissette v United States*, 342 U.S. 246, 250 (1952).

[16] See B Harcourt, 'Beccaria's *On Crimes and Punishments:* A Mirror on the History of Modern Criminal Law' in M Dubber (ed), *Foundational Texts in Modern Criminal Law* (Oxford, Oxford University Press, 2014) 39, 46 ('punishment must be related to the harm associated with the criminal offense, and the metric of harm, for Beccaria, is to be measured by the harm to society, not, as it is for retributivists, by the *mens rea* or the evil intent of the offender').

[17] See H Elmer Barnes, 'Historical Origin of the Prison System in America' (1921) 12 *Journal of the American Institute of Criminal Law and Criminology* 35; J Bressler, *The Birth of American Law: An Italian Philosopher and the American Revolution* (Durham, NC, Carolina Academic Press, 2014).

Enlightenment legacy intersected and ran parallel with another form of individualism: scientific individualism.

III. Between Libertarian and Scientific Individualism

The nineteenth century is considered the 'formative era' of American law.[18] It also featured laissez-faire capitalism and domination of the cultural ethos by an ideology that Alexis de Tocqueville in 1835 called 'democratic individualism'.[19] Through the glorification of single individuals who enjoyed equal powers of freedom and self-reliance within society, individualist ideology exacerbated a narrative of persons as self-governing and self-determinant of their own course. Individual autonomy became a key societal principle, and each and every individual was considered responsible for his or her own choices and self-cultivation of moral character. Accordingly, bad behaviour was viewed as a product of the individual's failure to cultivate his or her own character with adequate moral seriousness and of his or her consequently poor choices.

The glorification of the individual amid the democratisation of American culture entailed an increased emphasis on legal libertarianism. Jacksonian-Democrat codifiers such as Edward Livingston[20] sought to vindicate the rule of law and its master principles of liberty and equality. The reformers embraced such libertarian and equality-focused principles in calling for circumscription of criminal law to only those behaviours that were positively designated by statutes.[21] Criminal culpability was confined to statutory elements of the offence and deprived of any moral connotations. The guilty mind was conceived of in terms of descriptive mental states without also comprising arbitrary elements of moral fault. The logic of these principles suggests that criminal conviction occurred only when the relevant person had manifested guilt with respect to each and every one of the elements in a statute. No person should be subject to punishment without knowing that his or her conduct had violated a statute, and suck knowledge would indicate self-determination and choosing of his or her conduct.

Persons were presumed to understand the consequences of their actions and self-determine their behaviour; hence, they were most likely culpable of the acts that

[18] R Pound, *The Formative Era of American Criminal Law* (Boston, Little, Brown & Co., 1938).

[19] A de Tocqueville, *Democracy in America* (1835) H Mansfield and D Wintrop (eds and transl) (Chicago, The University of Chicago Press 2002) See also J Whitman, 'What Happened to Tocqueville's America?' (2007) 74 *Social Research, Punishment: The US Record* 251 (arguing that the American concept of democracy – which de Tocqueville exalted in his writings – is the ultimate cause of the harsh punitiveness that characterises today's criminal justice system).

[20] See SH Kadish, 'Codifiers of the Criminal Law: Wechsler's Predecessors' (1978) 78 *Columbia Law Review* 1098.

[21] See Leonard (n 13) 757.

they performed.[22] In this libertarian narrative of culpability, judging an individual's unlawful choice necessarily involved abstracting that individual from the context – the environment that conditioned or even caused that choice to an indeterminable degree.[23] In other words, the adjudication of culpability required that individuals were 'sealed off' from their social relations, context, and background, which possibly gave rise to action. Criminal liability was built on the assumption that culpability was personal insofar as it was founded on the individual's free choice.[24]

Overall, the doctrine of culpability partly continued the rationalist legacy of Enlightenment ideology that individuals and their reason were the ultimate causal locus of behaviour. Accordingly, culpability attributions remained substantially immune[25] to the pressures of a different type of individualism – scientific individualism – that was endorsed by the developing psychological, psychiatric, and criminological sciences. From phrenology to social Darwinism to Lombroso's positivism, the growing prestige of the behavioural sciences and their deterministic stances began to undercut the rhetoric of crime as an individual, autonomous choice. These scientific approaches viewed crime as the product of an individual's physical traits, personality, character, and biology, all which had to be subject to empirical investigation.[26] The narrative of 'differentness' between 'criminals' or 'delinquents' and law-abiding individuals became increasingly defined and popular in common sense, scientific, social, and criminal policy discourses[27] on crime with widespread political implications.[28]

Whereas scientific perspectives of human nature and crime did not influence the question of criminal culpability, they had a significant impact on criminal

[22] See OW Holmes, *The Common Law* (Boston, Little, Brown & Company, 1881) 253 (writing that legal standards 'take no account of incapacities, unless the weakness is so marked as to fall into well-known exceptions. Such as infancy or madness. They assume that every man is as able as every other to behave as they command').

[23] See C Haney, 'Criminal Justice and the Nineteenth-Century Paradigm: The Triumph of Psychological Individualism in the "Formative Era"' (1982) 6 *Law and Human Behavior* 191, 194.

[24] ibid, 209.

[25] ibid, 209–10. See also A Norrie, *Crime, Reason, and History: A Critical Introduction to Criminal Law* (Cambridge, Cambridge University Press, 1993) 178–9 (discussing conflicting views of crime between law and psychiatry during the nineteenth century and arguing that '[f]or the lawyers, a society of rational individuals with a propensity for evil was held in check by a firm penal code which punished the wrongdoer for purposes of deterrence and justice. [On the other hand] the development of medical science [...] suggested a new technological approach to social order, in which the problems of crime would be solved not by the punishment of an individual who could not help himself, but by isolating and treating the causes of crime within the psyche. [...] Psychiatrists did not just disagree with lawyers, they threatened to "relocate the symbols of the moral order" by abolishing evil and retribution') (citation omitted).

[26] See Haney (n 23) 212 ('Even attempts to explicitly acknowledge the role of external, environmental variables in crime causation drifted invariably towards the dispositional and individualistic').

[27] Holmes (n 22) ('stood on the moral grounds which are proposed for it, the first thing to be considered would be those limitations in the capacity for choosing rightly which arise from abnormal instincts, want of education, lack of intelligence, and all other defects which are most marked in the criminal classes').

[28] See Haney (n 23) 203.

justice and penal policy. In particular, punishment practices became oriented toward treating crime perpetrators as individuals of defective and deviant inner traits. The preventative penology of the Enlightenment was thus supplanted by a penology based on incapacitation, treatment, and reform. The penitentiary moved from a place in which people were incarcerated to be deterred into a site at which people were locked up to be fixed.[29] Thus, the penitentiary no longer served purely utilitarian/preventive goals and gradually assumed a more individualised dimension. The prison environment was initially structured to support character-building, reflection, and penitence. Gradually, it turned into a site that more heavily targeted harsh correctional treatment (too often correctional *mis*treatment) of incarcerated people through a state of social exclusion, precarious living conditions, and profound isolation.[30]

IV. The Rise and Fall of Treatmentist Rehabilitation: From Penal Modernism to the Model Penal Code

Scientific individualism remained dominant well into the first half of the twentieth century. During that period, which is commonly referred to as

[29] See H Franke, 'The Rise and Decline of Solitary Confinement: Socio-Historical Explanations of Long-term Penal Changes' (1992) 32 *British Journal of Criminology* 125, 137 ('the enthusiasm for solitary confinement cannot be seen in isolation from the highly individualistic concept of sin and evil avowed by the confessional politicians and members of the societies of for moral improvement of prisoners').

[30] C Haney, 'The Contextual Revolution in Psychology and the Question of Prison Effects' in A Liebling and S Maruna (eds), *The Effects of Imprisonment* (New York, Routledge, 2005) 66, 71–72 ('The rise of imprisonment during the 19th century was entirely consistent with the emphasis on individualism that was enshrined in the American legal system during the same period … [The prison form] came increasingly to embody the staunchly individualist view that the causes of behavior were internal. [P]rison continued to be the place where putatively damaged persons were taken to have their defects addressed. As the century progressed, "prison science" drew increasingly from the loose set of ideas that were being formalised under the rubric of psychology and science of human behavior. [S]cientific techniques quickly degenerated into outright mistreatment when their prisoner-changing programmes failed to produce the expected results'). See also S Shalev, 'Solitary Confinement and Supermax Prisons: A Human Rights and Ethical Analysis' (2011) 1 *Journal of Forensic Psychology Practice* 151, 152 (reporting that 'solitary confinement was first widely and systematically used on both sides of the Atlantic in the newly built "separate" and "silent" penitentiaries of the early to mid-nineteenth century, which were specially designed to enable the strict isolation of convicts from one another and from the outside world. Viewing crime as an infectious but curable disease, it was believed that once left alone with their conscience and the Bible, prisoners would engage in inner reflection, see the error of their ways, and be reformed into law-abiding citizens'). Solitary confinement was largely abandoned toward the end of the century due to the severe harm it caused to individuals and its inefficiency in inducing reformation. In *In re Medley* [134 U.S. 160 (1890)], the US Supreme Court famously acknowledged that solitary confinement was responsible for producing harmful effects on people's psychological health. As a result, solitary confinement was no longer to be universally applied to all people in custody; rather, it was to be reserved only for those whom other methods of discipline proved ineffective. As the use of solitary confinement was reduced in many prison systems across the country, so too were the debates over its reputed harmfulness. However, a combination of events in the twentieth century led to the resurgence and expansion of solitary confinement as a punitive and incapacitative practice.

'progressive era' or era of 'penal modernism',[31] criminal law experienced a wave of positivist penology. Legal thinkers were widely affected by the 'scientific' ideas that surrounded them. The majority of these thinkers affirmed ideas that were mostly compatible with a libertarian understanding of culpability, yet many still followed the lead of scientists in approaching crime in decidedly causation-based terms.

Enshrined in the works of authors such as Zebulon Brockway, Sheldon and Eleonor Glueck, and Albert Lévitt, penal modernism ultimately sought to understand crime and criminal law from a modern scientific perspective. Crime was framed as a complex empirical phenomenon that results from psychosocial cues; accordingly, criminal law was considered a dynamic instrument for addressing social problems. Punishment, which was relabelled as *treatment*, was conceived of as essentially therapeutic in character and supposed to be tailored to the characterological traits of individual perpetrators with the aim of rehabilitating those who could be rehabilitated and incapacitating those who were dangerous for as long as necessary. Thus, the ultimate goal of criminal law was the neutralisation – both physical and psychological – of the individual through peno-correctional treatments that sought to reform personality aspects that predisposed the individual to criminality.

Under penal modernism, the core matter of the criminal law was that the perpetrator and his or her physical and psychological structure renders him or her a danger to society. The criminal act was viewed as a symptom or manifestation of his or her dangerousness. The mental state with which the accused committed the offence was relevant to adjudication as a criterion to assess the accused's dangerousness.[32] Thus, findings of culpability served the end of indicating the level of social danger that the accused posed in order to identify individualised treatments that were tailored to his or her individual characteristics.

Penal modernism was key to reforming criminal justice and transforming it into a reformatory system of social defence and controls that hinged on individualisation.[33] During the aforementioned era, this ideology led to the introduction of indeterminate prison sentences, prison-based treatment programmes, probation laws, and parole release on the basis of treatment progress of the relevant individual.

[31] For a thorough historical and critical analysis of penal modernism, see M Pifferi, *Rethinking Punishment, A Comparative History of Criminology and Penology in the Nineteenth and Twentieth Centuries* (New York, Oxford University Press, 2016). See also J Whitman, 'The Case for Penal Modernism: Beyond Utility and Desert' (2016) 1 *Critical Analysis of Law* 143. For comments on Whitman's account of Penal Modernism, see eg L Farmer, 'Penal Modernism: An American Tragedy' (2014) 1 *Critical Analysis of Law* 189.

[32] A Levitt, 'Some Societal Aspects of the Criminal Law' (1922) 13 *Journal of Criminal Law and Criminology* 90 ('The mental characteristics of the accused indicate the nature and extent of the peril he represents').

[33] For a discussion about the meanings of 'individualisation' see Pifferi (n 31) 19; J Whitman, *Harsh Justice: Criminal Punishment and the Widening Divide Between America and Europe* (New York, Oxford University Press, 2003) 52.

Amid this ideological climate, in the 1930s, a reform movement that was led by the legal process jurist Herbert Wechsler[34] established the grounds for a *model* code that could systematise, rationalise, and scientise substantive criminal law against the excessive fragmentation of common law as well as detract criminal law from the arbitrariness of the judiciary.[35] The reform movement aspired to construe a model of criminal liability and punishment (*rectius*: treatment) that could limit excessive state intromissions into individual liberty while also ensuring crime prevention through deterrence and peno-correctional treatment.[36] Notwithstanding its commitment to a pragmatic utilitarianism, the model code project gauged criminal liability to the subjectivist principle that wrongdoings should be committed with a culpable mental state.[37] However, '[t]he code's "principle" of "culpability" [was] not a normative principle, a requirement of "morality" or "justice", but an insistence on scientific accuracy'. Indeed, *mens rea* states were intended to 'capture the harmful tendency of an act insofar as they reflect[ed] the dangerousness of the actor'.[38]

The Model Penal [and Correctional][39] Code, which is 'one of the great law reform projects of mid-twentieth century America',[40] was published by the ALI in 1962. The code remarkably introduced a 'model piece of legislation' that aimed to transfer criminal law-making powers to the statute law-making legislature as well as change conversations of criminal law nationwide.[41]

[34] Wechsler and his Columbia Law School mentor Jerome Michael co-authored a two-part article on the law of homicide which set the groundwork for many of the most prominent features of the Model Penal Code project and remained one of the most influential criminal law articles for a good part of the twentieth century. See H Wechsler and J Michael, 'A Rationale of the Law of Homicide: I' (1937) 37 *Columbia Law Review* 701, 703–08; J Michael and H Wechsler, 'A Rationale of the Law of Homicide II' (1937) 37 *Columbia Law Review* 1261.

[35] See M Dubber, 'The Model Penal Code, Legal Process, and the Alegitimacy of American Penalty' in M Dubber (ed), *Foundational Texts in Criminal Law* (New York, Oxford University Press, 2014).

[36] See Wechsler and Michael, 'The Rationale of the Law of Homicide: I' (n 34) 730 n 126 (explicitly eschewing retributive theory) However, Wechsler did not reject retributivist values altogether. For a discussion of Wechsler's evolving views regarding retributive theories of criminal law, see generally A Walker, 'American Oresteia: Herbert Wechsler, the Model Penal Code, and the Uses of Revenge' (2009) *Wisconsin Law Review* 1017.

[37] See D Wolitz, 'Herbert Wechsler, Legal Process, and the Jurisprudential Roots of the Model Penal Code' (2016) 51 *Tulsa Law Review* 633, 661 (noting the retributivist spirit of anchoring criminal conviction to a finding of culpability).

[38] See Dubber (n 35) 241. Against see Wolitz ibid.

[39] Today, this part of the Code is largely forgotten. Moreover, the ALI has revised and replaced its original commitment to rehabilitation with retributivist principles of blameworthiness and proportionality. The Code has affirmed such retributivist turn in 2017. See below section V.

[40] M Dubber, *The Dual Penal State: The Crisis of Criminal Law in Comparative-Historical Perspective* (New York, Oxford University Press, 2018) 216.

[41] ibid, 216 ('The majority of U.S. jurisdictions revised their criminal law in the wake of the Model Penal Code; some, like New York and Pennsylvania, adopted large chunks of the Code, others smaller bits. The Code also reenergised and reoriented American criminal law scholarship and teaching. With its extensive commentaries, it remains the best treatise on American criminal law to this day, over half a century after its completion'). See also M Dubber, 'The American Law Institute's Model Penal Code and European Criminal Law' in A Klip (ed), *Substantive Criminal Law of the European Union* (Antwerpen, Maklu, 2011).

It has been suggested (not without controversy) that the 1962 Code reflected the intentions of the reformers in the 1930s to reinterpret the basic principles of criminal law in light of prevention and peno-correctional treatmentism.[42] Notably, the Penal Code, which established general principles of substantive criminal law and describes specific offences, was construed to 'provide the diagnostic tools for assigning the treatment that is applied according to the Correctional code'.[43] Culpability criteria ultimately served as dangerousness criteria.[44] *Mens rea* states were framed as scalar 'indicators of that abnormal dangerousness which indicates the need for [individualised] peno-correctional treatment'.[45]

On the other hand, peno-correctional treatment could consist of either correctional rehabilitation or, in the event of its failure, incapacitation. Correctional rehabilitation included mandatory treatments and programmes that targeted the character traits, attitudes and predispositions of individual perpetrators with the objective of reforming their personality to enable re-entry into society. The Code's devotion to correctional rehabilitation – which was widely dominant during the 1960s – appeared to heavily promote the view that crime perpetrators are not like 'normal' people who do not break the law, but have a particular flaw that needs to be fixed. Otherwise, their crime-producing deficits will persist and produce the same outcome as in the past, namely criminal involvement.[46] If correctional rehabilitation was unsuccessful, an individual would be incapacitated (ie, neutralised through physical removal from society for an indefinite period of time) to preserve the safety of society.

Although the Code remarkably transformed and uniformed criminal law across jurisdictions, it was not immune to criticism and failures. From a

[42] See M Dubber (n 40). Against see G Lynch, 'Revising the Model Penal Code: Keeping It Real' (2003) 1 *Ohio State Journal of Criminal Law* 219, 222 (noting that 'the core provisions of the Code stand up remarkably well despite the resurgence of retributivism or just deserts thinking. If anything, indeed, they have solidified … [T]he general part of the Code Wechsler produced is quite consistent with Kantian notions of fairness and desert'). See also Wolitz (n 37) 661 (arguing that 'it would be a mistake … to see the Model Penal Code as the product of a strictly utilitarian or deterrence-based mindset. Retributive values were both explicit in the text, in the Commentaries, and in Wechsler's writings about the Code').

[43] M Dubber, 'Criminal Justice Process and War on Crime' in C Sumner (ed), *The Blackwell Companion to Criminology* (Oxford, Blackwell Publishing, 2004) 49, 60.

[44] But see D Brown, 'Penal Modernism in Theory and Practice' (2014) 1 *Critical Analysis of Law* 182, 182 ('The MPC made moral culpability a consistent requirement for all crimes. The MPC's sentencing code, which embraced judicial discretion, rested on that antecedent commitment. Modernists were committed to moral desert as the basis for criminal censure'). See also Wolitz (n 37) 670 (noting that 'the Code's determination that there is no place for imposing the moral condemnation of criminal conviction absent some finding of culpability was a powerful stand principled on retributivist grounds').

[45] Dubber (n 35) 241.

[46] See F Allen, 'The Decline of the Rehabilitative Ideal in American Criminal Justice' (1978) 27 *Cleveland State Law Review* 2 (Rehabilitation 'is the notion that the purpose of penal treatment is to effect changes in the characters, attitudes, and behaviors of convicted offenders, so as to strengthen the social defense against unwanted behavior, but also to contribute to the welfare and satisfaction of others').

substantive standpoint, the pragmatic and science-based approach of the Code was criticised for its theoretical limitations, including its disregard for the normative foundations of penal justice and lack of grounding in any particular theory of criminal law.[47] More importantly, the aspirations of the rehabilitative/treatmentist ideal were largely discredited by the early 1970s.[48] Many reasons have been advanced to explain the sudden decline of treatmentist/correctional rehabilitation after many years of ideological hegemony and universal support.[49] One critique was that correctional rehabilitation problematically viewed individual perpetrators as 'different' subjects who needed to be treated to be reformed. Moreover, the evidence-based rehabilitation programmes of the time were challenged for being flawed and ineffectual at preventing recidivism. A third, more straightforward criticism was that paternalistic and therapeutic approaches to crime were simply incompatible with the aims of criminal law, which is not intended to care for and cure people but rather to hold them culpable for their crimes and administer punishment.

In combination with a scholarly urge to clarify the tenets and aims of the criminal law,[50] the collapse of the rehabilitative ideal prompted growing efforts by a sustained group of legal scholars and philosophers to elicit the 'true' overarching theoretical foundations of culpability and punishment, including their underlying model of personhood. Such strains vigorously and successfully (re)turned understandings of criminal law (and of the Model Penal Code itself) to a normative-philosophical dimension, and removed it from the 'dangerous' domain of science.

V. Voluntarism and the Resurgence of Retribution

Amid the decline of penal treatmentism/rehabilitationism, a sustained group of legal theorists undertook an intellectual project to pinpoint the theoretical foundations of culpability and punishment. That intellectual project significantly

[47] Dubber (n 35) 241 ('The Model Penal Code was explicitly, intentionally, even programmatically, non-foundational. Wechsler had no patience for prolonged explorations of the theoretical, or even principled, foundations of criminal law; as a Legal Process man, he was interested in doing things with law'). See also M Dubber, 'Penal Panopticon: The Idea of a Model Penal Code' (2000) 4 *Buffalo Criminal Law Review* 53. Against see Wolitz (n 37).

[48] M Tonry, 'Can Twenty-first Century Punishment Policies Be Justified in Principle?' in M Tonry (ed) *Retributivism Has a Past: Has it a Future?* (New York, Oxford University Press, 2011) 3, 7–8.

[49] See F Cullen, 'Rehabilitation: Beyond Nothing Works, Crime and Justice' (2013) 42 *Crime and Justice in America 1975–2025* 299.

[50] Even the Supreme Court implicitly acknowledged the lack of (and possibly the need for) overarching theoretical foundations of culpability and punishment that could provide guidance in understanding and interpreting legal doctrine. See *Powell v Texas* 392 U.S. 514 (1968) (concluding that 'evolving aims of the criminal law and changing religious, moral, philosophical, and medical views of the nature of man' essentially were beyond the Court's province). According to Thomas Green, the Court in *Powell* 'left it to the scholars … to make sense of the human will's proper relationship to criminal culpability, although their conclusions thus were bound, in some regards, to remain as abstract commentaries on a law that, in practice, often appeared willfully untheorized'. See T Green, *Freedom and Criminal Responsibility in American Legal Thought* (New York, Cambridge University Press, 2014) 277.

influenced theoretical conversations of criminal law, legislations, and courts and laid the grounds for still-dominant paradigms of culpability and punishment.

Following the lead of prominent scholars such as Herbert Morris[51] and HLA Hart,[52] this scholarly movement – which was later labelled as 'voluntarism' – refined the core of culpability in terms of blameworthy choice, mental capacity, and situational opportunity.[53] Voluntarist scholarship revived Enlightenment and post-Enlightenment principles of penal egalitarianism and freedom and was therefore strongly committed to the idea that criminal law is morally obligated to treat individuals as *persons*, which necessitates respecting their freedom of choice, holding them responsible for their wrong choices, and punishing them for such choices.[54] In this way, criminal law displays respect for people as autonomous and rational beings.

As anticipated in the preceding chapter, voluntarism advances from the assumption that criminal law is fundamentally compatibilist. Thus, criminal law views the person as a choosing being who is able to self-determine his or her course through his or her practical reasoning powers, even if he or she is influenced by factors and circumstances beyond his or her control. Such a compatibilist understanding of personhood has allowed voluntarists to preserve and protect the normative essence of culpability and punishment from the deterministic pressures of social and psychological sciences, including their causal explanations of criminal behaviour. Notably, the argumentative strength of this legal-philosophical approach overshadowed other views in legal scholarship that were more sensitive to the ambiguous boundary between social injustice and crime and advocated for attributing an excusing relevance to difficult social conditions, including poverty and deprivation.[55]

The affirmation of voluntarism in legal scholarship entailed the resurgence of retributivism.[56] Although (neo)retributivism[57] can assume a variety of forms

[51] H Morris, 'Persons and Punishment' (1968) 52 *The Monist* 475.

[52] HLA Hart, *Punishment and Responsibility: Essays in the Philosophy of Law* (Oxford, Oxford University Press, 1998).

[53] See SJ Morse, 'New Neuroscience, Old Problems: Legal Implications of Brain Science' (2004) 6 *Cerebrum* 81, 81 (arguing that 'the law presumes that adults are capable of minimal rationality and responsibility and that the same rules may be applied to all, but this presumption can be rebutted in appropriate cases').

[54] See Morris (n 51) 48-49.

[55] As a paradigm article, see SJ Morse, 'The Twilight of Welfare Criminology: A Reply to Judge Bazelon' (1976) 49 *Southern California Law Review* 1247.

[56] There is some disagreement as to when the revitalisation of retributivism precisely began. For instance, Green attributes an early resurgence of retributivism to Herbert Morris's hugely influential 1968 article *Persons and Punishment* (n 51). See Green (n 50). Other accounts locate the revival of retributivism in the 1970s. See eg S Kadish, 'Fifty Years of Criminal Law: An Opinionated Review' (1999) 87 *California Law Review* 943, 978; RA Duff, 'Penal Communications: Recent Work in the Philosophy of Punishment' (1996) 20 *Crime & Justice* 1, 1–2 ('Penal theory in the 1970s was marked by a retributivist revival, in reaction against the consequentialist orthodoxies that had dominated penal thought in the postwar period').

[57] The Latin root of retribution is the verb '*re + tribuere*', which literally means 'to pay back'. One way to understand the notion of paying back is that it concerns paying debts that are owed. This understanding connects to the commonly shared retributive thought that a person who has been appropriately

and nuances,[58] its classical (and still popular) version justifies the rationale of punishment on 'just deserts' grounds. Such grounds uphold the deontological idea that people must be punished simply because 'they deserve it' – irrespective of the consequences of such punishment. Desert is in turn founded on two conditions: first, the person must have committed a wrongdoing; second, the person must have committed the wrongdoing with a culpable mind.[59] Punishment must not exceed what would be proportional to individual desert.[60] Hence, it must be commensurate to the seriousness of the offence committed and of 'what [the person] *did* rather than … what the sentence expects he will do if treated in a certain fashion'.[61] Such measurement depends on not only the magnitude of harm that was caused or risked but also the extent of the person's culpability. The more a person chooses to cause harm, the more he or she is culpable and deserves to be punished. Just deserts and proportionality ultimately depend on a combination of these two independent variables.[62] Culpable wrongdoing thus serves as a constraint on blame and punishment.

Voluntarist retributivism conceives of punishment as a means to *respect the human dignity* of people who break the law as autonomous and rational beings. Punishment respects human dignity because it treats persons who break the law

punished has 'paid his or her debt to society'. Relatedly, retributivism stands for the proposition that it is morally valuable for a person to suffer punishment in response to their wrongdoing. See eg J Rawls, 'Two Concepts of Rules' (1955) 64 *Philosophical Review* 3, 5 ('What we may call the retributive view is that punishment is justified on the grounds that wrongdoing merits punishment. It is morally fitting that a person who does wrong should suffer in proportion to his wrongdoing. That a criminal should be punished follows from his guilt, and the severity of the appropriate punishment depends on the depravity of his act. The state of affairs where a wrongdoer suffers punishment is morally better than the state of affairs where he does not; and it is better irrespective of any of the consequences of punishing him.'). See also I Primoratz, *Justifying Legal Punishment* (London, Humanities Press, 1989) 12 (noting that 'in its most complete form, retributivism contains five tenets: The moral right to punish is based solely on the offense committed; the moral duty to punish is also grounded exclusively on the offense committed; punishment ought to be proportionate to the offense; punishment is the "annulment" of the offense; and, punishment is a right of the offender').

[58] Many different accounts of retribution have been proposed over the years. Different versions of retribution include positive and negative retribution, mandatory and permissible retribution, pure and mixed retribution, character retribution. Moreover, retributionists also divide between moralistic and legalistic. For an exhaustive analysis of the diverse types of retribution, see R Christopher, 'Deterring Retributivism: The Injustice of "Just" Punishment' (2002) 96 *Northwestern University Law Review* 843.

[59] *Kansas v Hendricks*, 521 U.S. 346, 362 (1997) (retribution is dependent on having 'affix[ed] culpability', and criminal culpability, and hence retribution, requires an awareness of some wrongdoing.).

[60] A Von Hirsch, *Doing Justice: The Choice of Punishments, Report of the Committee for the Study of Incarceration* (New York, Hill and Wang, 1976) 51 ('[t]he penalty is … not just a means of crime prevention but a merited response to the actor's deed, "rectifying the balance" in the Kantian sense and expressing moral reprobation of the actor for the wrong'). See also Y Lee, 'The Constitutional Right Against Excessive Punishment' (2005) 91 *Vanderbilt Law Review* 677, 683 (suggesting that, as a principle of proportionality, retribution requires that 'one should not be punished more harshly than one deserves').

[61] C Goodhell, 'Preface' of Von Hirsch (n 60) xvii.

[62] See Hart (n 52) 231 (a retributive theory of punishment contains three elements: (1) a person may be punished if and only if he or she has voluntarily done something wrong; (2) the punishment must match, or be equivalent to, the wickedness of the offence; and (3) the justification for punishing persons is that the return of suffering for suffering for moral evil voluntarily done is itself just or morally good).

as *moral equals* who are sufficiently rational to know that there are rules – and consequences for breaking them – and to freely choose to act in breach of them. Furthermore, punishment respects human dignity because it recognises that persons who break the law are 'capable of understanding the wrongs they have committed and the fairness of the penal sanctions imposed on them by the state in response to those wrong' and able 'to comprehend and respond constructively to the reasons for which they are being punished'.[63] Accordingly, voluntarist retributivism justifies punishment with the *moral failing* of the person to act otherwise.[64] It further insists on structuring punishment to be, at minimum, consistent with treating and honouring a person as an end rather than as a means.[65] Thus, punishment is depicted as a fundamentally benign institution that is dedicated toward realising some good or the good – at least in theory.

The principle of respect for individual dignity has been vital to the affirmation of voluntarist retribution against rehabilitation. From the perspective of voluntarist retributivism, rehabilitation is a form of social control that purports to treat persons as passive subjects in the hands of the state. As such, rehabilitation profoundly disrespects the dignity of individuals as autonomous and rational creatures, as it ultimately treats them as patients who must be cured or as 'animals who must be conditioned'.[66] Moreover, approaching crime as a social pathology that must be cured poses the risk of dangerous manipulations under the mantle of being humane, merciful, and evidence-based.

The voluntarist-retributivist dismissal of rehabilitation as a legitimate justification for punishment is emblematically illustrated in Moore's work.[67] Moore has distinguished between two forms of rehabilitation. The first, which he has called 'non-paternalistic rehabilitation', is strongly tied to incapacitation and implies the infliction of harsh punishment to neutralise otherwise dangerous individuals either because they then become 'penitent, or because [they are] unwilling to risk again such an awful treatment'.[68] Such model of rehabilitation translates into a cost-effective means of keeping society safe; however, it is not intended to actually reform the individual perpetrator. The second type of rehabilitation is 'paternalistic' in that it aims to improve and reform the personality of perpetrators through the

[63] R Lippke, 'Retribution and Incarceration' (2003) 17 *Public Affairs Quarterly* 29, 43.

[64] See Hart (n 52) 46-47 (noting that one of the benefits of a choice-based theory of punishment is that it gives citizens the reassuring impression that they can avoid punishment by making prudent choices).

[65] See Morris (n 51) 490, 492-93 (suggesting that 'the primary reason to prefer a retributivist to a consequentialist system of punishment might be that the former does, and the latter does not, treat others as persons'. For Morris, two conditions must be satisfied to treat someone as a person: 'we treat a human being as a person provided, first, we permit the person to make the choices that will determine what happens to him and, second, when our responses to the person are responses respecting the person's choices').

[66] ibid, 487.

[67] M Moore, *Law and Psychiatry: Rethinking the Relationship* (Cambridge, Cambridge University Press, 1984) 234-35. See also Hart (n 52) 26-27.

[68] Moore (n 67) 234.

implementation of therapeutic treatments in humane settings. Paternalistic rehabilitation seeks not only to render an individual non-dangerous but also to enable them to be 'a flourishing, happy, and self-actualizing member of our society'.[69] Thus, this rehabilitative approach justifies punishment in the name of the offender, 'not in the name of all of us'.[70]

For Moore, who has expressed the same view as Hart, paternalistic rehabilitation is particularly unfit to provide a plausible justification for punishment for multiple reasons. First, it problematically implies a poor distribution of already-scarce social resources, as it takes them away from more deserving people (eg, people with disabilities) and redirects them to people who are the least deserving and often do not even want them.[71] The allocation of social resources to rehabilitate perpetrators could be plausible only if we also accept that 'criminals suffer distinctive disadvantages', that is, that criminal behaviour is a disease that needs to be cured, which makes the mistake of 'conflat[ing] illness with badness'.[72]

In a less drastic manner than Moore, Andrew von Hirsch, in his influential *Doing Justice*,[73] similarly insists that retribution is the only plausible goal of punishment if only because it critically grants the individual fundamental substantive and procedural guarantees. Notably, retributivist principles of just deserts and proportionality (which he calls the 'principle of commensurate proportionality') are critical side-constraints that forbid punishment of innocent individuals and disproportionate punishment of those who are guilty. According to von Hirsch's account, a criminal sentence communicates the degree of censure that the perpetrator deserves for his wrong by the severity of the sanction it imposes. Justice demands that we punish each person precisely according to the degree of censure that he or she deserves in virtue of his or her moral culpability for wrongdoing. Other considerations, such as encouraging rehabilitation and reintegration of the perpetrator back into society, are matters of secondary importance to be dealt with in whatever way might not interfere with the communication of the primary message of the criminal sentence. Moreover, rehabilitation enacts a prediction-based model of (potentially indeterminate and frequently abusive) enforced treatment, which is not only significantly more severe than punishment on the basis of commensurate desert but also potentially extremely unfair. Nevertheless, certain rehabilitative programmes, such as vocational training, education, and counselling, could be implemented during the execution of sentences as long as individuals can participate in them on a voluntary basis.

[69] ibid.

[70] ibid.

[71] M Moore, *Placing Blame: A Theory of Criminal Law* (New York, Oxford University Press, 1994) 86. Stephen Morse shares similar concerns. Although Morse acknowledges that punishment also serves utilitarian goals, he rejects that rehabilitation should figure as a justification for punishment. Adding on Moore's argument, Morse claims that rehabilitation 'is not a form of intentional infliction of pain … even if the offender experiences it as such'. Moreover, 'it is unfair to provide benefits to those who least deserve them and especially because the offender may not want the benefits'. See SJ Morse, 'Commentary: Reflections on Remorse' (2014) 42 *Journal of American Academy of Psychiatry and Law* 49, 53.

[72] Moore, ibid.

[73] Von Hirsh (n 60) 66-76.

In summary, by emphasising choice, autonomy, rationality, and the obligations and duties of the state when tasked with inflicting punishment, voluntarist retributivism appears to have reaffirmed the centrality of the individual as an autonomous and rational subject who should be held responsible for his or her choice to commit a wrongdoing *vis-a-vis* his or her intellectual faculties of practical reasoning and control. The individual has a right to be punished for his or her wrongs precisely because, through that punishment, he or she is recognised and respected as a person. Only a system of culpability and punishment that recognises and hinges on the individual's (capacity for) free and rational choice can be said to respect individual human dignity. Thus, such a system accords with and pays homage to a universal aspect of human nature that is widely considered definitional of the human being.

The strong liberal (and, in its own terms, progressive) commitment to blaming and punishing only those who act freely and rationally undeniably extols the virtues of voluntarist retributivism. According to Norrie, criminal '[l]aw [*must*] respect … autonomy and personhood, and this is a value in itself'.[74] Furthermore, such virtues partly explain why voluntarist retributivism has become the predominant ideology of culpability and punishment among legal academics, courts,[75] and policy-makers alike.[76] Over the past decades, the voluntarist/retributivist principles of culpability and punishment have been overarching subjects of theoretical conversations about criminal law, they have persuaded political discourses of criminal justice, and have been foundational to scholarly accounts and court interpretations of legal doctrines. To date, retribution – renamed as either desert or proportionality, and softened to accommodate utilitarian concerns – is central to modem sentencing.

In fact, the egalitarian and liberal model of voluntarist retribution has been adopted by many American jurisdictions[77] and has occupied a central spot in the

[74] A Norrie, 'The Limits of Justice: Finding Fault in the Criminal Law' (1996) 59 *Modern Law Review* 540, 541.

[75] See eg *Spaziano v Florida*, 468 U.S. 447, 461 (1984); *Gregg v Georgia*, 428 U.S. 153, 183-84; *Kansas v Hendricks*, 521 U.S. 346, 361-62 (1997); M Cotton, 'Back with a Vengeance: The Resilience of Retribution as an Articulated Purpose of Criminal Punishment' (2000) 37 *American Criminal Law Review* 1313, 1326–27 (2000) (citing *State v Morrow*, 492 N.W.2d 539, 546 [Minn. Ct. App. 1992]; *Adams v State*, 577 S.W.2d 717, 729 [Tex. App. 1979] *rev'd* on other grounds, 448 U.S. 38 [1980]).

[76] For other acknowledgments, by retributivism's critics, of retributivism's generally favoured status, see M Bagaric and K Amarasekara, *The Errors of Retributivism* (2000) 24 *Melbourne University Law Review* 124; D Dolinko, 'Retributivism, Consequentialism, and the Intrinsic Goodness of Punishment' (1997) 16 *Law & Philosophy* 507.

[77] See eg California Penal Code § 1170(a)(1) (West 1985) ('The Legislature finds and declares that the purpose of imprisonment for crime is punishment. This purpose is best served by terms proportionate to the seriousness of the offense with provision for uniformity in the sentences of offenders committing the same offense under similar circumstances'; no other purpose is given for the setting of prison terms'); Florida Statute § 921.002(1)(b) (2019) ('The primary purpose of sentencing is to punish the offender. Rehabilitation is a desired goal of the criminal justice system but is subordinate to the goal of punishment'); Pennsylvania Code Title 204 § 303.11 (2001) ('The sentencing guidelines provide sanctions proportionate to the severity of the crime [which] … establishes a sentencing system with a primary focus on retribution …').

revised version of the MPC. In fact, motivated in part by a desire to make the Code more relevant to actual sentencing law, the ALI embarked on a 15-years project of revising the Code's sentencing provisions, which has culminated in 2017.[78] Embracing Norval Morris's (today widely accepted)[79] theory of limiting retributivism,[80] the ALI has set retribution – phrasing it as proportionality based on the gravity of offences, the 'blameworthiness' of perpetrators, and the 'harms done to crime victims' – as the predominant criterion for sentencing and as a limiting principle that accommodates utilitarian aims.[81] Under the new Code's scheme, desert is set to prescribe upper (and perhaps lower) limits to the range of punishments that may be imposed in pursuit of these non-retributive goals. On the other hand, non-retributive goals such as rehabilitation, deterrence, and the reintegration of perpetrators into law-abiding community are secondary goals that can be achieved within the boundaries of proportionality and desert. This approach is not strictly retributivist, as it allows crime-preventive considerations to have a say in sentencing and possibly lead to increasing the penalty and tightening control if needed for non-retributive reasons. Yet, desert figures as the primary justification for imposing a sentence and serves an important role as a limiting condition on other sentencing considerations. Thus, although retribution is not treated as the exclusive rationale of a given punishment, it still looms large and afforded predominant relevance within sentencing determinations.

Altogether, voluntarist retributivism, and its underlying model of the person, is arguably perceived as the strongest grounds for the paradigms of culpability and punishment in present-day American criminal law.

VI. Backlashes

The onset of voluntarist retribution marks a fundamental milestone in criminal law. The liberal model of crime as free and rational choice that has been promoted by this scholarship has resisted medicalised views of perpetrators that represent the core of invasive criminal policies that raised post-war concerns about

[78] See American Law Institute, Model Penal Code: Sentencing, Tentative Draft No. 1, Part I. General Provisions (9 April 2007) 1; American Law Institute, Model Penal Code: Sentencing (approved on 24 May 2017).

[79] N Morris, *The Future of Imprisonment* (New York, Oxford University Press, 1974); See R Frase, 'Limiting Retributivism: The Consensus Model of Criminal Punishment' in M Tonry (ed), *The Future of Imprisonment in the 21st Century* (New York, Oxford University Press, 2003).

[80] Limiting retributivism is a 'mixed theory' of punishment which posits that retributive principles should set the outer bounds of a sentence, while the precise nature and duration of disposition should be designed to implement one or more independent criminal justice system goals.

[81] For sustained attacks to the ALI's retributivist turn, see J Whitman, 'A Plea Against Retributivism' (2003) 7 *Buffalo Criminal Law Review* 89; A Ristroph, 'How (Not) to Think like a Punisher' (2009) 61 *Florida Law Review* 727; A Ristroph, 'Desert, Democracy and Sentencing Reform' (2006) 96 *Journal of Criminal Law and Criminology* 1293.

authoritarianism.[82] The predominant conception of punishment shifted from a mandatory therapeutic treatment by the state to reform individuals whose personalities needed to be fixed to the 'intentional infliction by the state of consequences normally considered as unpleasant, or painful, on person[s] in response to [their] having been convicted of a crime'.[83] The ultimate condition that can justify the infliction of such punishment is a culpable wrongdoing that an individual freely and rationally chooses to commit. Altogether, this scholarly movement has imposed itself as a protective shield for the respect of the person as the central pillar of culpability attributions and punishment inflictions.

Notwithstanding the undeniable values of this scholarship, the rise of voluntarist retributivism has also prompted a series of backlashes in the actual practice of criminal justice.[84] In fact, the language of blame and retribution within this scholarship supposedly partly contributed to the generation of a pejorative narrative of crime and punishment, including the rhetoric that nothing can (or should) be done to rehabilitate justice-involved people.[85] Notably, it paralleled and intersected with the rise of a political rhetoric that hinges on punitiveness and control and with an increasing harshness of penal policies and practices – incarceration in particular – that advanced in the 1970s.[86] Such backlashes, which collectively represent so-called 'American penal exceptionalism',[87] are still tangible today.

A. Harsh Punitiveness

As widely documented,[88] the 1970s witnessed numerous developments: a dramatic rise in crime rates, urban and prison riots, and racial conflicts; the

[82] See Hart (n 52) 23 (suggesting that the choice theory of punishment is appealing in part because it protects citizens from excessive state interference with private lives).

[83] ibid 4-5; Von Hirsh (n 60) 81. See also L Zaibert, 'The Instrument of Abolition, or Why Retributivism is the Only Real Justification of Punishment' (2013) 32 *Law & Philosophy* 33, 45 (holding that culpable individuals 'deserve to suffer' for their wrongdoing); D Gray, 'Punishment as Suffering' (2010) 53 *Vanderbilt Law Review* 1619.

[84] See Brown (n 44) 187 (framing these backlash effects as 'the failure of retributivism').

[85] See eg M Gottschalk, 'Sentenced to Life: Penal Reform and the Most Severe Sanctions' (2013) 9 *Annual Review of Law & Social Science* 353, 370 ('[o]ver the past 40 years or so, retribution has become a central feature of U.S. penal policy, supplanting rehabilitation and even public safety as the chief aim.'). See also *Miller v Alabama*, 567 U.S. 460 (2012) (Anthony Scalia, J, oral argument at 18:49 and 19:07) ('modern penology has abandoned that rehabilitation thing, and they no longer call prisons reformatories … [P]unishment is the criterion now. Deserved punishment for crime. Rehabilitation is therefore "irrelevant"'), available at www.oyez.org/cases/2011/10-9646.

[86] See Brown (n 44) 187 (suggesting that 'contemporary retributivism has suffered from the same fault (or fate) that its adherents alleged of the modernist era: policies supposedly premised on a desert-based account of criminal punishment in fact reflect the infiltration of utilitarian policies unconstrained by moral proportionality').

[87] See generally K Reitz (ed), *American Exceptionalism in Crime and Punishment* (New York, Oxford University Press, 2017).

[88] For a review, see eg Green (n 50).

'nothing-works'[89] ideology in criminology; an intensifying over-criminalisation; an increasing overreliance on harsh incarceration; and an (abusive) application of severe correctional practices, such as solitary confinement. All of these social, criminological, political, and policy-making factors fuelled public fears of crime and opened a pathway to 'law-and-order' political strains which relied on a rhetoric of being 'tough on crime'[90] to support repressive laws and policies, such as War on Drugs laws, 'three-strikes' laws, a system of determinate sentencing with lengthy mandatory minimum sentences,[91] and supermax security regimes – all of which culminated between the 1980s and the 1990s and still apply today.[92]

While voluntarist/retributionist scholars have vigorously rejected any association of their scholarship with the increasingly harsh punitiveness of American criminal justice,[93] others have suggested that such harsh punitiveness should at

[89] The expression 'nothing works' was made famous by sociologist Robert Martinson. See R Martinson, 'What Works? – Questions and Answers About Prison Reform' (Spring 1974) *The Public Interest* 22. Critics argued that Martinson's conclusion was flawed for two reasons. First, the research methodology available was so inadequate that only a few studies warranted unequivocal interpretations, and second, the majority of studies examined programmes that were so poorly implemented they would hardly have been expected to affect criminal activities. See eg JQ Wilson, '"What Works?" Revisited: New Findings on Criminal Rehabilitation' (Fall 1980) 61 *The Public Interest* 3. Moreover, in 1979 Martinson published another paper that unequivocally withdrew his previous conclusion, declaring that 'contrary to my previous position, some treatment programs *do* have an appreciable effect on recidivism'. See R Martinson, 'New Findings, New Views: A Note of Caution Regarding Sentencing Reform' (1979) 7 *Hofstra Law Review* 243, 244. But then, the 'nothing works' narrative was entrenched in both popular and professional thinking. In 1983, a report issued by the US Senate Judiciary Committee calling for more stringent sentencing criteria cited Martinson's 1974 paper, without acknowledging neither his later reversal nor the subsequent work of other social scientists suggesting that specific rehabilitative programmes were effective. The Committee stated that '[r]ecent studies suggest that this approach has failed, and most sentencing judges as well as the Parole Commission agree that the rehabilitation model is not appropriate basis for sentencing decisions. We know too little about human behavior to be able to rehabilitate individuals on a routine basis or even to determine accurately whether or when a particular individual has been rehabilitated'. See Sentencing Reform Act of 1983: Report of the Committee on the Judiciary United States Senate, Washington 1983, 37.

[90] See eg RJ Cottrol, 'Hard Choices and Shifted Burdens: American Crime and American Justice at the End of the Century' (1997) 65 *George Washington Law Review* 506, 507–508 (book review) (noting that '[s]ince the mid-seventies retribution has come back with a vengeance, enjoying today a greater prominence in public discourse over crime and punishment than at any other time in post-war America. Nowhere is this mood better demonstrated than in the debate over the death penalty. Where once capital punishment was reluctantly defended as a necessary deterrent to the most heinous of murders, it has, in recent years, been eagerly embraced by politicians eager to adopt a "tough on crime" posture').

[91] Critiques of judicial discretion motivated calls for uniform, determinate sentencing, culminating in the 1987 Federal Sentencing Guidelines and guideline schemes in about half the states. See K Reitz, 'Sentencing Guidelines' in J Dressler (ed), *Encyclopedia of Crime and Justice* (New York, MacMillan Reference, 2002) 1429. See also A Dershowitz, *Fair and Certain Punishment: Report of the Twentieth Century Fund Task Force on Criminal Sentencing* (New York, McGraw-Hill, 1976); Von Hirsh (n 60).

[92] See M Tonry, 'Remodeling American Sentencing: A Ten-Step Blueprint for Moving Past Mass Incarceration' (2014) 13 *Criminology & Public Policy* 503, 514.

[93] Neo-retributivist scholars have vigorously rejected political interpretations of retribution – as vengeance, revenge, hate, or retaliation – claiming that they are based on a misleading understanding of retribution. See eg J Murphy, 'Retribution' in E Luna (ed), *Reforming Criminal Justice, Vol. 4: Punishment, Incarceration and Release* (Phoenix, Arizona State University, 2017) 7, 8–10 ('What is the cause of the deplorable state of the American penal system and what can be done about it? A variety of

least be framed as an *unintended and indirect*[94] consequence of the scholarship.[95] A notable proposition is that the message of the voluntarist/retributivist rhetoric (ie, 'punishment of a wrongdoer is justified for the reason that he or she deserves to be punished because he or she has chosen to do wrong') 'pour[ed] gasoline on the fires of American punishment'[96] by providing a 'moral cover'[97] that legitimised and justified harsh forms of justice in actual practice.

Scholars such as James Whitman have posited that even if the revived retributivism that arises from theoretical considerations has philosophical appeal, it cannot be divorced from the real-world implications of its claims, including the fact that the approval of retributivism underpinned the inhumane, vengeance-based, and harsh punishment that befell the US from the 1970s onward.[98] In his seminal work *Harsh Justice*,[99] Whitman suggests a subtle relationship between the principle of *respect for persons* as rational and autonomous beings, which animates both voluntarist retributivism and criminal law in general, and the harshness of American criminal justice. For Whitman, the way in which American law and justice 'respects persons' actually demonstrates a lack of respect in two main senses. On the one hand, such (dis)respect manifests in a commitment to *formal equality*, which is an ideal (preached by Enlightenment thinkers) that aims to treat all persons alike – *irrespective of and disregarding their individuality* (eg, personal history, social reality). On the other hand, the generalised tendency of American criminal law 'to surrender to the degrading aspects of punishment' results in a lack of respect for *all* persons who are involved in criminal justice. Therefore, Whitman

distinguished scholars and jurists … have suggested that the villain is easy to identify: retribution as the value now dominating the system. … I believe that this diagnosis … rests upon a misunderstanding of the concept of retribution … The claim that retribution represents a special fondness for harsh punishment is simply false … When the retributivist views punishments as justified suffering … the meaning of "suffering" at play here is not "pain". It is rather suffering in the sense of [non-painful] enduring'). See also G Bradley, 'Retribution: The Central Aim of Punishment' (2003) 27 *Harvard Journal of Law and Public Policy* 20–22 (addressing common misconceptions about retribution).

[94] See Whitman (n 81). See also T Green (n 50) 277 ('If theorists sometimes made use of arguments from their real-world counterparts, they mainly stood apart from the practices of that increasingly harsh penal domain and inhabited an intellectual world of their own – and one [in a manner of speaking] of their own making').

[95] D Garland, *The Culture of Control: Crime and Social Order in Contemporary Society* (Chicago, The University of Chicago Press, 2001) 9 ('[Just deserts retribution] has … re-established the legitimacy of an explicitly retributive discourse, which, in turn, has made it easier for politicians and legislatures to openly express punitive sentiments and to enact more draconian laws'). See also M Dubber, *An Introduction to the Model Penal Code*, 2nd edn (New York, Oxford University Press, 2015) 12 (suggesting that the MPC has survived shifts from treatmentism and retributivism 'adapting itself to each orthodoxy along the way' and adding that '[a]nother, less sympathetic way of making this point is that the Code proved remarkably compatible with the dramatic expansion of imprisonment in the United States in the 1960s').

[96] Whitman (n 81) 94.

[97] M Fondacaro and J O' Toole, 'American Punitiveness and Mass Incarceration: Psychological Perspectives on Retributive and Consequentialist Responses to Crime' (2015) 18 *New Criminal Law Review* 477.

[98] See Whitman (n 81).

[99] See Whitman (n 33) 42-43. For a partial criticism of Whitman's view, see C Flanders, 'Retribution and Reform' (2010) 70 *Maryland Law Review* 87.

concludes, 'in American criminal law persons just do not matter … all persons receive equal punishment, and all persons receive little respect'.[100]

In a similar vein, other authors have observed that the individualist choice-based narrative of voluntarist retributivism further legitimises state violence.[101] This (most likely Foucault-inspired) perspective asserts that placing the rationale of culpability and punishment on individual choice is a state *strategy* to inflict pervasive forms of violence upon individual citizens through legitimate punishment. When the law dictates that culpability and punishment depend entirely on an individual's free choice to do wrong, it implicitly grants the individual the power to legitimise the state to exert its punitive force against his or her in response to such choice. Thus, this criterion subtly gives the citizen an illusion of 'empowerment that it is "up to him [or her]" whether [s]he will be punished'. While anchoring culpability and punishment to individual choice imposes limits on state punishment, it also slyly renders state violence more acceptable and legitimate to the populace.

As part of such legitimate punishment, many people are executed, while others are permanently deprived of their liberty, excluded from society, separated from their families, and denied a second chance to live their lives profitably and successfully. This corollary, which is notoriously known as mass incarceration, is a prime example of state infatuation with the retribution-based rhetoric to avenge and violently respond to crimes. Tough determinate sentencing in the name of desert and proportionality has admittedly resulted in the rise of prison populations to the extreme of severe overcrowding, diminished services and heightened potential for violence. Since the increase of the prison population to the present day, the number of incarcerated people in the US is staggering.[102] The nation imprisons individuals not only at a much higher rate than that of other Western democracies but also in notoriously harsh conditions for years, decades, or lifetimes, which undoubtedly constitutes a form of state violence on a massive scale.

B. Social Exclusion and Stigmatisation

Another, consequential, backlash of retributive punishment can be ascribed to the factual fusion of the logic of deserts with the logic of social exclusion and

[100] ibid, 43.

[101] See eg P Arenella, 'Convicting the Morally Blameless: Reassessing the Relationship Between Legal and Moral Accountability' (1992) 39 *UCLA Law Review* 151, 1608 ('Perhaps all this legal rhetoric about just deserts and moral responsibility is just the law's way of legitimizing one form of human suffering that the state employs to defend itself').

[102] The total number of people in prison in 2018 was 1,465, 200. See U.S. Department of Justice, 'Prisoners in 2018' (NCJ 253516) (April 2020), available at www.bjs.gov/content/pub/pdf/p18_sum.pdf. Jails held 738,400 people nationwide at midyear 2018. See U.S. Department of Justice, 'Jail Inmates in 2018' (NCJ 253044) (March 2020), available at www.bjs.gov/content/pub/pdf/ji18_sum.pdf.

deprivation.[103] As said, the theory of retribution depicts punishment as the infliction of some form of suffering upon the individual on the part of the state. Standard retributive appeals to restoring a balance between the perpetrator, the victim and the community justify such suffering through the imposition of some losses or other deprivations upon perpetrators that are commensurate (ie, proportional) with their desert. Such losses of deprivations are imposed in a manner that expresses censure or blame.

Retributive theory does not clarify the type of losses or deprivations that punishment must or might entail, nor how such losses or deprivations should be enacted.[104] Differing positions exist among retributive scholars on this issue. On balance, it is plausible to frame such losses and deprivations in terms the (either temporary or permanent) loss or deprivation of certain rights (eg, liberty and property) and certain privileges of citizenship, all of which result in diminished opportunities for justice-involved individuals to live a life of their own choosing – in a way that is commensurate to their desert.

In practice, this retributive rhetoric of loss and deprivation in the name of desert has contributed to and legitimised a system of punishment that is fundamentally based on separation, exclusion, and marginalisation. It is a fact that the losses and deprivations and that people facing punishment suffer extend far beyond the right to freedom or to privacy, and encompass personal and social losses such as employment, education, family and community relationships, and other basic social rights. It is also a fact that people who faced punishment are at a higher risk of being excluded from a series of civil and political domains due to their prior conviction. Thus, while theoretical discourses of punishment rely on the rhetoric of imposition of some losses in proportion to the person's ill desert, in actual practice this rhetoric merges with impulses to exclude perpetrators from society – both physically and morally.

The legitimised losses inflicted in the name of desert and retribution are exacerbated when desert-based retributive considerations are combined with neutralisation-based considerations that are typical of incapacitation.[105] Despite their contradicting theoretical orientations, retribution and incapacitation 'support' each other in actual practice. Blame and retribution serve as a basis for legitimising the application of exclusionary penalties to serve neutralisation

[103] See R Weisberg, 'Barrock Lecture: Reality-Challenged Philosophies of Punishment' (2012) 95 *Marquette Law Review* 1203, 1241('The stock story of the recent politics of the incarceration boom focuses far more on retribution than incapacitation, but the common political rhetoric of 'public safety' surely implies that incapacitation is salient in the minds of the polity').

[104] D Brink, 'The Nature and Significance of Culpability' (2019) 13 *Criminal Law and Philosophy* 347 (supporting an account of 'predominant retribution' and claiming that 'though desert may *constrain* how we punish, because it constrains how much we should punish, it leaves the manner of punishment largely *underdetermined*'). See also E Rubin, 'Just Say No to Retribution' (2004) 7 *Buffalo Criminal Law Review* 17, 39 ('there is no inherent connection between retributivism and incarceration as a mode of punishment … retribution could be achieved by virtually any means of inflicting pain or suffering on the offender, and most obviously, by physical torture').

[105] See Rubin (n 104) 36-39.

goals.[106] On the other hand, social exclusion is a means to allow retribution to achieve its main goal of inflicting 'losses' on someone who deserves it. As has been observed, the combination of the narrative and goals of retribution and incapacitation is central to – and, in a sense, justifies – the application of harsh, exclusionary, and frequently prolonged sentences.[107] From this perspective, a culpable individual is inflicted deserved suffering because he or she freely chose to do evil. *De facto*, such suffering translates into an incapacitating outcome of physical, moral, and civil exclusion of the culpable individual from the rest of society.

These claims are most evident in the philosophy and excessive practice of the preferential crime response, namely incarceration. The notion that retribution and incapacitation are the primary justifications of incarceration is commonly accepted. A continuously popular message in support of such response is that incarceration, which is a prototypical means of deprivation and social exclusion, is that the suffering of detention in exclusionary conditions is a just consequence that certain people deserve for choosing to commit crimes as well as to protect the public from their alleged dangerousness. Incarceration physically removes people from society and deprives them of significant control over their lives, even of their own body. People who are incarcerated are deprived of family life, natural environments, variety in food, many forms of work and leisure, and so forth. Such losses may be deserved from a retributivist perspective, but they also serve to exclude and separate individuals from their social life. Thus, the logic of incarceration privileges deprivation, disempowerment, physical separation, and social and moral exclusion – often in precarious settings[108] – to presumably rationalise the infliction of just and effective punishment on an individual. Specific methods of detention, such as solitary confinement, maximise this logic of incarceration under the guise of furthering public safety and assigning just punishment that the perpetrator deserves to suffer for the crime that he or she chose to commit.

Furthermore, as Hanan has correctly expressed, the depriving and exclusionary logics of sentencing practices

> extend also beyond prison walls to a multitude of collateral consequences. Practices that prevent people with criminal records from living in public housing, obtaining professional licenses, and participating in other aspects of society limit their participation in civil life and, thus, thwart any meaningful reintegration into society … Exclusionary

[106] Ristroph 'Desert' (n 81)1335 ('So long as most of us agree on the very broad principle that criminals deserve punishment, desert can provide moral legitimacy to a wide range of sentencing policies whose specific details may be dictated by utilitarian arguments').

[107] ibid, 1336 ('[s]entencing policies originally motivated by utilitarian concerns may become immune to claims of disutility once we have convinced ourselves that the sentences are deserved. This vicious cycle may be evident with respect to long prison sentences for recidivists. The long policies were originally motivated by a perceived need to incapacitate dangerous offenders, but quickly justified in terms of desert as well').

[108] See Whitman (n 33) 59-60.

> practices can serve retributive … functions, but their hallmark is that they are designed to protect the public through incapacitating the offender.[109]

One corollary of such exclusionary practices lies with the stigmatisation of justice-involved individuals as social outsiders. Stigmatisation involves labelling justice-involved people as deviant and casting them out of the community. For example, access to the labour market, or financial aid for education is too often denied and other measures are taken that contribute to social marginalisation, including and preventing formerly justice-involved people from getting professional licences.

Stigmatisation implies what John Braithwaite has famously named 'disintegrative shaming.'[110] This kind of shaming – largely informed by labelling theory in criminology – has the effect of labelling people rather than actions as 'bad', so that *the whole person* is degraded – not only his or her acts. Slightly differently put, disintegrative shaming means shaming which stigmatises, where a justice-involved person is treated with disrespect, as an outcast or bad person. This is shaming which tears down the individual and makes no effort to reconcile him or her with the community. It involves disrespect, humiliation, and ceremonies to certify deviance for which there is no counterpart terminating such certification and to allow deviance to become a master status trait.

The ashamed person is largely denied the opportunity to participate in mainstream culture. According to Braithwaite, this may well incite feelings of deviancy in the individual, leading him or her to re-offend. A person who feels excluded is less willing to seek legitimate opportunities because such opportunities will be more difficult, so that the person may feel that he or she has been treated unjustly and problem subcultures may become more attractive as fitting with the imposed deviant identity.

Importantly, a voluminous body of knowledge from over 40 years research indicates that punitive and exclusionary practices that are applied in the name of retribution and incapacitation are ineffectual at reducing criminality. Such indication is proven by the high rate of recidivism (re-arrest and re-incarceration), which, at the national level, reflects that about 60 per cent of people who are convicted with non-violent offences and approximately 70 per cent of those who are convicted with violent offences are re-arrested within five years of their release.[111] Thus, the

[109] E Hanan, 'Incapacitating Errors: Sentencing and the Science of Change' (2019) 97 *Denver Law Review* 151, 152–53. See also M Mauer and M Chensey-Lind, *Invisible Punishments: The Collateral Consequences of Mass Imprisonment* (New York, The New Press, 2002).

[110] J Braithwaite, *Crime, Shame and Reintegration* (New York, Cambridge University Press, 1989).

[111] See eg, M Durose et al, 'Recidivism of Prisoners Released in 30 States in 2005: Patterns from 2005 to 2010', U.S. Department of Justice, available at www.bjs.gov/index.cfm?ty=pbdetail&iid=4986; M Alper et al, '2018 Update on Prisoner Recidivism: A 9-Year Follow-up Period (2005-2014)' (NCJ 250975), U.S. Department of Justice, available at www.bjs.gov/content/pub/pdf/18upr9yfup0514.pdf.

criminal justice system perpetuates policy and practice that are costly, ineffective, and, at worst, damaging. Yet, neither the crime rate nor recidivism has been appreciably reduced. Punitiveness and exclusion simply do not work.

VII. Conclusion

Dominant contemporary paradigms of culpability and punishment find their rationale in the American penchant for individualism. Indeed, these paradigms are premised on the myopic view that individual choice is the only relevant locus of behaviour. On the one hand, blame rests on the individual's choice to not do otherwise; on the other hand, a blameworthy individual deserves to be punished precisely because he or she did not choose to abide by the law. Blaming and punishing an individual for choosing to do wrong in the name of deserts is supposedly a means by which the criminal law recognises and respects individual autonomy, equality, dignity and personhood.

The undeniable value of the voluntarist/retributivist movement is that of rejecting therapeutic understandings of crime and (re)focusing discourses of culpability and punishment on 'the person' with a strong emphasis on individual choice, autonomy, and rationality and in the name of equality and individual dignity. Still, the valuable ideals of voluntarist retributivism have been counterbalanced by a series of backlashes in the real domain of criminal law and justice. The language of individual choice, blame, and retribution has yielded the (probably unintended) consequence of fuelling the increasing punitiveness of American criminal law by offering a moral cover for legitimising harsh and exclusionary yet ineffective practices of justice.

Obviously, the notorious punitiveness of American criminal law cannot be ascribed primarily or solely to its theoretical devotion to voluntarism and retribution. A complex matrix of racial, economic, social, and political factors has more heavily determined the intensifying harshness of this justice system.[112] Notwithstanding, I hold that one contributing factor to the collateral effects of voluntarist retribution on concrete applications of justice is its theoretical foundation, which notably lies in the normative model of the person at the core of this influential theory. In the next chapter, I address this issue in more depth.

[112] See eg M Alexander, *The New Jim Crow: Mass Incarceration in the Age of Colorblindness* (New York, Penguin Books, 2010); J Pfaff, *Locked In: The True Causes of Mass Incarceration and How to Achieve Real Reform* (New York, Basic Books, 2017); R Barkow, *Prisoners of Politics: Breaking the Cycle of Mass Incarceration* (Cambridge, MA, Harvard University Press, 2020); D Garland (ed), *Mass Imprisonment: Social Causes and Consequences* (London, SAGE Publications, 2001); B Harcourt, *The Illusion of Free Markets: Punishment and the Myth of the Natural Order* (Cambridge, MA, Harvard University Press, 2011); M Jouet, *Exceptional America: What Divides America from the World and Each Other* (Oakland, CA, University of Berkley Press, 2017).

3

Critiques of the Model of the 'Person' in Culpability and Punishment

I. Introduction

As the preceding pages have illustrated, the model of the (culpable) person that characterises the paradigms of culpability and punishment in criminal law theory and doctrine is rationalist and individualist. Both culpability and punishment revolve around and find their rationale in a model of the person as a practical, instrumental reasoner who has the capacity to grasp the prescriptive meaning of legal norms and conform his or her behaviour to them *vis-a-vis* his or her inner mental states. In view of such capacities, the individual is blamed and punished for freely and rationally choosing to commit an offence and, thus, for disregarding the opportunity to behave otherwise.

Over the years, this model of the culpable subject as a coldly rational and isolated agent has been criticised for proposing an excessively abstract and depersonalised representation of human beings. Several authors – and even some voluntarist/retributivist theorists[1] – have acknowledged that this model of personhood problematically promotes an atomistic and incomplete image of justice-involved people that is also profoundly detached from the real-world dynamics of human behaviour. Thus, this model of agency produces a thin and generalised account of human agency that negates our profound individuality and 'affixes … a mask to our face which has nothing to do with what we really are or resemble … that have nothing to do with the real needs and attributes of human beings'.[2]

Critiques have further emphasised that this incomplete normative model of personhood contributes to supporting and favouring the implementation of harsh

[1] Admittedly, some defenders of the voluntarist model of human agency and personhood have recognised its limitations. See eg A Ashworth, *Principles of Criminal Law* (Oxford, Oxford University Press, 1991) 132 (commenting 'how individualistic, even atomistic, are the assumptions implicit in the liberal theory which underlies the subjective principle'). See also M Moore, *Law and Psychiatry: Rethinking the Relationship* (Cambridge, Cambridge University Press, 1984) 112 ('The very abstract view of persons in terms of autonomy and rationality is of course radically incomplete as a picture of any person we know. In particular, left out is the life of the emotions where, if anywhere, the 'affection of other men' is gained. Yet the radical incompleteness of the law's view of a person is no argument that it is wrong. As far as it goes, the law's view of persons could be quite correct even if radically incomplete').

[2] A Norrie, *Crime, Reason, and History: A Critical Introduction to Criminal Law* (Cambridge, Cambridge University Press, 1993) 13.

forms of justice. The critique goes that rationalist and individualist depictions of the culpable person as an individual who freely and rationally chooses to perpetrate an offence for 'bad' reasons fuels an image of law-breakers as rational opportunists who commit crimes out of intrinsic badness. Accordingly, it has encouraged the identification of law-breaking with moralistic notions of individual wickedness, thereby leading criminal justice and public discourses of crime to be most deeply grounded in what Fondacaro and O'Toole have called an 'evil-doer theory of crime'.[3]

This evil-doer view of the culpable individual contributes to inciting 'moral-anger-based reactive attitudes'[4] to crime. It has legitimised 'punitive urges at individual and systemic levels' and, 'paradoxically to some, help[ed] to fuel the intensity and scope of punishment in the American criminal justice system'.[5] Specifically, it has informed and reinforced the narrative that perpetrators deserve to suffer for the crimes that they committed, and such suffering might be achieved through the pains of exclusion that can result from punishment.[6] Altogether, even if the rationalist and individualist rhetoric of culpability, blame, and retribution demands the assignment of blame and infliction of punishment on an individual based on his or her choice to commit a criminal act, this rhetoric in practice reverberates on the individual as a whole, including his or her negative identity and supposed evilness.[7]

II. A Thin Account of Human Agency

One of the most sustained *j'accuse* against criminal law concerns its reliance on and promotion of an abstract, partial and universalised view of human nature. Mainstream discourses of culpability and punishment are founded on a narrow idea of *abstract reasoning* that focuses predominantly on the individual's ability to reason instrumentally about his or her actions without also considering other fundamental aspects of human agency in morally salient social contexts.[8] Indeed,

[3] M Fondacaro and MJ O'Toole, 'American Punitiveness and Mass Incarceration: Psychological Perspectives on Retributive and Consequentialist Responses to Crime' (2015) 18 *New Criminal Law Review* 477, 482.

[4] G Caruso, 'Skepticism Against Moral Responsibility' in E Zalda (ed), *Stanford Encyclopedia of Philosophy* (Spring 2018), available at plato.stanford.edu/entries/skepticism-moral-responsibility/#ReacAtti.

[5] Fondacaro and O'Toole (n 3) 482.

[6] eg Justice A Kennedy, 'Speech Delivered at the American Bar Association Annual Meeting' (2003) 16 *Federal Sentencing Reporter* 126, 126 (acknowledging that moral support for retribution cannot support harsh punishment and suggesting that a social desire 'to degrade and demean the prisoner … is not acceptable in a society founded on respect for the inalienable rights of the people').

[7] L Keller et al, 'A Closer Look at An Eye for An Eye: Laypersons' Punishment Decisions are Primarily Driven by Retributive Motives' (2010) 23 *Social Justice Research* 99.

[8] See A Norrie, 'Practical Reasoning and Criminal Responsibility' in D Cornish and R Clarke, *The Reasoning Criminal: Choice Perspectives on Offending* (New Brunswick, NJ, Transaction Publishers, 2014) 217.

this idea of abstract reasoning 'decontextualizes actions and intentions from their context', as it 'focuses solely upon the existence of rationally formed intentions and excludes from its gaze questions of how individuals come to form them – their motives, their motives' contexts, and so on'.[9] Such abstractism has contributed to a narrative of the culpable person that is profoundly entrenched in moralistic notions of individual wickedness, which in turn supports punitive stances of justice.

According to this scholarly critique, a view of the culpable person that is grounded in a defensible vision of human nature cannot overlook other fundamental factors that critically concur in determining human behaviour. Accordingly, the paradigms of culpability and punishment should hinge on a broader and more realistic picture of persons that equally embraces key factors that influence human acts in social contexts. Two main elements have been particularly specified for re-consideration within current understandings of culpability and punishment at both theoretical and doctrinal levels: emotions and the social environment.[10] As demonstrated, both of these factors have been largely and artificially discredited in dominant paradigms of culpability and punishment.

A. A Flawed Conception of Emotions

As the preceding pages have explained, emotions are afforded an inconsistent and marginal weight in voluntarist criminal law theory and legal doctrine. They are foremost treated as mostly *a-rational* forces that distort practical reasoning and control (the so-called 'mechanistic conception of emotions'). While voluntarist criminal law recognises that individuals do experience emotions, it simultaneously presupposes and normatively expects[11] that individuals are typically capable of resisting the intrusive influence of emotions on their deliberations by employing their intellectual powers of reason and control. Nonetheless, such law grants mitigating relevance to certain (strong) emotions, such as intense anger or fear, as long as these emotions appear to incapacitate the individual's reasoning and control under the circumstances. On the other hand, voluntarist criminal law does not also require that individuals are capable of experiencing emotions. Indeed, the capacity to experience and adaptively respond to emotions is not viewed as a constitutive or necessary pre-condition of culpability. Furthermore, the emotional dimension of the accused receives inconsistent treatment in sentencing.

[9] ibid, 221.

[10] See V Nourse, 'Hearts and Minds: Understanding the New Culpability' (2002) 6 *Buffalo Law Review* 361, 362 ('The individual implied by the modern law of mens rea is bare and alone, the subject of observation but bereft of emotions and motives and relationships to others. This [is a] rather empty, mechanistic, image – man as rational calculator, foreseer of risk, and harborer of statistical probabilities …').

[11] N Finkel and W Gerrod Parrott, *Emotions and Culpability: How the Law Is at Odds with Psychology, Jurors, and Itself* (Washington DC, America Psychological Association, 2006) 137.

Overall, as Finkel and Parrot have noted, 'the folk category of emotion can appear to threaten the orderly rule of law, for it carries with it the irrationality of primate impulses and the indeterminacy of subjective states. These perceived threats account for why the law omits emotion in favour of more cognitive criteria'.[12] Moreover, the general reluctance to deal with emotion is linked to the effort of law to avoid subjective rules, standards, and judgements as much as possible.[13] Therefore, the law has opted for 'more mechanical, physical, bodily aspects of everyday emotion language'.[14]

Criminal law scholars and philosophers – mostly those ascribing to the character-based tradition in criminal theory[15] – have vigorously criticised the limited and inconsistent treatment of emotion (compared to cognition) in both voluntarism and legal doctrine. Notably, they have stressed that criminal law's view of emotions is profoundly at odds with the widely shared perspective in philosophy and psychology that emotions are a vital dimension of rational agency, especially in morally salient social contexts. Indeed, emotions provide substantial content for understanding the world of meanings, values, and reasons for action *au pair* of our beliefs. Thus, emotions have an important role in human life and are indeed partly constitutive of human choices and behaviour.

In their seminal 1996 work,[16] Dan Kahan and Martha Nussbaum contrast the 'falsity' of the mechanistic conception of emotions – which permeates criminal law theory and doctrine – with the 'truth' of the evaluative conception of emotions.

[12] ibid, 48 ('in the Law's folk psychology theory as well as in its normative expectations, there is the belief that control over one's emotions is psychologically possible and normatively expected').

[13] ibid, 83.

[14] ibid.

[15] Character-based theories locate the core of culpability in the character traits, values, attitudes and personality dispositions of the individual. Many versions of character-based theories have been proposed over the years. Their common core is that the primary object of responsibility is the individual's own character, and they view criminal actions as proxies for the character flaws such actions express. This means that the imposition of criminal punishment may be morally justified only when the wrongful act reveals a flaw in the actor's character. While character-based theories embrace a broader conception of personhood (including one's emotions, desires, values, aversions, ambitions) than theories based on choice, their view of criminal action as a proxy for a person's bad character or attitudes suggests a (problematic) identification of the criminal act with the perpetrator as a whole. Thus, the ultimate basis for holding people culpable lies in their failure to do something about the character traits or attitudes that prompt them to engage in morally and legally objectionable conduct. See eg M Bayles, 'Character, Purpose, and Criminal Responsibility' (1982) *Law and Philosophy* 1, 5; G Fletcher, *Rethinking Criminal Law* (Boston, Little Brown and Co., 1988); N Lacey, 'The Resurgence of Character: Criminal Responsibility in the Context of Criminalisation' in A Duff and S Green (eds), *Philosophical Foundations of Criminal Law* (Oxford, Oxford University Press, 2011) 151; N Lacey, *State Punishment* (London, Routledge, 1988) 68; P Arenella, 'Character, Choice and Moral Agency: The Relevance of Character to Our Moral Culpability Judgments' (1990) 7 *Social Philosophy and Policy* 59l; V Tadros, 'The Characters of Excuse' (2001) 21 *Oxford Journal of Legal Studies* 495; P Westen, 'An Attitudinal Theory of Excuse' (1992) 25 *Law and Philosophy* 289. In actual practice, character evaluations feature the sentencing stage of criminal trials, where considerations of an individual's blameworthiness merge with (or even prevail over) considerations of his or her social dangerousness based on his or her personality.

[16] D Kahan and M Nussbaum, 'Two Conceptions of Emotions in Criminal Law' (1996) 96 *Columbia Law Review* 269.

Such conception disavows the intuition that emotions are mere primitive states and instead argues that emotions have a cognitive dimension. It thus perceives emotions as rational phenomena that not only provide constructive information about personal values and priorities but also motivate and guide behaviour.

By applying this evaluative conception of emotions to selected doctrines, such as those of premeditation, provocation, and extreme emotional disturbance (EMED), Kahan and Nussbaum have highlighted that the focus of such doctrines is ultimately the *moral quality of the agent's emotional motivation* that moved him or her to act as he or she did. For instance, in their discussion of rage in provocation, they argue that rage is mitigating in this context not because it provokes a mechanical loss of control in the individual but because it conveys values that are proper (ie, reasonable) in the relevant situation. Thus, the normative excusing rationale of provocation is not that the individual lost control under extreme rage but rather that his or her rage expressed a reasonable assessment of the situation and prompted an appropriate response to the provocative event.[17]

The choice and emotion theorist Samuel Pillsbury[18] has outlined a similar view. In his compelling reinterpretation of the law of homicide, Pillsbury criticises two main aspects of the definitional and distinguishing criteria of types of homicide, including premeditated and passion homicides. First, the division between these types mostly concerns the presence or absence of strong emotions. Second, the mitigating relevance of emotions is based on their *intensity*, which reflects their impact on the person's control under the circumstances. In both cases, the law neglects the moral worth of emotions by failing to inquire into the individual's (moral) reasons for having such emotions and reacting to them by committing the killing.

For Pillsbury, the risk of this approach is twofold. First, the law fails to distinguish between apparently equal types of homicide (ie, those within the same category) that are morally distinguishable. In this way, the law provides equal treatment for homicides that are qualitatively different under a profile of moral blameworthiness. Second, the law grants mitigation to most violent crimes that are committed for the most despicable reasons simply because the actor lost control while in the grip of an overwhelming emotional state.[19] The overall risk is that culpability attributions in homicide 'result in morally erroneous downgrading of some homicides … and erroneous upgrading of others'.[20]

Pillsbury has proposed that the ultimate evaluative criterion for distinguishing between types of homicide should be precisely the moral quality of the agent's

[17] ibid, 306–7.

[18] S Pillsbury, *Judging Evil: Rethinking the Law of Murder and Manslaughter* (New York, New York University Press, 1998).

[19] Pillsbury's observations also rest on the heavy criticisms that the 'heat-of-passion' doctrine has received over the years. As is well known, heat-of-passion law has been the subject of ethical, and most especially, feminist attacks. Likewise, provocation law has been attacked on the ground that it devalues gay victims of violence.

[20] ibid, 106.

(emotional) motive to kill.[21] By introducing this additional element, criminal law would be able to operate a more accurate assessment of homicides, as it would consider the actual degree of moral disregard for and hostility to individual human value and the value of the community. Such disregard or hostility is precisely expressed and measurable by the quality of the individual's motives for action. According to Pillsbury, motive is relevant to culpability in homicide because it reveals the depth and nature of the perpetrator's attack on value. The worst motives for killing correspond to the strongest commitment to individual or community disregard.

Pillsbury's argument links with the broader and long-standing scholarly discussion of the (ir)relevance of motives in elemental *mens rea* analysis.[22] Modes of *mens rea* such as purpose or reckless are defined and distinguished by the presence and intensity of legally identified cognitive mental states that accompany the relevant conduct. These criteria do not include the motive that moved the actor to engage in that conduct. The latter is relegated to a mere background condition that bears no relevance in culpability assessments. In other words, *mens rea* analysis focuses solely on the existence of rationally formed mental states and does not pursue the question of why an individual forms them.[23] Thus, a person who commits theft is not more or less guilty because he or she was motivated by a hatred of the victim as opposed to a desire to be able to afford a better school for his or her child. According to this branch of scholarship, the exclusion of motives from *mens rea* is problematic because it unduly overlooks the fundamental moral dimension of crimes and of criminal law. In fact, limiting *mens rea* assessments to factual or descriptive criteria risks over-punishing acts that were committed for morally worthy or morally reasonable motives and that are therefore morally distinguishable (and less morally blameworthy) from other crimes that were committed in the same *mens rea* state.

Several commentators have also criticised the omission (especially in legal doctrine) of emotional competence from the relevant mental capacities that are necessary for culpability. According to these accounts, simply possessing the capacity for cognitive understanding is insufficient to qualify as a (potential) culpable agent. In endorsing the view that emotions have an equally important role as that of prototypical cognition in guiding rational behaviour, these authors have held that the legal determination that an individual is mentally capable should also – and more accurately – rest on the individual's capacity for emotionally understanding or appreciating the moral significance of his or her conduct.

[21] See Pillsbury (n 18) chs 7 and 8 (providing a critical analysis of *State v Anderson*, 70 Cal. 2d 15, 447 P2 942 [1968]; *State v Forrest*, 362 S.E.2 252 [N.C. 1987]; *State v Gounagias*, 153 P.9 [Wash. 1914]; *State v Ott*, 686 P.2d 1001 [Or. 1984]).

[22] See J Hall, *General Principles of Criminal Law*, 2nd edn (Clark, NJ, The Lawbook Exchange, 2005) 88 ('hardly is any part of penal law is more definitely settled than that motive is irrelevant'). See also *State v Asher*, 50 Ark. 427 (1887).

[23] D Husak, *The Philosophy of Criminal Law: Selected Essays* (Oxford, Oxford University Press, 2010) 58 ('[*Mens rea*] is interested in *what* action was performed, however, it is not also interested in the *why* a person acted').

The exact meaning of emotional appreciation or understanding is admittedly unclear and the subject of continuous scholarly discussions. Philosophers and legal scholars who support its inclusion among the general conditions of culpability have provided a variety of definitions of emotional capacity that include, for instance, the capacity to care for the interests of other human beings, the capacity to engage in the moral evaluation of one's self and experience moral emotions, such as guilt, shame, remorse, and resentment, the capacity to internalise the normative expectations of others, the capacity to respond to moral norms as a motivation for one's conduct, and the capacity to self-identify with moral norms. Collectively, emotional capacity is mostly framed in moral terms as a capacity to feel the significance of moral norms (eg, to self-identify with moral norms and be vulnerable to feelings of shame, guilt, and remorse when failing to conform one's conduct in accordance with them).

The third criticism concerns sentencing. The machinery of sentencing turns out to be little interested in the person's emotions. Although sentencing hearings are designed to provide space for remorse or apology, they eventually focus almost entirely on the defendant and his or her dangerousness.[24] Scarce consideration of history of trauma leads to misinterpretations of certain negative emotional expressions, such as lack of empathy or callousness, as symptomatic of characterological criminality rather than as trauma responses.[25] And when emotional trauma is properly taken into account, it most likely entails a quantitative penalty discount without a qualitative determination of the most appropriate options for responding to and addressing it.

Last, the emotional dimension of perpetrators, including their emotional needs, is hardly addressed during the execution of punishment. As implied above, justice responses to crime are constructed around a fear-based rhetoric: *the state must punish crime*. By virtue of this rhetoric, exclusionary and disempowering mechanisms in the execution of punishment prevail over the emotional needs of those who have harmed others. The emotional issues, traumatic experiences, and remorseful feelings of perpetrators simply 'vanish' once they enter the criminal justice system.[26]

B. The (Political) Exclusion of the Social Context

An omission that is more striking than that of emotional factors is the omission of socio-environmental factors and their effects on individual behaviour.

[24] See S Bibas, *The Machinery of Criminal Justice* (Oxford, Oxford University Press, 2012).

[25] See K Wayland, 'The Importance of Recognizing Trauma Through Capital Mitigation Investigations and Presentations' (2008) 36 *Hofstra Law Review* 923, 947–8.

[26] This claim finds further support in the body of prison research suggesting that incarcerated people suppress their feelings by uniting their traumatic life histories with their current lives in prison and that such suppressed emotions return through violence toward others and the self. See, eg B Laws, 'The Return of the Suppressed: Exploring How Emotional Suppression Reappears as Violence and Pain among Male and Female Prisoners' (2019) 21 *Punishment & Society* 560.

As discussed, voluntarist criminal law allocates culpability and punishment entirely to individuals' rational choices,[27] thereby ignoring questions of social context. Thus, it tends to overemphasise the influence of intrapersonal factors and underestimate the impact of situational/social circumstances when accounting for human acts.[28] Altogether, voluntarist criminal law overlooks the ineradicable relationship between the individual and his or her social context in terms of history, background, and living conditions.

According to Alan Norrie, while individualist paradigms of culpability and punishment overvalue the individual's power of agency over the circumstances, they also *fictitiously* obscure the motivational significance of the social context in which the individual operates.[29] The exclusion from legal inquiry of 'everything … which gives what the individual did meaning, and without which he would not have acted'[30] seems to either deny or disregard the fact that socio-environmental factors influence an individual's choices and behaviour to more easily meet the repressive goals of blame and punishment.[31]

Norrie has further claimed that the tendency to decontextualise personhood, agency and behaviour also emerges from the individualist structure of many fundamental doctrines.[32] He has cited the example of the exclusion of the context of motives for acting from *mens rea* assessments[33] (ie, the context in which the individual's motive for his or her behaviour matured). Likewise, he has emphasised that the conception of legal insanity obscures the mediating role of social factors in mental pathology and crime.[34] For Norrie, the omission of such contextual factors from culpability ascriptions is problematic precisely because it cannot be adequate to grasp the complex reality of human nature and social life, thereby offering a one-sided view of the individual as a 'solitary atom'[35] who acts in a vacuum.

[27] See H Zehr, *Changing Lenses: Restorative Justice for Our Times*, 25th Anniversary ed (Harrisonburg, VA, Herald Press, 2015) 75 (commenting on the voluntarist/retributivist account of culpability and observing that, under this account, 'offenders have had various choices and, having picked the wrong ones, they are guilty. [Therefore,] guilt is individual failing').

[28] ibid, 74 ('Although each of us is responsible for the choices we make, the social and psychological context in which we find ourselves certainly influences our actual or potential choices … but our individualistic concept of guilt ignores context') and at 76 ('Because guilt is narrowly defined, centering on individual behavior, it allows us to ignore the social and economic roots and contexts of crime. We thus attempt to create justice by leaving out many of the relevant variables. And since guilt is viewed in either-or terms, it encourages a simplistic view of the world that tends to see things as good and bad, them and us.'). See also D Dripps, 'Fundamental Retribution Error: Criminal Justice and the Social Psychology of Blame' (2003) 56 *Vanderbilt Law Review* 1383.

[29] A Norrie, 'The Limits of Justice: Finding Fault in the Criminal Law' (1996) 59 *The Modern Law Review* 540, 554 ('The problem for [criminal] law, for criminal justice, for the penal equation, is that it is one-sided in its treatment of people being in control. There is a double exclusion here: of the social conditions of selfhood and the structural conflicts which inform those conditions').

[30] Norrie (n 2) 171.

[31] ibid.

[32] ibid.

[33] ibid, 36–46.

[34] ibid, 187–94. See also L Johnston, 'Reconceptualizing Criminal Justice Reform for Offenders with Serious Mental Illness' (2019) 71 *Florida Law Review* 515, 523–35 (suggesting that current criminal law approach to mental pathology supports the criminalisation of mentally ill people).

[35] Norrie (n 2) 172.

Following the same line of criticism, Nicola Lacey has recognised that the voluntarist model of culpability is founded on a naïve and pre-social view of the human being[36] that artificially divorces his or her reasoning, judgement, and control abilities from his or her social environment. Lacey has utilised Hart's capacity-responsibility[37] model as a normative benchmark to suggest that the features of a subject's situation, environment, history, or circumstances – such as traumatic experiences, the quality of parenting and education, and so on – are objectively apt to exert several significant effects on the subject's cognitive and control capacities, which supposedly afford him or her the opportunity to behave in conformity with the law.[38] According to Lacey, voluntarism does not fail to recognise social factors because of their claimed irrelevance[39] to culpability as 'it would be simply irrational'[40] to consider them irrelevant. Thus, the reason is not found within this philosophical model of culpability itself. Rather, the reason is that the model hinges on and expresses a vision of the functions of criminal law primarily in terms of desert, blame, and stigmatisation as well as 'a weakening of the internal constraints set by the demands of legitimation where civil libertarian sentiments are robust'.[41] Yet, if this philosophical model was supported by a vision of the purposes of criminal law in terms of fostering positive goals, such as integration, reform, and even forgiveness, then no aspect of the model alone would preclude the assignment of weight to 'realistic as well as a respectful attempt[s] to understand the background to offending behavior'.[42]

In a more straightforward vein, Anders Kaye has offered a political critique of the modern compatibilist theory of personhood that is at the core of voluntarist criminal law.[43] He has notably contended that the claimed purity, equality, and neutrality of such a compatibilist approach to personhood masks conservative socio-political aims since the focus on the individual at the exclusion of social cues of behaviour reinforces economic class divisions and hinders social change.[44] While Kaye has acknowledged the many variations within modern compatibilist theory, he has also emphasised that their common aim is to 'salvage' the narrative of individual blame and punishment by marginalising the disruptive effects of difficult socioeconomic conditions on law-abiding behaviour. Thereby, compatibilist

[36] N Lacey, *State Punishment* (London, Routledge, 1988).

[37] See HLA Hart, *Punishment and Responsibility* (Oxford, Oxford University Press, 1968).

[38] N Lacey, 'Socializing the Subject of Criminal Law? Criminal Responsibility and the Purposes of Criminalization' (2016) 99 *Marquette Law Review* 541.

[39] See ch 1.

[40] Lacey (n 38) 553.

[41] ibid, 557.

[42] ibid, 556.

[43] A Kaye, 'The Secret Politics of Compatibilist Criminal Law' (2007) 55 *Kansas Law Review* 365.

[44] For a similar argument, see also A Ristroph, 'How (Not) To Think like a Punisher' (2009) 61 *Florida Law Review* 727, 746 ('[w]hatever the causal relationship between the concept of desert and race and class disparities in sentencing, desert may protect those disparities from efforts to eliminate them. Most individuals who receive criminal sentences have done something illegal, even if not the precise offense of conviction. Hence, even if desert is always based on a finding of illegal action, we can safely conclude that all those poor, black men in prison deserved at least some punishment').

criminal law ultimately leads the populace to be less sensitive to the connections between social conditions and crime, they 'slip into thinking that … the significant causes of [one's] crime are in [the relevant individual]',[45] and 'resign themselves to 'evil' itself'.[46] On the other hand, by excluding harsh social conditions from the host of factors that are relevant to culpability and punishment determinations, compatibilist criminal law inevitably punishes the disadvantaged more frequently and, through punishment, supports the infliction of further social losses that only perpetuate 'the disadvantaged status of the disadvantaged'.[47] Ultimately, voluntarist criminal law grounds blame in moral luck and eventuates in profound unfairness.

The second, linked branch of this criticism concerns an inconsistent consideration of social factors in sentencing determinations. As illustrated earlier, the penalty phase appears to be slightly more sensitive to the accused's psychosocial history. However, such sensitivity is left to the discretion of decision-makers and risks of discrimination-based disparities in regard to the accused's background, ethnicity, or education. According to Alice Ristroph, deserts considerations of moral blameworthiness often appear to obscure socioeconomic injustice or racial bias and to reproduce them into penal practice.[48] Recalling Marx's notion that 'philosophical theories are in peril if they are constructed in disregard of the nature of the empirical world in which they are supposed to apply', Ristroph has argued that retributive considerations dangerously fails to address 'the unjust world' that characterises modern society and encourages the justice system 'to ignore the relationship between [social disadvantage] and crime altogether'.[49] In view of this, she and other authors have recommended a more consistent inclusion of neglected and disadvantaged backgrounds in sentencing determinations. The sentencing system should be more attentive to the social stories of perpetrators,[50] and it should value and address the potential social inequalities, disadvantages and victimisations that many (if not most) justice-involved individuals have suffered prior to offending.

The third and last criticism concerns the exclusion of the relevance of social factors (notably, social bonds and relationships) during the execution of sentences. Punishment is by definition intended to exclude or separate an individual from

[45] Kaye (n 43) 413.

[46] ibid, 412.

[47] ibid, 420.

[48] A Ristroph, 'Deserts, Democracy, and Sentencing Reform' (2006) *Journal of Criminal Law and Criminology* 1293, 1297 ('The normative judgment that those who break the law are morally deserving of punishment renders irrelevant the more or less uncontroverted fact that the poor are much more likely to break the law').

[49] ibid.

[50] See M Gohara, 'In Defense of the Injured: How Trauma-Informed Criminal Defense Can Reform Sentencing' (2018) 45 *American Journal of Criminal Law* 1, 26 ('the exclusion of social history from sentencing consideration has hindered courts from learning the reasons that people break the law. It has prevented consideration of sound bases for proportionate punishment and opportunities for rehabilitation, while still producing disparate outcomes in numerous cases. Rather than seeing the pervasiveness of trauma in case after case as an opportunity to identify and treat a factor underlying many offenses, courts, constrained by guidelines and determinate sentences, have explicitly disavowed its consideration').

the rest of society. Social losses due to punishment – including loss of employment, family and community separation, and scarce access to education – have the effect of producing or aggravating social disadvantage, thereby creating a vicious cycle that is challenging to interrupt. Hence, many scholars, advocates, and legal practitioners have persistently advocated for a punishment system that values the social needs of justice-involved individuals. Punishment should grant as much inclusivity as possible in terms of community involvement, family support, and access to employment and education, which are all factors that not only permit an individual to be and feel like an active and productive member of societal life but also avoid that punishment leads to the civil death of an individual. The latter outcome is perhaps the worst sentence of all.

III. A Static View of the Culpable Person

Other than approaching (culpable) persons as subjects without a past, voluntarist criminal law also treats them as subjects without a (better) future. Indeed, voluntarist criminal law is notably indifferent to the idea that a person who commits an offence can and should be given the opportunity to (self-)change. This attitude is either implicitly or explicitly manifest in a series of criminal law and justice domains of both theoretical and practical nature.

First, this assumption is implicit in the relationship between criminal law's voluntarist view of persons as autonomous and rational choosing beings and the logic of culpability and retribution. Under voluntarist retributivist theory, culpability and punishment are static and backward-oriented. They build exclusively on the wrongful choice of the perpetrator at the moment of the offence. The timeframe to assess an individual's blame and desert is narrowly focused on the precise moment of the act and does not extend consideration to other contextual circumstances, such as the individual's history and development, the impact of punishment on him or her and his or her family, or his or her post-offence circumstances and changes. Thus, from a retributivist perspective, the individual's life and time is fixed in the very moment that he or she chooses to commit an evil act.[51] In slightly different terms, the fact that an individual can (and should be given the possibility to) change his or her lifestyle and behaviour is not part of deontological discourses on culpability and punishment.[52] Accordingly, a system that pursues retribution as its primary penological goal is fundamentally uninterested in whether sentences should be structured in a way that can or should promote positive individual change.

[51] Norrie (n 2) 172 ('The law focuses its attention on an isolated homunculus, an individual without past or future, a solitary atom').

[52] See also R Canton, '*Why Punish? An Introduction to the Philosophy of Punishment*' (London, Palgrave McMillan 2018) 118 ('Retribution … reduces an individual to "an offender", blithely ignoring the personal and social circumstances of her crimes or the implications for her of her punishment defining this persuasively as *justice*').

Such lack of interest for a person's positive change exacerbates when retributive considerations merge (as it quite often happens in reality) with incapacitative considerations. For one thing, retributive backward-looking considerations are indifferent to any prospects of change of the individual. The calculus of punishment on retributive grounds only encompasses the individual's desert, without also considering the effect that such punishment can have on such person. On the other hand, incapacitation rests on an understanding of perpetrators as inherently dangerous and likely to reoffend across different circumstances and situations. When retribution merges with incapacitation, the pains of punishment are inflicted upon an individual not only for committing a bad deed but also for *being* a bad person.[53] In short, punishment entails censuring evil as well as attributing it to the individual's personality.

The fusion of retributive and incapacitating rationales places barriers to the achievement of rehabilitative aims. Following the decline of the treatmentist rehabilitative ideal,[54] rehabilitation has re-gained its place within sentencing theory and practice and it does qualify as one of the aims of sentencing. Indeed, certain measures, such as probation, are expressly designed to promote the rehabilitation of the perpetrator.[55] Nevertheless, rehabilitation remains an altogether secondary goal of punishment and is largely disregarded in actual practice. Punishment is designed to give perpetrators what they deserve, to protect the public from crime and, *if conditions permit*, to provide opportunities for rehabilitation.

The exact meaning and scope of rehabilitation are heterogeneous and subject to different interpretations across statutes, courts, and legal scholarship.[56] At the statutory level, rehabilitation qualifies as a utilitarian and state-centred goal of punishment to be pursued for the sake of public safety and when there is a reasonable belief that such utilitarian benefit will be realised. The pursuit of rehabilitation is subordinated to its realistic efficacy, that is, it is pursued insofar as it is reasonable, it is achieved through reasonable means, and when there is a reasonable prospect for success in employing those means. Thus, the question of whether rehabilitation is reasonably feasible is at root an empirical one, conditioned on its efficacy at promoting special deterrence. Accordingly, rehabilitation should *not* be pursued based on an unsupported hope that a perpetrator can be rehabilitated. Altogether, punishment should aim for rehabilitation provided that rehabilitation

[53] See F Zimring and G Hawkins, *Incapacitation: Penal Confinement and the Restraint of Crime* (New York, Oxford University Press, 1995) 15 ('The implicit assumption that offenders are intractable and insusceptible to change serves to justify imprisonment for the purpose of restraint on both moral and practical grounds').

[54] See ch 2.

[55] For a discussion about the failures of 'mass probation' at promoting crime reduction and lowering incarceration rates, see M Phelps, 'The Paradox of Probation: Community Supervision in the Age of Mass Incarceration' (2013) 35 *Law & Policy* 51.

[56] Rehabilitation has taken variegated forms over the years, ranging from rehabilitation as training to rehabilitation as moral reform. For a review of different types of rehabilitation, see F McNeill, 'Punishment as Rehabilitation' in G Bruinsma and D Weisburd (eds), *Encyclopedia of Criminology and Criminal Justice* (New York, Springer, 2014) 4195, 4196–8.

is empirically feasible and capable of promoting public safety. From this state-centred perspective, the pursuit of rehabilitation is not an absolute or universal goal of punishment, but it is contingent upon its concrete effectiveness to avoid further crime.

The unsteady significance and scope of rehabilitation are also manifest in the jurisprudence of the Supreme Court. Over the course of the years, the Supreme Court has repeatedly acknowledged that rehabilitation is a purpose of punishment; however, its interpretation of the meaning and scope of rehabilitation within penalty has been largely inconsistent.[57] The Court's ambiguous approach to rehabilitation is particularly glaring within the body of constitutional jurisprudence about the pursuit of rehabilitation during incarceration. Foremost, while the Court has recognised that rehabilitation is a legitimate penological interest, it has rejected that people in prison are entitled to a positive right to rehabilitation.[58] Moreover, the Court has been unclear as for the exact meaning of rehabilitation. On some occasions, the Court has seemed to endorse an understanding of rehabilitation as training in terms of education or job opportunities. On other occasions, the Court has seemed to understand rehabilitation as ultimately a moral reform through which the perpetrator is induced to reflect and become a morally better person. Such interpretation of the concept of rehabilitation has led the Court to legitimise certain forms of deprivation under the mantle of being potentially instrumental to achieve the individual's moral reform. For instance, the Court's interpretation of rehabilitation as moral reform is glaring in *Beard v Banks*.[59] In that case, the Court endorsed a deprivation theory of rehabilitation and recognised that deprivation is a valid tool in promoting rehabilitation as it gives people in prison an added incentive to improve their behaviour.[60] Thus, prison regulations can legitimately – however within constitutional limitations – deprive incarcerated people of certain goods and benefits if such deprivations are meant and apt to pursue a rehabilitative goal.

The Court has manifested a striking emphasis on rehabilitation as a fundamental goal of punishment in its landmark constitutional decisions on juveniles[61] that

[57] See *Tapia v United States*, 131 S. Ct. 2382 (2011); *Pepper v United States*, 131 S. Ct. 1229 (2011) (providing different views about the use of rehabilitation under the Sentencing Reform Act). For a discussion of these two cases, see C Flanders, 'The Supreme Court and the Rehabilitative Ideal' (2015) 49 *Georgia Law Review* 383, 403–8.

[58] See *Powell v Texas*, 392 U.S. 514 (1968); *Rhodes v Chapman*, 452 U.S. 337 (1981). See also *Padgett v Stein*, 406 F. Supp. 287, 296 (MD Pa. 1975) (concluding that incarcerated people do not have a right to rehabilitation and government entities are not constitutionally compelled (ie, they do not bear a positive obligation) to rehabilitate them).

[59] 548 U.S. 521 (2006).

[60] It is interesting to note that this understanding of rehabilitation as moral reform figures also in the final draft of the MPC Sentencing Project, where the ALI has clarified that '[i]f an ex-offender is reformed because he found conviction and punishment to be painful and worth avoiding in the future, he is still reformed. The Code does not limit its understanding of rehabilitation to interventions that are voluntary, administered with kindness, or enjoyable'. See American Law Institute, Proposed Final Draft Model Penal Code: Sentencing, Comment to § 1.02(a)(ii) 6 (2017).

[61] *Graham v Florida*, 560 U.S. 48 (2010); see also *Miller v Alabama*, 567 U.S. 460 (2012); *Montgomery v Louisiana*, 136 S. Ct. 718 (2016).

banned the application of mandatory life imprisonment without the possibility of parole (LWOP) to adolescents. Unlike previous opinions that paid most attention to retribution and deterrence,[62] in *Graham v Florida* Justice Kennedy (writing for the majority) remarkably used rehabilitation as the key argument to find LWOP an excessively disproportionate punishment for adolescents convicted for crimes other than homicide. Regrettably, Justice Kennedy was unclear as to what he meant by rehabilitation, and just left open to 'the State, in the first instance, to explore the means and mechanisms for compliance' with the Court's instruction that adolescents must be given a 'meaningful opportunity' to obtain release.[63]

It is important to emphasise that the Court's argument about rehabilitation in *Graham* is implicitly premised on the constitutional protection of human dignity,[64] understood here as the intrinsic worth of children as human beings. A key guiding factor within the Court's reasoning has been the recognition that adolescents have a 'greater capacity for change',[65] compared to adults, in view of their ongoing (neuro)development and maturation. Considering such generalised possibility of change in adolescents,[66] the Court acknowledged that LWOP deprives them of 'the opportunity to achieve maturity of judgment and self-recognition of human worth and potential and forswears altogether the rehabilitative ideal'.[67]

Graham and its progeny have been reduced to a narrow 'juveniles are different' doctrine, which entails that juveniles can be rehabilitated because their ongoing development enables them to change.[68] In overlooking the far-reaching scope of these decisions, Courts and legal scholars have largely disregarded potential extensions of these principles to adult justice,[69] where the goals of retribution and incapacitation continue to prevail over the aim of rehabilitation. Adults are who they are and so less capable of rehabilitation. Thus, children are to be rehabilitated and adults are to be punished.

This generalised presumption of incapacity for change is most evident in a series of criminal justice practices and contexts. It is foremost apparent in mandatory LWOP and death sentences. These penalties, which find their ultimate rationale

[62] See *Roper v Simmons*, 543 U.S. 551 (2005).

[63] *Graham* (n 61) 73–74.

[64] See eg *Roper* (n 62) 578.

[65] *Graham* (n 61) 74.

[66] But see *Miller* (n 61) (banning automatic mandatory life imprisonment without the possibility of parole following murder convictions for all but the rarest adolescents who are assessed to be 'irreparably corrupt' and therefore 'incapable of rehabilitation and bound to continue to be a threat to society').

[67] *Graham* (n 61) 74.

[68] *Roper* (n 62) 570 ('[f]rom a moral standpoint it would be misguided to equate the failings of a minor with those of an adult, for a greater possibility exists that a minor's character deficiencies will be reformed').

[69] But see, eg R Frase, 'What's 'Different' (Enough) in Eighth Amendment Law?' (2013) 11 *Ohio State Journal of Criminal Law* 9; C Steiker and J Steiker, 'Graham Lets the Sun Shine In: The Supreme Court Opens a Window Between Two Formerly Walled-off Approaches to Eighth Amendment Proportionality Challenges' (2010) 23 *Federal Sentencing Reporter* 79; J Simon, 'Dignity and Risk: The Long Road from Graham v. Florida to Abolition of Life without Parole' in C J Ogletree, Jr. and A Sarat (eds), *Life Without Parole: America's New Death Penalty?* (New York, NYU Press, 2012) 282; M O' Hear, 'Not Just Kids Stuff? Extending Graham and Miller to Adults' (2013) 78 *Missouri Law Review* 1087.

in the principles of retribution and incapacitation, build on 'an irrevocable judgment about a person's value and place in society'[70] that *ab origine* and definitively negates the possibility that the person can and should be given the opportunity to change, repair his or her mistake, and reclaim his or her life as a member of the community.[71] Besides these extreme examples, criminal justice fails to acknowledge the capacity and potential for adult change through habitual offender statutes, its use of risk assessment tools for establishing individual dangerousness, and the implementation of other forms of exclusion (eg, felony disenfranchisement) that target people on the basis of their crimes or criminal records. Last, though certainly not least, the indifference of criminal law and justice to individual change also manifests in an overreliance on incarceration and its methods, including the negation of relevant social and institutional bonds, a scarcity of rehabilitation services, supermax detention regimes, and the application of prolonged solitary confinement in often precarious conditions. The paradox of these legitimised forms of suffering, exclusion and isolation is the presumption and expectation that they will allow an individual to re-enter and remain in society as a productive, cheerful, and law-abiding citizen.

IV. Dehumanisation

The analysed aspects of the model of personhood that underpins the dominant paradigms of culpability and punishment also warrant examination through the lens of dehumanisation. The concept of dehumanisation is highly complex and has been the subject of thorough investigation in psychological, sociological, and legal research over the past 40 years. In the most basic terms, 'dehumanisation' refers to the partial or whole denial of the humanity of a person or group of persons. Although it is possible to speak of degrees of dehumanisation, one general principle is constant: to perceive or treat someone as less human, not fully human, or subhuman is an act of dehumanisation, as is the total denial of the humanity of an individual or group. Accordingly, humanness consists of acknowledging and valuing *uniquely human qualities and capacities* in other individuals.

Empirical studies have described two main dehumanisation mechanisms: negation of human identity and negation of social belongingness (ie, moral and social exclusion). The first mechanism refers to denial of certain qualities of an individual that must be accorded to a person to perceive him or her as fully human. Herbert C Kelman wrote that humanness primarily entails a recognition

[70] *Graham* (n 61) 74.

[71] J Simon, 'Dignity and Risk: The Long Way from Graham v Florida to Abolition of Life Without Parole' in C Ogletree and A Sarat (eds), *Life Without Parole: America's New Death Penalty?* 282, 282 (observing that '[life without parole] defines the logic of contemporary [American] penality … in its embrace of a totalizing promise of prison incapacitation extended to the very limits of life, and unmediated by any further consideration of the prisoner as a distinct human being').

of another person's identity.[72] To accord a person identity 'is to perceive him [or her] as an individual, independent and distinguishable from others, capable of making choices' (ie, capable of agency).[73] From this perspective, dehumanisation corresponds to the negation of the agency of an individual.

Similarly, in his widely cited work,[74] the psychologist Nick Haslam has identified two distinct senses of humanness: 'human uniqueness' and 'human nature'. These two conceptual models of humanness correspond to two types of dehumanisation: animalistic dehumanisation and mechanistic dehumanisation. *Animalistic* dehumanisation is a process of dehumanisation whereby people are perceived to be lacking uniquely human characteristics, such as rationality, higher cognition, civility, refinement, and moral sensibility. By lacking such unique human characteristics, people are 'seen implicitly or explicitly to be animal-like' and thus 'uncultured, lacking in self-control, and unintelligent'.[75] On the other hand, *mechanistic* dehumanisation is a process of dehumanisation whereby people are considered devoid of the natural human characteristics of 'emotionality, interpersonal warmth, cognitive openness [e.g. flexibility] … and … depth'.[76] Consequently, they are perceived as 'inert and cold' and 'emotionally inert'.[77]

Besides the negation of human identity, dehumanisation occurs through the negation of a person's social belonginess (ie, sense of community). According to Kelman, to accord a person community, people need to live in an 'interconnected network' in which they 'care for each other … recognize each other's individuality and … respect each other's rights'.[78] To be dehumanised is to be excluded from this community, regardless of the severity of the consequences. With such exclusion, the individual is viewed by the 'in-group' as outside the moral kinship based on a perceived deviance from normalised standards of appearance or behaviour. By excluding a person or persons from the moral community, it becomes possible to act inhumanly toward them or else to allow them to be harmed by others without invoking any sense of moral inhibition or self-reproach. Psychological studies have indeed suggested that perceiving others as less human than ourselves increases opportunities for moral disengagement or indifference.[79] Studies have also found that such moral disengagement, of which dehumanisation is a part, not only allows

[72] H Kelman, 'Violence Without Restraint: Reflections on the Dehumanization of Victims and Victimizers' in GM Kren and LH Rappoport (eds), *Varieties of Psychohistory* (New York, Springer, 1976) 282.

[73] H Kelman, 'Violence Without Moral Restraint: Reflections on the Dehumanization of Victims and Victimizers' (1973) 29 *Journal of Social Sciences* 25.

[74] N Haslam, 'Dehumanization: An Integrative Review' (2006) 10 *Personality and Social Psychology Review* 252.

[75] ibid, 257.

[76] ibid.

[77] ibid, 258.

[78] Kelman (n 72) 48–9.

[79] A Bandura, 'Moral Disengagement in the Perpetration of Inhumanities' (1999) 3 *Personality and Social Psychology Review (Special Issue on Evil and Violence)* 193. See also M Ososfky et al, 'The Role of Moral Disengagement in the Execution Process' (2005) 29 *Law and Human Behavior* 371.

individuals to distance themselves from those that are perceived as less human but also leads to a heightened willingness to punish.

A growing number of studies have associated dehumanisation of offending behaviour and punitive tendencies. According to Vasilejvic and Viki,

> [b]y performing criminal acts, society may view offenders as having denied themselves the right to make choices on their own and also as having forfeited their right to be members of the community. By committing acts that are not condoned by the community, they are dehumanized and excluded from the human moral circle. Once expelled from the human moral circle, and assigned as savage subhumans, offenders can be harshly punished and ill-treated for what they have done.[80]

The relationship between dehumanisation of offending behaviour and punitive attitudes derives support from a series of studies that evidence a positive correlation between dehumanisation of the perpetrator and support for harsher punishment, including the death penalty. For instance, Giner-Sorolla et al[81] have advanced the idea that perpetrators are dehumanised and even demonised as malignant, evil, and incapable of reform. Such extreme dehumanisation incites or even mandates the enactment of extreme measures, including violence against perpetrators.

A study by Bastian et al[82] has more specifically tested Haslam's model of dehumanisation against the voluntarist model of personhood that is intrinsic to retributive theory of punishment. The study proposes that the extent to which people dehumanise perpetrators by not perceiving them as fully human beings influences the degree to which people display support for harsh punishment through their desire for retributive justice. The study indicates that people's reasoning about punishment outcomes is driven not only by a moral outrage about the harmfulness of a given offending behaviour but also by a perception of crime perpetrators as subhuman and not amenable to change. According to these authors, this perception of perpetrators as subhuman renders them seemingly more deserving of severe and coercive forms of punishment as well as less capable of re-joining society.

Another study by Bastian et al[83] has notably reported that when individuals are perceived as high in human uniqueness – that is, they are perceived as having the capacity for reason and inhibition – they are expected to act according to moral norms and are blamed and punished when they transgress. Consequently, denying people human uniqueness (through animalistic dehumanisation) leads to

[80] M Vasilejvic and G Tendayi Viki, 'Dehumanization, Moral Disengagement and Public Attitudes' in P Gain, J Vaes and JP Leyens (eds), *Humanness and Dehumanization* (New York, Routledge, 2013) 129, 133.

[81] R Giner-Sorolla et al, 'Dehumanization, Demonization, and Morality Shifting: Paths to Moral Certainty in Extremist Violence' in MA Hogg and DL Blaylock (eds), *Extremism and the Psychology of Uncertainty* (Boston, Wiley-Blackwell, 2012) 165.

[82] B Bastian et al, 'The Roles of Dehumanization and Moral Outrage in Retributive Justice' (2013) 8 *PLoS One* e61842.

[83] B Bastian et al, 'Blaming, Praising, and Protecting Our Humanity: The Implications of Everyday Dehumanization for Judgments of Moral Status' (2011) 50 *British Journal of Social Psychology* 469.

perceptions that they are unable to inhibit immoral behaviour and are less deserving of punishment. On the other hand, when individuals are viewed as possessing strong human nature characteristics, including emotional warmth, flexibility and communality, their rehabilitation and resocialisation receive heavier endorsement. Consequently, denying people human nature (through mechanistic dehumanisation) leads to perceptions that they are less deserving of rehabilitation and less capable of proactively contributing to the moral community. Altogether, characteristics that distinguish humans from animals are those that are believed to underlie our responsibility, namely practical reasoning and control. Yet, these qualities are also viewed as making us more deserving of punishment and potentially reduce the extent to which we are afforded the opportunity for rehabilitation and resocialisation.

The combination of various models and effects of dehumanisation mechanisms, including that of inciting stronger punitive attitudes in the name of retribution and incapacitation, has an interesting parallel with the characteristics and ambiguities of the voluntarist model of (culpable) personhood. Prima facie, the normative model of the person is humanising. In criminal law, a person is depicted as an equal moral agent who is automatically assigned the capabilities to make choices (practical reasoning and control) and behave in conformity with the law. In this sense, in Haslam's language, criminal law's person is principally afforded highly human uniqueness. Yet the law is more controversial in assigning such person human nature qualities, such as emotional warmth, depth, as well as cognitive flexibility. Even if the law presupposes that the person experiences certain emotions, such as rage or fear, it expects him or her to control them through his or her reason and control powers. On the other hand, the law is mostly indifferent as to other types of the person's emotions, such as self-reflective emotions like guilt, remorse, shame, as well as his or her empathy. Such indifference is particularly manifest in the insufficient weight that these emotions are delivered in the determination and administration of punishment – where, as we saw, considerations of blameworthiness and dangerousness prevail over the emotional dimension of individuals. From this perspective, the criminal law's person is depicted as uniquely human, however, his or her human nature characteristics are largely left behind.

As suggested,[84] such partial dehumanisation emerges once a person offends. When it is a matter of adjudicating culpability, the person is reduced to his or her cognitive abilities of knowledge, reasoning, and control under the circumstances, and the judgement ultimately revolves around the fact that he or she did not choose to behave otherwise at the moment of committing the crime – generally regardless of his or her motives, context, or background, which inform why he or she ultimately made that choice.[85] Once he or she is found to be culpable,

[84] Vasilejvjc and Viki (n 80) 133.

[85] By largely leaving contextual and motivational factors out of inquiry, one could even argue that culpability criteria are already dehumanising per se.

the person loses his or her moral status and is deserving of punishment precisely because he or she did not exercise his or her choosing abilities to abide by the law.

The loss of such moral status facilitates dehumanisation (animalistic, mechanistic, or both). It also promotes moral disengagement and prompts punitive and exclusionary responses. The culpable individual is disempowered of his or her ability to make choices; he or she is denied his or her flexibility and amenability to change, and his or her social identity is obscured by punitive mechanisms that are legitimised by the fact that he or she chose to commit an offence. Moreover, the culpable person is dehumanised through exclusion, which either denies or diminishes his or her social belongingness. This social exclusion contributes to and solidifies a collective perception of crime perpetrators as outsiders to societal and moral kinship who deserve little respect in view of their transgressions. Accordingly, it triggers mechanisms of distancing, shaming, stigmatisation, and discrimination without invoking any sense of moral self-reproach.

In summary, while voluntarist criminal law endorses an 'agentic' view of perpetrators by depicting them as rational and autonomous practical reasoners and choosing beings, it also promotes an image of 'essentialised difference'[86] that can justify vigorous support for punitive crime responses.[87] A person who is found guilty of a crime becomes an 'alien other'[88] whose behaviour manifests wantonness and amorality with minimal social value or resemblance to 'us'. This individualistic, abstract, and depersonalised view of the culpable person can be ascribed to the range of causes that have contributed to a rhetoric of the perpetrator as an evil-doer. The humanness of perpetrators is secondary to the punitive mechanisms of justice, which socially exclude individuals and, as a consequence, deprive them of their agency and leaves behind their social identities. Eventually, criminal law perpetuates a dehumanising model of people that fuels the maintenance of punitive attitudes to crime.

V. Conclusion

The common theme that cuts across the reviewed critiques of the dominant model of the criminal law's person is that such model promotes a distorted and pejorative narrative of justice-involved individuals. Such narrative contributes to the

[86] D Garland, *The Culture of Control: Crime and Social Order in Contemporary Society* (New York, Oxford University Press, 2001) 135.

[87] See E Hanan, 'Incapacitating Errors: Sentencing and the Science of Change' (2019) 97 *Denver Law Review* 151, 164 (reporting that 'the tendency to designate individuals and groups as characterologically criminal is certainly prevalent in U.S. discourse. Nicole Gonzalez Van Cleve, for example, documented how courtroom professionals in Chicago's criminal courts describe defendants as belonging in one of two categories: the "mopes" or the "monsters." While the "mopes" might deserve a break, assistance, and special services, the "monsters"' must be incapacitated. Of course, at any point the line between "mopes" and "monsters" can be moved to shrink the class of offenders') (citations omitted).

[88] Garland (n 86) 136.

culture of differentness and exclusion and overall perpetuates punitive attitudes to crime. Alternatively, a more significant or different consideration of other aspects of human agency and behaviour, such as emotions, the social environment as well as the capacity for change, has the potential to lead the criminal law and public discourses of crime to endorse a more realistic and humanising view of the 'culpable person', and possibly lead to a system of justice that is less punitive, less stigmatising, and less exclusionary.

Nevertheless, scholarly efforts to rethink the notion of human nature in culpability and punishment attributions have admittedly remained altogether marginal in theoretical and doctrinal conversations of criminal law and have been overshadowed by prevailing punitive tendencies of the justice system. Yet, the soundness of these efforts has, at least in principle, found support within – and, in a sense, is revived by – the body of behavioural and brain research that indicates critical roles of emotions and the social environment in determining moral and social behaviour. Indeed, by suggesting the fundamental ways in which emotions and social factors operate in the brain to inform behavioural outcomes, these findings offer valuable considerations to deeply rethink the idea of the person that underpins notions of culpability and punishment. Notably, this body of knowledge offers critical insights to encourage a profound reconsideration of the way in which criminal law conceives of and responds to crime.

4

Emotions, the Social Environment, and the Brain

I. Introduction

In *Women and Human Development*,[1] the philosopher Martha Nussbaum offers a rather objective list of universal 'functional capabilities' that she considers central to human life. Many of those capabilities are intimately connected to human experience, such as

> [b]eing able to have attachments to things and people outside ourselves; [n]ot having one's emotional development blighted by overwhelming fear and anxiety, or by traumatic events of abuse or neglect [Emotions]; [b]eing able to form a conception of the good and to engage in critical reflection about the planning of one's life [Practical Reason]; [b]eing able to … recognize and show concern for other human beings, to engage in various forms of social interaction; to be able to imagine the situation of another and to have compassion for that situation … Having the social bases of self-respect and non-humiliation [Affiliation].[2]

According to Nussbaum, these components are separate yet strictly interrelated. Moreover, they are of central and equal importance to being and behaving as uniquely and completely human.[3] Nussbaum's list embraces a multidimensional conception of the central capabilities that are innate to the nature of humans as fundamentally emotional and social beings. Notably, Nussbaum's account implicitly aligns with insights from moral and social psychology as well as moral and social neuroscience regarding the mental and situational factors that are implicated in deciding, choosing, and behaving morally in social contexts.

At odds with – and, in a sense, complementing – dominant views in criminal law theory and legal doctrine, these empirical disciplines have evidenced that our choice to behave prosocially toward others and in compliance with social and moral norms does not simply rely upon our faculties of knowledge, understanding, or reasoning about the nature of our actions with respect to normative standards of right and wrong. Rather, these fields have underscored the centrality of emotions and emotion-related abilities, such as empathy, coupled with and

[1] M Nussbaum, *Women and Human Development* (New York, Cambridge University Press, 2000).
[2] ibid, 79.
[3] ibid, 81.

under the influence of socio-environmental factors in informing the processes that lead to adaptive social behaviour.

Foremost and contrary to the traditional notion of criminal law that emotion and cognition (or rationality) are separate entities of the human mind that compete for control of behaviour, modern sciences have indicated that the divide between cognition and emotion is a myth.[4] Every choice that we make – from the most automatic to the most deliberate – is influenced by the integration of cognition and emotion; consequently, discerning the boundaries between the two can be difficult. How we think about a matter is influenced by how we feel about it, and vice versa. The mutual influence between 'thinking' and 'feeling' drives our decision-making and behaviour.

Behavioural and neuroscientific studies have particularly emphasised the critical role of emotions in moral judgements and behaviour. As the literature suggests, there is agreement that the moral motivation to act prosocially does not stem solely from knowledge or reasoning about principles of justice but also relies on an appreciation of the interpersonal significance of a given mode of conduct. Such appreciation is largely mediated by the interaction between certain social/moral emotions – notably certain self-conscious or self-reflective emotions – as well as emotion-related faculties, including empathy, and pre-existing conditions, such as goals, beliefs, contexts, and experiences.

The fact that our choices and behaviour are significantly driven by our emotions as well does not imply that we are slaves to our emotions. An increasingly accredited hypothesis in modern neuroscience[5] is that emotions are not necessarily automatic reactions that we passively experience. In much of social life, we build, alter, regulate, and adapt our emotions based on our goals and situational needs. Most people have such capacity. Granted, there are several pathological conditions in which the 'emotion system' is compromised to such an extent that the individual may find it almost or completely impossible to use his or her emotions adaptively. In many of such cases, social behaviour can be severely compromised regardless of whether or not one knows that their actions are socially or morally wrong.

On the other hand, emotional reactions – and, consequently, our behaviour – are largely determined by context. Specifically, the way in which each person experiences, expresses, and regulates emotions to orient their social and moral behaviour is influenced by a series of contextual factors, including the features of the current situation and, more broadly, their culture, background, and the living social environment.[6] Strong evidence to support the latter claim concerns

[4] See R Davidson,' 'Cognitive Neuroscience Needs Affective Neuroscience (and Vice Versa)' (2000) 42 *Brain and Cognition* 89, 91 ('[c]ognition would be rudderless without the accompaniment of emotion, just as emotion would be primitive without the participation of cognition'); see also L Pessoa, 'On the Relationship Between Emotion and Cognition' (2008) 9 *Nature Reviews Neuroscience* 148.

[5] L Barrett, *How Emotions are Made: The Secret Life of the Brain* (Boston, Houghton Mifflin Harcourt, 2017); L Barrett, 'The Theory of Constructed Emotion: An Active Inference Account of Interoception and Categorization' (2017) 12 *Social Cognitive and Affective Neuroscience* 1.

[6] K Greenaway et al, 'Context is Everything (in Emotion Research)' (2018) 12 *Social Personality Psychology Compass* e12393.

the neurobiological, psychological, and behavioural impacts of severe socio-environmental factors, such as exposure to traumatic experiences and adverse experiences resulting in toxic stress over a long period of time. As this chapter demonstrates, research has found that chronic exposure to traumas and toxic stressors may entail a multitude of adverse effects for the emotional well-being of individuals, all of which may have negative repercussions on prosocial behaviour.

The ineradicable relationship between emotions, the environment, and moral behaviour also emerges from another, perhaps even more crucial perspective, namely the idea that humans have the capacity to change their behaviour over the entire course of their life. The human brain has the amazing ability to re-organise itself and adapt in response to changing environments and behavioural interactions. This ability, which is known as neuroplasticity, allows individuals to learn from new experiences, create memories and lose others, rewire their emotions, and adjust their behaviour and lifestyles accordingly. Crucially, healthy environments and social connections, including meaningful social relationships, stable social bonds, social inclusion, and perceived belongingness, have been found to foster positive changes in the brain regions that support the emotional processes that are involved in morality and prosocial behaviour. Meanwhile, social exclusion (both emotional and physical) can either precipitate or aggravate problematic neurobiological patterns in the same brain regions, which poses dramatic implications for prosociality, psychological well-being, and mental health.

This chapter analyses these aspects in turn with the aim of highlighting several gaps in the current architecture of (broad) culpability as well as dominant ideas and practices of punishment. Ultimately, the discussion of scientific findings within the following pages emphasises that criminal law conceives of and treats humans in a way that runs against their nature as fundamentally emotional and social beings.

II. The Emotional Brain

A. Definition(s) of Emotions

Emotions are essential to human life. Without emotions, life occurrences would be perceived as random, meaningless, and colour-blind events. Through emotions, we make meaning and sense of the external world. Emotions help us navigate our social environment as well as develop and maintain social relationships. They are an integral part of our social thinking, decisions, and actions and essential components of the social mind. Most notably, emotions maintain the social functionality of the brain and preserve its health.

The word 'emotion' derives from the Latin words *ex* (out) and *movere* (to move). Its etymology is consistent with the core function of emotions, namely that they move us to act and interact with the external environment. Other terms that closely correspond to 'emotion' can be found in other ancient languages.

For instance, the ancient Greek term *pathos* has the original meaning of 'experience' or 'suffering'. Eventually, the word *pathos* came to identify the quality of anything that either excites or stimulates feelings, such as pity or sorrow. Aristotle described *pathos* as a mode of persuasion alongside *logos* (logical argumentation) and *ethos* (virtuous character). Notably, he defined *pathe* as 'those things on account of which people change and differ in regard to their judgments, and upon which attend pain and pleasure'.[7] Aristotle's valence-based understanding of emotion can be considered one of the first influential explicit definitions of emotion and has attracted support in modern sciences.

Over the centuries, many definitions of 'emotion' have been offered across disciplines, though a consensus has not yet been reached. Indeed, 'what is an emotion?' is an ongoing conceptual question in scientific research that seems to correspond to a never-ending attempt to define emotion. Fehr and Russell have highlighted the difficulty of producing an explicit definition of emotion in stating that 'everyone knows what an emotion is, until asked to give a definition. Then, it seems, no one knows'.[8]

While an absolute definition of emotion is still absent,[9] modern psychology and neuroscience agree in understanding emotions as multicomponent phenomena of a brief duration that are elicited by environmental or interoceptive salient stimuli and involve three main interrelated sets of processes: neurophysiological processes (ie, autonomic nervous system activity leading to physiological changes, such as in the heartbeat); bodily/expressive processes (eg, facial expressions); and cognitive-experiential processes (ie, subjective feelings).[10] According to many authors, emotion is a type of 'action readiness' that urges an individual to act in specific ways (motivations) in response to perceived or received environmental stimuli.[11] For instance, danger provokes the emotion of fear, which determines the tendency to flee, somatic responses in preparing to flee, actual fleeing, and feelings of fear.

All emotions can be organised along two dimensions: valence and intensity.[12] Valence refers to the nature (or quality) of an emotion (ie, how good or bad an emotion is for us on a spectrum from avoidance to approach). In terms of intensity, emotions range along a continuum from a mild form to an extremely high

[7] Aristotle, *Rhetoric (Book II)*, ch 1, 1378a, in W Rhys Roberts (trans), *The Rhetoric and the Poetics of Aristotle*, (New York, The Modern Library, 1990).

[8] B Fehr and J Russel, 'Concept of Emotion Viewed from a Prototype Perspective' (1984) 113 *Journal of Experimental Psychology: General* 464, 464.

[9] See eg P Kleinginna and A Kleinginna, 'A Categorized List of Emotion Definitions, with Suggestions for a Consensual Definition' (1981) 5 *Motivation and Emotion* 345.

[10] But see Barrett, *How Emotions are Made* (n 5) (suggesting a computational theory of constructed emotion).

[11] See C Izard, 'The Many Meanings/Aspects of Emotion: Definitions, Functions, Activation, and Regulation' (2010) 2 *Emotion Review* 363.

[12] See L Barrett and JA Russell, 'The Structure of Current Affect: Controversies and Emerging Consensus' (1999) 8 *Current Directions in Psychological Science* 10.

level. For instance, anger is negative in the valence dimension, which indicates that it is an intrinsically unpleasant experience. When anger is extremely intense, it results in rage. Notably, the valence and intensity of emotions are both determined by several appraisals of the ongoing situation.

It is important to note the key distinction between emotions and feelings. In common language, emotions are normally referred to as 'feelings' (ie, something that is felt). However, in scientific language, feelings are understood as one component of emotions. To maintain such distinction, the term 'emotion' is often used to refer only to the bodily state that is elicited by a given stimulus, whereas the term 'feeling' is employed to refer to the conscious experience (ie, the mental representation) of such emotional state. Indeed, the terms 'feeling', 'emotional consciousness', and 'emotional experience' are typically applied interchangeably in the literature.

(Neuro)scientists have assumed heterogeneous positions on the exact relationship between emotions and feelings. According to LeDoux, emotions and feelings serve radically different functions. Emotions are automatic survival responses to relevant environmental challenges; however, they may not contribute to the emotional life of an individual.[13] Meanwhile, a feeling is the aware and self-reported experience of an emotional response. Feelings are a matter of consciousness and are notably supported by working memory.[14] Thus, consciousness makes us emotional.[15] Ralph Adolphs[16] has likewise suggested that emotions are biological functional states that regulate behaviour and allow us to cope with environmental challenges. In their turn, emotion states can cause the conscious experience of emotions (ie, feelings). In this way, feelings are derivative of emotion states. From a slightly different perspective, Antonio Damasio[17] has argued that feelings are natural evolutions of emotions. Because feelings are a natural sequence of emotions, an individual's feeling of a given emotion is ultimately the emotion per se. Thus, the two states can be referenced by the same name. Crucially, Damasio has suggested, emotions affect 'the mind' only when they evolve into feelings.

Altogether, emotion states are functional states that regulate complex behaviour in response to stimuli that instantiate recurrent environmental themes. These functional states, in turn, can also cause subjective conscious experiences

[13] J LeDoux, 'Feelings: What are They and How Does the Brain Make Them?' (2015) 144 *Daedalus, Journal of American Academy of Arts and Science* 96, 100.

[14] ibid, 102.

[15] In a more recent co-authored article, LeDoux has maintained that emotions, or feelings, are not innately programmed into our brains, but are cognitive states resulting from the gathering of information. As a result, emotions are 'higher-order states' embedded in cortical circuits. Therefore, agreeing with Barrett (n 5) and contrasting present theories, LeDoux sees emotional states as similar to other states of consciousness. See J LeDoux and R Brown, 'A Higher-Ordered Theory of Emotional Consciousness' (2017) 114 *PNAS* E2016.

[16] R Adolphs, 'How Should Neuroscience Study Emotions? By Distinguishing Emotion States, Concepts, and Experiences' (2017) 12 *Social Cognitive and Affective Neuroscience* 24, 27.

[17] A Damasio, *The Feeling of What Happens: Body and Emotion in the Making of Consciousness* (San Diego, Harcourt Brace, 1999) 36.

(feelings). Nevertheless, emotions do not necessarily translate into feelings. We do react automatically to many situations with our emotions without any awareness of doing so, but in some situations – especially those that are socially complex – we normally gain an awareness of our emotions in that we 'feel' them. When this case applies, we 'take ownership' of our emotions by consciously using them to guide our choices and behaviour. Furthermore, we modulate and regulate our emotional reactions depending on the situation. Given that the line between emotion and feeling may be significantly ambiguous, and to avoid confusing the reader, I adopt the style of many authors and use the term 'emotion' to also refer to feelings throughout this chapter.

B. Modern Theories of Emotions: The Emotion/Cognition Ambiguous Divide

Early theories of emotions investigated emotions as essentially physiological phenomena.[18] Such theories viewed emotions as solely automatic or reflexive (and therefore uncontrolled) processes that may occur either before or after an individual's physiological responses to environmental stimuli. By this logic, as purely unconscious phenomena, emotions were assumed to modulate human behaviour in a way that is unmediated by thinking. At the neurological level, these theories assumed that *all* emotions are generated and processed by the most primitive subcortical regions of the brain, including the limbic system and, notably, the amygdala.[19]

Whereas early theories assumed that emotions are animalistic-laden states over which an individual has no control, they viewed cognitive functions (supported by the neocortex) as the 'engine' of conscious, rational, and controlled behaviour. For decades, psychologists and neuroscientists have maintained a net separation between emotion and cognition within human thought and behaviour,[20] wherein cognition rules and is involved in emotion insofar as it is used to stop or block emotions from emerging.

Beginning in the 1960s, studies in cognitive and social psychology began to support the view that emotions are more than mere bodily sensations and physiological reactions over which we have no control. In contrast to the earlier

[18] W James, 'What is An Emotion?' (1884) 9 *Mind* 188; Cf. WB Cannon, 'The James-Lange Theory of Emotions: A Critical Examination and an Alternative Theory' (1927) 39 *The American Journal of Psychology* 106.

[19] J Papez, 'A Proposed Mechanism of Emotion' (1937) 79 *Archives if Neurology and Psychiatry* 725; P McLean, 'Psychosomatic Disease and the Emotional Brain: Recent Developments Based on Papez's Theory' (1949) 11 *Psychosomatic Medicine* 338.

[20] See G Loewenstein and J Lerner, 'The Role of Affect in Decision-making' in RJ Davidson, KR Scherer and HH Goldsmith (eds), *Series in Affective Science. Handbook of Affective Sciences* (New York, Oxford University Press, 2003) 619.

perspectives, these studies have indicated that the generation and processing of emotions also and essentially involve cognition. Since these findings were revealed, emotions have come to be viewed as cognitively constructed phenomena. Cognitive theories of emotions are numerous and propose slightly varying accounts of the emotion-cognition interaction in the generation of emotions. For instance, Schachter-Singer's two-factor theory of emotion[21] suggests that a stimulus from the environment leads first to various physiological responses (eg, change in the heartbeat, trembling). Then, the individual cognitively interprets this physiological response and labels it as a given emotion. Hence, in this account, emotions emerge as a result of a specific situation and the cognitive interpretation of such situation.

Another major cognitive theory of emotion is cognitive appraisal theory. Regardless of the various nuances between different versions of this theory,[22] its central tenet is that emotions are causally preceded by cognitive activity, which serves an emotion-activating function. According to this approach, when we receive or perceive inputs from the environment, we first appraise them with cognitive mechanisms that assign meaning to them in terms of personal significance and value. This appraisal process results in and is constitutive of the experience of emotion. In turn, the latter orients our response to the environmental inputs. This account also posits that emotions result from a specific situation and the cognitive interpretation of such situation. The cognitive interpretation of the stimulus precedes the physiological response to it.

According to a third account, namely the psychological construction model of emotion,[23] emotion is a construction that results from the interplay of more basic psychological processes that are not dedicated to emotion. In the psychological construction model, emotions are not special mental states but instead caused by other mental states, such as core affect (ie, states experienced as simply feeling good or bad), cognition, and perception. One version of the psychological construction model that is called the 'conceptual act model',[24] describes emotions as mental states that emerge when people make meaning of sensory input from the body and from the world by using knowledge of emotion that is based on prior experiences.

[21] S Schachter and J Singer, 'Cognitive, Social, and Physiological Determinants of Emotional State' (1962) 69 *Psychological Review* 379.

[22] See A Moors et al, 'Appraisal Theories of Emotion: State of the Art and Future Development' (2013) 5 *Emotion Review* 119. A critical dilemma for adherents to the cognitive appraisal theory is the definition of 'cognition'. Some see cognition as constituting emotion, others view it as merely playing a part, though an important part, in emotion generation. See eg GL Clore, 'Why Emotions Are Felt' in Ekman P, R Davidson (eds), *The Nature of Emotion: Fundamental Questions* (New York, Oxford University Press, 1994) 103. *cf* R Solomon, *Not Passion's Slave: Emotions and Choice* (New York, Oxford University Press, 2003) 92.

[23] eg L Barrett, 'Psychological Construction: A Darwinian Approach to the Science of Emotion' (2013) 5 *Emotion Review* 379.

[24] See L Barrett, 'Solving the Emotion Paradox: Categorization and the Experience of Emotion' (2006) 10 *Personality and Social Psychology Review* 20.

In the conceptual act model, emotions are 'situated conceptualisations'[25] because the assigned meaning is tailored to the immediate environment and prepares the person to respond to the input in such a way that is specific to the situation.

While myriad models of emotion have been proposed, most of them agree that automatic and cognitive emotion processes can be thought of as complementary. Notably, as Helion and Ochsner have emphasised,

> current research suggests that emotions result as much from controlled [cognitive] processes as they result from automatic [uncontrolled] ones, and that controlled processes play roles in all kinds of affective processes.
>
> On the automatic side, emotional processes can be rapid and reflexive … non-consciously tied to representations of individuals and their actions … On the controlled side, higher cognitive processes [aid in] the elaboration of the meaning of a stimulus, as well as the monitoring and reporting of emotion … [Such evaluations] can change how the emotional value of a stimulus is construed, how we categorize and perceive our affective states, and how they will inform our future behavior. Together, controlled and automatic processes both create and change affect, and the meaning derived from a situation and subsequent emotional responses are the product of both of these processes working in tandem … These automatic and controlled processes are bidirectional, and can interact in a number of ways to produce distinct affective experiences and evaluations.[26]

When they are either automatic or controlled, emotions prepare us to act with specific relational aims. Notably, emotions are associated with action tendencies,[27] which represent a propensity to engage in certain actions or refrain from acting when experiencing a specific emotion. Action tendencies correspond to the motivational aspect of the emotional response. Indeed, several emotion researchers have suggested that 'emotions are motivating'[28] and that they are 'closely and intimately related to action by way of their nature as motivational states'.[29] For instance, anger may promote antagonistic tendencies that are designed to restore control, seek redress, or remove obstruction.

From this perspective, emotions help people prioritise and organise their behaviour in ways that optimise their adjustment to the demands of their physical and social environment. Consequently, emotions modulate people's behavioural responses by appropriately aligning such responses with the demands or opportunities that the environment offers. Ultimately, people's behaviours are adaptive responses to their emotions and reflect (either automatic or controlled) appraisals of features of the environment that are significant for their well-being.

[25] ibid.

[26] C Helion and K Ochsner, 'The Role of Emotion Regulation in Moral Judgments' (2018) 11 *Neuroethics* 297, 300.

[27] N Frijda, 'Emotion, Cognitive Structure and Action Tendency' (1986) 1 *Cognition and Emotion* 115.

[28] E Rolls, *The Brain and Emotion* (New York, Oxford University Press, 1999).

[29] N Frijda, 'Emotions and Action' in ASR Manstead, N Frijda and A Fischer (eds), *Feelings and Emotions* (Cambridge, Cambridge University Press, 2004) 158, 159.

Modern theories of emotions acknowledge the importance of the environment or context[30] by asserting that a stimulus is always appraised (either automatically or cognitively) in context and as a function of the current needs and goals of the individual. Emotions result from and represent the significance of the transaction[31] between the person and their environment. The type of situation that the individual encounters is of immense importance to the generation and differentiation of emotions. Altogether, emotions are conceived of as flexible, malleable, goal directed, and contextually bound.

C. From Emotion Generation to Emotion Regulation: Insights from Neuroscience

The cognitive dimension of emotions has found critical support in modern neuroscience, wherein research has highlighted that emotion processes (from the generation to the experience and regulation of emotions) involve a broad constellation of brain regions. A key insight is that these brain regions work together in both automatic and controlled emotion processes.[32] As an individual gains explicit awareness of his or her emotional states in a given situation, interaction among these brain regions increases.

Within this network, four brain regions appear to be particularly implicated: the limbic system, including the amygdala and the hippocampus; the anterior insula (AI), the anterior cingulate cortex (ACC); and the prefrontal cortex (PFC), especially the medial PFC (mPFC). The amygdala 'orchestrates emotion[s]'[33] by providing received or perceived stimuli with a given affective quality and linking unconscious and conscious aspects of emotion experience. The hippocampus is involved in vital functions of spatial mapping and consolidating sensory information into memory, and it also contributes to the interpretation of environmental cues that are likely to produce an emotional response.[34] The AI is thought to be implicated in the subjective awareness of

[30] See Barrett (n 5). See also C Wilson-Mendenhall et al, 'Situating Emotional Experience' (2013) *Frontiers in Human Neuroscience*, available at doi.org/10.3389/fnhum.2013.00764 (suggesting that emotional experience is situated and dynamic).

[31] See R Lazarus et al, 'Emotion: A Cognitive-Phenomenological Analysis' in R Plutchik and H Kellerman (eds), *Theories of Emotion*, Vol. I (New York, Academic Press 1980) 189, 195; C Smith and R Lazarus, 'Emotion and Adaptation' in LA Pervin, (ed), *Handbook of Personality Theory and Research* (New York, Guilford Press) 609.

[32] See Helion and Ochsner (n 26).

[33] E Kandel, *The Disordered Mind: What Unusual Brains Tell Us About Ourselves* (New York, Farrar, Straus and Giroux, 2018) 180.

[34] D Perry et al, 'Projecting Memories: The Role of the Hippocampus in Emotional Mentalizing' (2011) 54 *Neuroimage* 1669; KA Muscatell, 'Self-involvement Modulates the Effective Connectivity of the Autobiographical Memory Network' (2010) 5 *Social Cognitive and Affective Neuroscience* 68; N Eisenberger et al, 'Functional Magnetic Resonance Imaging Responses Relate to Differences in Real-world Social Experience' (2007) 7 *Emotion* 745.

all feelings (ie, emotional awareness).[35] The mPFC, including the dorsomedial prefrontal cortex (dmPFC) and ventromedial prefrontal cortex (vmPFC), and the orbitofrontal cortex (OFC) appear to contribute to the representation and valuation of emotional stimuli as well as the modulation of emotional responses, sensitivity to reward, and motivation.[36] The ACC has an important role in the integration of neuronal circuitry for emotion regulation.[37] In fact, this area has extensive connections with regions that are known to be essential for emotion arousal (eg, the amygdala), memory (eg, the hippocampal region), and reward (eg, the OFC).[38]

These (and other) brain areas work together during the generation, experience, and regulation of emotions through ascending (bottom-up) and descending (top-down) connections. As Lewis and Todd have explained, subcortical and cortical regions maintain a reciprocal relationship in emotional processes whereby 'cortical activities regulate subcortical activities through executive modulation of prepotent appraisals and emotional responses; [while] subcortical systems regulate the cortex by tuning its activities to the demands or opportunities provided by the environment.'[39] Thus, bottom-up processes from the subcortex and the limbic system in particular encode the affective valence of emotionally salient environmental stimuli and thus feature and elicit responses to such stimuli. On the other hand, top-down processes allow cognitive processes of the cortex to elaborate on and make attributions regarding the emotional meaning of environmental stimuli and experiences, thereby regulating emotional responses. This top-down hierarchical organisation appears to be consistent with the view that cognitive

[35] eg AD Craig, 'How Do You Feel–Now? The Anterior Insula and Human Awareness' (2009) 10 *Nature Reviews Neuroscience* 59.

[36] eg M Kringelbach, 'The Human Orbitofrontal Cortex: Linking Reward to Hedonic Experience' (2005) 6 *Nature Review Neuroscience* 691; WA Cunningham et al, 'Orbitofrontal Cortex Provides Cross-modal Valuation of Self-generated Stimuli' (2011) 6 *Social Cognitive and Affective Neuroscience* 286; K Ochsner and JJ Gross, 'The Neural Bases of Emotion and Emotion Regulation: A Valuation Perspective' in JJ Gross and R Thompson (eds), *The Handbook of Emotion Regulation*, 2nd edn (New York, Guilford Press, 2014) 23.

[37] Emotion regulation is the unconscious or conscious (automatic or controlled) process used to increase, maintain, or decrease one or more components of an emotional response. Conscious emotion regulation entails processes by which individuals influence which emotions they have, when they have them, and how they experience and express these emotions. Emotion regulation involves several strategies, such as reappraisal (reinterpreting the valence of a stimulus in order to change the way in which we respond to it) or distancing. See eg JJ Gross, 'Emotion and Emotion Regulation' (1999) in LA Pervin and OP John (eds), *Handbook of Personality: Theory and Research*, 2nd edn (New York, Guilford, 1999) 525; J Powers and K LaBar, 'Regulating Emotion Through Distancing: A Taxonomy, Neurocognitive Model, and Supporting Meta-Analysis' (2019) 96 *Neuroscience and Biobehavioral Review* 155; C Helion et al, 'Emotion Regulation Across the Life Span' in MD' Esposito and JH Grafman (eds), *Handbook of Clinical Neurology*, Vol. 163 (New York, Elsevier 2019) 257; SJ Banks et al, 'Amygdala-frontal Connectivity during Emotion Regulation' (2007) 2 *Social Cognitive and Affective Neuroscience* 303.

[38] F Stevens et al, 'Anterior Cingulate Cortex in Cognition and Emotion' (2011) 23 *Journal of Neuropsychiatry and Clinical Neuroscience* 121.

[39] M Lewis and R Todd, 'The Self-Regulating Brain: Cortical-Subcortical Feedback and the Development of Intelligent Action' (2007) 22 *Cognitive Development* 406, 412.

attributions and appraisals can influence the dynamic 'construction' of emotions[40] in response to a given situation.

It is crucial to emphasise that regulating emotions does not entail controlling or blocking emotions from occurring. As mentioned, emotions (or feelings) possess key organising, motivating, and adaptive functions. Thus, they are not intended to be tightly controlled. Rather, regulating emotions involves accurately recognising and appraising one's own emotions as well as altering or modulating them adaptively in response to a given situation.[41] Interestingly, the skills that are required to effectively regulate emotions have also been linked with the relatively recently introduced construct of emotional intelligence.[42] Individuals who present deficits in emotional intelligence manifest difficulties in accurately appraising and expressing emotion, engaging in the effective regulation of emotion, successfully comprehending the feeling of others, and using such feelings to guide their behaviour. Difficulties with adaptive emotion regulation are considered a significant risk factor for aggressive behaviour as well as a potential precursor of psychopathology.[43]

D. Emotion and Decision-making

In 1957, the Nobel Laureate Herbert Simon launched a revolution in decision theory by introducing the concept of bounded rationality.[44] This concept was proposed to question that of global or perfect rationality, thereby refining the model of rational choice to include cognitive and situational constraints. Global rationality perceives the individual as a *homo oeconomicus* whose cognitive capacity for knowledge grants him or her complete information about the options that are available for choices, perfect foresight of the consequences from selecting those options, and the wherewithal to solve an optimisation problem that identifies an option that maximises the individual's personal utility. In contrast to this idea, Simon maintained that the real-world individual is bounded by cognitive limits of the mind, including an incompleteness of information, difficulty with anticipating the consequences of future actions, and scarce knowledge of all possible options. In addition to these cognitive limits, the individual operates in a social

[40] See C Wilson-Mendenhall et al (n 30).

[41] eg K Ochsner et al, 'Functional Imaging Studies of Emotion Regulation: A Synthetic Review and Evolving Model of the Cognitive Control of Emotion' (2012) 1251 *Ann New York Academy of Science* E1; JJ Gross, 'Emotion Regulation: Current Status and Future Prospects' (2015) 26 *Psychological Inquiry* 1.

[42] D Goleman, *Emotional Intelligence: Why It Can Matter More than IQ* (New Delhi, Bloomsbury, 1995).

[43] eg T Roberton et al, 'Emotion Regulation and Aggression' (2012) 17 *Aggression and Violent Behavior* 72; T Ehring, 'Emotion Regulation and Psychopathology' (2012) 4 *Journal of Experimental Psychology* 448.

[44] H Simon, *Models of Man. Social and Rational. Mathematical Essays on Rational Behavior in Social Settings* (New York, Wiley, 1957).

environment that affects his or her decision-making. As a cumulative effect of bounded rationality, people conclude 'satisficing' rather than optimal decisions. With such decisions, the chosen alternative is satisfactory insofar as it meets a given situational need (or a threshold), though it does not maximise the expected utility.

While endorsing this theory, Simon nonetheless acknowledged that 'in order to have anything like a complete theory of human rationality, we have to understand what roles emotion plays in it'.[45] As this quotation suggests, Simon was aware that his theory would be incomplete until the role of emotion was specified, thus presaging the crucial role that contemporary science has been recently assigning emotion in decision research. Indeed, the quest to identify the effects of emotion on decision-making has become a central issue across (neuro)scientific disciplines.

Psychologists and neuroscientists have developed numerous theories of emotions in order to understand the rationality of emotions within human decision-making. These theories vary extensively, but they largely impugn the view that emotions are mere primitive or a-rational states that only distort rational decision-making. There is a consensus in the literature that emotions are implicated in all of our decisions – from the simplest to most complex decisions that concern social life. Emotions constitute powerful and predictable drivers of decision-making across contexts, as they influence various decision-making components, including judgement and choice. In summary, emotion and decision-making are innately connected.[46]

Emotions affect and inform decision-making both directly and indirectly. In this regard, behavioural literature has distinguished between integral emotions and incidental emotions.[47] The former are emotions that directly relate to the situation and are elicited by the decision itself. They encompass the influences of feelings that are normatively relevant to present judgements and choices. For example, anticipated regret when evaluating a gamble has been evidenced to influence the degree to which a person is willing to gamble.[48] Other works have suggested that experiencing regret about a decision changes the behaviour of a person when facing the same decision again.[49] Likewise, anticipated anxiety (which emerges from fear) when thinking through a risky decision might be a sign of caution, which may lead one to be more risk-averse than risk-seeking with the decision. On the other hand, incidental emotions are emotions that we carry with us and are neither related to the situation nor elicited by the decision. They 'encompass the (sometimes) puzzling influence of feelings that should be normatively

[45] H Simon, *Reason in Human Affairs* (Stanford, Stanford University Press, 1983) 29.

[46] See eg N Schwartz, 'Emotion, Cognition, and Decision-making' (2000) 14 *Cognition and Emotion*, 433; J Lerner et al 'Emotion and Decision-making' (2015) 66 *Annual Review of Psychology* 33.1.

[47] For a review, see eg Lerner et al (n 46); JF Yates, 'Emotion Appraisal Tendencies and Carryover: How, Why, and … Therefore?' (2007) 17 *Journal of Consumer Psychology* 179.

[48] See eg Loewenstein and Lerner (n 20).

[49] T Connolly and M Zeelenberg, 'Regret in Decision-making' (2002) 11 *Current Directions in Psychological Science* 212.

irrelevant to present judgments and choices'.[50] Even though incidental emotions derive from other sources, they are nonetheless considered in a decision-making process and experienced as the decision is made. This incidental carryover may even occur when decision-makers are unaware of such emotional influences or when concrete outcomes are at stake. While reliance on incidental emotions can indeed be dysfunctional, integral emotions provide valid information, and attending to this information is highly adaptive, as indicated by a large body of research on emotional intelligence and the role of feelings in decision-making.[51]

The influence of emotions on judgements, choice, and decision-making is well-supported in the literature.[52] For instance, Schwartz and Clore's influential feeling-as-information hypothesis[53] suggests that people attend to their integral emotions (or to changes in such emotions) as a source of information to orient their judgements, thoughts, and decisions about a situation. This hypothesis postulates that the way we feel provides a crucial assessment (feedback) about the value of a situation that is needed during 'cognitive' processes such as judgements and decisions. Thus, feelings inform us of the nature of our current situation to attune our thoughts, judgements, and decision-making processes to meet situational requirements. In brief, our thought process about a matter is necessarily coupled with our feelings about it. Notably, recent work has further illustrated that such emotion-cognition interaction is dependent on context and situated in nature.

Neuroscientific research has yielded a significant additional contribution to understanding the role of emotion in decision-making processes.[54] Neuroscientists agree that the regions of the brain that are involved in emotional processes are substantially recruited during decision-making. Functional interactions between subcortical (eg, the amygdala) and cortical brain regions mediate emotional influences on decision-making processes as well as the cognitive regulation of emotions during decision-making. As Johnston and Olson have explained,

> the so-called cognitive brain functions, such as attention, perception, learning and memory, and decision-making can no longer be seen as separate and distinct from

[50] JS Lerner et al, 'Feelings and Consumer Decision Making: Extending the Appraisal Tendency Framework' (2007) 17 *Journal of Consumer Psychology* 181.

[51] See L Barrett and P Salovey (eds), *The Wisdom in Feeling: Psychological Processes in Emotional Intelligence* (New York, The Guilford Press, 2002).

[52] eg M Zeelenberg et al, 'On Emotion Specificity in Decision-making: Why Feeling Is for Doing' (2008) 3 *Judgment and Decision Making* 18.

[53] See N Schwartz and GL Clore, 'How Do I Feel about It? The Informative Function of Mood' in K Fiedler and J Forgas (eds), *Affect, Cognition, and Social Behavior* (Toronto, Hogrefe, 1988) 44; GL Clore and J Palmer, 'Affective Guidance of Intelligent Agents: How Emotion Controls Cognition' (2009) 10 *Cognitive System Research* 21; N Schwartz, 'Feeling as Information' in P Van Lange, A Kruglanski, and E Higgins (eds), *Handbook of Theories of Social Psychology* (Oaks, CA, SAGE Publications, 2011) 562.

[54] See eg, E Phelps et al, 'Emotion and Decision-making: Multiple Modulatory Neural Circuits' (2014) 37 *Annual Review of Neuroscience*, 263; X Chen et al, 'The Neural Dynamics Underlying the Interpersonal Effects of Emotional Expression on Decision-making' (2017) 7 *Scientific Reports*, available at doi: 10.1038/srep46651; N Naqvi et al, 'The Role of Emotion in Decision Making: A Cognitive Neuroscience Perspective' (2006) 15 *Cognitive Directions in Psychological Science* 260.

> emotions; instead, they are inextricably infused with emotional assessments and feelings that accompany them.[55]

Lesion studies have provided compelling evidence of the centrality of emotions in decision-making. Much of this evidence originates from emotionally impaired patients who sustained injuries to the vmPFC, which, as noted above, is a key area of the brain for integrating emotion and cognition. Studies have found[56] that such neurological impairments reduce the ability of patients to feel both emotion and the optimality of their decisions in ways that cannot be explained by simple cognitive changes.

Antonio Damasio's famous work on his young patient, Elliot, supports the latter claim. Elliot had undergone a radical personality change after a surgery to remove a brain tumour on the surface of his frontal lobe.[57] Elliot's intelligence remained substantially intact after the operation.[58] However, he became disinhibited, undisciplined, and unemotive.[59] According to Damasio, in post-surgery tests, 'Elliot emerged as a man with a normal intellect who was unable to decide properly, especially when the decision involved personal and social matters'.[60] Damasio gave Elliot a test that revealed one additional post-operation change: Elliot's vmPFC damage had compromised his ability to feel and process emotion and, thus, to make personal and socially appropriate decisions.[61] According to Damasio, '[t]he cold-bloodedness of Elliot's reasoning prevented him from assigning different values to different options, and made his decision-making landscape hopelessly flat'.[62]

Following Elliot's case, other research[63] on patients with similar damages to that of Elliot have provided further support of this initial finding. Strikingly, many of these patients exhibited no deficits in conventional cognitive tests on, for example, language, knowledge, or memory. Yet, they appeared to suffer from the same issue: a difficulty experiencing emotion and processing information that is evocative of emotions. These findings confirm the hypothesis that a disruption to the experience and processing of emotions may lead to tremendous difficulty making decisions.

[55] E Jonhston and L Olson, *The Feeling Brain: The Biology and Psychology of Emotions* (New York, Norton Professional Books, 2015) 306–7.

[56] For a review, see B Schneider and M Koenigs, 'Human Lesion Studies of Ventromedial Prefrontal Cortex' (2017) 107 *Neuropsychologia* 84.

[57] A Damasio, *Descartes' Error: Emotion, Reason, and the Human Brain* (New York, Avon Books, 1994) 36.

[58] ibid.

[59] ibid, 38.

[60] ibid, 43.

[61] ibid, 38–51.

[62] ibid, 51.

[63] See eg H Damasio, 'Disorders of Social Conduct Following Damage to Prefrontal Cortices' in JP Changeux, AR Damasio and W Singer (eds), *Neurobiology of Human Values* (Heidelberg, Springer, 2005) 37.

III. Emotions, Empathy, and Moral Behaviour

Traditionally, emotions have been conceptualised and studied primarily as individual phenomena, and research has focused on cognitive and expressive components as well as physiological and neurological processes that underlie emotional reactions. However, the last decades have witnessed increasing scholarly awareness that emotions are inherently social, as they tend to be elicited by other people, expressed toward other people, and regulated to influence other people or comply with social norms. Morality is one social domain in which emotions appear to be particularly central.

For a long time, research on moral behaviour was mostly concerned with 'typical' cognitive functions. Influential work[64] on the psychology of morality during the 'cognitive era' studied morality in terms of abstract moral reasoning as a result of mainly cognitive processes to the relative neglect of the role of emotions in guiding moral conduct. However, this enduring perspective has been reversed by findings in evolutionary psychology that interpret emotions as mental states that are central to the origins of human morality and social behaviour. Thus, the cognitive revolution was complemented by an affective revolution. This affective revolution changed the scientific perspective of the role of emotions by gradually indicating that emotions are heavily involved in moral judgements, decisions, and behaviour.

Although research on the exact engagement of emotions in first-person moral judgements is ongoing,[65] a growing consensus exists that emotion and emotion-related faculties, such as empathy, are inescapably involved in moral judgements and motivate morally relevant behaviour. Notably, there is agreement that the moral motivation to act prosocially does not stem solely from knowledge or reasoning about principles of justice but also relies on an appreciation of the interpersonal significance of a given mode of conduct. Such appreciation is largely mediated by the interaction between certain social/moral emotions – notably certain self-conscious or self-reflective emotions – as well as emotion-related faculties, including empathy, and pre-existing conditions, such as goals, beliefs, contexts, and experiences. As Jamil Zaki has stated,

> Principles are difficult to abide on an empty stomach or under other states that tax people's psychological energy … [T]o the extent that people can tune [emotions and empathy] to match their principles, they gain access to a … emotional engine for powering prosocial behavior. Emotion-based moral behavior might confer benefits that other

[64] J Piaget, *The Moral Judgment of the Child* (New York, Harcourt, Brace, Jovanovich, 1932); L Kohlberg, *Essays on Moral Development, Vol. 2: The Psychology of Moral Development* (San Francisco, Harper and Row, 1984).

[65] For a review of different perspectives on the role of emotions in moral judgements, see Helion and Ochsner (n 26).

> moral behaviors do not … In sum, emotions in general – and empathy in particular – add weight both to the efficiency of prosocial actions and to their benefits.[66]

A. Social/Moral Emotions

Emotion theorists have provided numerous taxonomies of emotions.[67] These taxonomies classify emotions based on their nature, features, and functions within the behaviour. Emotion categories often overlap, and a certain emotion can belong to many categories.

In social/moral domains, a category of emotion that has received particular attention is that of social emotions. This category – which may be alternatively known as moral emotions, depending on the relevant taxonomy – includes emotional states and processes that are typically elicited by social situations and intrinsically linked to the interests or welfare of either society as a whole or persons other than the agent. Social/moral emotions develop after childhood and are influenced by culture; therefore, their antecedents, subjective experience, and consequences vary across cultures. Notably, these emotions serve to regulate social and moral behaviour, elicit social attitudes in others, and attain complex social goals.

Social/moral emotions are 'cognitively complex', that is, they are generated and processed cognitively based on specific cognitive antecedents.[68] The latter include processes of awareness and representation (either self-directed, other-directed, or both, depending on the relevant emotion), which stimulate an evaluation of the situation and, in light of such evaluation, elicit the relevant emotion.[69] For instance, (moral) anger is related to disapproval of someone else's blameworthy action (reproach) and displeasure with the related undesirable event (distress). This emotion is determined by several appraisals of the situation in terms of, for example, the degree of judged blameworthiness, deviations of the agent's actions from person or role-based expectations, and the degree to which the event is undesirable.

Notwithstanding the various classification proposals, social/moral emotions have been divided into four main categories: self-conscious or self-reflective emotions (guilt, shame, embarrassment, pride, and regret); other-condemning

[66] J Zaki, 'Empathy Is a Moral Force' in K Gray and J Graham (eds), *Atlas of Moral Psychology* (New York, The Guilford Press 2018) 49, 52 (citations omitted).

[67] For a review, see D Sander, 'Models of Emotions: The Affective Neuroscience Approach' in J Harmony and P Vuilleumier (eds), *The Cambridge Handbook of Human Affective Neuroscience* (New York, Cambridge University Press, 2013) 5.

[68] See J Tracy and R Robins, 'The Self in Self-conscious Emotions: A Cognitive Appraisal Approach' in J Tracy, R Robins and J Tagney (eds), *The Self-conscious Emotions: Theory and Research* (New York, Guilford Press, 2007) 3.

[69] ibid.

emotions (anger, disgust, and contempt); other-praising emotions (love and elevation); and other-suffering emotions (compassion). Research has suggested that some of these emotions – particularly guilt, regret, and compassion – are powerful drivers of moral behaviour.[70] Overall, these emotions have been found to profoundly influence one's 'adherence to moral standards'[71] because they function to keep behaviour within the constraints of social norms and encourage prosocial action toward others.

Each of these social emotions conveys different information about various perceived events and shapes moral judgements by prioritising specific sociomoral concerns.[72] For instance, several studies have identified the moral function of compassion[73] in motivating altruism and providing a genuine prosocial motivation to alleviate the suffering of others. Other studies have outlined that regret[74] discourages choices when the outcomes are harmful or non-optimal for another person (when regret is anticipated) and, *post factum*, fosters personal accountability, reparative actions, and more appropriate behaviour in the future.

Another part of the literature focuses on the adaptive function of guilt in promoting prosocial behaviour when an individual's decisions pose relevant consequences for others.[75] The feeling of guilt occurs when individuals evaluate their behaviour as negative.[76] Hence, when feelings of guilt precede a potentially harmful behaviour, such as harming others, people simply avoid engaging in the behaviour that might cause them to feel guilty and suffer the negative consequences of such potential misbehaviour. When a feeling of guilt follows harmful behaviours, people are more prone to feel remorse for the harm they caused, take responsibility for it, make amends, and attempt to repair the damage.[77] Overall, guilt serves an adaptive function in most people by protecting them from the risk of engaging in inappropriate behaviour and suffering its negative consequences.[78]

[70] eg R Teper et al, 'How Emotions Shape Moral Behavior: Some Answers (and Questions) for the Field of Moral Psychology' (2015) 91 *Social & Personality Psychology Compass* 1, 5.

[71] J Price Tangney et al, 'Moral Emotions and Moral Behavior' (2007) 58 *Annual Review of Psychology* 345, 357.

[72] See eg E Horberg et al, 'Emotions as Moral Amplifiers: An Appraisal Tendency Approach to the Influences of Distinct Emotions upon Moral Judgment' (2011) 3 *Emotion Review* 237, 238.

[73] G Coricelli et al, 'Brain, Emotion, and Decision-Making: The Paradigmatic Example of Regret' (2005) 11 *Trends in Cognitive Science* 258.

[74] K Preckel et al, 'On the Interaction of Social Affect and Social Cognition: Empathy, Compassion, and Theory of Mind' (2018) 19 *Current Opinion in Behavioral Science* 1.

[75] See eg RF Baumeister et al, 'Guilt: An Interpersonal Approach' (1994) 115 *Psychological Bulletin* 243; J Tangney et al, 'Moral Emotions and Moral Behavior' (2007) 58 *Annual Review of Psychology* 345. *cf* N Harris, 'Reassessing the Dimensionality of Moral Emotions' (2003) 94 *British Journal of Psychology* 457; J Sabini and M Silver, 'In Defense of Shame: Shame in the Context of Guilt and Embarrassment' (1997) 27 *Journal for the Theory of Social Behavior* 1.

[76] Tagney et al (n 71).

[77] ibid.

[78] ibid.

The adaptive functions of guilt are usually contrasted with the maladaptive functions of shame. Shame has been defined as 'the intensely painful feeling or experience of believing that [*oneself is*] flawed and therefore unworthy of love and belonging'.[79] Shame occurs when individuals evaluate *themselves* as failures.[80] Thus, shame may involve intense feelings of humiliation, powerlessness, worthlessness, poor self-esteem, and low self-respect, all of which result from global evaluations of one's self-concept.[81] When the experience of shame is extremely intense or unacknowledged (so-called 'dysfunctional shame'), this emotion is likely to lead to other intense negative emotional reactions by the individual (eg, rage,) as well as maladaptive action tendencies (eg, hostility, aggression), cognitive distortions (eg, avoidance, neutralisation of negative behaviour), and the externalisation of blame.[82]

At the neurological level, the neural organisation of social/moral emotions in the human brain is not fully understood, and more research is necessary. Some studies[83] have attempted to identify uniquely neural structures of individual social/moral emotions. Furthermore, neuroimaging studies have investigated and detected the neural correlates of many moral emotions.[84] For instance, some studies have indicated that the OFC has a critical role in the processing of regret-related outcomes in a decision-making task.[85] They have also illustrated an enhanced amygdala response to regret-related outcomes when such outcomes are associated with self-blame.[86] On the other hand, several studies have emphasised the particular involvement of the vmPFC in the processing of emotions such as guilt or compassion.

Other work has highlighted the neural substrates of cognitive processes that accompany the generation, processing, and regulation of social/moral emotions. With reference to self-conscious moral emotions, Beer[87] has evidenced neural underpinnings of antecedent processes that provoke the experience of emotions,

[79] B Brown, *I Thought It Was Just Me (But It Isn't): Making the Journey from 'What Will People Think?' to 'I Am Enough'* (New York, Gotham Books, 2007) 29.

[80] Tagney et al (n 71).

[81] See, eg, P Velotti et al, 'Faces of Shame: Implications for Self-Esteem, Emotion Regulation, Aggression, and Well-Being' (2017) 151 *The Journal of Psychology* 171.

[82] JP Tangney et al, 'Shame, Guilt and Remorse: Implications for Offender Populations' (2011) 22 *The Journal of Forensic Psychiatry & Psychology* 706; J Stuewing et al, 'Shaming, Blaming, and Maiming: Functional Links Among the Moral Emotions, Externalization of Blame, and Aggression' (2010) 44 *Journal of Research in Personality* 91.

[83] eg M Gilead et al, 'Neural Correlates of Processing 'Self-conscious' vs. 'Basic' Emotions' (2016) 81 *Neuropsychologia* 207.

[84] C Bastin et al, 'Feelings of Shame, Embarrassment, and Guilt, and their Neural Correlates: A Systematic Review' (2016) 71 *Neuroscience and Biobehavioral Reviews* 455.

[85] eg G Coricelli, 'Regret and its Avoidance: A Neuroimaging Study of Choice Behavior' (2005) 8 *Nature Neuroscience* 1255.

[86] A Nicolle et al, 'Amygdala Involved in Self-blame Regret' (2011) 6 *Social Neuroscience* 178.

[87] J Beer, 'Neural Systems of Self-conscious Emotions and Their Underlying Appraisals' in J Tracy, R Robins and J Tagney (eds), *The Self-conscious Emotions: Theory and Research* (New York, Guilford Press, 2007) 53.

namely self-perception (ie, awareness of the self), person inference (ie, awareness of others), and knowledge of social norms. These processes apparently involve neocortical regions, such as the mPFC (including the OFC and vmPFC), the amygdala, and the ACC. These findings suggest that these emotions are heavily implicated in social cognition and, notably, theory of mind. Furthermore, they imply that these emotions are closely connected to the experience of empathy, which is considered fundamental to moral behaviour.

B. Empathy

Lay conversations of emotions – especially in social or interpersonal situations – often involve empathy. In common thinking, empathy is often considered an emotion through which we feel what others feel. We are emotional insofar as we are empathic. Accordingly, when we are unempathetic, we are often criticised for being 'unemotional'.

Empathy is not an emotion. While its experience is admittedly related to that of emotions, it is not an emotion itself. Despite the lack of unanimous agreement about a precise definition of empathy, it is predominantly understood as a multi-dimensional process that consists of 'gaining information about the internal affective representations of others'[88] and consequently eliciting vicarious emotional responses. Empathy enables us to insert ourselves into 'the mental shoes' of other people to understand, feel, and care about their feelings without encountering confusion between ourselves and them.

Compelling evidence supports the hypothesis that empathy is a critical component of social cognition and moral judgements and does have an overall bearing on prosocial behaviour.[89] Empathy prompts aversion to the pain or distress of others, which in turn provides an intuitive 'compass' that guides moral action. Empathy promotes other-humanisation and caregiving behaviour, and it leads to inhibition and aversions to violence.[90]

As mentioned, empathy is not a unitary process but instead encompasses several dissociable components. Under the dominant view in the literature, empathy includes three main components: an affective component (defined interchangeably as affective sharing, empathic arousal, or emotion contagion), a cognitive component (defined interchangeably as perspective-taking or mentalising), and a motivational component (defined alternatively as empathic concern, empathic motivation, or prosocial concern).[91] Each component serves its own

[88] See MH Davis, 'Measuring Individual Differences in Empathy: Evidence for a Multidimensional Approach' (1983) 44 *Journal of Personality and Social Psychology* 113.

[89] See Zaki (n 66).

[90] J Decety and J M Cowell, 'Empathy, Justice, and Moral Behavior' (2015) 6 *AJOB Neuroscience* 3.

[91] See J Zaki and K Ochsner, 'The Neuroscience of Empathy: Progress, Pitfalls and Promise' (2012) 15 *Nature Neuroscience* 675.

function in empathic processes and appears to be supported by distinct neural correlates. Moreover, researchers have suggested that each component serves unique functions in prosocial behaviour. Affective sharing reflects the process of being affectively aroused by others' emotions. Through the detection of another person's motivational and emotional states, it can elicit an adaptive response (eg, caring or helping) by the observer. Therefore, it instils a primary motivation to act in a prosocial manner.[92] Perspective-taking is the process of consciously situating oneself in the mind of another person and imagining how that person is feeling. It has been found to heighten an individual's perception of the needs of others and, thereby, to elicit concern for others, including out-group members.[93] Finally, empathic concern corresponds to the motivation to care for another's welfare based on feelings such as compassion. As such, it is largely involved in altruistic behaviour in response to witnessing someone in distress.[94]

Empathy has been further associated with emotion regulation. There is disagreement over whether emotion regulation should be included as a fourth component of empathy. However, research has interestingly indicated that the neural processes that support the affective, cognitive, and motivational aspects of empathy are closely related to the processes that are involved in emotion regulation. Notably, researchers have hypothesised that both empathy deficits and empathic hyperresponsivity are potential triggers of emotion dysregulation, which results in dysfunctional behaviours.[95]

In the literature, empathy is often understood as a capacity that results from nature and nurture, which encompass biological bases, socialisations (ie, parental care, affective communications, social attachments), and cognitive development. The general belief is that people cannot control empathy, as it is an automatic ability, and it therefore 'just happens'. When empathy is present, it seems to lead to prosocial behaviour. Conversely, an absence or scarcity of empathy produces socially dysfunctional outcomes. Striking confirmation of this account derives from studies of certain psychiatric diagnoses that are characterised by empathy impairments, including psychopathy[96] and frontotemporal dementia (FTD).[97]

[92] See eg N Eisenberg and J Strayer, 'Critical Issues in the Study of Empathy' in N Eisenberg and J Strayer (eds), *Cambridge Studies in Social and Emotional Development. Empathy and Its Development* (Cambridge, Cambridge University Press, 1987) 3.

[93] eg M Shih et al, 'Perspective taking: Reducing Prejudice Towards General Outgroups and Specific Individuals' (2009) 12 *Group Processes & Intergroup Relations* 565.

[94] eg O FeldmanHall et al, 'Empathic Concern Drives Costly Altruism' (2015) 105 Neuroimage 347, 352–54.

[95] For further discussion, see also M Schipper and F Petermann, 'Relating Empathy and Emotion Regulation: Do Deficits in Empathy Trigger Emotion Dysregulation' (2013) 8 *Social Neuroscience* 101.

[96] See RD Hare, *The Hare Psychopathy Checklist-Revised* (Toronto, Multi-Health Systems, 1991).

[97] eg J Snowden, 'Empathy in Frontotemporal Dementia' (2018) 31 *Cognitive and Behavioral Neurology* 111.

The capacity-based account of empathy has attracted some criticism.[98] The predominant critique emphasises that empathy does not always lead to prosocial behaviour and may even be a source of immoral conduct. Admittedly, when we notice others in distress, we do not always empathise with them. If we did, it would be difficult to explain why humans often voluntarily inflict pain on one another through allegedly corrective punishments, or out of mere spite. Moreover, empathy can also be parochial. It can spur concern for the well-being of some people but not others by, for instance, skewing prosocial behaviour unfairly toward in-group members at the expense of those who are perceived as out-group members. Altogether, the capability for empathy is not symptomatic of acting prosocially across all situations. Empathic responses are not universal and can be modulated by a number of factors, such as the target, the reason for the target's emotional state, and contextual appraisal. In this regard, context is a fundamental modulator of human empathy.

To respond to criticism and fill the gaps in the capacity-based account, several authors have proposed a motivation-based account of empathy. According to this understanding, which has been notably supported by the neuroscientist Jamil Zaki,[99] empathy leads to prosocial behaviour in most cases insofar as it is *chosen*. Most of us are capable of empathy, but we are not empathic across all situations or toward everybody. Rather, we 'activate' empathy selectively based on the motives that we might have for doing so. This perspective primarily frames empathy as a choice – either explicit or implicit – which 'reflects people's goals in a given context and … can be carried out through multiple strategies'.[100] Since empathy is a choice, we can opt for or reject it according to the relevant circumstances and through different strategies. For instance, we can choose not to empathise with other people by refusing to connect with their emotions altogether. In addition, people can 'de-activate' empathy through mechanisms of moral disengagement in order to belittle the suffering of others.[101] In these and many other cases, people fail to empathise not because they are incapable of it but because they are unmotivated to share, understand, or generate concern for the lives of others.[102]

Whether perceived as a capacity or a choice, empathy is a critical vehicle for prosocial behaviour. Furthermore, both branches of empathy research have heavily emphasised that empathy, like social emotions, is malleable and flexible. As such, empathy can be built, trained, and motivated to augment, extend, and expand the circle of concern of an individual with positive effects in terms of prosociality. I discuss this point further later in this chapter.

[98] See J Decety and JM Cowell, 'Friends or Foes: Is Empathy Necessary for Moral Behavior?' (2015) 9 *Perspectives on Psychological Science* 525.

[99] Zaki (n 66).

[100] ibid, 52.

[101] A Bandura, 'Moral Disengagement in the Perpetration of Humanities' (1999) 3 *Personality and Social Psychology Review, Special Issue on Evil and Violence* 193.

[102] Zaki (n 66).

C. The Neuromoral Network

Insights into the relationships among social/moral emotions, empathy, and moral judgements have been further complemented by advances in neuroscience regarding the neural correlates of moral judgements. Evidence from neuroscience lends support to the hypothesis that emotions, empathy, and moral judgements are mutually bound. Brain scans alone can hardly determine precisely which emotions are at stake when we decide, judge, or act morally; yet, studies that use neuroimaging techniques have critically evidenced 'a striking overlap between the regions involved in both automatic and controlled emotional processes [including moral emotion and empathy processing][103] and those implicated in moral judgment'.[104]

The growing body of investigations of the neural bases of morality have formulated a complex, constructivist view that integrates affective and cognitive systems that are supported by frontal, temporal, and subcortical brain regions.[105] Some researchers have conceptualised these integrated systems as a 'neuromoral network'.[106] This network appears to be constantly and significantly involved in moral judgements. The 'emotion-related component' of this network spans from subcortical to higher cortical regions and includes the amygdala,[107] the insula, the ACC,[108] the OFC,[109] and, notably, the vmPFC,[110] which is also perceived as the 'integrative center for innate morality',[111] especially in so-called 'care-based morality'.[112]

The considerable implication of emotions in moral judgements at the brain level has received strong support from lesion studies. For instance, studies of vmPFC patients have reported that patients who had lesions of the vmPFC manifested a series of morality-related deficits, including low empathy, poor decision-making, a failure to plan ahead, and a diminished sense of guilt. In one of these studies, Koenigs et al[113] administered personal[114] and non-personal moral dilemma tests

[103] eg J Blair & K Fowler, 'Moral Emotions and Moral Reasoning from the Perspective of Affective Cognitive Neuroscience: A Selective Review' (2008) 2 *European Journal of Developmental Science* 303, 314.

[104] Helion and Ochsner (n 26).

[105] See eg, L Pascual et al, 'How Does Morality Work in the Brain? A Functional and Structural Perspective of Moral Behavior' (2013) 7 *Frontiers in Integrative Neuroscience* 1.

[106] See MF Mendez, 'The Neurobiology of Moral Behavior: Review and Neuropsychiatric Implications' (2009) 14 *CNS Spectrum* 608.

[107] *See* J Blair, 'The Amygdala and the Ventromedial Prefrontal Cortex in Morality and Psychopathy' (2007) 11 *Trends in Cognitive Science* 387.

[108] ibid.

[109] See Blair (n 107).

[110] See ibid; L Young and M Koenigs, 'Investigating Emotion in Moral Cognition: A Review of Evidence from Functional Neuroimaging and Neuropsychology' (2007) 84 *The British Medical Bulletin* 69; C Hu and X Jiang, 'An Emotion Regulation Role of Ventromedial Prefrontal Cortex in Moral Judgment' (2014) *Frontiers in Human Neuroscience* 873.

[111] See D Marazziti et al, 'The Neurobiology of Moral Sense: Facts or Hypotheses?' (2013) 12 *Annals of General Psychiatry* 6.

[112] Blair and Fowler (n 103) (describing care-based morality as those forms of moral reasoning that concern actions that harm others).

[113] M Koenigs et al, 'Damage to the Prefrontal Cortex Increases Utilitarian Moral Judgments' (2007) 446 *Nature* 908.

[114] These tests give participants solutions that require personally harming someone in order to achieve the greater good.

to vmPFC-damaged patients. While these patients provided the same utilitarian responses to non-personal harm dilemmas as the control subjects, they demonstrated a far more marked utilitarian reasoning in personal moral dilemmas compared to the control subjects.[115] With a similar study that used the 'trolley dilemma',[116] which is an iconic experiment in moral philosophy, Gleichgerrcht and Young have further indicated that participants with vmPFC dysfunctions exhibited low levels of empathic concern and were more likely to endorse utilitarian solutions to personal moral dilemmas.[117] In addition to confirming the crucial role of the vmPFC in attributing emotional meaning to moral considerations, these researchers have also observed that normal utilitarian reasoning in impersonal dilemmas confirms that vmPFC patients retained intact cognitive intellectual abilities of knowledge and abstract reasoning.

Further evidence has emerged from studies of certain psychiatric populations.[118] One example concerns frontotemporal dementia (FTD), which is a neurodegenerative disease that results from deterioration of the prefrontal and anterior temporal cortex. Patients with this disease exhibit changes in personality and mode of interaction with others. Notably, these patients exhibit deficits in recognising emotions in others as well as abnormal emotion suppression, emotion generation and experience of self-conscious emotions. FTD induces general problems with correctly processing social context information, which may lead to blunted emotion, disregard for others, and engagement in inappropriate behaviours, such as moral transgressions, including in public. Moreover, they struggle to process the contextual details that are needed to understand social events. FTD reportedly affects the vmPFC[119] and can significantly impair moral judgements. For instance, in a study that administered moral dilemmas, Mario Mendez et al[120] have found that patients with FTD exhibited a pronounced tendency to adopt the utilitarian alternative in addressing personal moral dilemmas. Notably, the authors have stated that '[t]he FTD patients retained knowledge of moral rules and norms and could reason about the right and wrong of a

[115] Koenigs et al (n 113) 910.

[116] J Jarvis Thomson, 'Killing, Letting Die, and the Trolley Problem' (1976) 59 *The Monist* 204.

[117] E Gleichgerrcht and L Young, 'Low Levels of Empathic Concern Predict Utilitarian Moral Judgment' (2013) 8 *PLoS One* e60418. See also L Young et al, 'Damage to Ventromedial Prefrontal Cortex Impairs Judgment of Harmful Intent' (2010) 65 Neuron 845; I Patil and G Silani, 'Reduced Empathic Concern Leads to Utilitarian Moral Judgments in Trait Alexithymia' (2014) 5 *Frontiers in Psychology* 501.

[118] A caveat is needed here. A direct link between the brain, mental illness, and crime is scientifically contestable and epistemologically untenable. However, neuroscientific studies with psychiatric populations have been key to lending further support to the idea that emotions and emotion-related abilities are critical to certain aspects of decision-making and behaviour.

[119] Other studies have implicated the anterior insular cortex and its connection with the medial prefrontal cortex. See eg J Van den Stock and F Kumfor, 'Behavioural Variant Frontotemporal Dementia: At the Interface of Interoception, Emotion and Social Cognition?' (2017) *Cortex* 1.

[120] M Mendez et al, 'An Investigation of Moral Judgement in Frontotemporal Dementia' (2005) 18 *Cognitive and Behavioral Neurology* 193.

situation. In contrast, they appeared to have diminished emotional identification with others and solved moral dilemmas in an impersonal fashion'.[121]

Studies involving the controversial category of patients with a psychopathic disorder have yielded similar results.[122] Despite heterogeneity in the findings,[123] the core brain regions that have been consistently implicated in psychopathy (notably the vmPFC and the amygdala) are the same regions that contribute to the 'emotional circuitry' of the brain network that is involved in moral judgements. Some researchers[124] have proposed that impairments in these brain areas seem to explain why patients who are affected by this disorder, present severe moral and emotional deficits that are marked by reductions in guilt and empathic concern. Such effects result in reduced emotional response to the pain and distress of others (eg, the suffering of the victims) in 'care-based transgressions' (ie, transgressions that involve harming others).[125]

Individuals with psychopathy do seem to retain a cognitive understanding of moral and legal wrongs.[126] However, as one study has suggested,[127] individuals with psychopathy treat the word 'wrong' in a purely conventional way as if it simply means 'prohibited by local authorities'. Thus, even if individuals with psychopathy are capable of propositionally distinguishing rightness from wrongness – and, therefore, of knowing the moral meaning of an action – they tend to make morally poor decisions because their access to the kind of emotional information that drives moral behaviour in healthy individuals is profoundly reduced.

D. Emotions, Morality, and Self-regulation

The role of emotional processes in moral behaviour is also relevant in terms of another aspect: self-regulation.[128] Self-regulation is critical to our adaptive social

[121] ibid, 195–96.

[122] While psychopathy represents less than 1% of the general population, neuroscientific research on psychopathy has become one of the main vehicles to suggest that emotions and empathy are key factors for morality and prosocial behaviour.

[123] A Raine and Y Yang, 'Neural Foundations to Moral Reasoning and Antisocial Behavior' (2009) 1 *Social Cognitive Affective Neuroscience* 203; FA Espinoza et al, 'Aberrant Functional Network Connectivity in Psychopathy from a Large (N=985) Sample' (2018) 39 *Human Brain Mapping* 2624.

[124] See eg Raine and Yang (n 123).

[125] J Blair, 'Emotion-based Learning Systems and the Development of Morality' (2017) 167 *Cognition* 38.

[126] See eg N Levy, 'The Responsibility of the Psychopath Revisited' (2007) 14 *Philosophy, Psychiatry & Psychology* 129, 132 (claiming that psychopaths know their actions 'are widely perceived to be wrong … they are unable to grasp the distinctive nature and significance of their wrongness').

[127] RJ Blair, 'A Cognitive Developmental Approach to Morality: Investigating the Psychopath' (1995) 57 *Cognition* 1.

[128] See A Bandura, 'Selective Moral Disengagement in the Exercise of Moral Agency' (2002) 31 *Journal of Moral Education* 101 (holding that morality is rooted in self-regulation rather than dispassionate abstract reasoning).

functioning.[129] Without it, people could be impulsive, lash out at the smallest provocation, blurt out the first idea that comes to mind, and engage in any behaviour that feels good at the time. All humans have an impressive capacity for self-regulation; however, failures are common, and people lose control of their behaviour in a wide variety of circumstances, including legally relevant ones.

According to an accredited definition in the literature, self-regulation consists of the dynamic ability to adaptively alter and regulate thoughts, feelings, and behaviours in a way that serves goal striving, whether the goal is set by the self, the society or both. Hence, self-regulation involves both the initiation and maintenance of behavioural change in addition to inhibiting undesired behaviours or responding to situational demands. According to Bandura, self-regulation not only mediates the effects of most external influences, but provides the very basis for purposeful action.

Scientific research on self-regulation (including in moral contexts) is ongoing, but a significant bulk of research has achieved considerable progress in identifying the individual factors and situational circumstances that either foster or impair self-regulation. Although a clear-cut taxonomy of self-regulation is lacking, and many models have been proposed,[130] there is a common understanding of self-regulation as a multidimensional ability that occurs in degrees and involves a series of interacting (and overlapping) cognitive, affective, and motivational states and processes, including emotion perception, appraisal, cognitive/executive control, emotion regulation, and reward/delayed gratification.[131] These processes collectively contribute to an individual's self-regulation and preserve inhibitory control.[132] Moreover, self-regulation is flexible in nature, and its implementation also depends on situational features.

The processes that interact during self-regulation are supported by a balanced coordination system in the brain, which encompasses a wide network of regions. This network involves and connects the activity of subcortical regions (including the amygdala, the ventral tegmental area, and the *nucleus accumbens*) and neocortical regions (notably the dorsolateral prefrontal cortex [DPFC], the dorsal ACC [dACC], the OFC, and the VmPFC), which serve the interdependent functions of

[129] See eg L Lazarus et al, 'The Roles of Impulsivity, Self-regulation, and Emotion Regulation in the Experience of Self-Disgust' (2019) 43 *Motivation & Emotion* 145, 147. While some authors use the term self-regulation and self-control interchangeably, others consider self-control to be a subset of self-regulation or vice versa. See eg W Hofmann et al, 'Executive Functions and Self-regulation' (2012) 16 *Trends in Cognitive Science* 174, 174 (defining self-regulation as 'goal-directed behavior' and self-control as 'a narrower subset of self-regulatory processes [aiming] to override unwanted, prepotent impulses or urges …'). *cf* J Buckholtz et al, 'A Neuro-Legal Lingua Franca: Bridging Law and Neuroscience on the Issue of Self-Control' (2016) 5 *Mental Health & Policy Journal* 1, 15–6 (referring to the ability to delay immediate gratification in favour of long-term outcomes as a specific domain of self-control); R Baumeister et al, *Losing Control: How and Why People Fail at Self-regulation* (San Diego, Academic Press, 1994) (using 'self-regulation' and 'self-control' interchangeably).

[130] Buckholtz et al (n 129) 13.

[131] eg J Metcalfe and W Mischel, 'A Hot/Cool System Analysis of Delay of Gratification: Dynamics of Willpower' (1999) 196 *Psychological Review* 3.

[132] See Lewis and Todd (n 39) 406.

emotion processing, emotion regulation, reward, and inhibition in goal-directed behaviour.[133] These cortical and subcortical regions operate in a reciprocal relationship during self-regulation so that 'cortical activities regulate subcortical activities through executive modulation of prepotent appraisals and emotional responses; [while] subcortical systems regulate the cortex by tuning its activities to the demands or opportunities provided by the environment'.[134]

From this perspective, 'emotions' help us remain in control as much as 'cognition'. On the one hand, emotions provide anticipated feedback about the (in)appropriateness of a given action as a response to a valanced situational demand.[135] Therefore, they prompt our behavioural response in accordance to that feedback. On the other hand, cognitive faculties, including high-level executive functions or cognitive control, regulate emotional responses to further adapt our behaviour to situational demands. Hence, various levels of regulation are implicated: emotions may act as regulators or be regulated themselves, or it could, at any rate, be desirable to regulate them in social interactions.[136] Granted, an alteration in either level of regulation may endanger self-regulation altogether.[137]

The relevance of emotions to self-regulation, especially in social/moral contexts, has emerged from the body of neuropsychological studies that have been conducted with patients who have damage to the vmPFC, which, as noted above, is typically involved in (moral) emotion processing, decision-making, and moral judgements. The vmPFC functions as the 'site of interaction' of 'valuation and self-control processes'[138] during decision-making, and such interaction seems 'to facilitate successful self-control'.[139] Damage to this region of the brain often results in a deficiency in incorporating feedback from others and social norms to conclude appropriate behavioural choices in social contexts, which results in social disinhibition and inappropriate approach behaviour toward other individuals.[140] In most cases, these changes are marked by disinhibited and often inappropriate behaviour and, sometimes, a severe loss of motivation in the absence of any observed cognitive impairment.

[133] ibid.

[134] ibid.

[135] NH Frijda, 'Emotions are Functional, Most of the Time' in P Ekman and RJ Davidson (eds), *The Nature of Emotions* (New York, Oxford University Press, 1994) 112, 118 ('[a]ctual emotion, affective response, anticipation of future emotion can be regarded as the primary course of decisions').

[136] B Rimé, 'Interpersonal Emotion Regulation' in JJ Gross (ed), *Handbook of Emotion Regulation* (New York, The Guilford Press, 2007) 466.

[137] See S Penney, 'Impulse Control and Criminal Responsibility: Lessons from Neuroscience' (2012) 35 *International Journal of Law and Psychiatry* 99, 100.

[138] E Miller et al, 'Delay Discounting: A Two-Systems Perspective' in JJ Gross (ed), *Handbook of Emotion Regulation*, 2nd edn (New York, Guilford Press, 1995) 93, 102.

[139] ibid.

[140] eg, J Beer et al, 'The Regulatory Function of Self-conscious Emotion: Insights from Patients with Orbitofrontal Damage' (2003) 85 *Journal of Personality and Social Psychology* 594; L Clark et al, 'Differential Effects of Insular and Ventromedial Prefrontal Cortex Lesions on Risky Decision-making' (2008) 131 *Brain* 1311.

Damage to the VmPFC leads patients to appear unable to regulate their social, affective, or appetitive behaviours.[141] Such patients might become aggressive or antisocial, and they can exhibit hypersexuality, engage in excessive overacting, and make risky decisions.[142] All of these cases reveal that VmPFC damage entails a general dysregulation of social behaviour along with difficulty controlling primary physiological drives. Notably, most patients appear to be fully aware of the impropriety of their actions, yet they are unable to effectively apply that knowledge to action.[143] Likely, as one study has highlighted, '[w]ithout the restraint of intuitive moral emotions and self-other conjoining ... [vmPFC] patients may not be able to deter an impulse to act in an unacceptable manner, even as they know right and wrong and understand the nature of their acts'.[144]

Dysfunctions in the vmPFC may also manifest when the damage occurs in a brain region that is closely connected to it. For instance, a study by Hampton et al has indicated that patients with amygdala damage exhibited a profound change in vmPFC activity related to reward expectation and behavioural choice, which implies that information concerning behavioural choice in vmPFC relies directly on input from the amygdala.[145] Hence, abnormal functioning in the amygdala may negatively impact emotional information processing at a cognitive level, which culminates in poor control over behavioural responses.[146]

Further evidence has derived from OFC lesion studies. A paradigmatic (though rare) case study in the literature concerns patients with so-called acquired paedophilic disorder. Reportedly, individuals with this disorder develop uncontrollable hypersexual urges of a paedophilic type (either exclusive or non-exclusive) following brain tumours that damage their OFC. This OFC syndrome appears to severely compromise the individual's inhibition and impulse control, although it leaves the individual's cognitive capacities of knowledge and understanding substantially intact. Thus, individuals with this condition know that their actions are wrong. Such dysregulation and diminished response disinhibition have been associated with a scarce affective capacity to appreciate or 'feel' the wrongness of their behaviour, which results in 'decision making that emphasizes immediate reward rather than long-term gain, impairing the subject's ability to appropriately navigate social situations'.[147]

[141] For a review, see D Wagner and T Heartherton, 'Giving in to Temptation: The Emerging Cognitive Neuroscience of Self-regulatory Failure' in K Vohs and R Baumeister (eds), *Handbook of Self-Regulation: Research, Theory and Applications*, 2nd edn (New York, Guilford Press, 2011) 41.

[142] See eg A Bechara et al, 'Characterization of the Decision-Making of Patients with Ventromedial Prefrontal Cortex Lesions' (2000) 123 *Brain* 2189.

[143] JL Saver and A Damasio, 'Preserved Access and Processing of Social Knowledge in a Patient with Acquired Sociopathy Due to Ventromedial Frontal Damage' (1991) 29 *Neuropsychologia* 1241.

[144] Mendez (n 106) 611.

[145] A Hampton et al, 'Contributions of the Amygdala to Reward Expectancy and Choice Signals in Human Prefrontal Cortex' (2007) 55 *Neuron* 545.

[146] See S Penney, 'Impulse Control and Criminal Responsibility: Lessons from Neuroscience' (2012) 35 *International Journal of Law and Psychiatry* 99, 100.

[147] J Burns and R Swerdlow, 'Right Orbitofrontal Tumor with Pedophilia Symptom and Constructional Apraxia Sign' (2003) 60 *Archives of Neurology* 437, 440. See also F Gilbert and F Focquaert, 'Rethinking

Overall, psychological and neuroscientific research on self-regulation provides three key points of information. Foremost, self-regulation is not a unitary capacity[148] that either exists or does not exist. It can hardly be said that a person totally lacks it. Rather, a multitude of complex and sometimes interrelated processes are involved self-regulation abilities. These processes involve brain mechanisms that are not purely or solely cognitive but form complex circuits in which affective and motivational processes also have a prominent role in the evaluation, information processing, regulation, and appropriate reaction to salient situations. Thus, as researchers have observed, since abilities of self-regulation appear to depend on a multitude of dissociable processes, preserved functioning in one of these processes may still be accompanied by poor functioning in others.[149] Although this scenario does not imply a *total* lack of control, such ability may nevertheless be compromised to a significant extent.

Second, dysregulation does not occur only when an individual is emotionally hyper-responsive but also when he or she is emotionally hypo-responsive. Indeed, poor processing of emotion information may entail difficulties with incorporating feedback about a situation as a basis for making adaptive choices and regulating inappropriate impulses accordingly.

Last but not least, the power of individuals to choose which conduct to engage in within a given context, which involves regulating their impulses, is not necessarily an automatic consequence of their faculties of knowledge and understanding. The studies reported above reflect that the mechanisms of self-regulation (and dysregulation as a consequence), especially in interpersonal contexts, support cognitive, motivational, and emotional processes, which serve distinct – yet related – functions in governing self-regulating faculties. A disruption to either process (eg, maladaptive emotional responses or deficient regulation) can *equally* endanger a choice of appropriate behaviour in response to a certain stimulus. On the whole, neither emotion, motivation, nor cognition alone guarantees self-regulation or subsequent impulse control, as they need to work together.

IV. From the Emotional Brain to the Social Brain: How the Social Environment Becomes Embedded and Informs Social Behaviour

As noted above, the relationship between the 'emotional brain' and human behaviour, including moral behaviour, is not directly balanced, and it is mediated by socio-environmental contexts. Contextual factors are among the major

Responsibility in Offenders with Acquired Paedophilia: Punishment or Treatment?' (2015) 38 *International Journal of Law and Psychiatry* 51.

[148] See Buckholtz et al (n 129) 13.

[149] ibid.

determinants of human emotions and behaviour; thus, the specific meaning or appropriateness of an emotion, emotional response, or behavioural reaction varies by context. In other words, the reason for and way in which people appraise and respond to salient stimuli with specific emotional and behavioural reactions depends on the socio-environmental context.

The concept of socio-environmental context not only encompasses the immediate context that the individual operates in or interacts with at a given time but also extends more broadly to include more constant and longitudinal factors, such as family, peers, neighbourhood, cultural factors, and life experiences. From this (social ecological)[150] perspective, the reason why a person feels, thinks, and behaves as he or she does on a particular occasion is based on the ongoing, dynamic transaction between the person and all of these contextual aspects. As the British psychologist John Bowlby said in 1986, 'what goes on in the internal world is a more or less accurate reflection of what an individual has experienced in the external world'.[151]

One critical vehicle to explain why human behaviour is a product of bidirectional and dynamic interactions between the person and the socio-environmental context concerns the social function of the brain. The brain is a social organ, as many researchers have suggested.[152] It is clearly an individual organ with discrete biological boundaries; however, in a functional sense, the brain only operates in conjunction with other brains and the outside social environment. At the same time, the outside environment profoundly shapes brain processes. Thereby, the social environment operates as a modulator resembling an interpersonal 'thermostat' that continually influences a person's brain function in modulating emotions, thoughts, and behaviours, and vice versa. Thus, unlike the criminal law that views the person as an 'isolated' agent and locates human behaviour solely in individual choice, human research depicts a broader perspective. Such perspective frames human behaviour as a function of *both* personal and situational influences and considers the 'power of the situation'[153] to be a major determinant of an individual's behaviour.

Concerning the relationship between longitudinal contextual cues, emotions, and moral behaviour, research has revealed that specific social, economic, and environmental factors (eg, secure attachments, positive social engagement, exposure to positive environments, and social acceptance) are essential to the development and functionality of the numerous competencies that are linked to morality and

[150] U Bronfenbrenner, *The Ecology of Human Development* (Cambridge, MA, Harvard University Press, 1979).

[151] J Bowlby et al, 'An Interview with John Bowlby on the Origins and Reception of His Work' (1986) 6 *Free Associations* 36, 43.

[152] eg D Siegel, *The Developing Mind: How Relationships and the Brain Interact to Shape Who We Are* (New York, Guildford Press, 2020); M Lieberman, *Social: Why Our Brains Are Wired to Connect* (New York, Crown, 2013).

[153] See C Haney et al, 'Interpersonal Dynamics in A Simulated Prison' (1973) 1 *Journal of Criminology and Penology* 69.

prosocial behaviour.[154] Notably, studies have documented a positive relationship between these factors and the healthy development and functionality of key brain regions that are involved in the experience of adaptive moral emotions as well as adaptive emotion processing and regulation.[155] Thus, cross-disciplinary evidence supports the idea that healthy environments and relationships aid in healthy development and physiological function of the brain circuits that correlate socio-emotional competencies that are implicated in morality and prosocial behaviour, which exerts beneficial and enduring effects on social functioning.

On the other hand, social psychology and social neuroscience studies have indicated that unhealthy social factors (eg, emotional neglect, disorganised attachments, and social isolation, extreme environmental deprivation)[156] as well as experiences of traumatic life events (eg, physical abuse and chronic exposure to violence)[157] may induce significant and long-standing alterations in the brain pathways that govern judgement; impulse control; empathetic responding; regulation of emotions; interpretation of stimuli, experience and social cues; perception of threat[158] – all of which are critically involved in social functioning. In fact, these dysfunctions have been associated with a heightened risk of maladaptive action tendencies and behaviours, including hostility, rule-breaking, aggression, and violence.[159]

These psychological and behavioural conditions have been associated with alterations occurring in the brain. For instance, a sustained body of studies have indicated that childhood traumas such as abuse or neglect completely change the trajectory of the developing brain and have long-term effects on adult behaviour.[160]

[154] EH Telzer et al, 'Social Influence on Positive Youth Development: A Developmental Neuroscience Perspective' (2018) 54 *Advances in Child Development and Behavior* 215.

[155] L Cozolino, *Neuroscience of Human Relationships: Attachment and the Developing Social Brain*, 2nd edn (New York, WW Norton & Company, 2014).

[156] AN Schore, 'Early Relational Trauma, Disorganized Attachment, and the Development of a Predisposition to Violence' in D Siegel and M Solomon (eds), *Healing trauma: Attachment, Mind, Body, and Brain* (New York, WW Norton & Company, 2003) 107.

[157] C Smith and T Thornberry, 'The Relationship Between Childhood Maltreatment and Adolescent Involvement in Delinquency' (1995) 33 *Criminology* 451; CS Widom, 'Does Violence Beget Violence? A Critical Examination of the Literature' (1989) 106 *Psychological Bulletin* 3; A Wall and R Barth, 'Aggressive and Delinquent Behavior of Maltreated Adolescents: Risk Factors and Gender Differences' (2005) 8 *Stress, Trauma, & Crisis* 1.

[158] B Van Der Kolk, *The Body Keeps the Score: Brain, Mind, and Body in the Healing of Trauma* (New York, Penguin Books 2014) 170; J Douglas Bremner, 'Traumatic Stress: Effects on the Brain' (2006) 8 *Dialogues in Clinical Neuroscience* 445.

[159] Criminological research converges on the same conclusion: social contexts can influence one's tendency to experience specific moral feelings in given situations, and drive behaviour accordingly. See eg Haney et al (n 153). See also K Matsuda et al, 'Gang Membership and Adherence to the 'Code of the Street' (2013) 30 *Justice Quarterly* 440; C Melde and F Esbensen, 'Gang Membership as a Turning Point in the Life Course' (2011) 49 *Criminology* 513.

[160] eg E McCrory et al, 'The Neurobiology and Genetics of Maltreatment and Adversity' (2010) 51 *Journal of Child Psychology and Psychiatry* 1079; B Van der Kolk and E Rita, 'Childhood Abuse and Neglect and Loss of Self-regulation' (1994) 58 *Bulletin of the Menninger Clinic* 145; V Misheva et al, 'The Effect of Child Maltreatment on Illegal and Problematic Behaviour: New Evidence on the 'Cycle of Violence' Using Twins Data' (2017) 30 *Journal of Population Economics* 1035, 1046.

Other studies have suggested that chronic exposure to toxic stressors, such as extreme poverty,[161] as well as the experience of traumas such as constant exposure to and victimisation by violence, produce dysregulating outcomes in the individual's biological stress response that have long-term negative effects on the brain, mental health, and social behaviour. In fact, cumulative and repeated exposure to toxic stressors and traumas over time produces alterations in stress responses that have physiological effects on the brain. These effects impact psychological functioning in ways that can even be damaging to physical and mental health.[162]

For instance, several neuroscientific studies have explored the relationship between cortisol levels (ie, biological stress response), toxic environmental stressors, and violence, especially in adolescence and young adulthood.[163] Taken together, these studies associate exposure to violence and contextual stressors with elevated cortisol levels, hypervigilance, and hyperresponsivity to threats in the long term. Chronic or long-lasting hyper-responsivity to threats seems to explain why people (especially youth) who live in disadvantaged communities may become more vulnerable to aggressive reactions or even experience 'pathological adaptations', including a desensitisation to violence.[164] Likewise, traumatic experiences such as abuse and maltreatment have been associated with elevated cortisol levels in both adolescents and young adults.[165]

It is important to note that these neurobiological changes can alter brain structure and function in the long term in several brain regions such as the hippocampus, the amygdala, and various regions of the PFC, especially the mPFC.[166] As indicated, alterations in these brain regions have been found to negatively affect social functioning by hampering self-regulation, emotion regulation, and impulse control as well alter adaptive moral emotion- and empathic responding. All of these factors have been associated with problematic decision-making under risk conditions[167] and a higher risk of engaging in maladaptive behaviours, including those involving aggression and violence.

[161] G Evans et al, 'Stressing Out the Poor: Chronic Physiological Stress and the Income Achievement Gap' (2011) *Pathways, Winter* 16; P Kim et al, 'Effects of Childhood Poverty and Chronic Stress on Emotion Regulatory Brain Function in Adulthood' (2013) 110 *Proceedings of the National Academy of Sciences* 18442.

[162] A Danese and B McEwen, 'Adverse Childhood Experiences, Allostasis, Allostatic Load and Age-Related Disease' (2012) 106 *Physiology & Behavior*, 29; S Lupien et al, 'Effects of Stress throughout the Lifespan on the Brain, Behavior and Cognition' (2009) 10 *Nature Reviews* 434.

[163] See eg S Aiyer et al, 'Exposure to Violence Predicting Cortisol Response During Adolescence and Early Adulthood: Understanding Moderating Factors' (2014) 43 *Journal of Youth Adolescence* 1066.

[164] See J Garbarino et al, 'Mitigating the Effects of Gun Violence on Children and Youth' (2002) 12 *The Future of Children* 73.

[165] See Aiyer et al (n 163).

[166] eg JD Bremner, 'Traumatic Stress: Effects on the Brain' (2006) 8 *Dialogues in Clinical Neuroscience* 445.

[167] eg AJ Porcelli and MR Delgado 'Acute Stress Modulates Risk Taking in Financial Decision-making' (2009) 20 *Psychological Science* 278; K Starcke et al, 'Anticipatory Stress Influences Decision Making under Explicit Risk Conditions' (2008) 122 *Behavioral Neuroscience* 1352.

Altogether, constant exposure to traumas and toxic stress induces adverse biological, structural, and functional changes in the brain that risk alterations to psychological balance and social functioning, which is likely to produce negative effects on the behavioural level, including a higher risk of engaging in criminal conduct. As Nee and Verhnam have claimed,

> [t]he chaotic and impoverished background of most offenders is unlikely to offer the neurological prerequisites desired to foster cognitive, behavioural and interpersonal competencies. Sufficient nutrition, rest, a stimulating and loving environment; ample opportunity to observe prosocial behaviour; consistent rewards for the incremental development of self-regulation and empathy for others; a childhood free from physical violence and access to toxic substances; are not the typical context of the child more likely to become an offender. These prerequisites of emotion regulation, impulse control and empathy are often sadly lacking.[168]

Granted, not all individuals with similar exposures develop the same vulnerabilities; some are more resilient or have access to buffers or supports, or they may use more effective coping strategies to mitigate the potential effects of such stressors. The longitudinal effects of toxic stress and trauma on behaviour also depend on individual variables, notably age. A dominant hypothesis that links toxic stress, trauma, and problematic social behaviour focuses on the level, variety, frequency, and duration of stressful experiences and traumas[169] and the extent to which they are buffered by social supports in the form of emotional or instrumental resources that are provided by or shared with others as well as by individual ways of coping. When these resources are lacking, toxic stress and traumatising experiences are more likely to impose adverse effects on the brain, thus endangering psychological well-being and, in many cases, social behaviour accordingly. These factors can further augment the risk of psychopathologies such as post-traumatic stress disorder (PTSD), complex PTSD, depression, all of which entail dysfunctions at the neurological and social behavioural level.[170]

The negative effects of toxic stressors and traumas on social behaviour, including also a heightened risk of engaging in antisocial conduct, have further been observed in unhealthy populations. While a direct link between the brain, mental illness, and crime is scientifically contestable and epistemologically untenable,

[168] C Nee and Z Verhnam, 'Expertise and its Contribution to the Notion of Protective Factors in Offender Rehabilitation and Desistance' (2017) 32 *Aggression and Violent Behavior* 37, 40.

[169] eg J Garbarino, 'Forward: Pathways From Childhood Trauma to Adolescent Violence and Delinquency' (2002) 6 *Journal of Aggression, Maltreatment, and Trauma* xxv; V Ardino, 'Offending Behaviour: the Role of Trauma and PTSD' (2012) 3 *European Journal of Psychotraumatology*, 10.3402/ejptv3i0.18968; J Briere and C Scott, 'Complex Trauma in Adolescents and Adults Effects and Treatment' (2015) 38 *Psychiatry Clinics of North America* 515.

[170] See eg JD Bremner et al, 'Structural and Functional Plasticity of the Human Brain in Posttraumatic Stress Disorder' (2008) 167 *Progress in Brain Research* 171; Z Marinova and A Maercker, 'Biological Correlates of Complex Posttraumatic Stress Disorder – State of Research and Future Directions' (2015) 6 *European Journal of Psychotraumatology*, available at doi: 10.3402/ejpt.v6.25913.

adverse socio-environmental factors appear to mediate[171] the effects of mental illness on criminal behaviour. Contributing factors may be that individuals with mental illness who do not receive proper social support are at a higher risk of being exposed to social exclusion, economic disadvantage, isolation, or victimisation. For instance, several scholars have reported that social and economic disadvantages, under-education, unemployment, paucity of positive social relationships, discrimination, and stigma are all risk factors for criminal justice involvement among persons with mental illness.[172] On the whole, as Lea Johnston has observed, research suggests that the same social risks and needs that lead individuals without mental illness to engage in criminal conduct also drive those with mental disorders to commit crimes.[173]

Overall, empirical research reflects that chronically stressful, traumatising, and unhealthy social environments can be profoundly deleterious for the brain and the psychological mechanisms that support prosocial behaviour. Adverse contextual factors can have dramatic effects on the neurological and psychological well-being of an individual as well as heighten the risk of adverse behavioural outcomes, including justice involvement. Nevertheless, a more positive insight is that the negative neurological, psychological, and behavioural effects of dysfunctional backgrounds can be mitigated or even reversed throughout the entire lifespan. As I discuss in the next section, cross-disciplinary evidence from social psychology and neuroscience supports the notion that engagement with healthy environments and positive relationships as well as the reception of social support can reshape the brain circuits that are responsible for the socio-emotional competencies that are implicated in prosocial behaviour, which has beneficial and enduring effects on social functioning. Such evidence has consistently indicated that emotions and social-emotional skills are powerfully dynamic and malleable factors that can promote resilient functioning and protect people from the negative outcomes that are typically associated with a dysfunctional background.

V. Emotional Plasticity, Social Connections, and Positive Behavioural Change

Until some time ago, a common assumption was that the adult brain is static and mostly unaltered by the environment or behavioural interactions. Today, it has been firmly established that the brain is constantly in flux and thus constantly changes.[174] Although there may be key periods in its development and sensitivity

[171] For a discussion, see L Johnston, 'Reconceptualizing Criminal Justice Reform for Offenders with Serious Mental Illness' (2019) 71 *Florida Law Review* 515.

[172] For a review of these studies, see ibid.

[173] ibid.

[174] J Power and B Schlaggar, 'Neural Plasticity Across the Lifespan' (2017) 6 *Wiley Interdisciplinary Review of Developmental Biology* e216.

to change – such as during childhood and adolescence – the brain continues to create and alter neural pathways throughout one's life, as its structure and function are ceaselessly moulded by socio-environmental and behavioural influences.[175] Changes that occur in the brain as a result of plasticity allow individuals to learn from new experiences, store new information, create new memories and lose others. Consequently, they further allow individuals to reframe their thoughts, modify their feelings, and change their habits and behaviour.

Neuroscience research has critically revealed the marked plasticity of the brain's circuits that are involved in the experience and regulation of emotions in response to new experiences and changing environments.[176] These changes have been found to positively affect moral reasoning and prosocial behaviour. Hence, by virtue of ongoing neuroplasticity, people can 'rewire' their emotions and socio-emotional skills that connect to moral and social behaviour, even in later stages of life.

Some work has stressed the positive repercussions of compassion training for prosocial attitudes. Research from psychology[177] has illustrated that compassion promotes social connectedness, augments positive affect and emotional resilience, and fosters emotion regulation. Moreover, compassion strengthens feelings of perceived self-other similarity[178] and enhances altruistic feelings of concern for others. Hence, compassion naturally induces feelings of positivity, empathy, and prosociality toward others. Consistent with the behavioural perspective, neuroscientific work on the effects of compassion training on the brain[179] has reported that this practice induces positive changes in brain regions that are involved in social cognition and empathic responses, including the ACC and the insula, the medial OFC, the striatum, and the amygdala. These results suggest that compassion training changes the brain, and an increase in other-concerned behaviour may result from the heightened engagement of neural systems that are implicated in understanding the suffering of other people, executive and emotional regulation, and reward processing. These results align with behavioural studies[180] finding

[175] See A Sale et al, 'Environment and the Brain: Towards an Endogenous Pharmacotherapy' (2014) 94 *Physiological Review* 189.

[176] R Davidson et al, 'Emotion, Plasticity, Context, and Regulation Perspectives from Affective Neuroscience' (2000) 126 *Psychological Bulletin* 890.

[177] eg K Neff et al, 'Self-compassion and Adaptive Psychological Functioning' (2007) 41 *Journal of Research in Personality* 139; E Inwood and M Ferrari, 'Mechanisms of Change in the Relationship between Self-compassion, Emotion Regulation, and Mental Health: A Systematic Review' (2018) 10 *Applied Psychology Health Well Being* 215.

[178] eg C Oveis et al, 'Compassion, Pride, and Social Intuitions of Self-other Similarity' (2010) 98 *Journal of Personality and Social Psychology* 618.

[179] eg O Klimecki et al, 'Functional Neural Plasticity and Associated Changes in Positive Affect after Compassion Training' (2013) 23 *Cerebral Cortex* 1552; A Lutz et al, Regulation of the neural circuitry of emotion by compassion meditation: Effects of Mediative Expertise' (2008) 3 *PLoS One* e1897; T Singer and O Klimecki, 'Empathy and Compassion' (2014) 24 *Current Biology* R875; G Desbordes et al, 'Effects of Mindful-attention and Compassion Meditation Training on Amygdala Response to Emotional Stimuli in an Ordinary, Non-meditative State' (2012) 6 *Frontiers in Human Neuroscience* 292.

[180] S Stosny, *Treating Attachment Abuse: A Compassion Approach* (New York, Springer, 1995); C Murphy et al, 'Change in Self-esteem and Physical Aggression during Treatment for Partner Violent Men' (2005) 20 *Journal of Family Violence* 201.

that interventions that aim to increase compassion ultimately reduced aggression among people with violent tendencies.

Meanwhile, other work has underscored the positive effects of mindfulness[181] on emotional responding, emotional resilience, and psychological well-being. For instance, through the use of anatomical magnetic resonance imaging (MRI), Hölzel et al[182] have indicated that mindfulness increases the grey matter concentration in brain regions such as the posterior cingulate cortex, the temporo-parietal junction, and the cerebellum. Activity in these brain regions has been associated with increased emotion regulation, self-referential processing, and empathic perspective-taking.

In a functional MRI study, Goldin et al[183] have identified a positive link between mindfulness programmes, reduced amygdala activity, and increased activity in the prefrontal regions that are implicated in attentional deployment. These authors have likewise indicated that mindfulness training may reduce negative emotional experiences while enhancing emotion regulation. These results have been replicated in other studies. For instance, in one longitudinal study of incarcerated adolescents between 16 and 18 years of age, Umbach et al[184] have concluded that 'regular' incarceration entails a decline in cognitive functioning skills, including emotion recognition, emotion regulation, and cognitive control, all of which are protective factors against antisocial behaviour. Meanwhile, alternative prison programmes that employ a combination of mindfulness and cognitive behavioural therapy appeared to buffer such decline. These findings complement and support the body of behavioural research[185] that has demonstrated the beneficial effects of mindfulness-based programmes on incarcerated people with histories of violence and aggression. This research has reported enduring improvement in anger and hostility, relaxation capacity, self-esteem, and optimism. By extension, cross-disciplinary evidence reflects that mindfulness might be beneficial for prosocial behaviour.

Positive emotional and behavioural change have been crucially attributed to the cultivation of positive social connections[186] and healthy environments.

[181] J Davidson and BS McEwen, 'Social Influences on Neuroplasticity: Stress and Interventions to Promote Well-being' (2012) 15 *Nature Neuroscience* 689.

[182] B Hölzel et al, 'Mindfulness Practice Leads to Increases in Regional Brain Gray Matter Density' (2011) 191 *Psychiatric Research* 36.

[183] P Goldin and J Gross, 'Effects of Mindfulness-based Stress Reduction (MBSR) on Emotion Regulation in Social Anxiety Disorder' (2010) 10 *Emotion* 83. See also A Doll et al, 'Mindful Attention to Breath Regulates Emotions via Increased Amygdala-Prefrontal Cortex Connectivity' (2016) 134 *Neuroimage* 305.

[184] R Umbach et al, 'Cognitive Decline as a Result of Incarceration and the Effects of a CBT/MT Intervention: A Cluster-Randomized Controlled Trial' (2017) 45 *Criminal Justice and Behavior* 31.

[185] eg A Perelman et al, 'Meditation in a Deep South Prison: A Longitudinal Study on the Effects of Vipassana' (2012) 51 *Journal of Offender Rehabilitation* 176.

[186] Social connection indicates a person's subjective sense of having close and positively experienced relationships with others in the social world. Social engagement is interacting with others, feeling connected to other people, doing purposeful activities with others and/or maintaining meaningful social relationships.

In a seminal article, Baumeister and Leary[187] have posited that human beings are programmed to form and maintain interpersonal bonds because they are motivated by their innate need to belong. The authors have characterised this need as the need to form and maintain strong, stable interpersonal relationships. Moreover, they have crucially argued that such need is satisfied by frequent human contact and genuine bonds of caring between individuals. Baumeister and Leary have proposed nine criteria to assess whether a given human need is a fundamental motivation for human behaviour. Specifically, the relevant need should achieve the following:

> produce effects readily under all but adverse conditions, (b) have affective consequences, (c) direct cognitive processing, (d) lead to ill effects (such as on health or adjustment) when thwarted, (e) elicit goal-oriented behaviour designed to satisfy it (subject to motivational patterns such as object substitutability and satiation), (f) be universal in the sense of applying to all people, (g) not be derivative of other motives, (h) affect a broad variety of behaviours, and (i) have implications that go beyond immediate psychological functioning.

Hence, the authors have reviewed a large body of evidence that demonstrates that belonging and social connection meet all of these criteria. On this basis, they have concluded that the need to belong is indeed a fundamental human need.

Baumeister and Leary's arguments are in line with a robust body of studies in evolutionary and social psychology that have largely demonstrated that humankind exhibits an ineradicable biological need for social bonds and relationships. Notably, these studies have emphasised the importance of positive human social connection for mental and physical health, psychological well-being as well as prosocial tendencies.

Social connection appears to exert a buffering effect in contending with life stressors.[188] It may allow people to regulate their emotions and maintain a state of well-being via the help of others.[189] For instance, the feeling that others will provide support has the effect of protecting one from stress by changing the appraisal of a situation that was formerly perceived as stressful. An important finding emerging from psychological data is that 'social contact is not sufficient to reap benefits; rather, it is the affective quality of the relationship that is significant'.[190] This finding supports the accredited hypothesis that an *emotional connection* is among the most crucial elements of social connection.

[187] R Baumeister and M Leary, 'The Need to Belong: Desire for Interpersonal Attachments as a Fundamental Human Motivation' (1995) 117 *Psychological Bulletin* 497.

[188] S Cohen and T Willis, 'Stress, Support and the Buffering Hypothesis' (1985) 98 *Psychological Bulletin*, 310, 314; PA Thoits, Social Support as Coping Assistance' (1986) 54 *Journal of Consulting and Clinical Psychology* 416, 421.

[189] See E Seppala et al, 'Social Connection and Compassion: Important Predictors of Health and Well-being' (2013) 80 *Social Research: An International Quarterly* 411.

[190] ibid, 417.

Psychological research has further revealed that social connection is malleable, which implies that it is possible to alter levels of social connection and that social connection can be cultivated for mental and physical health and well-being as well as societal welfare. For instance, Twenge et al[191] have found that inducing connection after a social threat of exclusion provides a buffer against antisocial feelings and tendencies that are associated with exclusion.[192] Their study has illustrated that when social connection was evoked in some way after the social exclusion manipulation, the aggressive reactions disappeared. These findings suggest that social connection can preclude aggressive tendencies that result from social rejection. They further indicate that social connection not only serves an emotion regulatory function but also helps to fend off antisocial behaviour.

The sustained body of psychological evidence on the fundamental importance of healthy social connections for well-being and social functioning has found crucial support in social neuroscience research. Critical insights emerge primarily from research that was conducted with animal models. Studies with rodents[193] have notably emphasised that rodents that were reared in 'enriched environments' and surrounded by their peers exhibited normal developmental pathways in the structure and function of several brain regions, including those that support a variety of functions ranging from learning and memory to emotion regulation. Moreover, these animal samples exhibited normal sociable tendencies. Further evidence derives from human research. Key human research on brain plasticity has revealed that positive social connections induced positive changes in the neural circuits that underlie cognitive functions, socio-affective skills (eg, empathy and emotion regulation)[194] and social behaviour over the entire lifespan.[195] These changes have been associated with higher cognitive performance, emotional responsiveness, psychological well-being, and prosocial behaviour.[196] Hence, by virtue of ongoing neuroplasticity, positive experience as well as healthy social and environmental influences have the potential to (re)shape the emotions and socio-emotional skills that connect to moral and social behaviour, even in later stages of life. Chapter six explains that this perspective is also consistent with studies that have investigated the individual and social factors that relate to crime desistance.

[191] JM Twenge et al, 'Social Exclusion Decreases Prosocial Behavior' (2007) 92 *Journal of Personality and Social Psychology* 56.

[192] See below.

[193] MR Rosenzweig and EL Bennett, 'Cerebral Changes in Rats Exposed Individually to an Enriched Environment' (1972) *Journal of Comparative and Physiological Psychology* 304; S Neal et al, 'Enriched Environment Exposure Enhances Social Interactions and Oxytocin Responsiveness in Male Long-Evans Rats' (2018) *Frontiers in Behavioral Neuroscience*, available at doi:10.3389/fnbeh.2018.00198. There is a general consensus among the scientific community that the brain and social developmental pathways are similar in human and non-human primates.

[194] R Eisler and DS Levine, 'Nurture, Nature, and Caring: We Are Not Prisoners of Our Genes' (2002) 3 *Brain and Mind* 9.

[195] See Sale et al (n 175); eg S Valk et al, 'Structural Plasticity of the Social Brain: Differential Change after Socio-affective and Cognitive Mental Training' (2017) 3 *Science Advances* e1700489.

[196] See eg Eisler and Levine (n 194).

VI. The Pain of Social Exclusion

The relevance of emotions, social connections and positive environments for promoting positive behavioural change is further apparent from behavioural and neuroscientific studies that have explored the adverse psychological and neurobiological effects of social exclusion. In scientific terms, social exclusion refers to the experience of physical or emotional social isolation. The former type of isolation consists of *objective* isolation, which entails the objective physical state of being deprived of social interactions. Emotional isolation is a *subjective* form of isolation that is associated with social rejection, loneliness, and the loss of emotional attachments and meaningful social relationships.

Social exclusion of either type has been associated with a series of psychological issues and negative effects on behaviour, including problematic interpersonal behaviour. People who are and/or feel socially excluded may engage in less prosocial behaviour and exhibit more aggression.[197] Furthermore, social exclusion has been generally associated with a higher propensity to commit antisocial acts, such as criminal offences.[198]

One of the most heavily investigated psychological effects of social exclusion is social pain, which refers to the painful feeling of being socially excluded. The experience of social pain relates to the nature of humans as fundamentally social beings. As explained above, humans have a biological and universal need for social connection and belongingness. From an evolutionary standpoint, this natural need likely originates from the lengthy period of critical need for maternal attachment, care, and nurturance among mammalian infants in order to survive.[199] Based on this survival need, it is possible that 'the social attachment system – which ensures social connection – may have piggybacked onto the physical pain system, borrowing the pain signal to indicate when social relationships are threatened'.[200] Thus, the experience of social pain may be understood as an adaptive means of preventing and surviving the threat of social exclusion and rejection.[201] From a psychological standpoint, social pain has been associated with a variety of psychological symptoms and negative action tendencies that include emotional distress, anxiety, humiliation, lack of self-esteem, greater rejection sensitivity, emotion

[197] See eg J Twenge and R Baumeister, 'Social Exclusion Increases Aggression and Self-Defeating Behavior while Reducing Intelligent Thought and Prosocial Behavior' in D Abrams, M Hogg and J Marques (eds), *Social Psychology of Inclusion and Exclusion* (New York, Psychology Press, 2005) 27; M Leary et al, 'Interpersonal Rejection as a Determinant of Aggression' (2006) 10 *Personality and Social Psychology Review* 111.

[198] See eg R Baumeister et al, 'Social Exclusion Impairs Self-Regulation' (2005) 88 *Journal of Personality and Social Psychology* 589.

[199] N Eisenberger, 'Why Rejection Hurts: What Social Neuroscience Has Revealed About the Brain's Response to Social Rejection' in J Decety and J Cacioppo (eds), *The Oxford Handbook of Social Neuroscience* (New York, Oxford University Press, 2011) 586.

[200] ibid.

[201] ibid.

dysregulation, blunted affect, and aggression. Moreover, several studies have linked the experience of social pain with a stronger predisposition to develop physical diseases or mental issues and even a higher risk of mortality. Therefore, regardless of whether the traumatic effects of social pain are immediately visible, they may manifest and grow over time.

Over the past decades, social neuroscience research has started to examine the neurological representations of social pain. According to an influential account in the literature, namely the 'shared representation hypothesis',[202] social pain is neurologically akin to physical pain, which is the pain that follows a physical injury. This account holds that, in a neurological sense, social pain shares the same affective component as that of physical pain. Specifically, it appears to recruit the same neural circuitry, including the dACC and the AI.[203] According to other studies,[204] physical pain and social pain actually involve distinct neural representations within and across brain regions; thus, the neurological overlap between these two types of pain seems to occur only at a gross anatomical level. Overall, social pain and physical pain possibly consist of diverse affective experiences, which entail unique psychological consequences and require different interventions. Nonetheless, physical pain and social pain may be functionally related and mutually influential. For instance, evidence indicates that individuals who suffered emotional trauma are at a higher risk of developing pain disorders.

As for the relationship between social exclusion and social pain, several laboratory studies have explored the link between the experience of social pain and social disconnection via neural activity in the brain regions that support the experience of this form of pain. Importantly, functional MRI studies have recently examined the effects of social pain on aggression by way of activation in the AI and dACC.[205] One study has reflected a positive correlation between increased activity in these two brain regions, which are associated with the experience of social pain, as well as heightened levels of aggression in socially rejected individuals who exhibited less executive functioning. Another study[206] has tested the socio-emotional mechanisms that link low expression of monoaminoxidase genetic polymorphism (MAOA-L) to aggression by measuring neural activity in response to social rejection. The study found that, compared to participants with high expression of MAOA, MAOA-L participants exhibited heightened sensitivity to negative social experiences, as evidenced by increased dACC reactivity to social exclusion.

[202] N Eisenberger, 'The Neural Bases of Social Pain: Evidence for Shared Representations with Physical Pain' (2012) *Psychosomatic Medicine* 126.

[203] N Eisenberger, 'The Pain of Social Disconnection: Examining the Shared Neural Underpinnings of Physical and Social Pain' (2012) *Nature Reviews of Neuroscience* 421.

[204] C Woo et al, 'Separate Neural Representations for Physical Pain and Social Rejection' (2014) *Nature Communications*, available at doi: 10.1038/ncomms6380.

[205] D Chester et al, 'The Interactive Effect of Social Pain and Executive Functioning on Aggression: An fMRI Experiment' (2014) 9 *Social Cognitive Affective Neuroscience* 699.

[206] N Eisenberger et al, 'Understanding Genetic Risk for Aggression: Clue's from Brain Response to Social Exclusion' (2007) 61 *Biological Psychiatry* 1100.

According to the authors of this study, these findings indicate that the higher risk of aggression in MAOA-L individuals is not due to a lack of social concern or a blunted affect but is instead tied to heightened socio-emotional sensitivity, such as rejection sensitivity, to negative social experiences, which likely prompts these individuals to respond to these experiences with aggressive behaviour.

Although more brain-based research is needed, these results lend support to the perspective that social pain is a contributing factor to aggressive reactions among socially rejected individuals.[207] For instance, Elison et al[208] have suggested a psychobiological chain linking shame to anger and aggression via the experience of social pain. These authors have qualified shame as a strategy for coping with the threats of social exclusion. When people experience a feeling of shame, this experience is both physically and emotionally painful; in turn, physical and emotional pain elicit anger and aggression. As a result, anger that is expressed through aggression is a (mal)adaptive coping strategy or psychological defence for handling shame due to social exclusion.

The adverse psychological and neurological consequences of social exclusion are most glaring in the case of objective isolation, especially when such isolation occurs in impoverished environments. Compelling evidence from human and animal research suggests that increased social isolation in impoverished environments contributes to or reinforces problematic neurobiological patterns, even within a short period of time. This body of research collectively reveals that objective isolation has negative repercussions for both brain structure and function, including reduced cortical volume, diminished neuronal connections in cortical areas and the hippocampus, decreased myelin production, and altered activity in the reward system and amygdala.[209] These cerebral alterations have been connected to detachment from the environment, hostility toward others, high levels of aggression, blunted affect, and an increased risk of susceptibility to several behavioural conditions that emulate psychiatric diseases and disorders, including neurodegenerative disorders and schizophrenia.[210] Morphological and functional changes in the brain may occur even after a short period of time in extreme isolation and appear to continue after the reintroduction of the subject into the social environment.[211]

[207] ibid.

[208] J Elison et al, 'Shame and Aggression: Theoretical Considerations' (2014) 9 *Aggression and Violent Behavior* 447.

[209] eg J Liu et al, 'Impaired Adult Myelination in the Prefrontal Cortex of Socially Isolated Mice' (2012) 15 *Nature Neuroscience* 1621; J Djordjevic et al, 'Effects of Chronic Social Isolation on Wistar Rat Behavior and Brain Plasticity Markers' (2012) 66 *Neuropsychobiology* 112; E Castillo-Gómez et al, 'Early Social Isolation Stress and Perinatal NMDA Receptor Antagonist Treatment Induce Changes in the Structure and Neurochemistry of Inhibitory Neurons of the Adult Amygdala and Prefrontal Cortex' (2017) 4 *eNeuro* 0034; K Fone and M V Porkess, 'Behavioural and Neurochemical Effects of Post-weaning Social Isolation in Rodents – Relevance to Developmental Neuropsychiatric Disorders' (2008) 32 *Neuroscience & Biobehavioral Review* 1087.

[210] See Fone and Porkess (n 209).

[211] eg M Makinodan, 'A Critical Period for Social Experience–Dependent Oligodendrocyte Maturation and Myelination' (2012) 337 *Science* 1357.

One of the most significant findings concerns the deleterious effects of chronic stress due to increased isolation. Studies with rodents[212] have revealed that rodents that are housed alone (in contrast to those that are housed in enriched environments) develop a smaller cerebral cortex and shorter synapses in the brain areas that are involved in spatial information processing, memory, social information, and emotion regulation, including the hippocampus and the amygdala. In addition, some studies have associated morphological and functional diminutions of the hippocampus with decreased hippocampal neurogenesis.[213] Such damages have been linked to the experience of long-term mental health conditions in humans, such as memory loss, cognitive decline, depression, and PTSD. Although more research with human samples is needed, reliable evidence exists that 'increased social isolation and diminished physical contact contribute to and reinforce problematic neurobiological patterns'.[214]

This important body of research reported in this Section sheds a critical light on the adverse neurobiological mechanisms that underlie psychological and socio-behavioural issues that may either emerge or increase during and after incarceration. Abundant psychological research has widely reported that the act of imprisonment – as well as the restrictive, traumatising, depriving, and exclusionary conditions of prison life – can produce or aggravate a number of affective, cognitive, and behavioural deficits, including affective disturbances such as decreased affect, lack of self-esteem, increased feelings of rejection and humiliation, chronic anger and rage, and problems with self-regulation, among others. A crucial observation is that incarceration can re-traumatise and stimulate the same negative emotional feelings (eg, dysfunctional shame) and behavioural tendencies that have consistently qualified as risk factors for antisocial conduct, especially violence.[215]

Although brain-based research about the effects of incarceration on the brain remains scant, the adverse psychological effects of incarceration most likely follow from adverse neurobiological mechanisms. As researchers have suggested, the socially scarce and exclusionary conditions of a prison setting are likely to 'generate or exacerbate neurobiological deficits and maladaptive behaviors … [T]his becomes a significant issue, especially for individuals who are chronic offenders, where existing neurobiological vulnerabilities are intensified in settings of confinement and segregation, thereby reinforcing maladaptive patterns of behavior'.[216]

[212] Djordjevic (n 209); F Mumtaz et al, 'Neurobiology and Consequences of Social Isolation Stress in Animal Model – A Comprehensive Review' (2018) 105 *Biomedicine and Pharmacotherapy* 1205; A Ieraci et al, 'Social Isolation Stress Induces Anxious-Depressive-Like Behavior and Alterations of Neuroplasticity-Related Genes in Adult Male Mice' (2016) *Neural Plasticity*, available at doi: 10.1155/2016/6212983.

[213] See S Cacioppo et al, 'Toward a Neurology of Loneliness' (2014) 140 *Psychological Bulletin* 1464.

[214] A Baskin-Sommers and K Fontaneau, 'Correctional Change Through Neuroscience' (2016) 85 *Fordham Law Review* 403, 428.

[215] J Gilligan, 'Punishment and Violence: Is Criminal Law Based on a Huge Mistake?' (2000) 67 *Social Research* 745.

[216] Baskin-Sommers and Fontaneau (n 214) 428.

Thus, the experience of social exclusion in often impoverished or even precarious environments that is typical of incarceration potentially damages the brain. Such damage could have devastating effects on mental health, psychological well-being, and prosociality, and they may be long-lasting or even permanent.

These insights reflect the vital importance of constant positive interactions in stimulating environments for mental health, psychological well-being, and the cultivation of prosocial attitudes. These factors act as positive incentives for neural growth and activity in the brain circuits that support the socio-emotional competencies that are fundamental to social and moral life. Most importantly, these factors fundamentally allow individuals to keep and feel their sense of humanity.

VII. Conclusion

The above-discussed empirical insights suggest that the dominant models of culpability and punishment are at odds with the nature of humans as emotional and social beings. The illustrated findings highlight that these models rely on an excessively narrow model of human agency and personhood. They specifically emphasise that dominant models of culpability and punishment are founded on an incomplete understanding of the dynamics that underlie social behaviour, as they fail to account for factors that actually (and critically) contribute to an individual's choice to act in breach of or in accordance with social norms. Thus, the rationalism and individualism of culpability and punishment offer an ideal and partial representation of human agency and personhood by artificially decontextualising individuals from relevant factors that influence their social behaviour. Adjudicating and responding to crime on the basis of a choice that is dictated by knowledge and reasoning faculties – to the relative neglect of the role of emotions and socio-environmental factors within human agency – is evidently contradictory to how human beings behave socially. Human behaviour is not entirely an intrapsychic matter, as rationalist and individualist theories of culpability and punishment assume. People do not suppress their emotions to weigh the pros and cons of different courses of action in view of standards of right and wrong and then freely decide whether to engage in an (im)moral action. Furthermore, people do not operate as isolated (moral) agents who are impervious to the contexts in which they operate and the realities in which they are enmeshed.

An even more critical aspect that has emerged from the above discussion concerns the dynamic nature of the human brain. As noted, the human brain has the amazing ability to change as a function of changing environments and behavioural interactions, thereby allowing individuals to learn from new experiences and modify their feelings, thoughts, and behaviour. Crucially, positive stimuli, healthy environments, and social connections, including meaningful social relationships, stable social bonds, social inclusion, and perceived belongingness, have been found to foster positive changes in the brain regions that support the emotional processes that are implicated in moral and prosocial behaviour. Meanwhile, social exclusion can either precipitate or aggravate problematic neurobiological patterns in the same brain regions, which presents dramatic implications for an individual's prosociality, psychological well-being, and mental and physical health. These insights imply that the generalised view of 'law-breakers' in their adulthood – especially those who commit the worst acts – as people with little capacity for change does not at all accurately reflect the reality of human biology. Moreover, these insights highlight that socially excluding individuals is biologically devastating and causes counterproductive effects at both psychological and behavioural levels.

How could these aspects of the influence of emotions and the social environment on human behaviour be used to inspire a rethinking of the model of the person that underpins dominant paradigms of culpability and punishment? And how could they be employed to reconsider culpability criteria as well as ideas and practices of punishment? In the next two chapters, I delve into these issues and provide one approach to respond to these complex questions. It is my hope that the following arguments can resituate criminal law's understanding of and responses to crime on more rational and humane grounds.

5

Holistic and Situated Culpability

I. Introduction

Behavioural and neuroscientific insights into the engagement of emotions and social influences in moral behaviour lend compelling empirical support to the scholarly criticism of the model of the person in criminal law. Notably, the body of insights that I have reported in the previous chapter suggests that the normative model of the (culpable) person provides a narrow and, in a sense, inaccurate picture of the relevant aspects and factors that govern human decision-making and behaviour in moral contexts. In fact, the idea that moral agents effect choices based on an instrumental practical reasoning offers a partial view of the mental processes implicated in moral behaviour in social contexts. This idea decontextualises people from other relevant factors that influence their decisions to behave either in conformity or in breach of social and moral values, and offers an altogether ideal representation of human agency. Stated in another way, science confronts us with the fact that the manner by which the law conceives of us when it adjudicates our behaviour is not entirely correspondent to how we 'work' as moral agents, that is, how we reason, decide, and act morally in social contexts. In short, the law artificially denudes us of other critical aspects of our moral and social mind.

An important point to emphasise – since now – is that nothing within the body of empirical knowledge I have previously reported suggests that human decisions and behaviours are not the product of people's choices and reasons. Even if the law accepted that human actions are governed by brain and psychological mechanisms, it should not abandon its intuition that humans are agents who decide and act for reasons. However, science importantly boosts the law's awareness of the complexity and contingency that surround decision-making processes and actions in social settings, and can help it frame human behaviour through a more multifaceted lens. The law may want to consider empirical information and revise the substance of its criteria accordingly, while simultaneously remaining fundamentally committed to the normative assessments of human behaviour.

This consideration for empirical knowledge within the law neither equates to attributing a normative significance to science, nor to claiming that science could erode the nature of foundational legal notions. Nevertheless, scientific insights can provide some correctives to certain tendencies to which the law is prone in understanding human behaviour. From this perspective, empirical knowledge may become crucially integral to discussions of culpability (and the lack thereof) insofar as the information it provides has an impact on the standard determinants of culpability. The law may want to take this information into account and handle it within the existing canons of culpability and excuse. Altogether, properly understood, science can have a significant bearing on the normative theory of culpability, without necessarily revolutionising its foundational notions.

Although I, similar to the vast majority of legal scholars, hold the view that science cannot and should not supplant legal notions, I believe that science – and more specifically the body of science I have analysed – can offer important insights to move the law to reconsidering its way of looking at humans, by grasping and affording relevance to further aspects and nuances of human behaviour in moral and social contexts. One reason is that science can inform the law's understanding of the relation between emotion, cognition, and morality, and prompt the law to re-think its conventional understanding of emotions in mechanistic terms. Considering the centrality of emotions to morality, the law may intend to reconsider its treatment of emotions within culpability assessments and afford emotions the same normative relevance that it provides to 'cognitive' states and capacities of knowledge and understanding. Another reason is that science may also help the law in recognising the absurdity of separating individual agency from the social environment, and may invite the law to consider the context of a crime to a greater extent.

In the pages that follow, I embark on a cautious endeavour to incorporate this body of scientific information within the current voluntarist paradigm of culpability. In particular, I propose several changes within the articulation of the current components of this paradigm to requalify the normative relevance of emotions and social factors within their criteria. Before I proceed with my normative evaluation of culpability, I begin my discussion with a re-interpretation of rationality and autonomy – *quo* fundamental features of the person in criminal law – as multidimensional notions, in which emotions and the social environment figure as their essential aspects. Hence, the chapter focuses on the revision of the current model of culpability, which is based on a holistic and situated view of human behaviour. The proposed normative model draws on David Brink and Dana Nelkin's conception of the architecture of culpability and expands it to give more prominence to emotional and social factors in its criteria. I subsequently examine the potential implications that such a re-thought theoretical model of culpability can have for legal doctrines. This part of the analysis initially focuses on the potential revision of the criteria of legal insanity and then underscores the potential provision of a 'generic partial excuse' – following Stephen Morse's lead – the normative excusing condition of which lies in a person's non-culpable limited choice to do otherwise. In the final section, I discuss the personal guilt principle to support the normative relevance of a culpability model that embraces a holistic and situated view of human behaviour.

II. Autonomy and Rationality as Multidimensional Concepts: Reframing the 'Person' in Criminal Law

In chapter one, I discussed that the predominant criminal law's theory of the person, which is also largely reflected in legal doctrine, conceives of such person as an autonomous and rational agent. The paradigm person in the law is a self-governing agent who effects choices in the light of an instrumental practical reasoning against the normative standards of right and wrong. As I emphasised, the conception of rationality and autonomy endorsed by voluntarism is rationalist and individualist. The paradigm person in the law is indeed depicted as an individual who has an ability for moral deliberation and rational transcendence of emotion and is largely abstracted from his or her social context. As I also clarified, voluntarism neither denies that the culpable person has emotions nor indicates that he or she may be influenced by his or her social background. Nonetheless, the feeling and social dimensions of such person are conceived of as distinct aspects of his or her personhood, that is, as separated entities from the person's autonomy and rationality. Under this conception, people are presupposed to be rational and autonomous as long as they are able to act for reasons and control their behaviour. Such ability also entails that people are able to keep their emotions at the margins and resist situational pressures. In this picture, emotions are thus a type of raw data of nature to be controlled by 'reason'.[1] By contrast, the individual's powers of autonomy and rationality stand in isolation from the influences of the social environment.

A consideration of the empirical insights illustrated in the previous chapter can allow us to draw a different picture. This picture suggests that both emotions and the social context are inescapable components of individual autonomy and rationality. That is, both emotions and the social context are integrating components of the individual's capacity to master his or her own actions and to be responsive to the reasons for such actions. Moreover, the involvement of emotions and the social context in human behaviour is particularly glaring in moral behaviour.

Beginning with emotions, the assumption that emotions are states that operate within the human mind unmediated by thinking, and to be possibly controlled by thinking, has been generally dismissed. The purported dichotomy between emotion and cognition has emerged as simply false. Indeed, every single decision people make entails an integrated participation of mutually influencing and often overlapping cognitive and emotional processes.

In this picture, emotions play a preponderant role in informing human decision and behaviour. Emotions provide a bridge between our abstract thinking and the outside environment; they provide a meaning to external occurrences and motivate our choices and reactions to cope with them. In other words, emotions are states that people experience, regulate, and use to motivate and guide their

[1] See ch 1.

behaviour and adaptively cope with social demands. From this perspective, emotions are both products and reasons of our deliberations, as they reflect our judgements about things in the world and inform behavioural reactions. Accordingly, the qualitative distinction between 'emotion' and 'cognition' appears to be implausible, as emotions have cognitive contents and are critical triggers of choices and behaviours. Thus, emotions do have a positive bearing on our rational choices, as they are an integral part of them. Furthermore, emotions consequently help us to be in control and choose among different courses of action to adaptively behave in social situations. Emotions are therefore central to our capacity for self-governance and self-determination.[2]

The view of emotions as an integral part of individual autonomy has found traction in several philosophical accounts. For instance, the philosopher David Shoemaker posits that an action is autonomous when it is determined by the agent's most central cares with respect to that situation, where cares are defined in terms of emotional reactions. The fact that we care for the outcome of our actions prompts us to deliberate about what to do.[3] For Shoemaker, our cares are ours in so far as they result from well-functioning cognitive/emotional mechanisms and are not the product of manipulations. These mechanisms include critical reflection and self-evaluation, as well as mechanisms that allow our cares and our motivations to be sensitive to our thoughts. For our cares to constitute our real autonomous selves, they ought to have developed naturally, on the basis of a normal unfolding of our emotional and cognitive capacities.

As essential components of human choices, emotions are also vital elements of human practical reasoning, especially in moral contexts. According to Patricia Greenspan,[4] emotions factor in practical reasoning in two main ways. First, emotions reinforce non-emotional reasons such as desires and beliefs. By evaluating brute facts (ie, environmental stimuli) through the attachment of positive or negative valences, emotions yield further non-emotional reasons 'to sustain the conditions that make the evaluation appropriate'.[5] This postulation implies an understanding of emotions in normative terms, that is, as mental factors that provide or constitute reasons for actions. For Greenspan, all experienced emotions combine belief- and desire-like aspects. Thus, emotions are relevant to moral reasoning in the way that beliefs and desires are relevant. For instance, feeling guilty at the prospect of wronging others can involve a negative moral judgement that the act is wrong, along with an aversion to the act of wronging. This guilt feeling can be an input to our desires and beliefs, and hence to our overall moral reasoning up to our behavioural response. Second, emotions make an individual 'hold in

[2] See also A Bandura, 'Selective Moral Disengagement in the Exercise of Moral Agency' (2002) 31 *Journal of Moral Education* 101.

[3] See D Shoemaker, 'Caring, Identification, and Agency' (2003) 114 *Ethics* 88.

[4] P Greenspan, 'Practical Reasoning and Emotion' in A Mele and P Rawling (eds), *The Oxford Handbook of Rationality* (New York, Oxford University Press, 2004) 206.

[5] ibid.

mind'[6] the content of the evaluation of environmental stimuli. More specifically, emotions provide *evaluative propositions* (eg, that something might cause harm) and anticipate the practical eventualities of actions or situations, thereby prompting an individual to react accordingly. In this picture, emotions consequently serve as the anticipatory 'self-evaluation'[7] of actions in view of certain normative standards, that is, they provide anticipated feedback about the (in)appropriateness of a given action against certain standards and as a response to a valanced situational demand.

This account aligns with the reviewed empirical studies, which suggest that people do not decide and act morally on the sole basis of a 'cognitive' reasoning about abstract principles of justice (ie, what is right and what is wrong). As we observed, moral decisions and behaviours also require an appreciation of the interpersonal significance of a given mode of conduct. In other words, moral decisions and behaviours also entail an inescapable participation of emotion-related processes, through which the individual assesses the interpersonal significance of a given situation and regulates his or her behaviour to fit the moral demands of a given context. Such appreciation chiefly involves an interaction between specific social/moral emotions – notably certain self-conscious or self-reflective emotions – as well as emotion-related faculties, including empathy, and pre-existing conditions such as goals, beliefs, contexts, and experiences. Altogether, emotions and emotional capacities are centrally relevant to responding to and adaptively behaving in social-moral contexts. Emotions have a bearing on practical rationality in moral contexts because they provide people with the motivation for acting morally under the circumstances. Thus, the ability to act for normative reasons, or to be normatively rational, does not simply require knowledge or understanding of the moral appropriateness of one's behaviour against the normative standards of right and wrong. People can be considered as rational not only insofar as they are able to know or recognise normative reasons for actions but also to the extent that they are able to 'feel' them.[8]

Furthermore, individual autonomy and rationality are not entirely 'intra-psychic' matters, but stand in interaction with context. People's reasoning and choosing faculties are intertwined with contextual factors, including the features of the immediate contexts and, more broadly, with life experiences and ongoing social environments.[9] Thus, to understand why a person feels, thinks, reasons,

[6] ibid.

[7] See also Bandura (n 2).

[8] See also R Slovenko, 'Psychiatry, Criminal Law, and the Role of the Psychiatrist' (1963) *Duke Law Journal* 395, 397 ('The dictum, "Cogito, ergo sum", "I think, therefore I am", is, however, the formula for the schizoid intellectual's struggle to possess an ego. A healthy human being would be more likely to start from "I feel, therefore I am."'); see also A Duff, 'Psychopathy and Moral Understanding' (1977) 14 *American Philosophical Quarterly* 189, 194 ('An understanding of moral concepts and values requires not just an intellectual recognition of the criteria by which others make moral judgments, but a concern for such values').

[9] See S Wolf, *Freedom Within Reason* (New York, Oxford University Press, 1990) 69 (defining the ability to act in accordance with Reason as the ability 'to be sensitive and responsive to relevant changes in one's situation and environment – that is, to be flexible').

chooses, or behaves the way he or she does, one cannot overlook the ongoing relationship between the individual and aspects of his or her social environment. As we observed, empirical insights into the social nature and function of the brain suggest the presence of a mutual influence between person and environment in shaping individual reasoning and conduct. On the one hand, the individual is provided with the capacity to critically think of and respond to situational demands through his or her choices and practical reasoning skills. On the other hand, contexts principally influence people's minds and behaviours, including their practical reasoning, emotional needs, and reactions to adaptively cope with situational demands. From this perspective, we should conceive of rationality and autonomy as notions that are tied to circumstances and social contexts.[10]

The idea of the individual acting in isolation from the social context, which the criminal law primarily endorses, provides a partial picture of human nature and 'a means of evading the truth of how individuals reason practically in social contexts'.[11] Otherwise, as Mark Fondacaro has argued, the criminal law's predominant focus on the individual in attempting to understand and assess human nature and behaviour is 'analogous to trying to understand and analyse the nature of water by focusing exclusively on hydrogen atoms'.[12] This abstraction can serve as a more or less coherent defence of the practice of attributing criminal responsibility and inflicting punishment, but it is not respondent to the reality of human behaviour.

The richness of behavioural and brain science research clearly indicates that human behaviour is best understood when it is judged in context, as human behaviour is a function of a dynamic interplay between personal and situational influences. Admittedly, to be human is not solely to choose and act for practical reasons. To be human is to choose and act for practical reasons in the context of a social situation. Hence, a fuller picture of human rationality and autonomy requires that human reasons and actions are also 'located' within the ongoing social context of the individual.

If we accept such multidimensional view of individuals *as* autonomous and rational actors, then we can also see that the traditional individualist and rationalist picture of the 'culpable agent' is unnecessarily abstract and narrow. We cannot assess human reasoning and choice without also considering the role that emotions and the social environment play in them. If the very nature of persons entails a connection to their affect and social context, then an image of the culpable agent that is based on a defensible view of human nature should afford a more significant weight to these aspects of human behaviour. A more comprehensive picture of

[10] See also J Doris, *Talking to Our Selves: Reflection, Ignorance, and Agency* (2015) (Oxford, Oxford University Press, 2015) (proposing a 'collaborativist' theory of human reason and agency, and suggesting that optimal human reasoning and action are substantially social: people reason and act best when they reason in interaction with others rather than in isolation).

[11] A Norrie, 'Practical Reasoning and Criminal Responsibility: A Jurisprudential Approach' in D Cornish and R Clarke (eds), *The Reasoning Criminal: Rational Choice Perspectives on Offending* (New Brunswick, NJ, Transaction Publishers, 2014) 217, 225.

[12] M Fondacaro, 'Toward an Ecological Jurisprudence Rooted in Concepts of Justice and Empirical Research' (2000–2001) 69 *UMCK Law Review* 179, 192.

humans may probably lead to an assessment of culpability based on criteria that grasp a fuller conception of humanness rather than an abstraction of it.

III. Holistic and Situated Culpability: Revising the Architecture of the Current Paradigm

Rethinking the ideas of autonomy and rationality through the lines I sketched above may support a revision of the criteria of culpability in a way that embraces a holistic and situated understanding of individual reasoning that results in a choice to engage in criminal wrongdoing. By *holistic*,[13] I mean that culpability determination should consider aspects of practical reasoning and decision-making that also and more extensively embrace the motivational and affective aspects of human conduct. Such an understanding entails a deeper inquiry into the content and quality of an agent's reason for acting as he or she did.

By *situated*, I suggest that the determination of culpability needs to 'locate' the reason for acting, and the behaviour accordingly, to the social context of the individual. As has been observed, 'the social context provides the material conditions within which the individual acts, and the individual's reasoning power serves to mediate between himself or herself, his or her subjective agency and his or her social context'.[14] Hence, a situated understanding of culpability is one that recognises individual autonomy and rationality but situates individual agency within a given social context. Such an understanding entails that culpability assessments go beyond the traditional focus on individual capacities or mental states and assesses agents and their behaviours in contexts and circumstances.

A voluntarist conception of culpability that can accommodate such a holistic and situated view of a person's decision-making and behaviour is the model proposed by the legal philosophers David Brink and Dana Nelkin.[15] The peculiarity of their modified conception of broad culpability is that it 'brings together'[16] the mental and situational components of human behaviour. As I explained in chapter one, (broad) culpability is predicated on two main conditions: mental capacity and a fair opportunity to do otherwise. In other words, the relevant individual *quo* autonomous and rational actor needs to possess specific mental capacities and act under circumstances that afford him or her a fair opportunity to avoid wrongdoing. Under the dominant account, mental capacity and fair opportunity are conceived of and treated as jointly sufficient yet independent variables

[13] *cf* K Ferzan, 'Holistic Culpability' (2007) 28 *Cardozo Law Review* 2523 (understanding 'holistic' as a combination of descriptive and normative levels of culpability).

[14] Norrie (n 11) 217.

[15] D Brink and D Nelkin, 'Fairness and the Architecture of Responsibility' in D Shoemaker (ed), *Oxford Studies in Agency and Responsibility, Vol. 1* (New York, Oxford University Press, 2013) 284.

[16] ibid, 285.

of culpability. Mental capacity is conceived of as a status condition of the individual to qualify as a rational and therefore responsible agent. On the contrary, fair opportunity is conceived of as the situation in which individuals find themselves and exert their behavioural choice. The separation between mental capacity and fair opportunity is also evident in legal doctrine. Consider the two main excuses, namely insanity and duress. In legal insanity, the individual is excused because he or she 'lacks' the requisite mental capacity to qualify as a rational actor. In duress, the individual is excused because he or she acted under circumstances (extreme threat or coercion) that did not afford him or her a fair opportunity to choose to do otherwise.

Brink and Nelkin have endorsed the idea that the separation between the mental and situational components of culpability is more blurred than predominant accounts assume. Indeed, these two components do (though not always) interact with each other.[17] Brink and Nelkin further re-qualify the situational component of culpability as 'situational control' and position 'fair opportunity to do otherwise' as the 'unifying element'[18] between normative competence and situational control, as well as the 'guiding principle'[19] underlying culpability/responsibility. In their view, the fair opportunity to choose to do otherwise is the core of culpability 'because [the] failure of either normative competence or situational control violates the norm that blame and punishment be reserved for those who had a fair opportunity to avoid wrongdoing'.[20]

Although their scholarship rejects situationist challenges to criminal responsibility,[21] Brink and Nelkin acknowledge that 'how much and what sorts of capacity one needs depend on situational features'.[22] They further recognise that the relationship between normative competence and situational control varies across individuals in view of certain variables. In other words, the influence of situational pressures on individual behaviour depends on the baseline level of normative competence, which varies across individuals. Altogether the requisite levels of normative competence and situational control are not invariant, but they need to be contextualised.[23]

Moreover, Brink and Nelkin have suggested that these two components need to be framed within a perspective that 'admit[s] of degree'.[24] Notably, they observe that both normative competence and situational control are scalar concepts that

[17] From this perspective, Brink and Nelkin's view seems to be more in line with Hart's capacity–responsibility account, according to which responsibility is predicated on the mental capacities of the actor and the situation in which the actor finds himself or herself: such a situation must afford the actor a fair chance to use his or her capacities to avoid wrongdoing. See ch 1.

[18] Brink and Nelkin (n 15) 305.

[19] ibid, 308.

[20] ibid.

[21] See D Nelkin, 'Freedom, Responsibility, and the Challenge of Situationism' (2005) 29 *Midwest Studies in Philosophy* 181; D Brink, 'Situationism, Responsibility and Fair Opportunity' (2013) 30 *Social Philosophy & Policy* 121.

[22] Brink and Nelkin (n 15) 304.

[23] See below.

[24] Brink and Nelkin (n 15) 309.

cannot be bifurcated through an all-or-nothing approach (ie, either one has them or does not). Thus, they propose the adoption of a trivalent system of culpability, one that reflects different degrees of its components and recognises partial excuses as a third verdict option at the guilt stage of the criminal process.[25]

Brink and Nelkin's proposed framework of the architecture of culpability is a solid ground to rethink culpability in holistic and situated terms. Foremost, the framework allows for a re-consideration of emotional competences within normative competence. Furthermore, the framework also provides a basis to factor the social context into the discourse of situational control. In the remainder of this section, I analyse the components of Brink and Nelkin's conception of culpability and contextually integrate emotional and social factors in their respective substances.

To recapitulate the model under analysis before I proceed: culpability hinges upon the fair opportunity to do otherwise. In its turn, the fair opportunity to do otherwise is factored in two components: normative competence (or mental capacity, which is subdivided into cognitive and control capacities) and situational control. Importantly, mental competence and situational control are often interacting; such interaction varies across individuals and depends on the context. Moreover, both normative competence and situational control are scalar concepts that admit degrees. Hence, they need to be viewed on a continuum rather than through a bifurcated lens.

A. Normative Competence

Consistent with most accounts across the literature and the law itself,[26] Brink and Nelkin factor mental competence in cognitive capacity and control capacity. In line with the dominant view, the authors interpret cognitive capacity as the ability to recognise and be responsive to normative reasons for actions based on a moral understanding of right and wrong.[27] Brink and Nelkin subsequently frame control capacity as the capability to regulate one's actions in accordance with [such] normative judgement.[28]

The empirical and normative discussions I made above entail that both capacities include emotional components. The literature I have analysed clarifies with little margin for doubt that any decision we make, especially in moral contexts, involves the inescapable participation and integration of emotion and cognition. Thus, the separation of emotion from cognition in moral behaviour is an obsolete assumption that has been largely discredited by more recent findings.

First, I discussed that the capacity to think, decide, and act morally is primarily driven and motivated by the individual's responsivity to the emotional-moral aspects of the situation and his or her conduct, that is, by an appreciation of

[25] ibid, 310.
[26] See ch 1.
[27] Brink and Nelkin (n 15) 292–5.
[28] ibid, 292.

the interpersonal significance of one's own conduct within a given situation. Such capacity mostly draws upon the experience and regulation of social/moral emotions such as guilt and regret, and empathy when responding to social cues.

The experience of social/moral emotions and empathy appears to be principally implicated in our competence to behave morally within a social context. Furthermore, I underscored that social emotions and empathy do not arise automatically, unmediated by thinking or out of our control. The experience of these emotions and of empathy is largely cognitive and strictly tied to an assessment of our beliefs, goals, and motivations in a given context. In short, in acting morally and refraining from hurting others we choose to engage and be driven by these emotions. Most of us have such capacity. Hence, not choosing to engage with these emotions to guide behaviour or to refrain from engaging in wrongful behaviour does not mean lacking the capacity to feel these emotions and be empathetic. It more simply signifies the absence of the motivation to engage with these emotions on a particular occasion, thereby prioritising other goals and considerations.[29]

Indeed, cases (due to psychopathology) can emerge in which the capacity to experience and appropriately regulate such emotions and empathy is substantially compromised to the point that an individual cannot 'feel' the moral wrongness of his or her behaviour. Such incapacity is not merely a typical feature of the controversial category of psychopathy, but it can be symptomatic of other (and perhaps less disputed) conditions such as (untreated) schizophrenia[30] or frontotemporal dementia. In many of such cases, people keep a general capacity to understand the factual and moral significance of their behaviour in a given situation; however, they are incapable of adaptively responding to the relevant emotional aspects of the situations and of their conduct as a consequence. From this perspective, it is not implausible to claim the 'capacity to *understand* right from wrong' and be responsive to normative reasons for actions in social situations is in part rooted not simply in the capacity to care about or to have internalised moral norms enshrined by criminal law, as several authors maintain,[31] but more fundamentally in the capacity to adaptively respond to the emotional relevance of situations.[32]

[29] See my discussion about empathy in ch 4.

[30] eg, Z Kristof, 'Mentalization and Empathy as Predictors of Violence in Schizophrenic Patients: Comparison with Nonviolent Schizophrenic Patients, Violent Controls and Nonviolent Controls' (2018) 268 *Psychiatric Research* 198. For a hypothetical situation linking moral emotional flatness and offending behaviour in a person acting under a psychotic delirium, see H Fingarette, *The Meaning of Legal Insanity* (London, University of California Press, 1972) 188.

[31] See ch 3. See also Ferzan (n 13) 2534 ('Moral agents are not merely prudential risk and reason calculators. They are persons who appreciate what hurting other people means and are generally moved by these considerations. Thus, when someone who can appreciate a moral norm fails to be moved by it, the actor's decision is a culpable one. Hence, while we can describe reasons in mechanical terms, we should not ignore the affective aspect of practical reasoning. Beliefs, goals, and desires do normative work because an agent should be moved to avoid harming others. Part of what makes an agent culpable is that she has the capacity to be moved by moral reasons, but is not so moved. Her culpability has an affective component').

[32] Brink and Nelkin similarly acknowledge that emotions should factor in cognitive competence. However, their discussion qualifies emotions as elements that 'may block normative competence by compromising cognitive capacity', thereby persisting in the assumption that emotions incapacitate cognition. See ibid, 296.

The idea that a person needs to actually empathise enough or feel anticipatory guilt at the prospect of wronging someone else is certainly not required. A general capacity to feel these emotions is sufficient to render the agent normatively rational. Indeed, feeling no empathy for another person on a given occasion is not equivalent to a general incapacity to feel empathy. Thus, unless an agent is able to affectively put himself or herself in another's shoes, to have a sense of what a potential victim will feel as a result of his or her conduct, and is able to emotionally respond to situational cues in an adaptive way, he or she will 'lack' the capacity to grasp and be guided by the reasons for complying with normative expectations.

Regarding the control component of mental competence, Brink and Nelkin's perspective aligns with the body of scholarly views that hold that control capacity is not a proxy for the cognitive capacities of knowledge, reasoning, or understanding. As the authors correctly note, 'rationality conceptions of normative competence need not reject the volitional [ie, control] dimension of normative competence. There may be more to rationality than correct belief or knowledge'.[33]

To reiterate, Brink and Nelkin define control capacity as the ability to regulate one's actions in accordance with normative judgement. Interestingly, the authors deem that this type of control capacity requires 'emotional and appetitive capacities'[34] that allow individuals to conform their actions to judgements. The authors further list conditions such as 'paralyzing fears', 'clinical depression', and 'damage to the prefrontal cortex of the brain',[35] in which agents have considerable difficulty in conforming to their own judgements. Each of these cases certainly involves significant control impairment, as agents experience a substantial difficulty in implementing or conforming to the normative judgements that they form.

This view of the control prong finds support in the body of empirical insights into self-regulation and impulse control that I outlined in chapter four. As explained, the 'capacity for self-control' involves a balanced coordination among a multitude of dissociable cognitive, emotional, and motivational mechanisms and processes. Hence, preserved functioning in one of these processes may still be accompanied by poor functioning in others. Although this scenario does not imply a *total* lack of control, such ability may be compromised to a significant extent. Thus, the notion that a person *totally* lacks the capacity for self-control is empirically impossible. However, it is possible to determine that a person's capacity for self-control can be diminished to a substantial degree, and still be unable to control his or her behaviour and conform it to social standards. Within such processes, emotions play a protective role in that they are largely involved in the evaluation of, information processing, regulation, and appropriate reaction to salient situations. In reality, dysregulation occurs not only when individuals are emotionally hyper-responsive but also when they are emotionally hypo-responsive. The poor processing of

[33] ibid, 298.
[34] ibid, 297.
[35] ibid.

emotion information may entail difficulties with incorporating feedback about a situation as a basis for making adaptive choices and regulating inappropriate impulses accordingly.

The most significant insight for the aims of this discussion is that the capacity for self-control is not necessarily 'parasitic' to a cognitive capacity of knowledge or understanding. As we observed, cases may occur in which individuals retain the knowledge and understanding of the social and moral inappropriateness of their behaviour, yet – by reasons of dysregulation – are unable to apply that knowledge to action. From this perspective, it is plausible to claim that control capacity stands on its own.

B. Situational Control

The other component of Brink and Nelkin's model of culpability is situational control. As mentioned, Brink and Nelkin have proposed using situational control instead of fair opportunity to do otherwise to suggest a more individualising understanding of the situational component of culpability. Although the authors do not provide an explicit definition of situational control, the latter can nevertheless be understood as an individual's ordinary ability to resist situational pressures. When situational pressures are so constraining that individuals find themselves on the whole incapable of choosing differently, then they lack situational control. This interpretation of the situational control component is consistent with Brink and Nelkin's understanding of the rationale of duress. Situational duress excuses conduct in situations in which the threatened harm is substantial, but it is inferior to the harm contained in the wrongdoing. In such instances, the excusing rationale of duress lies with the situational pressure that a person 'could [not] and should [not] be expected to resist',[36] which suggests that the assessment of situational control should not be confined to the objective features of the ongoing situation but should more broadly expand to also consider certain variables inherent to the individual. In the case of duress, the moral balance of evils needs to be assessed by employing agent-centre prerogatives rather than the features of the objective context alone.

Thus, whether the individual can resist situational pressures is a judgement that goes beyond the objective features of the situation, but should also consider other variables inherent to the person.

Such individualised interpretation of the situational component of culpability is indicative of the core aspect of Brink and Nelkin's model, which is the possible interaction between the situational and individual (capacity) components of culpability. Importantly, such interaction depends on context. As this aspect is more crucial for the purposes of the present discussion, I explore it in the next section.

[36] ibid, 303.

C. Situational Control and the Role of Context: *Situating* the Fair Opportunity to do Otherwise

Brink and Nelkin endorse the view (with which I concur) that normative competence and situational control are scalar concepts that can interact with each other. Such interaction is clearly bidirectional and varies across individuals. On the one hand, the amount of situational control that one can be expected to exhibit depends on 'differential normative competence'.[37] As an example, the authors compare resistance to criminogenic peer pressure in adolescents and adults. By virtue of their ongoing development, adolescents purportedly have less independence of judgement and are less capable of resisting peer pressure, that is, their situational control is diminished due to their reduced level of normative competence.[38] By contrast, adults are by definition less susceptible to peer influence because they have developed independence of judgement. In the case of group pressure, we subsequently expect and require from adults a higher level of situational control precisely because their normative competence is presumed to be fully present.

On the other hand, 'how much and what sorts of capacity one needs [to exert situational control] can vary according to situational features'.[39] For instance, situational duress entails an engagement of certain capacities that are not required when a rational individual chooses to commit an offence in a deliberate and unconstrained manner. Even in this case, the interaction between situational pressure and normative competence is not invariant but 'context-dependent'.

What Brink and Nelkin exactly mean by 'context' is admittedly unclear, as they do not provide any explanation of it.[40] However, it is not implausible to think that their idea of 'context' may include both individual and circumstantial variables. If this interpretation is accurate, then the notion of context against which to measure the interaction between normative competence and situational control can also extend to the social context of the individual.

Consider people who live in severely disadvantaged conditions and experience chronic toxic stress and persistent traumatising events. As I discussed in chapter four, the combination of toxic stressors and persistent traumatic experiences, especially when they are combined, may affect the brain and psychological mechanisms involved in self-regulation, judgement, and interpretation and responsiveness to social cues. Stressors and experiences that are systemic and unbuffered can significantly influence a person's appraisal of the nature of the immediate situations and circumstances that he or she experiences in life. Another likelihood is that they can produce some symptoms of chronic post-traumatic stress. Altogether, these factors can have negative repercussions on individuals'

[37] ibid, 305.

[38] See also E Scott et al, 'Brain Development, Social Context and Justice Policy' (2018) 57 *Washington University Journal of Law & Policy* 13.

[39] ibid, 304.

[40] See Brink and Nelkin (n 15) 305.

emotional well-being, and they condition the thinking, feeling, and behavioural styles of people.[41]

More broadly, the adverse psychological impact of chronically adverse socio-environmental circumstances on the individual derives from the choice-limiting effects[42] of such circumstances. In addition, research suggests that these choice-limiting effects, rather than the psychological condition they trigger, precisely constitute objective situational pressures toward illegal conduct. Prima facie, one might argue that people who engage in illegal conduct that links with their social situation have less situational control by virtue of their diminished capacity to conform their behaviour to the requirements of law. On the contrary – and that is the argument I endorse – people who engage in illegal conduct that links with their social situation have diminished situational control because they are subject to constant situational pressures that impact their psychological and emotional well-being, and condition their behaviour accordingly – without necessarily entailing a rationality or control 'defect'.

The latter case presents a situation akin to (however less severe than) situational duress. A person acting under situational duress presumably behaves under strong, however transient or episodic, stress triggered by the fear that something unpleasant might happen if he or she does not engage in illegal conduct. In such cases, the individual remains a rational subject who acts upon a rational assessment of the circumstances. Absent the threat, the individual would not engage in illegal conduct. The same logic applies to an individual who is subject to constant and serious situational pressures, and chooses to engage in illegal conduct to cope with or survive them. A key question consequently arises: Why should transient stress due to an episodic pressure receive practical and normative relevance as opposed to the chronic, inescapable systemic stress faced by people who live in seriously deprived or traumatising conditions?

Ongoing and unbuffered severe deprivations place individuals in circumstances in which they face authentically hard choices. Such conditions of sufficiently hard choices impact the psychological well-being of people to the point that their behaviour can even be conditioned, even if their mental capacity to conform their behaviour to the law is not compromised.[43] Of course, people living in extreme social deprivation *usually* do have options – indeed, many or most of such individuals do live crime-free lives. Nonetheless, many 'persistently encounter moderate to strong temptations to illegal conduct', especially in contexts where there are

[41] See ch 4.

[42] M Bagaric, 'Rich Offender, Poor Offender: Why It (Sometimes) Matters in Sentencing' (2014) 33 *Law & Inequality: A Journal of Theory and Practice* 1, 12.

[43] *cf* RG Wright, 'The Progressive Logic of Criminal Responsibility and the Circumstances of the Most Deprived' (1994) 43 *Catholic University Law Review* 459, 476 n. 49 (1994) ('[i]t may well be … that most severely deprived criminal defendants are capable of practical reason, in the sense of being perfectly sane, or possessing creative, resourceful, resilient or adaptive traits. … [This] should not detract from the various ways in which a person may be deprived of the capacity for responsibility').

'few viable opportunities to legally advance their interests'.[44] Moreover, criminal behaviour may be, in areas where social deprivation is acute, even considered as a legitimate response to people's plight.[45]

What I am suggesting is that people living in emotionally and socially depriving conditions must be viewed as rational actors who make choices. However, they constantly face choices that need to adapt to problematic situations and social environments. Slightly differently stated, people in such cases might be capable of recognising moral reasons for acting, but their responsiveness to those reasons might be disrupted by ongoing situational pressures. We can continue to argue that people living in such conditions who engage in offending behaviour do so out of their choices and practical reasoning skills – which is certainly true – but we would continue to lose sight of the very issue at stake: these practical reasons apply to contexts in which choice is limited.

For instance, individuals who are chronically exposed to violence and receive no social and emotional support to buffer the adverse effects of chronic violence exposure may be afflicted with the constant fear to survive and may develop heightened stress responses and hyperresponsivity to threat. As an example, consider people in their young adulthood who join gangs because their societal realities dictate this association as a viable course of self-protection and survival in the neighbourhood,[46] which eventually leads to criminal activity. In many of such cases, young people joining gangs are themselves victims of repeated domestic abuses and emotional and financial deprivation. Thus, gang joining can be considered as not only a (fear-based) mode of surviving and adapting to problematic neighbourhoods but also a way to gain an (unhealthy) means of self-affirmation and affective acceptance that they may not fully find at home.[47] We are of course tempted to hold that the reasons for such illegal conduct is the person's choice to be a gang member rather than not. Viewed in context, however, the person who becomes a gang member uses his or her rationality skills to adapt and survive a pathological situation. In other words, he or she has reasons for remaining in this unhealthy social environment and a reduced motivation to engage with the law.

Taking all of these matters into account, a vital question emerges: Is it reasonable to expect individuals in such circumstances to refrain from wrongdoing?

[44] R Lippke, 'Diminished Opportunities, Diminished Capacity: Social Deprivation and Punishment' (2003) 29 *Social Theory & Practice* 459, 466. See also R Lippke, *Rethinking Imprisonment* (New York, Oxford University Press, 2017) 184–98.

[45] Lippke 'Diminished Opportunities' (n 44) 465.

[46] ibid.

[47] See ch 4. See also C Haney, 'Evolving Standards of Decency: Advancing the Nature and Logic of Capital Mitigation' (2008) 36 *Hofstra Law Review* 835, 872 (suggesting the term 'criminal embeddedness' to refer to 'the degree to which people living in criminogenic contexts – contexts of the sort that are more likely to be created in poor neighborhoods – are immersed in a network of interpersonal relationships that increase their exposure to crime-prone role models. … Early exposure to harmful risk factors also can lead people to adopt dysfunctional coping mechanisms that prove to be damaging and disruptive later in life-strategies that provide short-term relief from the emotional pain they feel but which have the long-term effect of making their lives worse rather than better').

As I sought to demonstrate, there are valid empirical and normative arguments to respond: 'not entirely'. If a person's opportunities and options have been compromised and limited by his or her exposure to toxic environments and life experiences – all forces he or she did not choose and over which he or she had little or no control – then deprivation, trauma, and other life-altering experiences may gain practical and normative significance in terms of diminished blameworthiness.[48] For this normative reason, in cases where situational control or capacity is limited by situational pressures such as living in extreme deprivation, people have a diminished fair opportunity to do otherwise and therefore should be less culpable when they commit crime.

This consideration brings me to another point of discussion, namely the meaning of *fairness*. Hart and his progeny have based the understanding of fairness on a conception of society as a form of cooperation for mutual advantage among free and equal individuals. Under his account, the word 'fair' is to be taken as signifying equitable rather than just. As he wrote,

> [t]he protection of the law on terms which are fair, [rests] not only [on] a framework of reciprocal rights and duties, but also [on the view that] within this framework each individual is given a fair opportunity to choose between keeping the law required for society's protection or paying the penalty.[49]

As has been observed, Hart's conception of fairness hinges upon 'a conception of society in which people live together sharing the same values and being subject to rules of conduct that work to everyone's advantage'.[50] This conception appears too far off base in the case of individuals who live in depriving and traumatising social conditions. Although even the least advantaged members of society may be said to enjoy some benefits from living under the law, including a certain degree of personal protection, these people cannot be said to enjoy the benefits of social cooperation, which are distributed under the law's protection. From this perspective, the claim that each person in society is given a fair opportunity to choose between 'keeping the law or paying the penalty'[51] is highly questionable.[52] Perhaps

[48] See also Bagaric (n 42) 14 (similarly arguing for the lesser blameworthiness of socially disadvantaged people 'because, relatively speaking, well-off individuals find it easier to comply with the criminal law and have a greater motivation to do so').

[49] HLA Hart, *Punishment and Responsibility: Essays in the Philosophy of Law* (Oxford, Oxford University Press 1968) 22–23.

[50] G Mousourakis, 'Character, Choice, and Criminal Responsibility' (1998) 39 *Le Cahiers Du Droit* 51, 71.

[51] Hart (n 49). Note, however, that Hart acknowledged the problem of deeply disadvantaged people. See ibid, 51 ('[t]he admission that the excusing condition may be of no value to those who are below a minimum level of economic prosperity may mean, of course, that we should incorporate as a further excusing condition the pressure of gross form of economic necessity'). Unfortunately, Hart did not develop this argument further and it is unclear which situations he would have exonerated from criminal responsibility.

[52] See eg J Murphy, *Retribution, Justice and Therapy* (Dordrecht, D. Reidel Pub, 1979) 107 (holding that the fairness/choice theory is built upon a 'gentlemen's club' understanding of justice); see also M Tonry, 'Can Desert be Just in an Unjust World?' in A Simester et al (eds), *Liberal Criminal Theory: Essays for Andreas von Hirsch* (Portland, Hart Publishing, 2014).

a truly fair criminal law should acknowledge the objective inequalities that affect people who live in a determinate set of substandard, depriving, and traumatising circumstances and recognise that these people have objectively fewer opportunities to comply with the law.[53] I further this argument in my discussion about the provision for a 'generic partial excuse'.

IV. Implications for Legal Doctrine

The revised model of culpability that I outlined above may be supportive of a wide range of implications at the doctrinal level. Overall, such a model may allow for a rethinking of single culpability-related doctrines in a way that affords a greater normative relevance to the motivational aspects of offending behaviour, including a deeper inquiry into the context of such motives and of individuals themselves. Such revisions can range from a different valuation of motives within *mens rea* analysis, to a reinterpretation of the nature and rationale of mitigations such as extreme emotional disturbance (EED) and heat of passion, and to a reconsideration of the rationale of duress.

However, space does not allow me to analyse each doctrine in detail.[54] To remain within the salient aspects of my theoretical discussion, I narrow down my analysis to two macro doctrinal implications that might follow through the revised model of culpability proposed above. The first implication concerns an adjustment of legal insanity standards to afford a greater weight to emotional competences within their criteria. The second implication pertains to the provision of a partial excuse that may accommodate situations in which the relevant individual acted under a diminished opportunity to do otherwise. The partial excuse I propose draws upon Stephen Morse's proposed 'generic partial excuse'[55] doctrine and enriches it with considerations that value more broadly the social context of the

[53] See also RA Duff, 'Blame, Moral Standing, and the Legitimacy of Criminal Trial' (2010) 23 *Ratio* 123 (arguing that a state that perpetrates social injustice lacks the *standing* to punish victims of such injustice who commit crimes).

[54] A noteworthy aspect is that the revised model of culpability I propose can provide a theoretical framework for accommodating proposals made by several authors to reconsider the role of emotions in such doctrines, and for affording a greater normative weight to contextual factors within culpability determinations. See eg, S Pillsbury, *Judging Evil: Rethinking the Law of Murder and Manslaughter* (New York, NYU Press, 1998) (reconsidering the role of motives in *mens rea* evaluations in homicide); E Spain, *The Role of Emotions in Criminal Defences: Necessity and Duress* (Cambridge, Cambridge University Press, 2011) (suggesting a reinterpretation of the rationale of duress based on the cognitive appraisal theory of emotions); A Duff, 'Criminal Responsibility and the Emotions: If Anger and Fear Can Exculpate, Why Not Compassion?' (2015) 58 *Inquiry: An Interdisciplinary Journal of Law and Philosophy* 189 (proposing an Aristotelian account of emotions to afford justificatory relevance to emotional motivations); R Griffith Fontaine, *The Mind of the Criminal: The Role of Developmental Social Cognition in Criminal Defense Law* (New York, Cambridge University Press, 2012) (suggesting a reinterpretation of provocation law informed by social-cognitive theory).

[55] SJ Morse, 'Excusing and New Excuse Defenses: A Legal and Conceptual Review' (1998) 23 *Crime and Justice* 323; SJ Morse, 'Diminished Rationality, Diminished Responsibility' (2002) 1 *Ohio State Journal of Criminal Law* 289.

individual. The underlying normative condition of such generic partial excuse, as will be made clear, is that the individual is a substantially rational individual who acts for reasons. However, his or her ongoing contextual circumstances unfairly limit or diminish his or her opportunity to choose to do otherwise.

A. Legal Insanity

A model of legal insanity that is consistent with the model of normative competence suggested above involves three dimensions: a factual dimension, a moral/interpersonal dimension, and a control dimension. The factual dimension, which entails the capacity to comprehend the nature and quality of one's own conduct – that is, the ability 'to respond to [the] physical relevance' of the situation and of the conduct, using Fingarette's words[56] – remains fundamentally cognitive. The moral/interpersonal dimension, which relates to an individual's capacity to appreciate the moral/interpersonal relevance of the situation and of the conduct, involves an integration of purely cognitive and emotional competences. The control dimension, which entails the individual's capacity to regulate one's actions in accordance with his or her normative judgement about the factual and moral relevance of the situation and of his or her conduct, figures as an autonomous prong and necessitates self-regulation competences. In the remainder of this section, I focus my discussion on moral/interpersonal capacity and control capacity and their representation in current insanity standards.

i. Moral Capacity Test

In my discussion about normative competence, I argued that a more comprehensive understanding of the 'cognitive' capacity to recognise and be responsive to normative reasons for actions requires that people are fully able to comprehend the wrongness of violating the rights of others and use such understanding as a reason for refraining. Such full comprehension requires not only that the individual is able to appreciate that his or her conduct violates moral norms but, more profoundly, also ascertains whether the relevant person is able to appreciate the interpersonal relevance of his or her behaviour and to use such as a reason for refraining from wrongdoing. Consequently, people are excusable as long as they demonstrate that they are unable to perceive the wrongness of their actions due to an impaired or substantially compromised capacity to respond to the interpersonal significance of their conduct with respect to the rights of others.

An expanded understanding of 'cognitive capacity' within normative competence supports an expansion of the notion of moral capacity within insanity standards. Under this approach, the moral capacity test entails an assessment of

[56] See Fingarette (n 30) 187.

certain 'emotional' competences of the individuals, which are typically involved in moral judgements and behaviour (eg, their empathy capacities) to evaluate whether the relevant individual was able to perceive, or appreciate, the significance of the criminal act he or she committed.

Such a reinterpretation of the moral capacity test may necessitate several adjustments within the current standards of legal insanity. Turning first to M'Naghten,[57] the moral capacity test it contains requires that a 'defect of reason' arising from 'a disease of [the] mind' must impair the defendant's ability 'to know' that the act was wrong. The two key concepts of the test that are relevant for this discussion are 'reason' and 'know'. In fact, an expansive understanding of moral capacity, as I outlined above, entails a reinterpretation of each of them.

Let us begin with 'reason'. Under an accredited interpretation in the literature, the concept of 'reason' is to be understood as capacity for rationality.[58] The capacity for rationality identifies with the ability to recognise and be responsive to reasons for actions. Traditionally, similar to the notion of reason itself, the capacity for rationality has been ascribed to the cognitive capacities of knowledge, awareness, or abstract reasoning. The preceding discussion has instead suggested that a full comprehension of the moral significance of the conduct requires that people are able to comprehend the wrongness of violating the rights of others and use such comprehension as a reason for refraining insofar as they are also capable of figuring the moral/interpersonal significance of their behaviour, that is, to the extent that they are capable of responding to the relevant emotional-moral aspects of their conduct within a given situation. The latter capacity requires that the individual possesses certain emotion-related capacities (eg, the capacity for empathetically responding to others' concerns). Framed in this manner, the scope of the 'defect-of-reason clause' expands to also encompass the latter capacity to the ability to understand and respond to reasons, while incorporating a broader notion of the capability for moral rationality: one that similarly embraces moral-emotional competences.

A broadening of the notion of 'reason' leads to an expansion of the scope of the verb 'to know' in a way that gives more weight to moral-emotional competences. Indeed, a notion of moral knowledge that is more suited to the understanding of capacity for rationality that I have suggested is compatible with a broader interpretation of knowledge in terms of appreciation. This interpretation aligns with scholarly views that have suggested that the verb 'to know' does not simply refer to a verbal or propositional knowledge that something is wrong, but it pertains to an actual understanding of the normative meaning of the conduct.[59] On the contrary, this interpretation further expands the meaning of knowledge

[57] *R v M'Naghten* [1843] 8 Eng. Rep. 718.

[58] See ch 1.

[59] R Bonnie et al, *A Case Study in the Insanity Defense: The Trial of John Hinckley, Jr.*, 3rd edn (New York, Foundation Press, 2008) 12; see also A Goldstein, *The Insanity Defense* (London, Yale University Press 1967) 49–50.

(i.e., understanding) to also include a capacity to be responsive to the interpersonal relevance of the conduct under the circumstances.

As mentioned, the M'Naghten test primarily includes a factual test (ie, a test measuring a person's capacity to know the material circumstances of the conduct). This test, which is by definition a separate test from the moral capacity test, asks whether the individual was able to know or understand the physical aspects of the situation and of his or her behaviour, including its material consequences. In contrast to the moral capacity test, the factual test simply requires an assessment of the individual's cognitive competences.[60] Thus, perhaps a more precise formulation of the test that retains both prongs could keep the verb 'to know' (to be possibly interpreted as actual understanding, rather than an abstract awareness) in the factual test, and use the verb 'to appreciate' in the moral test. The test would thereby keep the current formulation regarding the factual test and reconsider its provision for the moral capacity test in more encompassing terms such as the capacity to appreciate that the act was wrong. Another (perhaps simpler) option could be that of replacing altogether the verb 'to know' with the verb 'to appreciate'. Hence, a revised formulation of the M'Naghten rule that is in line with the arguments made above could read as:

> To establish a defense on the grounds of insanity, it must be clearly proved that, at the time of the committing of the act, the party accused was laboring under such a defect of reason, from disease of [the] mind, as not to know the nature and quality of the act he or she was doing, or, if he or she did know it, that he or she did not *appreciate* he or she was doing what was wrong.

or:

> To establish a defense on the grounds of insanity, it must be clearly proved that, at the time of the committing of the act, the party accused was laboring under such a defect of reason, from disease of [the] mind, as not to *appreciate* the nature and quality of the act he or she was doing, or, if he or she did *appreciate* it, that he or she did not *appreciate* he was doing what was wrong.

Regarding the American Law Institute (ALI) test, the current formulation seems to be more consistent with such an expanded understanding of moral competence. The verb 'to appreciate' is broad enough to accommodate the expanded understanding of moral capacity that I suggested above. Similar to what I have posited regarding the M'Naghten rule, such test requires an assessment of a person's capacity to appreciate the wrongfulness of his or her conduct in terms of an appreciation of both the material circumstances of the conduct and of the moral significance of conduct, including the emotional/interpersonal aspects of it. Accordingly, the wording of the MPC appreciation test remains unaltered, but its meaning also encompasses relevant emotional competences.

[60] See also C Korponay and M Koenigs, 'The Neurobiology of Antisocial and Amoral Behavior' in S Moratti and D Patterson (eds), *Legal Insanity and the Brain* (Oxford, Hart Publishing, 2016) 10, 31.

Admittedly, an expanded interpretation of the 'appreciation prong' in the first paragraph of the ALI test to also include moral-emotional responsiveness appears to challenge, prima facie, the caveat paragraph contained in Section 4.01(2). As noted in chapter one, the paragraph was included to explicitly exclude from the range of legal insanity cases the classes of individuals who manifest repeated antisocial conduct due to alleged pathological predispositions to do so, including individuals with sociopathy and psychopathy. Indeed, this aim of the caveat paragraph has been a factor that pushed for an understanding of the appreciation prong of the test in purely 'cognitive' terms – in partial contrast to the initial intentions of the drafters.[61]

Under the approach I propose, the caveat paragraph would not have to be eliminated and instead should continue serving its deterrent function. Admittedly, neither all the 'repeated manifestations of criminal or otherwise antisocial conduct' are symptomatic of pathological emotional deficits,[62] nor do emotional deficits necessarily engender antisocial behaviour. For emotional deficits to potentially exculpate defendants, the fact that they are sufficiently severely pathological to have seriously compromised an individual's capacity for moral judgement at the time of the crime must be convincingly proven. Ultimately, the jury would be responsible for assessing the seriousness and the normative relevance of emotional dysfunctions under the normative standard within the domain of insanity pleas. This type of assessment is not new compared to what is regularly conducted in insanity evaluations.

ii. Control Capacity Test

The model of culpability advanced above is compatible with the provision of an autonomous control prong in legal insanity standards. As discussed in chapter one, the control prong in insanity tests plays a secondary role in comparison to the cognitive prong. The M'Naghten test does not include a control test at all, thereby entirely placing the burden of insanity on the cognitive and moral capacity tests. On the contrary, the Model Penal Code (MPC) standard does require that agents are capable of controlling their behaviour and conforming it to the law.[63] However, the notion of 'conforming behaviour to the law' is poorly defined and can potentially encompass a wide range of cases with control problems; indeed, the control prong of the MPC test is highly contested. Altogether, the autonomy of the control prong proves to be mostly theoretical and poorly applied.

In the model of culpability that I proposed above, control capacity is defined as the capacity to conform one's behaviour to one's normative judgement.

[61] See ch 1.

[62] See also *Wade v United States*, 426 F.2d 64, 72–73 (9th Cir. 1970) (pointing out that '[i]t is practically inconceivable that mental disease or defect would … be manifested *only* by repeated criminal or otherwise antisocial conduct').

[63] American Law Institute, Model Penal Code § 4.01 (1962).

This definition aligns with the empirical explanations about self-regulation and impulse inhibition I provided in chapter four. As I explained, such capacities rely upon a multitude of intertwined cognitive, emotional, and motivational processes, each of which contributes to an individual's self-regulating abilities. Furthermore, the processes involved in control capacity may be irrespective of an individual's normative judgement that something is either right or wrong. Indeed, people who are seriously dysregulated due to a pathological condition may have poor abilities to control their impulses, even when they are able to grasp the social and moral appropriateness of their actions.

Accepting that control capacity can figure as an autonomous capacity that relies upon its own processes and is not necessarily dependent on an individual's knowledge or appreciation faculties of one's conduct, supports insanity standards that also provide for a separate control test. Admittedly, it can further clarify their language and make it sound more specific to the juries. Let us consider the MPC test. The MPC control test can certainly accommodate the proposed understanding of control capacity; however, the language of its formulation should be reconsidered. As it reads now, the test defines control capacity as a capacity to conform behaviour to the law. This formulation is certainly too broad, as it potentially encompasses a wide range of conditions in which an individual had substantial difficulties in conforming his or her behaviour to normative requirements due to a mental disease. Moreover, even a substantial impairment to the capacity to appreciate the wrongfulness of one's behaviour renders an individual unable to conform his or her behaviour to the law – with the result that both prongs of the test revolve around the same criterion. The language used for defining the control test therefore requires a more specific definition.

A definition of control capacity as a capacity to conform behaviour to one's normative judgement in the sense explained above would maintain the broader understanding of control incapacity than merely an incapacity to control irresistible impulses,[64] and would bind the meaning of control to a more transparent and specific definition. Thus, I suggest that the MPC standard can be reformulated as follows:

> A person is not responsible for criminal conduct if at the time of such conduct, as a result of a mental disease or disorder, he or she was *unable to conform his or her behavior to the requirements of law due to* a substantial incapacity to appreciate the criminality [wrongfulness] of his or her conduct or *to conform his or her behavior to such appreciation.*

As is clear, the reformulation of the standard positions the inability to conform one's behaviour to the law (due to a pathological condition) as its core normative requirement. It then clarifies that such inability must emanate either from a substantial incapacity to appreciate the wrongfulness of the behaviour (to be possibly interpreted under the meaning expressed above) or from a substantial capacity

[64] See also Brink and Nelkin (n 15) 299–302 (criticising the excessive narrowness of approaching control incapacity as simply a matter of 'irresistible impulses or uncontrollable urges').

to conform behaviour to such appreciation. This reformulation of the standard does not alter the test's original formulation in any significant manner. However, it frames the standard through a more logical and a more coherent scheme and makes its language more specific, thereby overcoming the conceptual imprecisions that the current text contains and leaving less space for interpretive uncertainty.

Granted, the amount of control capacity that needs to be compromised to meet the normative criteria is an entirely normative assessment, which falls beyond the scope of empirical sciences. The empirical sciences lend support to the plausibility of viewing control capacity as not necessarily parasitic on an individual's knowledge or appreciation of his or her conduct. However, the law, through courts, ultimately determines whether an individual is capable of conforming his or her behaviour to its requirements.

B. Diminished Opportunity, Diminished Culpability: A Re-interpretation of Stephen Morse's Proposed 'Generic Partial Excuse' Doctrine

In the preceding theoretical discussion, I emphasised that criminal culpability – including its normative competence and situational control components – should be understood as a multivalent concept that admits degrees. Sharing Brink and Nelkin's view, I underscored the need for more nuanced forms of culpability assessment, ones in which the individual meets the minimum thresholds to be held accountable for his or her behaviour but deserves some forms of mitigation.

The theoretical support for the provision of more nuanced forms of responsibility does not fully reflect on the doctrinal level, as the provisions for partial excuses are quite limited in the current substantive criminal law. The only type of 'partial excuse' currently existing includes the heat of passion and the MPC's extreme mental and emotional disturbance (EMED) to reduce a homicide that would otherwise be murder to manslaughter.[65] Mitigations that apply to all the crimes are only considered to determine punishment at the sentencing stage of criminal proceedings, indicating that they are not subjected to a normative assessment of criminal responsibility by the jury, but their concession largely falls within the discretion of the judge.

In a paper published in 1998 (and in following works),[66] Stephen Morse famously proposed the introduction of a 'generic partial excuse' (GPR) as a new doctrine aimed at partially excusing individuals who acted under mild to moderate forms of mental illness or in conditions posing sufficiently hard choices, or a hybrid of the two. Morse acknowledges that contrary to the 'all-or-nothing doctrines' adopted by the current criminal law, capacities for rationality and

[65] See ch 1.

[66] See generally Morse (n 55).

control, and hard choices are continuum concepts.[67] In view of the fact that people 'display an enormously wide range of rational and control capacities',[68] and they are confronted with various degrees of hard choices,[69] a truly fair judgement of culpability must consider the types of impairments or situational constraints that affect an individual's capacity for rationality and control, as well as choice to some significant degree, even if they do not entirely compromise them.[70]

Contra his previous scholarship,[71] Morse maintains that these situations deserve normative consideration and potentially support a responsibility mitigation. Furthermore, considerations of conditions that limit responsibility should apply to all types of crime. As Morse contends, limiting responsibility mitigation to homicide alone is pointless, considering that any crime can be committed by a person whose rational and control capacity, and choices, are to some degree impaired.[72] With this point in mind, Morse proposes the adoption of an additional verdict, namely the GPR verdict. He frames GPR as a new general partial affirmative defence that warrants lesser culpability and punishment.[73] Moreover, GPR should apply in all cases of less severe rationality and control defects, as well as less severe hard choices, regardless of the crime committed.[74]

Morse advances compelling normative reasons (with which I concur) for which the current criminal law should include a generic partial excuse. First, the capacity for rationality, the capacity for control, and hard choice are all continuum concepts. Second, the lack of a partial excuse has triggered the rise of a wide variety of 'syndrome defences'.[75] Such syndrome defences do not fall within the strict parameters of excuses (indeed, they are barely successful), although they are ultimately rooted in rationality defects. The third argument lies with the retributivist goal of justice and the need for proportionate punishment. If punishment is to be proportional to wrongdoing – as retribution requires – a partial excuse

[67] Morse 'Diminished Rationality' (n 55) 296.

[68] ibid.

[69] ibid.

[70] ibid, 302 ('Perhaps the law should adopt a generic mitigation that would consider degrees of rationality and responsibility diminution').

[71] eg SJ Morse, 'Undiminished Confusion in Diminished Capacity' (1984) 75 *Journal of Criminal Law and Criminology* 1, 28–36.

[72] Morse, 'Diminished Rationality' (n 55) 296 ('Compromised rationality and its effect on culpability are not limited to homicide. Fairness and proportionality require that doctrinal mitigation should be available in all cases in which culpability is substantially reduced').

[73] ibid, 299–304.

[74] ibid, 295–8 ('I claim that the best interpretation of our moral and criminal law excusing practices is that there are only two basic excusing conditions: diminished rationality and 'hard choice.' … [T]here is a limited need for an excuse based on an impaired capacity for self-control. The capacity for rationality, the "hardness" of choice, and the capacity for control are all continuum concepts. Nonetheless, with precious few exceptions, present criminal law contains doctrinal all-or-nothing, bright line tests. … Present law is unfair because it does not sufficiently permit mitigating claims. … The solution to all these problems of potential doctrinal deformation is a generic mitigating excuse').

[75] See Morse, 'Excusing and New Excuse Defenses' (n 55) 363 (listing battered woman syndrome, Vietnam syndrome, child sexual abuse syndrome, Holocaust survivor syndrome, urban survival syndrome, rotten social background, adopted child syndrome, and road rage syndrome).

is subsequently warranted in all those cases in which an individual does not fully meet strict responsibility standards due to diminished rationality. Fourth, partial responsibility is a normative judgement, and normative judgements are properly a function of community representatives (the jury) before conviction, not the sentencing judge after conviction. Fifth, a partial responsibility verdict would imply a fixed reduction in sentence in inverse proportion[76] to the seriousness of the crime committed, thereby avoiding the vagaries of judicial judgment on punishment. Under the current law, judges need not reduce sentences for diminished responsibility: the decision is discretionary.

Although Morse's initial proposal for a GPR seemed to include cases involving either diminished mental capacity or sufficiently hard choice,[77] his subsequent works on GPR only considered the hypothetical provision of this defence in cases involving diminished mental capacity, and notably mild to moderate forms of mental illness that are not eligible for an insanity defence. Morse eventually left unexplored the discussion about the provision of GPR in cases involving situational hard choices.

Morse frames the range of cases in which the GPR applies as cases in which a person non-culpably suffers from 'substantially diminished rationality … and which substantially affected the defendant's criminal conduct'.[78] As this passage suggests, Morse remains intentionally vague about the types of mental impairments that may meet the requirements of the generic partial excuse he proposes.[79] He concedes that the defendant's rationality may be substantially impaired by a wide variety of factors, including stress, fatigue and mental disorder not supporting existing excuses.[80] Thus, he correctly separates questions of responsibility from arbitrary categorisations of conduct and focuses the inquiry on the essential normative issue at stake – substantially diminished rationality – regardless of whether the origin of such issue is medical, situational, or a combination of the two.[81]

Although Morse's proposal recalls a form of partial insanity (a typical doctrine in European legal systems), he suggests a potential GPR formula that adopts the language of the MPC's EMED.[82] As he claims, the language of the EMED is

[76] Morse, 'Diminished Rationality' (n 55) 401 ('I propose an inverse sliding scale between the seriousness of the crime and the amount of the reduction: The fixed reduction would be smaller for more serious crimes and vice versa').

[77] See Morse, 'Excusing and New Excuses' (n 55) 397.

[78] ibid, 300.

[79] ibid, 301 ('I would trust legislative judgment or the common law process to identify which rationality-diminishing factors would be justified').

[80] ibid, 294.

[81] See Morse, 'Diminished Rationality' (n 55) 301.

[82] Morse, 'Excusing and New Excuse Defenses' (n 55) 400 ('Any formula that expressed the central excusing notion would work. I rather like the Model Penal Code's formula: 'extreme mental or emotional disturbance for which there is reasonable explanation or excuse') See also Morse, 'Diminished Rationality' (n 55) 295 ('Provocation/passion and extreme mental or emotional disturbance as partially excusing mitigating doctrines are best explained by the theory that these conditions non-culpably reduce the capacity for rationality').

appropriate, as it 'addresses the underlying, normative excusing condition, uses common sense terms, and is not tied to any limiting model of why a defendant suffered from the requisite disturbance'.[83] A defendant could consequently use 'any relevant evidence that might satisfy the underlying reasons for excusing',[84] namely that he or she was less capable of rationality. Hence, GPR assessments would not be bound to rigid categories, but they would consist of normative and case-by-case inquiries that consider all relevant circumstances.

As an articulation of Morse's proposed doctrine (which is undeniably quite unusual for the voluntarist/retributivist panorama), Elizabeth Lambert has recently presented an argument applying the GPR to cases involving people living in severe poverty.[85] With the aim of affording normative relevance to poverty without relying upon stigmatising ad hoc defences[86] that are based on normatively flawed premises,[87] Lambert has suggested that poverty can fit in GPR as a situational factor that can diminish the rationality of the individual.

Lambert uses Mullainathan and Sharif's theory of scarcity, which accounts for scarcity as the subjective experience of 'having less than you feel you need',[88] and suggests a relationship between poverty, cognitive overload, and diminished executive function. Hence, Lambert advances the idea that scarcity creates a situational link between poverty and cognition. She also argues that the cognitive overload caused by the struggles and limitations of people living in severe economic disadvantage may acquire normative excusing relevance insofar as it affects cognitive bandwidth, meaning that it reduces both rational thinking and executive control.

According to Lambert, scarcity theory provides a viable means of establishing a connection between severe financial need and impaired normative capacity. Hence, evidence of diminished rationality and executive function may allow some defendants to adduce evidence of deprivation to demonstrate that their criminal acts were committed under an excusing condition. Lambert ultimately grounds the excusing force of poverty in the relevant person's defective rationality rather than the circumstances surrounding the offending act per se.[89]

Beyond its consistency with Morse's scholarship, Lambert's proposal is implicitly consistent with Brink and Nelkin's view that normative competence and

[83] Morse, 'Excusing and New Excuse Defenses' ibid.

[84] ibid, 390.

[85] E Winston Lambert, 'A Way Out of the Rotten Social Background Stalemate: 'Scarcity' and Stephen Morse's Proposed Generic Partial Excuse' (2018) 21 *University of Pennsylvania Journal of Law and Social Change* 297.

[86] ibid, 317 ('the fact that GPR would not be limited to poor people might be seen as both a weakness and a strength: it is a weakness in that it does not single out economic deprivation as a uniquely significant factor in the moral calculus of guilt; it is a strength in that it does not stigmatize the poor as morally 'different' from other human actors').

[87] ibid, 302–08 (discussing and criticising the various proposals to account for poverty and social deprivation as ad hoc defences).

[88] Lambert (n 85) 318 (citation omitted).

[89] Note, however, that Lambert is attentive to the situational component of poverty. Notwithstanding, she argues that poverty can lead to partially excusing behaviour as long as (and because) it impairs normative capacity.

situational control should more accurately be viewed as often interacting concepts, and that the assessment of such interaction varies across individuals based on context. Notably, Lambert's argument seems to endorse the view that situational factors such as poverty should be excusing because and insofar as they provoke a rationality defect in the individual.

Although I find Lambert's argumentations solid and coherent, I hold that chronic, hard, and distressful social situations such as poverty can also ground GPR *quo* conditions that give an individual a sufficiently hard choice to comply with the law. Notably, such situations can gain practical and normative relevance as situational pressures, which can severely diminish an individual's situational control and leave him or her with an altogether reduced opportunity to behave otherwise.

This 'situational prong' of the generic partial excuse combines the logic of duress with that of the EED and embraces all cases in which an individual engages in a given offence as a result of his or her substantial emotional and psychological distress for which there is a reasonable explanation or excuse, all of which substantially limited his or her choice to comply with the law. The focus of the judgement is not strictly the defendant's mind but the adverse contextual factors and their impact on the defendant's mind and behaviour. Consistent with Morse's proposal[90] to frame the GPR excuse by adopting the MPC's EED language, the situational prong of the GPR can be positivised through the following formula:

> The jury may find the defendant GPR if, at the time of the crime, the defendant acted under a non-culpable state of substantial psychological distress for which there is a reasonable explanation or excuse.

Cases that could fall under such situational prong of the generic partial excuse involve all types of situations in which a person acts under situational pressures that provoke a sufficiently serious level of mental distress, thereby prompting him or her to face an adequately hard choice to do otherwise. Amongst others, such situational pressures may include social and material adversity. By social adversity, I mean acute or chronic exposures to adverse social experiences which hypothetically impact on psychological well-being mainly by directly threatening salient relationships (eg, social isolation, exposure to threat or violence). By material adversity, I mean exposure to unfavourable circumstances mainly related to the immediate physical environment or the financial situation (eg, financial strain). Note, once again, that in such cases the normative partially excusing condition does not lie in a defect of the person's mental capacity, but rather in the fact that the person acts under substantial psychological distress within a context in which his or her choices are non-culpably constrained.

[90] *cf* Morse, 'Diminished Rationality' (n 55) 300 (suggesting the following GPR formula: 'The jury may find the defendant GPR if, at the time of the crime, the defendant suffered from substantially diminished rationality for which the defendant was not responsible and which substantially affected the defendant's criminal conduct').

A topical example includes abused women (either physically or psychologically) who commit petty crimes to escape an abusive environment (eg, stealing a car to escape from an abusive relationship, committing welfare or cheque fraud, or going along with their partner's fraudulent activities because of economic needs). As Angela Moe explains,[91] interpersonal domestic violence creates a context that shapes a woman's choice, or a substantial lack thereof, to engage in crime. Such context seems to be an important situational factor precipitating criminality for women, especially when help-seeking resources are unavailable, inaccessible, or unhelpful. In such situations, engaging in illegal activity seems reasonable, or rational, to survive and resist victimisation.

A person who is abused (physically, psychologically, or financially, or a combination of these forms of abuse) is a rational actor whose choices are made in a pathological situation.[92] We can certainly agree that the condition of abuse can have enduring psychological effects on the person.[93] However, this is far from saying that these effects lead the person to 'lose' his or her capacity for rationality. Most people living in abusive relationships do not suffer from any substantial impairment in mental capacity. Their perception of limited options is not delusional, as they can appreciate the significance of their conduct and retain sufficient self-control. Even the absence of a pathology does not diminish the gravity of the situation in which they live. The real issue in this case is that their control over the situation is diminished to the point that they have objectively limited choices.[94]

The motives that induce people living in abusive relationships not to leave such relationships are well documented in the literature. Such motives prompt abused people to rationally assess and decide to remain in the abusive relationship. Nonetheless, a person's presence in such a relationship does not mean that the person intends to stay. Many people stay because they reasonably fear that leaving would place them in greater danger. Many people repeatedly attempt to leave their batterers only 'to be hunted down and dragged back to heightened abuse and threats that the next escape attempt will be fatal … These [people] have good reasons to fear leaving'[95] and will not leave. They also frequently seek institutional help to no avail. In other cases, the reasons for staying may embrace

[91] See A Moe, 'Blurring the Boundaries: Women's Criminality in the Context of Abuse' (2004) 3 *Women's Study Quarterly* 116 (reporting and analysing incarcerated women's narratives of their crime involvement as a result of abusive situations).

[92] For a solid argument for viewing battered survivors as rational actors – rather than people suffering from a pathology – see AS Burke, 'Rational Actors, Self-Defense, and Duress: Making Sense, Not Syndromes, Out of the Battered Woman' (2002) 81 *North Carolina Law Review* 211.

[93] See ch 4. See also, eg, T Link and C Oser, 'The Role of Stressful Life Events and Cultural Factors on Criminal Thinking among African American Women Involved in the Criminal Justice System' (2018) 45 *Criminal Justice and Behavior* 8.

[94] See Moe (n 91) 135 ('The women who committed … crimes in the context of abuse perceive few, if any, alternative options. They were victims of heinous assaults they did not deserve. They became "criminals" for becoming active agents in their lives. They made decisions based on the limited set of options they perceived to be available at a given time, options we as a society placed before them').

[95] Burke (n 92) 268.

sustained financial worries.[96] In such instances, a person is not cognitively incapable of either knowing or appreciating that escape options are available; rather, the person either 'lack[s] … viable escape options'[97] or recognises that escape options exist but makes a rational decision not to escape based on an assessment of the circumstances.[98] Thus, the facts contributing to a belief by battered people that they cannot control the violence, stop it, or successfully flee are not products of delusional thinking or a defective appreciation of the situation. They are rational persons, living in pathological circumstances, who respond to a survival situation as many reasonable individuals in those circumstances would.

Affording normative relevance to adverse situational factors neither signifies that such factors (eg, being socially deprived or being victims of violence) cause someone to commit a crime, nor that acting under such conditions alone is sufficient to partially excuse. In the same manner as not all people with schizophrenia commit crimes, nor is schizophrenia alone a sufficient ground for a successful insanity defence. An absolute one-to-one link in either case is lacking. Similar to people with schizophrenia, individuals who purportedly act under the pressure of severely problematic situations need to meet normative excusing criteria. Indeed, this generic partial excuse cannot apply to cases where the link between the situation, the crime, and the normative excusing condition is objectively inexistent, such as sex crimes committed by people living in socially deprived conditions.[99]

Consistent with the propositions of Morse and Lambert, the normative evaluation of this partial excuse is to be conducted case-by-case, and on the basis of an assessment of the factual circumstances and the impact that such circumstances have had on the individual's choice and behaviour. The combination of these factors must convincingly demonstrate that the individual had a substantially reduced situational control to behave differently than he or she did. Ultimately, this defence inquiries into a defendant's reason for acting as he or she did, as well as into whether the reason was appropriately arrived at under the circumstances.

Both lines of inquiry require that the preponderance of evidence of convincing quality confirms that a direct link exists between a given situation, the person's state of mind (including his or her beliefs and motivations, or his or her psychological condition), an objectively diminished control over the situation, and the offence committed. First, the defendant would need to prove the existence of the factual condition or circumstance (eg, chronic exposure to violence, ongoing abuse, extreme poverty, or a combination of these situations when they are present) that will serve as the objective foundation for his or her claim of severe distress. This objective threshold of severe distress might be met in any number of ways, either documental and testimonial.

[96] ibid, 271.

[97] ibid, 268.

[98] ibid, 296.

[99] *cf* Bagaric (n 42) (suggesting that the evidence of child abuse at sentencing can have a mitigating effect except in cases involving violent and sex offences).

Subjectively, defendants would be asked to provide evidence linking the factual circumstances to their distressed state of mind due to the situation, as well as the motivating force of such distressed state of mind about the situation to prompt him or her to engage in illegal activity. Expert witnesses can provide a testimony about the reality of the person's state and motivations. They can even provide evidence about the person's psychological condition due to the situation of distress, and additionally educate the jury about the impact of severe and chronic stress on the brain, psychology, and behaviour of individuals under the relevant circumstances at stake (eg, educate about the neurobiological and psychological and behavioural impacts of prolonged exposure to traumatic stress due to victimisation). Consistent with the spirit of the EMED defence, the jury's determination of the defendant's conduct must be made initially by determining the situation in which the defendant found himself or herself, including the circumstances as he or she believed them to be at the time. Then, the jury should determine whether, from the viewpoint of a person in that situation, the condition of psychological distress, and the defendant's response to it, provides a reasonable ground to excuse the defendant's behaviour under the circumstances. Altogether, the jury would be asked to weight the defendant's motivation to engage in wrongdoing considering the context of his or her behaviour.

Knowledge of the defendant's ongoing situation (and, possibly, his or her history) would help the jury to view the defendant's behaviour in context. That is, it would allow the jury to contextualise the state of mind of the person at the time he or she committed the crime to assess the reasonableness of his or her behaviour. The presentation of such a narrative would directly speak to the claim that persons whose actions derive in part from their situations or to a whole host of other powerful forces and factors that can shape choice and behaviour, and over which they have diminished control, may be less culpable as a result. As Lambert correctly observes, one reason to favour an expanded version of 'the EMED formulation, especially in light of its subjective qualification of the reasonableness standard, [is that] it invites the defendant to engage in the kind of narrative that inspires empathy'.[100] In other words, through such narrative, jurors are required to empathise with the defendant's story and attempt to put themselves in his or her 'mental shoes' (ie, the situation in which the defendant found himself or herself when he or she committed the offence).

The provision of a situational generic partial excuse is a powerful means of bringing situational factors into the discourse of culpability. First, it makes the criminal law more responsive to the circumstances of the many people who live in substandard conditions that they neither caused nor deserve. Second, such provision shifts the crime narrative by re-directing the attention of fact-finders from the individual to the circumstances of the individual. Third, the provision addresses more fairly the criminal acts of many people who suffer the situational pressures

[100] Lambert (n 85) 326.

of hard social conditions, without the need of pathologising them to excuse them. One may be tempted to think that there is always a way out and such people can always choose to do otherwise; nonetheless, the unfortunate reality is that these situations are more complicated than one might think. I believe that the criminal law should be more sensitive to these situations, which are the most numerous, the most invisible, and the most unfairly treated.

V. Holistic and Situated Culpability, and the Personal Guilt Principle

Before I conclude this discussion, I raise a crucial normative question that is worth exploring: What is the normative justification that may support a notion of culpability, which is grounded in a holistic and situated view of the individual? In other words, why should criminal law doctrines expand to also afford normative relevance to an individual's emotional capacities or his or her social context?

In chapter one, I stated that culpability finds its ultimate normative rationale in the principle of personal guilt and provided two main interpretations of the predicate 'personal'. According to the first interpretation, a guilt finding requires that the individual be the material author of the relevant offence. In the second one, a guilt finding requires a psychological relation between the act and the actor, and such relation is described in terms of the belongingness of the act to the mind of the individual. This understanding of personal guilt as mental belongingness entails that the individual's mental state is expressive of his or her choice to engage in offending behaviour. More broadly, a criminal act can be said to 'belong' to the mind of the individual when he or she acts under 'ideal decision-making conditions'.[101] The ideality of the individual's decision-making conditions allows us to assess the quality of his or her deliberation and make the normative judgement that his or her behaviour manifested insufficient concern or disregard for the interests of others.

Dominant views (and the law itself) identify this ideality in the fact that the individual acts upon his or her practical reasoning skills, supported by his or her capacity to know or understand the significance of his or her conduct with respect to the normative parameters of right and wrong, and acts free of coercion. Nonetheless, gaining knowledge about the fundamental role that emotions and contextual factors play in (moral) decision-making invites us to shift the parameters of 'ideality' to also embrace these factors. First, it summons us to view practical reasoning not only in mechanical terms but also in terms of its affective aspect.[102] Moral agents are not merely prudential risk and reason calculators. These persons appreciate what hurting others means, and they are generally motivated by these

[101] See Ferzan (n 13) 2534.
[102] See also ibid.

considerations. Second, gaining the aforementioned knowledge induces us to view such conditions in context. From this perspective, decision-making conditions are likewise 'ideal' when they occur absent the contextual factors that limit an individual's choice to a significant extent and disrupt his or her responsiveness to moral reasons to abide by the law. This condition emerges not only when a person acts free of coercion (ie, when he or she must either break the law or endure dreadful consequences) but also, more broadly, when a person acts free of persistent pressures and hardships that unfairly limit his or her choices to comply with the law to a relevant extent. Such pressures and hardships are not comparable, quantitatively speaking, to the ones inflicted on an individual who breaks the law in conditions of extreme threat. However, the psychological toll they can impose upon an individual can be sufficiently severe – albeit not fatal – to suggest that he or she is confronted with a sufficiently hard choice and has an altogether diminished opportunity to behave otherwise.

If the personal guilt principle mandates that blame is fairly assigned insofar as an individual acts under ideal decision-making conditions (ie, indicative of the actor's lack of concern for the interests of others), then a notion of culpability that is better suited to this principle should be predicated on a more comprehensive and contextualised view of human actions – one that affords a normative relevance to *all* the significant individual and contextual aspects of an individual's decision-making and practical reasoning, which lead him or her to reasons to break the law under the circumstances. In other words, a notion of culpability that is more consistent with the idea that guilt must be personal should expand its inquiry to a more thorough consideration for the *quality* of the reasons that have led an individual to break the law, and lends itself to a broader evaluation of a person's actual opportunity to do otherwise under the circumstances. If generalised or abstract legal assumptions about human nature persist in providing the moral justification for attributing blame (and imposing a sanction as a consequence), then this attribution is not only misguided but also inconsistent with a foundational principle of the law.

This interpretation of the personal guilt principle I am proposing appears to suit scholarly views arguing for a more comprehensive and reality-based understanding of crime in contrast to a purely abstract conception as a discrete species of public wrong that is perpetrated against the law of the state. At least three competing conceptions suggest viewing crime through a more encompassing perspective. The first conception calls for viewing crime as a moral type of action, that is, it is an 'action[s] that follows or breaks moral rules, and is guided by what is right and what is wrong to do'.[103] As such, crimes are complex types of actions that involve a combination of a certain environment, or setting, and the individual's moral perceptions, that is, 'the identification of action alternatives and their moral

[103] See PH Wilkström and K Treiber, 'The Role of Self-control in Crime Causation' (2007) 4 *European Journal of Criminology* 237, 246.

qualities in response to particular motivations in a particular setting'.[104] Under this conception, crimes are framed not only in terms of reasons but also in terms of the relationship between reasons and exogenous (environmental) factors that lead the individual to perceive crime as a valid behavioural alternative to adapt to a certain setting.

The second conception[105] suggests a view of crime as a social phenomenon or a specific type of social behaviour. Considering its ineradicable social nature, crime does not emerge as an opportunity to achieve personal gain or as an impulsive reaction to an external stimulus. More accurately, crime (even when it is impulsive) arises from a 'complex set of mental operations by which one's social environment and ways through which to navigate it are evaluated'.[106] Thus, a more accurate assessment of crime requires a more thorough consideration for the individual and social dynamics.

The final conception views crime as a negative interpersonal interaction or a 'violation of people and [social] relationships'.[107] Under this relational understanding of crime, crime is a complex and multifaceted phenomenon that includes various dimensions of harm: to the victim, to interpersonal relationships, to the perpetrator, and to the community. Considering this multifaceted nature of crime, which also embraces the dimension of harm to the perpetrator, this perspective suggests a more comprehensive assessment of responsibility – one that affords a greater value to the motives that moved a person to disrupt social relationships, and recognises the role of social context in individual choice without denying personal responsibility.

An understanding of culpability that hinges upon a rationalist and individualist view of the human mind appears inadequate to grasp each of these alternative interpretations of crime, as it reflects a partial comprehension of the relevant conditions that contribute to an individual's decision to do wrong. Human behaviour is the result of a dynamic interaction between individual and contextual factors, all of which must receive consideration in assessing an individual's conduct to act in breach with social and legal values. Accordingly, a notion of culpability that is based on a defensible view of humans entails the assignment of more prominence to the individual and social dynamics that actually and critically contribute to adaptive social behaviour in morally relevant contexts. If criminal law is meant to treat individuals as rational and autonomous agents who choose to either act or not to act in compliance with the law's prescriptions, such law should take account more deeply of all such relevant factors that contribute to an individual's behavioural choices.

The issue of whether we should favour an expanded understanding of the personal guilt principle certainly depends on how we think of criminal law. We can think of criminal law as rule plus sanction, as an expression of state power, which imposes a duty of knowledge upon its subjects and requires them to conform their

[104] ibid.
[105] Griffith Fontaine (n 54) 259–60.
[106] ibid.
[107] H Zehr, *Changing Lenses: Restorative Justice for Our Times*, 25th Anniversary ed (Harrisonbourg, Herald Press, 2015) 184–8.

behaviour to its requirements. Under this conception, people must only be capable of understanding the criminal law as constituting a set of constraints according to which their conduct will be scrutinised by legal authorities. In other words, it is a conception that is consistent with individuals having only an external perspective of the law. If we maintain this conception of criminal law, then the fact that individuals must exhibit any particular emotional feature or act free of hardships and pressures is admittedly irrelevant to legal inquiry. Alternatively, as I and other scholars do, we can think of criminal law more broadly as a rule 'whose basic thrust acquires its force and meaning by virtue of expressing, however imperfectly, [the] essential aspects of collective moral conscience',[108] and whose aim is to 'protect … community values and social cohesion'.[109] If we espouse this concept of criminal law, then the idea that a person should be in the conditions (both individual and social) to be fully responsive to the moral force of the law becomes imperative.

In chapter three, I discussed that treating a person as a human involves acknowledging *human qualities and capacities*. To accord a person humanness is to perceive him or her as an individual who is independent and distinguishable from others and capable of making choices.[110] By contrast, humanness also signifies viewing the person as a part of an interconnected network, that is, as an individual whose life is constantly embedded in social units and who interacts in a process of adjustment and response to his or her own social reality. Contrary to its rationalist and individualist counterpart, this definition of humanness is more compatible with the holistic and situated understanding of culpability I have proposed in this chapter. The attribution of guilt is predicated on the commission of a criminal act by a person *quo* human. Framing the idea of the 'culpable person' through generalised, rationalist, and individualist assumptions about human behaviour in social contexts – while leaving emotional, and motivational and contextual factors out of the inquiry – not only risks resulting in unfair judgements of blameworthiness but also displays an indifference to an individual's humanness. Humanising the culpable agent does not mean dismissing his or her responsibility altogether. Rather, it implies adjudicating his or her behaviour from a broader perspective – one that affords consideration to other and more humane aspects of his or her decision to break the law. In other words, such humanisation indicates shifting 'the frame of reference … from one of "autonomous individualism" to one of "social individuality"'.[111]

I said that culpability represents the normative image of the human mind.[112] Even so, I hold that an important position is to ensure that the essence of this doctrine reflects a defensible view of this mind, one that is more responsive to the contingencies that surround an individual's choice to act in breach with the law. Perhaps, a more comprehensive and nuanced conception of the human mind,

[108] Fingarette (n 30) 189.
[109] S Bibas, *The Machinery of Criminal Justice* (New York, Oxford University Press, 2012) 15.
[110] See my discussion about 'Dehumanisation' in ch 3.
[111] Fondacaro (n 12) 193.
[112] See ch 1.

in contrast to a metaphor for it, is more suitable to provide the law with a more rational ground to establish whether an individual had a truly fair opportunity to do otherwise.

VI. Conclusion

In this chapter, I proposed several revisions to the current dominant paradigm of culpability to also factor emotions and socio-environmental aspects in the normative criteria. As I discussed, a revision of the parameters of culpability based on a more comprehensive view of human nature may afford normative and practical relevance to the individual and contextual aspects of human behaviour, which appear to critically contribute to an individual's choice and capacity to conform his or her behaviour to the law. As I have argued, affording relevance to such factors may make the criminal law fairer and more responsive to the individual and social dynamics that underpin offending behaviour. Notably, it would lead the criminal law to embrace a normative narrative of the person, which grasps a fuller conception of humanness rather than an abstraction of it.

However plausible the normative arguments I proposed can be, they are insufficient to settle the ultimate question of criminal responsibility: that of asking why we aim for holding people culpable, where 'why' stands for the goals that the imposition of a sanction upon a culpable person should pursue. As I discussed in chapter two, the current model of the culpable agent is the product of philosophical, normative, and political ideas that have consolidated over decades. This model is not an absolute or immutable truth, but it depends on a very precise ideology about the functions of criminal law. Hence, the question of whether culpability assessments should afford more relevance to the person's motivations or traumatising socio-environmental factors depends not only on whether these aspects of humanness can plausibly fit in the normative discussions of culpability (as we saw, they possibly do). More fundamentally, it depends on the ideological interpretations of the functions of criminal law with respect to the achievement of justice. To recall Lacey's words,

> it depends, at root, on whether we see the functions of criminal law primarily or solely in terms of desert, blame, and stigmatization; or whether we believe that criminal law should aspire more broadly to foster positive goals such as integration, reform, or even forgiveness – aspirations which surely depend on [and are compatible with] a realistic and respectful attempt to understand more thoroughly the [individual and social variables] of offending behavior.[113]

The next chapter focuses on the development of a paradigm of punishment, which positions social rehabilitation as its core principle, thereby precisely endorsing the latter view.

[113] N Lacey, 'Socializing the Subject of Criminal Law? Criminal Responsibility and the Purpose of Criminalization' (2015) 99 *Marquette Law Review* 541, 556.

6

Social Rehabilitation[1]

I. Introduction

In the preceding chapter, I traced a model of culpability grounded in a holistic and situated view of the 'person'. The revised paradigm of culpability I proposed remains fundamentally anchored to voluntarist notions of rationality, autonomy, capacity, and opportunity. However, the revisions I proposed discard the rationalist and individualist substance of these notions, and enrich and expand their substance to also embrace emotional and socio-environmental factors that influence human behaviour in social domains.

The acceptance of a holistic and situated view of the person that assigns more weight to the emotional and social dimensions of human agency can further reflect changes on the conception and practice of punishment. In the preceding pages, I have emphasised that human behaviour is the result of an ongoing dynamic relationship between the individual and the social environment. By virtue of this dynamic interaction, people can reframe their preferences, skills, priorities and values, and behavioural styles, across time and situations – potentially throughout life – independent of their past behaviour or background. Tellingly, emotional shifts coupled with interactions with healthy social environments appear to critically support prosocial change in individuals. As we saw, one critical vehicle to explain prosocial change lies with the marked plasticity of the brain's circuits that are involved in the socio-emotional skills that connect to moral and social behaviour.

What is more, studies on neuroplasticity have further evidenced that social exclusion, and negative environments and experiences can profoundly alter the brain pathways that are involved in the cognitive functions and emotional processes that support moral and social behaviour. Accordingly, these alterations have been found to affect negatively the individual's capacity to behave in socially functional and morally adaptive ways. In the long term, such alterations can provoke severe psychological deteriorations with tremendous effects at the socio-behavioural level.

[1] This chapter draws on my article, F Coppola, 'Valuing Emotions in Punishment: An Argument for Social Rehabilitation with the Aid of Social and Affective Neuroscience' (2018) *Neuroethics* available at doi.org/10.1007/s12152-018-9393-4. The discussions about crime desistance and restorative justice are incorporated integrally.

The insights into the innate human capacity for growth and positive change stand in opposition with the narrow and static narrative of justice-involved individuals that lies at the core of predominant rationales and ideas of punishment. First, these insights run against the assumption that an individual who has chosen to wrong is himself or herself wrong and hardly changes. Second, and consequently, they challenge the rationality and fairness of a punishment that either discourages or is indifferent to the prospect that an individual facing conviction should be provided with opportunities for change. Furthermore, and most importantly, these insights suggest that precluding individuals from engaging with healthy environments and meaningful relationships through responses that are punitive, disempowering and exclusionary not only entails a basic deprivation of their autonomy, but also a risk compromising their status as rational agents.

On the other hand, empirical insights into individual change are consistent with, and lend support to, the body of modern conceptions of rehabilitation[2] that are grounded in an integrated and dynamic view of the person and aim to challenge wrongdoing through a more empowering and inclusionary approach. One such theory that has found support both in the literature and international domains is *social* rehabilitation.[3] Centred on the individual and his or her powers of self-determination and self-change, social rehabilitation is a non-paternalistic conception of rehabilitation that aims to ensure that people facing conviction are granted opportunities to return to (or remain in) society with an improved chance to live a self-supporting and crime-free life as full members of the community. To this end, social rehabilitation values the power of individual autonomy and the importance of social connections to pave the way for constructive pathways of change and reintegration in the least restrictive settings necessary to ensure public safety. Critically, social rehabilitation recognises that all persons are potentially capable of change and views them as agents of their own change process. Thus, it considers the capacity for change as the core informing assumption for any responses to wrongdoing.

Drawing connections between the reviewed (neuro)scientific knowledge, views in the literature, and domestic and international jurisprudence, in this chapter I advance a model of punishment that positions social rehabilitation as its overarching principle. I begin by tracing the penological aspects of the proposed social rehabilitation-oriented model, including its features, its normative justification, and its relationship with other justifications for punishment. I then analyse the practical corollaries that such a model of punishment might entail in several areas of criminal justice. Regrettably, space does not allow me to analyse every single implication that might follow from a rethinking of punishment in

[2] See eg, F McNeill, 'Four Forms of "Offender" Rehabilitation: Towards an Interdisciplinary Perspective' (2012) 17 *Legal and Criminological Psychology* 18.

[3] Also labelled 'resocialisation' or 'resettlement' or 'relational reintegration'. See R Canton, *Why Punish? An Introduction to the Philosophy of Punishment* (London, Palgrave McMillan, 2018) 102–24.

social-rehabilitative terms. Thus, my discussion focuses on the analysis of the implications for selected areas of criminal justice, including sentencing, life imprisonment without the possibility of parole, incarceration, and solitary confinement.

The ultimate intention of this chapter, which concludes the book, is to advance a paradigm of punishment that is grounded in a different narrative of the person that takes account of and is respondent to the (neuro)biological nature of humans as dynamic emotional and social beings. Rethinking punishment through such different lenses does not foreswear penological goals of certainty, proportionality, and public safety, but ensures that the person facing conviction is valued in all his or her dimensions and provided with the individual and social means that are necessary to preserve his or her social individuality in view of a healthy and safe return to the community. Ideally, a model of 'punishment' that recognises and values the fundamental humanity and multifaceted dimension of individuals subject to it, including their capacity for change, has a better chance of turning criminal justice into a more equal, less punitive, inclusionary and non-stigmatising system.

II. Dynamic Personhood

People change with time and experience. Personalities, values, skills, preferences and behaviours shift incrementally as people accrue life experience, discover new sources of meaning, form or lose memories, and are confronted with changing environments. Eventually, accumulated psychological changes not only reshape how someone relates to the world about him or her, but also who he or she is as a person. However tightly we hold on to the people we are today, at some tomorrow we inevitably find ourselves changed.

Psychologists and neuroscientists now know that the ordinary processes of growth, maturation, and decline alter us all in fundamental respects. Through growth and experience, human beings have a unique capacity to change their mind. They have the ability to reframe the narrative of past experiences, reconsider the significance of actions, build resilience and reverse traumas that negatively impacted their behaviour.[4] Further, people can change their social attitudes.

Individual change largely implicates shifts in the emotional landscape of the person. Through positive changes in their emotions, people can reframe their perceptions of environmental occurrences, they can better regulate their responses to environmental demands, and they can behave more adaptively across time and situations. Empirical studies also indicate that the individual processes involved in prosocial change are strongly influenced, and at times even determined, by favourable environmental stimuli. Notably, social connections and healthy social

[4] eg G Bonanno, 'Loss, Trauma, and Human Resilience: Have We Underestimated the Human Capacity to Thrive After Extremely Aversive Events?' (2004) 59 *American Psychology* 20.

environments have been found to be powerful triggers for the mental processes involved in prosocial change.

Nevertheless, change is not an automatic or uncontrolled process, nor is it the result of passive experience. Empirical studies converge on the view that change is primarily a matter of self-determination and self-efficacy; it is the result of a series of experiential and behavioural steps[5] that the individual must actively take.[6] Since '[p]eople are self-organizing, pro- active, self-regulating, and self-reflecting' beings, they are 'contributors to their life circumstances, not just products'.[7] Thus, change is the outcome of a process that involves significant participation by the individual who, in many respects, acts as his or her own change agent.

On the other hand, empirical studies also suggest that change does not occur on its own. It is at least illusory to expect people to choose to pursue change without having a proper motivation, favourable conditions, and support to do so. As extensively argued, people – with their brains, minds, emotions, and behaviours – do not exist in a vacuum, but always in relation to others and in a constant and active interaction with the environment. As Nicola Lacey wrote:

> Our conception of ourselves as persons is inextricably linked with our relationships with others – with friends, family, fellow citizens, colleagues, neighbors – and with social institutions. … [R]elationships, interpersonal contacts, understanding, mutual support and fulfillment of obligations are among the things which human beings tend to regard most highly … but also, and more fundamentally, that we actually define ourselves to an important extent in terms of those relations …[8]

Extending Lacey's argument, if social connections are key for making individuals feel as persons, then social connections are also key for individual change precisely because they foster a sense of belongingness, acceptance, and self-affirmation, all of which prompt the individual to feel socially bound and to value these bonds more highly than acts that can potentially break them. Healthy and meaningful social environments are, therefore, fundamental to trigger and sustain positive individual change. Such environments can act as powerful motivators for the individual to outdistance himself or herself from past wrong behaviours, and to (re)value their social identities that allow him or her to restore his or her relationship and place within the community.

[5] See JO Prochaska et al, 'The Transtheoretical Model and Stages of Change' in K Glanz, BK Rimer and FM Lewis (eds), *Health Behavior and Health Education: Theory, Research, and Practice*, 3rd edn (San Francisco, CA, Jossey-Bass, Inc., 2002); JO Prochaska et al, 'In search of how people change: Applications to the addictive behaviors' (1992) 47 *American Psychologist* 1102; Jo Prochaska et al, 'Measuring processes of change: Applications to the cessation of smoking' (1988) 56 *Journal of Consulting and Clinical Psychology* 520.

[6] See ibid.

[7] A Bandura, 'Toward a Psychology of Human Agency' (2006) 1 *Perspectives on Psychological Science* 164.

[8] N Lacey, *State Punishment* (London, Routledge 1988) 172.

Altogether, empirical literature supports the claim that the capacity for change is inherent to all humans and an exalted expression of their agency. A robust acknowledgment that individuals are potentially capable of change – as long as they find themselves in the conditions to do so – entails a full recognition of the nature of humans as rational and autonomous beings. This dynamic (and holistic) understanding of agency, one that locates the capacity for change also in the emotional and social landscapes of the individual, is key for supporting a model of punishment that positions social rehabilitation as its overarching principle.

III. Social Rehabilitation: Theory, Pillars, and Normative Value

Empirical insights into the dynamic nature of personhood and agency implicitly support approaches to punishment that aim to encourage individual change through empowerment, social cohesion, and belongingness, in order to guarantee a person's safe and healthy return to society. Such approaches figure in the body of rights-based[9] accounts of rehabilitation, international documents[10] and foreign laws,[11] which position rehabilitation as an overarching goal of punishment. Although these accounts have used similar terms and expressions to describe such an understanding of rehabilitation,[12] the label that best captures and epitomises the sense of rehabilitation that I propose in this chapter is social rehabilitation.

In what follows, I analyse different aspects of social rehabilitation, including a description of its features, its view of human agency, and its normative value as a principle grounded in the respect for human dignity. I further analyse the relationship between social rehabilitation and other justifications for punishment and suggest a rethinking of the punitive and exclusionary aspects of such justifications through a constructivist approach that aims for social reintegration. Moreover,

[9] eg, E Rotman, *Beyond Punishment: A New View on the Rehabilitation of Offenders* (Westport, Connecticut, Greenwood Press 1990); E Rotman, 'Do Criminal Offenders Have a Constitutional Right to Rehabilitation?' (1987) 77 *Journal of Criminal Law and Criminology* 1023; S Lewis, 'Rehabilitation: Headline or Footnote in the New Penal Policy?' (2005) 52 *Probation Journal* 119; B Quigley and S Godchaux, 'Prisoner Human Rights Advocacy' (2015) 16 *Loyola Journal of Public Interest Law* 359; MR Gardner, 'Youthful Offenders and the Eighth Amendment Right to Rehabilitation: Limitations on the Punishment of Juvenile' (2016) 83 *Tennessee Law Review* 455.

[10] eg International Covenant on Civil and Political Rights (adopted 16 December 1966, entered into force 23 March 1976) 999 UNTS 171 (ICCPR), art 10.3; Council of Europe Recommendation No. R (84) 10. On the Criminal Record and Rehabilitation of Convicted Persons (1984); UN General Assembly, 'Standard Minimum Rules for the Treatment of Prisoners', Res. 70/175 (17 December 2015), Rule 59.

[11] German Prison Act 1976, §§ 2–4; Italian Constitution 1948, art 27.3; The Netherlands Penitentiary Principles Act 1998, art. 2.2.

[12] Typical expressions in the literature and across legislations include 'resocialisation', 'social reintegration', 'humanistic or anthropological rehabilitation', 'relational rehabilitation', and 'reeducation'.

I illustrate the relationship between social rehabilitation and restorative justice, a model of justice that is increasingly present in legal debates and penal policy.

A. Definition and Distinguishing Features

Social rehabilitation is a non-paternalistic type of rehabilitation that aims for the social reintegration of people facing conviction. The aim of social rehabilitation is to ensure that these individuals are granted fair opportunities to return to (or remain in) society with an improved chance to live a self-supporting and crime-free life. Importantly, social rehabilitation values and hinges upon the power of human connections to motivate and empower justice-involved individuals to shift away from crime and live as positive members of the community, with the rights and responsibilities that this entails. Moreover, social rehabilitation aims to ensure that individual rights are fully repristinated upon completion of the lawfully imposed sentence.

Social rehabilitation views human behaviour as a function of people's motivations, abilities, and opportunities. It does not reject (actually, it promotes) the idea of individuals as autonomous choosing agents, but recognises that behaviour is largely shaped by the social environment and life experiences (ie, it views choices, behaviour and people in context). Social rehabilitation values the power of social connections to promote positive change. It seeks to (re)establish positive relationships between justice-involved people and the rest of society by encouraging personal growth and change based on relational processes. To this aim, social rehabilitation addresses 'not only individual behaviour but also social and structural advantages relevant to him or her',[13] which include social bonds, employment, education, and other opportunities.

Social rehabilitation is compatible with an idea of punishment as the imposition of a sanction that is proportional to the seriousness of the offence committed and is also compatible with the idea that sanctions should also promote public safety. Yet, social rehabilitation affirms the need for humane principles to guide approaches to punishment. From this perspective, social rehabilitation is neither backward-looking nor forward-looking in a purely instrumental sense: it is, instead, functional. Its approach is likely to be functional to addressing successfully change in people who are affected by the criminal justice system and to provide them with fair opportunities to remain or become fully participating members of their families and their communities. Consistent with Rotman's humanistic or anthropological account,[14] social rehabilitation 'does not seek to achieve individual transformation through subtly imposed paradigms. It assumes instead

[13] A Ashworth et al (eds), *Principled Sentencing: Readings on Theory and Policy*, 3rd edn (Portland, Hart Publishing, 2009) 4.

[14] Rotman (n 9).

that significant change can result only from the individual's own insight and uses dialogue to encourage self-discovery'[15] and personal growth.

Therefore, social rehabilitation is individual-centred, not state-centred.[16] Thus, its pursuit is not conditioned on the discretion of the state in conceding it is based on utilitarian considerations. Instead, social rehabilitation prioritises the individual, his or her rights and needs, and places them at the centre of rehabilitation and resocialisation processes. Accordingly, it considers the effectiveness of rehabilitation to satisfy utilitarian goals of special deterrence and public safety to be secondary, although it does not disregard them. So framed, social rehabilitation positions itself as an overarching principle of punishment, rather than as a *stricto sensu* justification for punishment, one that is to be guaranteed universally at the outset. Therefore, the pursuit of social rehabilitation must not be subordinated to utilitarian considerations of effectiveness or 'reasonable feasibility'[17] in view of reducing recidivism.[18]

Another crucial aspect of social rehabilitation consists of maximising choice and voluntarism. Social rehabilitation recognises the powers of self-determination and self-efficacy[19] of the individuals in their process of (self)change; hence, it attributes to them an active role within the reconstruction of their individual and social life. Accordingly, social rehabilitation does not entail coercive impositions of rehabilitation programmes, nor is its pursuit subordinated to its success at accomplishing individual change to achieve social goals of special deterrence.[20] Admittedly, one of the most frequent criticisms of utilitarian rehabilitative approaches concerns the risk that they ultimately translate into subtle forms of coercion, ones that leave the freedoms and rights of the individual much more vulnerable and that open up new prospects of abuses that are justified in the putative public interest. While discourses about voluntariness within the penal context are, admittedly, complex and conditioned on a variety of practical circumstances,[21] social rehabilitation values the respect of the autonomy of justice-involved individuals as one of its

[15] Rotman, *Beyond Punishment* (n 9) 77.

[16] Above (n 9).

[17] See Model Penal Code: Sentencing Project 2017.

[18] E Rotman 'Beyond Punishment' in A Duff and D Garland (eds), *A Reader on Punishment* (Oxford, Oxford University Press, 1994) 292 (drawing distinctions between humanistic and authoritarian [utilitarian] models of rehabilitation and clarifying that '[t]he authoritarian model of rehabilitation is really only a subtler version of the old repressive model, seeking compliance by means of intimidation and coercion. Rehabilitation in this sense is essentially a technical device to mould the offender and ensure conformity to a predesigned pattern of thought and behaviour … The anthropocentric or humanistic model of rehabilitation, on the other hand, grants primacy to the actual human being rather than metaphysical fixations or ideologies, which long served to justify the oppressive intervention of the state.').

[19] See A Bandura, 'Self-efficacy' in VS Ramachaudran (ed), *Encyclopedia of Human Behavior Vol. 4* (New York Academic Press, 1994) (defining self-efficacy as 'the belief in one's ability to influence events that effect one's life and control over the way these events are experienced').

[20] See F Cullen and K Gilbert, *Reaffirming Rehabilitation*, 30th Anniversary edn (Waltham, MA, Anderson Publishing, 2013) 147.

[21] See G Bazemore (1999), 'After Shaming, Whither Reintegration? Restorative Justice and Relational Rehabilitation' in G Bazemore and L Walgrave (eds), *Restorative Juvenile Justice: Repairing the Harm of Youth Crime* (Monsey, Criminal Justice Press, 1999) 155.

primary pillars: individuals are entitled to choose how to utilise rehabilitative opportunities and to have a voice in the rehabilitation process. Thus, social rehabilitation aims to ensure that the essential human attribute of human agency is fully protected.

Social rehabilitation rejects punitiveness, deprivation, coercion, and exclusion as ways to challenge wrongdoing.[22] Instead, the concept espouses a constructivist approach to social reintegration that hinges on individual and social needs, fosters social connections, and prompts inclusion and support. Thus, social rehabilitation replaces the punitive and exclusionary aspects of the traditional model of punishment with an empowering and constructive approach to self-change and social reintegration. For some, this approach will mean the restoration of a former state; for others, this will mean the acquisition of knowledge and skills, as well as the establishment of rank, rights, and responsibilities previously denied. For still others, this will entail a process of reversion and overcoming of traumas and victimisations. For others, this will imply a process of accountability through an appreciation of the interpersonal and normative values they violated that may serve as a guidance for future behaviours. Altogether, while the aim of social rehabilitation (ie, social reintegration) is unitary, the possible means to achieve it are various and multifaceted because of individual and structural factors inherent to the relevant person.

B. Social Rehabilitation, Dynamic Personhood, and Crime Desistance

A critical aspect of social rehabilitation, which finds support in the body of (neuro) scientific knowledge I reviewed, lies with its view of human agency in relation to individual change. Foremost, social rehabilitation understands human agency as a multidimensional, or holistic, concept that is determined by individual and social factors. Therefore, it acknowledges that the choice to engage in offending behaviour results from an interaction between cognitive, emotional, and social aspects, all of which must receive the same weight in informing justice responses to crime.

Second, social rehabilitation acknowledges that personhood is dynamic, that is, it changes across time and situations. First, it rejects viewing the people who are involved in the justice system as irredeemable or hardly redeemable individuals with fixed characters. Thus, it rejects identifying a person's wrongdoing with his or her moral character and vice versa. Instead, social rehabilitation maintains a strict separation between a person and his or her actions and values the multiple aspects of a person's social identity and roles, going beyond his or her misdeeds. Furthermore, this account promotes individual change by including the powers of

[22] See eg Rotman, *Beyond Punishment* (n 9).

self-efficacy and self-determination of individuals; hence, it attributes to people an active role within the reconstruction of their life.

From this perspective, social rehabilitation adopts an empowerment approach,[23] which presents justice-involved individuals as active decision-makers in the (re)construction of their lives, and addresses not what their deficits are but rather what positive contribution they can make.[24] This approach stands in sharp contrast with the two reigning narratives of human agency and punishment that, as I illustrated in chapter two, have alternated over the years. According to the first narrative, which is typical of the retributivist and deterrent approaches, the individual is depicted as a rational and autonomous agent who chooses to offend, presents an ongoing risk to society, and must be punished and controlled. The second narrative, which characterises incapacitation and treatmentist approaches to rehabilitation, depicts the individual as driven by biological, psychological or sociological forces beyond his or her control and in need of help or treatment. Both paradigms present justice-involved individuals as passive recipients (of either control and punishment or help and treatment) and both are deficit models (ie, they emphasise wrongdoers' problems). On the other hand, the narrative of social rehabilitation presents justice-involved individuals as rational and autonomous beings – like retribution. However, this narrative espouses a broader, diachronic and integrated understanding of rationality and autonomy, one that also acknowledges the individual's innate capacity for change and flexibility, and it views emotional and social factors as powerful drivers and motivators for individual change. Accordingly, social rehabilitation aims to allow justice-involved individuals to harness their strengths to reconsider, widen, and value their contributions to the community, thereby restoring their relationships and their place within society.

Beyond recognising individual power to change, social rehabilitation places a significant emphasis on the social dimension of change. It notably recognises that people are hubs of relationships, and that secure and positive ties are key for encouraging change. Thus, social rehabilitation highlights the importance of maintaining or developing positive social bonds and relationships that may encourage feelings of belongingness and, consequently, motivate people to expand their circle of concern and opt for acting in prosocial ways towards others. The importance of social connections within the rehabilitation process is clear. People who feel socially connected and included are more motivated to re-engage morally with the community and to refrain from breaking community values. Hence, the element of social inclusion – understood as acceptance, meaningful social relationships,

[23] eg S Maruna and T LeBel, 'The Desistance Paradigm in Correctional Practice: From Programmes to Lives' in F McNeill, P Raynor and C Trotter (eds), *Offender Supervision: New directions in Theory, Research and Practice* (Cullompton, Willan Publishing, 2010) 65.

[24] R Brunett and S Maruna, 'The Kindness of Prisoners: Strengths-based in Theory and in Action' (2006) 6 *Criminology and Criminal Justice* 83.

and the establishment of stable social bonds such as education or employment – is warranted to provide healthy opportunities for personal growth and change, as well as to grant the successful (re)integration of the individual into society. Altogether, social rehabilitation opposes the 'top-down' approach of more popular utilitarian models of rehabilitation and instead locates human agency behind change in social networks and within the individual himself or herself rather than in passive treatment.

The empowerment model that lies at the basis of social rehabilitation is consistent with and finds support in studies on crime desistance.[25] The study of crime desistance falls within the scope of positive criminology, namely a new perspective in criminology that focuses on identifying positive individual and social influences – so-called 'dynamic factors of protection'[26] – that contribute to the prevention or discouragement of continued criminal behaviour.[27] The core argument that most desistance research has advanced is that individual choice coupled with proper social and emotional support[28] can prompt individuals who have offended to reconsider their self-image and self-worth and to recognise their own ability to change and to create a future identity without crime. Notwithstanding the different approaches and perspectives, studies on desistance have consistently emphasised the importance of feelings and emotions coupled with meaningful social relationships and social bonds in the process of desistance. These factors appear to be central to the processes that lead people to leave behind one identity (associated with criminal wrongdoing) and adopt more prosocial ways of being.

Desistance from crime has been linked to a series of shifts in the emotional and psychological processes of the individual, as well as changes in the social and environmental landscape. Most theories of desistance heavily incorporate personal agency,[29] self-identity,[30] and self-efficacy[31] and frame desisters as 'active participants in constructing their lives'.[32] Second, desistance research powerfully challenges the traditional individualistic lens of criminal law and justice that has dominated for centuries. Indeed, it emphasises the power of social relationships to encourage positive lifestyle change.

[25] B Bersani et al, 'Desistance from Offending in the Twenty-first Century' (2018) 1 *Annual Review of Criminology* 311.

[26] C Nee and Z Vernham, 'Expertise and Its Contribution to the Notion of Protective Factors in Offender Rehabilitation and Desistance' (2017) 32 *Aggression and Violent Behavior* 37.

[27] In other words, the key question in desistance research is not 'Why do people commit crimes?', but rather 'Why do people *stop* committing crimes?'.

[28] B Weaver, *Offending and Desistance: The Importance of Social Relations* (New York, Routledge, 2016).

[29] D Healy, 'Changing Fate? Agency and the Desistance Process' (2013) 17 *Theoretical Criminology* 557.

[30] R Paternoster and S Bushway, 'Desistance and the 'Feared Self': Toward an Identity Theory of Crime Desistance' (2009) 99 *Journal of Criminal Law & Criminology* 1103.

[31] A Bandura, *Self-efficacy: The Exercise of Control* (New York, Freeman, 1997).

[32] J Laub and R Sampson, *Shared Beginnings, Divergent Lives: Delinquent Boys to Age 70* (Cambridge, Harvard University Press, 2003).

Traditional work on desistance has mostly focused on the role of social structures – marriage, parenthood, employment, completed education – in assisting an individual's decision to desist.[33] Other studies have focused on the affective aspects of refraining from crime in an attempt to clarify the subjective processes associated with desistance. Giordano et al,[34] for instance, proposed that part of the desistance process (especially the initial stage) entails an emotional transformation that implies the diminution of negative emotions originally connected to crime; the gradual diminution of positive emotions connected to crime; and the management or regulation of negative emotions (eg, anger). In addition, social factors – so-called 'hooks for change'[35] – that include the formation of secure and healthy attachments (prosocial spouse) and bonds (education, stable jobs) incentivise or amplify these processes of emotional growth. Hence, the authors suggested that targeting emotional areas can foster the development of one's (positive) emotional self and 'increase the likelihood that individuals will be able to benefit from positive hooks for change that do become available within the environment'.[36]

More individual-focused accounts of desistance have emphasised the transformative power of emotions within the individuals' reconstruction of their past and future lives. Vaughan,[37] for instance, has stressed the evaluative and motivational functions of emotions within the internal narrative[38] of desistance. He reported that the narrative of desistance involves some reflexive moral assessment of past behaviours from an external perspective to allow the would-be desister to reconstruct his or her present and future identities in such a way that allows for the maintenance of nonoffending behaviour. The moral assessment implicated in narrative thinking elicits specific emotional responses including regret, shame, or guilt for the harm done, which lead the agent to acknowledge the significance of his or her actions, create a distance between the agent and his or her past life, and ultimately condition his or her current dispositions to change.[39]

Another line of research has adopted an interdisciplinary focus on the role of self-conscious moral emotions in triggering the change process involved in desistance. Some authors have stressed the role of regret.[40] As we have discussed, feelings of regret clarify the seriousness of one's misbehaviour and encourage an acceptance of personal responsibility. Since regret imparts a lesson that a different choice could

[33] See eg ibid.

[34] P Giordano et al, 'Emotions and Crime over the Life Course: A Neo-Meadian Perspective on Criminal Continuity and Change' (2007) 112 *American Journal of Sociology* 1603.

[35] ibid, 1606.

[36] ibid, 1649.

[37] B Vaughan, 'The Internal Narrative of Desistance' (2007) 47 *The British Journal of Criminology* 390.

[38] P Goldie, 'One's Remembered Past: Narrative Thinking, Emotion, and the External Perspective' (2003) 32 *Philosophical Papers* 301.

[39] Vaughan (n 37) 398–9.

[40] G Coricelli et al, 'Brain, Emotion, and Decision-making: The Paradigmatic Example of Regret' (2007) 11 *Trends in Cognitive Science* 258.

have led to other outcomes, it induces a disposition toward behavioural change. Similar arguments have been made regarding feelings of guilt.[41] As discussed in chapter four, studies have indicated that guilt has a powerful ability to dissuade individuals from making immoral choices. Moreover, guilt promotes accountability for one's own transgressions and encourages reparative actions and a desire to rectify matters. Feelings of guilt are also positively linked to empathy and negatively associated with an externalisation of blame and hostility. These insights have led some researchers to suggest that the experience of guilt might entail protective elements for individuals who have offended. On the other hand, work in criminology has examined the effects of shame in encouraging desistance.[42] Although the beneficial effects of shame for prosocial behaviour are disputed, supporters of the shame-desistance relationship have emphasised that the experience of shame can be beneficial insofar as it is combined with social acceptance. Therefore, as long as positive expectations toward acceptance accompany feelings of shame, shame can create responsibility, be acknowledged and expressed, and lead to further steps toward redefining oneself and the reframing of their social identities.

C. Social Rehabilitation, Human Dignity, and the (Neuro) Science of Change

Social rehabilitation finds its strongest normative foundation in the respect of the right to human dignity.[43] The concept of human dignity is complex and multifaceted, and many competing definitions are provided within the literature. A salient and omni-comprehensive understanding of human dignity rests on the intrinsic worth of human beings.[44] Such a robust sense of human dignity has a universal value and requires that each human be treated with respect just for being a human, beyond the single acts they commit. This universal conception of human dignity has three main ramifications: first, humans are entitled to be recognised as humans;[45] second, they are entitled to have the conditions in which they can

[41] eg J Tangney et al, 'Shame, Guilt and Remorse: Implications for Offender Populations' (2011) 22 *Journal of Forensic Psychiatry and Psychology* 706.

[42] eg J Braithwaite, *Crime, Shame and Reintegration* (New York, Cambridge University Press, 1989); TJ Scheff, and SM Retzinger, *Emotions and Violence: Shame and Rage in Destructive Conflicts* (Lincoln, iUniverse Inc, 1991).

[43] Universal Declaration of Human Rights (adopted 10 December 1948 UNGA Res 217 A(III) (UDHR), Preamble. For a discussion, see A Ploch, 'Why Dignity Matters: Dignity and the Right (or Not) to Rehabilitation in International and National Perspectives' (2012) 44 *International Law and Politics* 887.

[44] J Feinberg, *Social Philosophy* (Englewood Cliffs, NJ, Prentice Hall, 1993) 94.

[45] B Beyleveld and R Brownsword, *Human Dignity in Bioethics and Biolaw* (New York, Oxford University Press 1993) 17.

experience their own dignity, that is, the conditions that allow them to experience self-worth;[46] and third, they are to be empowered to exercise the distinctive human capacities that account for their dignity.[47]

A violation of a person's right to respect for their dignity can manifest in the following ways: first, if one were treated as having no worth or less than equal worth as a human relative to other humans; second, if one were treated as though one lacked distinctive human capacities; and three, if one were treated as a mere thing or object. In each case, human dignity is violated because a human is treated as if he or she is not a human or less than a human.

Respect for human dignity requires that justice-involved individuals are treated in a way that fully comports with their inherent worth as humans, that is, in a way that empowers them to exercise fully their human capacities for autonomy and rationality and enables them to keep or restore a sense of self-worth and self-esteem. To this end, penal policies must be structured in a way that they do not deteriorate nor diminish the mental and physical integrity of individuals. Second, penal policies must provide for the genuine fulfilment of the basic individual and social needs of justice-involved individuals, including the continuation or development of social connections with family and the community, and grant access to the resources of the civil society including education, employment, voluntary psychotherapy, and medical treatment. All these needs go beyond mere physical survival and provide opportunities for growth, change, and reintegration into social life. Moreover, respect for human dignity mandates that penal policies must favour a healthy and stable re-entry, thereby removing the risk of collateral consequences or barriers that could prevent a person from reintegrating into the community as a full member of its social and political life.

Although the notion of human dignity is largely omitted in US penal laws and policies,[48] human dignity is the core concept of the Eighth Amendment.[49] Under the Eighth Amendment, every citizen is entitled to human dignity, against which all sentences and conditions of confinement should be assessed.[50] Although human dignity has factored into constitutional analyses of punishment in some instances,[51] the weight it has been assigned to protect justice-involved individuals from state abuses has proved to be fragmented and inconsistent.[52] Over the years, the Supreme Court has clearly adopted a narrow and formalistic approach

[46] D Shultziner and I Rabinovici, 'Human Dignity, Self-worth and Humiliation: A Comparative Legal–Psychological Approach' (2012) 18 *Psychology, Public Policy, and Law* 105.

[47] Beyleveld and Brownsword (n 45) 15.

[48] See Ploch (n 43).

[49] U.S. Constitution amend. VIII ('Excessive bail shall not be required, nor excessive fines imposed, nor cruel and unusual punishments inflicted').

[50] *Weems v United States* 217 U.S. 349 (1922); *Trop v Dulles*, 356 U.S. 86, 100 (1958).

[51] eg *Furman v Georgia* 408 U.S. 238 (1972); *Roper v Simmons* 534 U.S. 551 (2005).

[52] For a discussion, see E Nilsen, 'Decency, Dignity, and Desert: Restoring Ideals of Humane Punishment to Constitutional Discourse' (2007) 41 *University of California Davis Law Review* 111.

to the Eighth Amendment; thus, 'abdicating its responsibility as a guardian of [its] protections',[53] especially in non-capital cases. Notably, the Court has demonstrated a weak and inconsistent approach to human dignity within constitutional scrutiny of punishment, turning the value of human dignity into a mere rhetorical argument rather than a subject of substantial constitutional protections.[54] As Nilsen criticised, the Court's jurisprudence heavily disregards the value of 'a convicted person as a human being with innate dignity [in terms of] punishment as it is actually experienced'.[55] Furthermore, the Court's 'excessive deference to legislatures leaves out conscience or moral compunction in its decisions'.[56]

Despite such a regrettable predominant attitude, the Court has displayed a willingness to consider a more robust constitutional conception of human dignity in the series of Eighth Amendment decisions banning the death penalty and mandatory life imprisonment without parole (LWOP) for adolescents.[57] In *Roper*, the Court explicitly and vigorously reaffirmed that dignity and individual freedom are fundamental values of the US Constitution and 'are central to the American experience'.[58] Turning its focus to foreign and international laws and practices, the Court judged that punishing a child with the death penalty is in sharp contrast to global standards of dignity, decency, and humanity that characterise any democratic society and stands against the rights and principles enshrined in the Eighth Amendment.

By analogising and extending the rationale in *Roper*, the Court, in *Graham*, implicitly reaffirmed the value of human dignity and linked it with the paramount importance of hope for rehabilitation and release in punishment determinations.[59] As discussed previously, a key factor that led the Justices to afford a central relevance to rehabilitation in juvenile justice, compared with incapacitation and retribution, was an acknowledgment of the capacity for change of adolescents in view of their particular neuropsychological malleability. According to the Court, a punishment that, at the outset, denies such change can happen disparages any hope for rehabilitation and release; thus, it entails a severe violation of the intrinsic worth (dignity) of children's lives.[60]

Leaving aside the relevant penalty at stake (to which I return later in this chapter), the *Graham* opinion advances a broader principle of justice with significant

[53] ibid, 175.

[54] See eg *Gregg v Georgia* 428 U.S. 153 [1976]; *Harmelin v Michigan* 501 U.S. 917 (1991); *Solem v Helm* 463 U.S. 277 (1983); *Rummel v Estelle* 445 U.S. 263 (1980); *Ewing v California* 538 U.S. 11 (2003).

[55] Nilsen (n 52) 115.

[56] ibid, 116.

[57] *Roper* (n 51); *Graham v Florida* 560 U.S. 48 (2010); *Miller v Alabama* 567 U.S. 460 (2012); *Montgomery v Louisiana* 136 S. Ct. 718 (2016).

[58] *Roper* (n 51) 578.

[59] *Graham* (n 57) 76 ('the State … must … give defendants like Graham some meaningful opportunity to obtain release based on demonstrated maturity and rehabilitation').

[60] ibid, 53, 79; see also *Montgomery* (n 57) 725–26, 736–37; *Miller* (n 57) at 477–79.

implications, namely that *individual change, rehabilitation and social re-entry should be of paramount importance within punishment determinations, as these concepts are intrinsically connected to respect for the dignity of persons facing criminal conviction.* As other authors have suggested,[61] this broader principle of justice is potentially extensible to adults also. Primarily, it is extensible to adults through a recognition that adults are also capable of change. As discussed thoroughly, modern neuroscience suggests that the human brain is programmed to shape, change, and adapt to changing environments. Neuroscience suggests that the brain retains this capacity at any stage of one's life, and that change directions depend on both individual variables and external circumstances. Thus, limiting the paramount importance of the principle of rehabilitation to adolescents, based on the generalised presumption that adults cannot change or hardly change, lacks empirical foundations.

Another argument is that 'human dignity is not an age-dependent principle. A person cannot forfeit his or her dignity by turning eighteen years old and entering adulthood, as dignity is rooted in the inherent worth of a human being'[62] and entails the full recognition of human capacities and the preservation of an individual's self-worth. If the capacity for change is fully recognised as a capacity that belongs to every human being and is vital to preserve an individual's self-worth, all persons must be offered opportunities to change and be entitled to rehabilitation with a view to return to society.

From another perspective, several authors have suggested that the rationale in *Graham* can be further extended to conditions of confinement in adult facilities.[63] If a prison system that withholds counselling, education, and rehabilitation programmes 'becomes complicit to the lack of an [adolescent] offender's development'[64] and hinders his or her pathway to change, rehabilitation, and re-entry, it is at least illogical to hold that the same principle should not also extend and adapt to conditions of confinement for adults. The (neuro)science of adult change suggests that positive change process is more likely to occur when an individual is confronted with healthy social environments and is provided with opportunities to enhance his or her skills. However, such a process is thwarted when these opportunities are lacking or when the individual is confronted with degrading social environments. For this and other reasons, incarcerated adults

[61] See eg C Flanders, 'The Supreme Court and the Rehabilitative Ideal' (2015) 49 *Georgia Law Review* 383, 428–30; M Jouet, 'Mass Incarceration Paradigm Shift?: Convergence in an Age of Divergence' (2019) 109 *Journal of Criminal Law and Criminology* 703; E Hanan, 'Incapacitating Errors: Sentencing and the Science of Change' (2019) 97 *Denver Law Review* 151; M O'Hear, 'Not Just Kids Stuff? Extending *Graham* and *Miller* to Adults' (2013) 78 *Missouri Law Review* 1087.

[62] Jouet (n 61) 712.

[63] A Ristroph, 'Hope, Imprisonment, and the Constitution' (2010) 23 *Federal Sentencing Report* 75, 77 (claiming that this holding of *Graham* 'could lead to greater scrutiny of solitary confinement, security classifications, and other dimensions of prison conditions that render a sentence more severe without necessarily extending its duration').

[64] *Graham* (n 57) at 79.

should never be deprived of rehabilitation opportunities and live in conditions that treat them as incorrigible, diminish their sense of self-worth, are damaging for their well-being, reinforce bad habits, and produce destructive changes in their personality.

This claim aligns with the body of lower courts' opinions[65] that have relied upon rehabilitation to find that debilitating prison conditions entail Eighth Amendment violations. Endorsing the principle that the conditions of incarceration must comport with 'broad and idealistic concepts of dignity, civilized standards, humanity, and decency',[66] several lower courts have considered the lack of provision of rehabilitation services as an element that accounts for unconstitutional conditions of confinement. More than one court has found that prison conditions are unconstitutional 'when they make it impossible to maintain acquired social skills or continue efforts of self-rehabilitation'.[67] The argument is that such impossibility is not only deteriorating for the individual, but also makes a reduction in recidivism unlikely.[68] Ultimately, these courts have attributed a central role to rehabilitation when accounting for the 'totality of conditions'[69] of confinement and their effects on the imprisoned,[70] and stated that rehabilitation programmes are constitutionally mandated to counteract the harmful and counterproductive effects inherent to incarceration. Altogether, these (admittedly few) opinions are suggestive that a heavier consideration of human dignity and rehabilitation would bolster broader interpretations of the Eighth Amendment and lead to closer scrutiny of prison conditions to counteract the innate destructive effects of hostile prison environments on the neurological, mental, and physical well-being of individuals.

D. Social Rehabilitation and Other Justifications for Punishment

Social rehabilitation is compatible with the hybrid, or mixed, function of punishment. Framed as an overarching principle, social rehabilitation acts in combination with other justifications for punishment and, at the same time, it informs them under its unitary goal of social reintegration. Thus, while the essential attributes and functions of each justification for punishment remain unvaried, they are re-interpreted in a way that fits the ultimate goal of social reintegration – to which these justifications must conform. In this section, I analyse the relationship

[65] eg *Laaman v Helgemoe*, 437 F.Supp., 269, 323 (1977); *Holt v Sarver*, 309 F. Supp. 362 (E.D. Ark. 1970). For a discussion of these and other cases, see Rotman, *Beyond Punishment* (n 9) at 79–85.

[66] *Hutto v Finney* 437 U.S. 678, 685 (1978) (citations omitted).

[67] Rotman, *Beyond Punishment* (n 9) 81.

[68] ibid.

[69] *Laaman* (n 65); see also *Rhodes v Chapman* 452 U.S. 337, 364 (Brennan, J, concurring) (1981).

[70] *Rhodes* ibid. (Justice Brennan, concurring) (citing *Laaman* (n 65)) ('In determining when prison conditions pass beyond legitimate punishment and become cruel and unusual, the touchstone is the effect upon the imprisoned').

between social rehabilitation and justifications for punishment. Notably, I highlight that the potential acceptance of social rehabilitation as an overarching principle of punishment has the potential to counteract and buffer the risk of punitiveness that is innate to retribution; to reduce greatly the exclusionary scope of incapacitation; and to re-orient the meaning of special deterrence.

i. Retribution

At a first glance, social rehabilitation may seem to reject retribution in its entirety. However, this interpretation is mistaken. As mentioned, social rehabilitation espouses a functional approach to punishment, one that goes beyond backward-looking or forward-looking considerations and aims more broadly to ensure that individuals facing conviction are granted fair opportunities to return (or remain) in society as safely as possible. This aim means ensuring that an individual facing conviction is granted opportunities for individual change and for restoring (or maintaining) social relationships. Furthermore, this aim means ensuring that the individual facing conviction is not deprived of the relevant social skills, basic individual and social needs and, more broadly, his or her capacities to fulfil his or her obligations as a full member of the society.

Against this backdrop, social rehabilitation does not reject the retributivist premise that punishment can only follow a crime conviction; nor does it reject that punishment be determined based on proportionality criteria. Furthermore, social rehabilitation is in principle compatible with retributive ideas of autonomy and rationality, that is, punishment is justly assigned as long as an individual freely and rationally chooses to commit the offence. However, as we have seen, social rehabilitation rejects the traditional individualist and rationalist understanding of human agency, and instead espouses a multidimensional and contextualised view of it, one that embraces and values dynamic emotional and social aspects of choice and behaviour.

Nevertheless, while sharing these retributive premises, social rehabilitation places limits on the punitive tendencies of retribution by informing its principles with the ultimate aim of social reintegration. Three main aspects of retribution are relevant for and can be informed by social rehabilitation. The first aspect concerns the *preservation of the capacity for autonomy and rationality of the individual*. As discussed in chapter two, (voluntarist) retribution is indifferent to the effects of a given penalty for an individual. However, retribution insists on structuring legal punishment so that it is, at minimum, consistent with treating justice-involved individuals as rational and autonomous beings. Based on this presupposition, retributive punishment aims to ensure that perpetrators are 'capable of understanding the wrongs they have committed and the fairness of the penal sanctions imposed on them by the state in response to those wrongs'.[71] Accordingly,

[71] R Lippke, 'Retribution and Incarceration' (2003) 17 *Public Affairs Quarterly* 29, 43.

retribution does not require that punishment erodes the capacities that constitute rational and autonomous personhood, such as 'physical and psychological health, and interaction with others'.[72] From a retributive perspective, these capacities and dispositions need to be regularly exercised to respect the ability of people facing punishment 'to comprehend and respond constructively to the reasons for which they are being punished'.[73]

From this line of reasoning, a punishment that imposes suffering and excludes people has the 'paradoxical' effect of contradicting this fundamental aspect of retribution, for it risks compromising the affective and cognitive abilities that support choice and practical reasoning skills,[74] and can 'cause further atrophy of what may have already been weak capacities to identify with and feel for others'.[75] Overall, harsh punitiveness and social exclusion not only results in a deprivation of basic human agency, but even in its deterioration. In short, harsh and exclusionary punishments disrespect the perpetrator as a rational and autonomous agent.

The positioning of social rehabilitation as the overarching goal of justice counteracts this 'paradoxical', yet existing, effect of retribution by mandating that individuals facing punishment must be always granted opportunities for social reintegration, with all the corollaries it entails. Admittedly, a punishment that values and respects the perpetrator as a rational moral equal cannot just 'reduce' him or her to a wrong act committed in the past but should also regard his or her personal and social life in view of his or her future. Put this way, social rehabilitation does not oppose but *enhances* the substance of this fundamental tenet of retribution. While retribution is limited to 'respecting' an individual's agency through the infliction of punishment, social rehabilitation is committed to 'preserving' the individual's agency during the execution of punishment, an aspect that pure retribution eventually disregards.

The second, and related, aspect concerns the *respect for the dignity of the person*. As discussed in chapter two, proponents of (neo)retribution strongly invoked a recognition of the equality and inherent dignity of all human persons. The egalitarian model of respect of dignity endorsed by (voluntarist) retributivists emphasises the universal dignity of all humans, law-abiding or otherwise. Theorists argue that it is a commitment to equality that requires retributive punishment in the first place. As has been correctly pointed out, '[s]uch theory though leaves retributive theorists with the paradoxical claim that we respect perpetrators by treating them worse than we do non-offenders …. Moreover, the retributivist claim that punishment is respectful seems particularly inconsonant with contemporary American

[72] ibid, 33.

[73] ibid.

[74] See also W Hirstein et al, *Responsible Brains: Neuroscience, Law, and Human Culpability* (Cambridge, MA, MIT Press, 2018) 222–24.

[75] Lippke (n 71) 44.

penal practices'.[76] Harsh and exclusionary punishment entails a profound lack of respect for human dignity, an aspect that contradicts the egalitarian spirit of fairness that lies at the core of (voluntarist) retributivism. As Ristroph put it, '[n]ot everyone will agree that convicted criminals are entitled to any form of respect at all. But assuming that some measure of respect is appropriate, it is a fact [that] retributive respect is weak in its aspirations and unfulfilled in practice'.[77]

Social rehabilitation invites a vastly different conception of respect for the dignity of wrongdoers, one that is both broader and more substantial. Since punishment entails by definition an intrusion on human freedom, agency and self-preservation, the only way to respect the dignity and humanity of those we punish is to acknowledge that all individuals facing criminal conviction are entitled to a fair opportunity to be reintegrated. From this perspective, social rehabilitation espouses a far more egalitarian notion 'respect' for human dignity and rejects punitive and exclusionary practices, which are degrading or humiliating, and promotes crime responses that are inclusionary, functional and dignifying, aiming to ensure that the person can safely return to society. Once again, this approach does not mean that crime should not call for a state response, but it largely avoids the risk that such response entails that the individual becomes a disempowered subject in the hands of the punitive power of the state.

The third and final aspect concerns *proportionality*. To date, the principle of proportionality is, arguably, viewed as a definitional feature of retribution.[78] Under the proportionality principle, the intrusions of punishment must never be greater than are merited by the gravity of the offence and the offender's degree of culpability. As currently conceived, proportionality analyses of punishment are limited to the consideration of these factors (gravity of the offence plus degree of culpability) without also considering further factors inherent to the person, including the effects that a given penalty could have on his or her psychological and social life. The outcome of such a disregard is that individuals with profoundly different situations receive exactly the same 'equal' treatment.

Social rehabilitation entails viewing proportionality more broadly as a limit upon punishment considerations based solely on desert criteria and expanding the scope to include considerations about the effects of a given punishment for the individual based on personal and social variables and in view of his or her social reintegration. Moreover, social rehabilitation also strives to counter the potential

[76] A Ristroph, 'Respect and Resistance in Punishment Theory' (2009) 97 *California Law Review* 601, 626.

[77] ibid, 628.

[78] But see A Ristroph, 'Proportionality as a Principle of Limited Government' 55 (2005) *Duke Law Journal* 263 (suggesting that proportionality should be viewed as an overriding principle that limits the punitive power of the state, without being attached to any specific justification for punishment); see also E Rubin, 'Just Say No To Retribution' (2003) 7 *Buffalo Criminal Law Review* 17, 49–50 (similarly suggesting that proportionality should be abstracted from the realm of retribution and viewed as an independent and subsidiary principle of punishment).

unintended effects of punishment (deprivation, hardship, loss of job, stigma), which make punishment unjust and disproportional – a goal that retributivists should view favourably.

Hence, proportionality under such an approach not only aims at limiting excessive punitiveness based on desert considerations, but, more broadly, at limiting that such desert considerations lead to a punishment that can have negative repercussions on the individual in view of his or her social reintegration. Accordingly, a punishment qualifies as excessive or disproportionate, not only in light of symmetrical considerations between the offence and the penalty, but also when such considerations entail the infliction of a punishment that hinders the possibility of social reintegration based on individual and sociable variables inherent to the relevant person. A punishment that disregards the human dimension of the individual based on solely desert considerations becomes inevitably disproportionate. Importantly, such an expanded and individualised view of proportionality is warranted because only a punishment that also pays respect and values the person and his or her life can be perceived as fair. A sanction that is experienced individually as fair can constitute a valid motivational basis for 'responding constructively to the reasons for which [an individual] is being punished',[79] thereby favouring processes of reconciliation between the individual and the community, and encouraging constructive pathways to change and reintegration.[80]

ii. Incapacitation

In principle, incapacitation is entirely at odds with social rehabilitation both empirically and theoretically. This contrast is inherent to the nature, assumptions, and outcomes of incapacitation. Incapacitation explicitly endorses (to a larger extent than retribution) a static view of the individual. The notion builds on the view that justice-involved individuals are 'characterologically criminal',[81] whose traits, dispositions, and attitudes cannot change regardless of the social context; that is, they are consistent across different situations. Thus, proponents of incapacitation view justice-involved individuals as inherently dangerous and likely to reoffend regardless of where they are put. Assuming that people cannot change their character and behaviour regardless of the situation, incapacitation operates via predictive criteria of dangerousness that are largely based on an individual's personality. Based on such personality-based predictions, incapacitation operates on the assumption that an individual will not continue to offend

[79] Lippke (n 71) 43.

[80] According to defiance theory, individuals who experience a sanction as unfair and stigmatising are more likely to react with shame and rage, which increases the chances of reoffending. See L Sherman, 'Defiance, Deterrence, and Irrelevance: A Theory of the Criminal Sanction' (1993) 30 *Journal of Research in Crime and Delinquency*, 445; see also G Robinson and F McNeill, 'Exploring the Dynamics of Compliance with Community Penalties' (2008) 12 *Theoretical Criminology* 431, 444.

[81] Hanan (n 61) 154.

once he or she is incapacitated. Thus, the notion works to remove (ie, socially exclude) an individual to neutralise the risk of future offences. Furthermore, as Binder and Notterman[82] correctly observed, incapacitation presupposes that the current prison environment does not generate criminal behaviour and is, therefore, indifferent to preventing crime in prison. Given the reality of prison environments, which can be rife with violence, sexual assaults, intimidation, and coercion, the public welfare purpose of incapacitation merges with a 'retributive strategy' of redistributing crime to the guilty, so that 'people in prison deserve not just their prescribed crime, but also an increased risk of being victimized'.[83]

Abundant literature has revealed the questionable empirical assumptions of incapacitation.[84] Primarily, incapacitation lends itself to the 'situationist critique'[85] – largely endorsed throughout this book – in which situations play a major and often dominant role in shaping character and behaviour. This critique has two main ramifications: first, the character and behaviour of an individual are strongly (and, at times, more largely) influenced by the relevant social environment than by solely 'innate' dispositions. Second, an individual's character and behaviour are not fixed, but change across time and situations. Psychologists have demonstrated that while 'individual responses to specific situations are surprisingly consistent across persons',[86] one person's behaviour across different situations is extremely variable. How a person behaves as an employee may differ dramatically from how he or she behaves as a parent, friend, or lover. Therefore, a person's 'character traits' at a given time cannot be taken as an absolute criterion of his or her future behaviour, nor are they indicative of his or her identity.

The situational critique of incapacitation finds further support in the body of evidence on brain plasticity and the social environment. This evidence further contradicts the incapacitation-based assumption by suggesting that the brain is capable of change over time and in response to different environmental stimuli. Thus, this evidence strengthens the claim that it is hardly possible to predict with any accuracy who is likely to prove dangerous in the future. Given that change is influenced by environmental stimuli and variables among individuals, it is difficult

[82] G Binder and B Notterman, 'Penal Incapacitation: A Situationist Critique' (2017) 54 *American Criminal Law Review* 1, 4.

[83] ibid.

[84] ibid; see also Hanan (n 61); H Wermink et al, 'Crime Preventive Effects of Incapacitation' in G Bruinsma and D Weisburd (eds), *Encyclopedia of Criminology and Criminal Justice* (New York, Springer, 2018); K Auerhahan, 'Selective Incapacitation and the Problem of Prediction' (2006) 37 *Criminology* 703; A Piquero, 'Youth Matters: The Meaning of Miller for Theory, Research, and Policy Regarding Developmental/Life-Course Criminology' (2013) 39 *New England Journal on Criminal and Civil Commitment* 347, 356–57; A Piquero and A Blumstein, 'Does Incapacitation Reduce Crime?' (2007) 23 *Journal of Quantitative Criminology* 267.

[85] See Binder and Notterman (n 82).

[86] ibid.

to predict whether 'a thirty-year-old person will … be a different person at forty-five years old'.[87]

Moreover, the discussed studies[88] provide evidence that the effects of toxic stressors and traumatising environments alter neurobiological responses to threat and produce a series of mental functions and abilities, including self-regulation, impulse control, and emotion regulation, thereby precipitating or heightening the risk of maladaptive action tendencies and dysfunctional behaviours, including aggression and violence. This evidence aligns with the body of prison studies evidencing the high rates of institutional violence[89] and high recidivism rates within several years of release.[90] Taken together, such evidence suggests that prisons are far from making individuals substantially less likely to commit crimes either in prison or upon their release. Thus, the incapacitation-based assumption that a prison is the ideal solution to neutralise the risk of future offending is profoundly flawed.

In addition to these empirical aspects, incapacitation stands in sharp contrast to the ultimate goal of social rehabilitation, namely the social reintegration of justice-involved individuals through as much inclusion as possible. As has been observed, 'incapacitation constitutes an expressive practice of segregating and stigmatizing justice-involved individuals on the basis of status and disposition. Incapacitation results in a segregation regime, which both prevents offenders from associating with other members of society, and stigmatizes them as unworthy to do so'.[91] This outcome not only makes any possibility of successful reintegration more difficult to achieve, but also compromises it.

Altogether, the assumptions that underpin and legitimise incapacitation as a justification for punishment are not only at odds with empirical sciences but, more broadly, contrast with the tenets and aims of social rehabilitation. Under a social rehabilitation approach, incapacitation should be largely precluded from rationally justifying sentences and should never be a legitimate justification for sentencing enhancement. I further expand my argument against incapacitation in the following section, arguing for the categorical ban of mandatory life imprisonment without the possibility of parole.

[87] Hanan (n 61) 183.

[88] See ch 2.

[89] B Steiner and C Cain, 'The Relationship Between Inmate Misconduct, Institutional Violence, and Administrative Segregation: A Systematic Review of the Evidence' in *Restrictive Housing in the U.S.: Issues, Challenges, and Future Directions* (NCJ-250320) (Washington DC, Department of Justice, National Institute of Justice, 2017).

[90] M Alper et al, '2018 Update on Prisoner Recidivism: A 9-Year Follow-up Period (2005–2014)' (NCJ 250975), U.S. Department of Justice, available at www.bjs.gov/content/pub/pdf/18upr9yfup0514.pdf.

[91] Binder and B Notterman (n 82) 4.

iii. Special Deterrence

Unlike utilitarian understandings of rehabilitation, social rehabilitation is not immediately instrumental for special deterrence as its main goal is not that of reducing crime. As mentioned above, social rehabilitation focuses on the individual and ensures that the individual facing conviction is respected and provided with opportunities to live a self-supporting life as an active member of the community. Thus, the pursuit of social rehabilitation goes beyond its efficacy at reducing crime, nor is it to be conditioned according to its efficacy at reducing crime.

The separation between social rehabilitation and special deterrence helps silence the many criticisms directed toward the possible failure of rehabilitation programmes at achieving special deterrence. This utilitarian understanding of rehabilitation contradicts the quintessence of social rehabilitation as a principle of justice, which is the protection of the perpetrator against punitive abuses by the state. Social rehabilitation prioritises the perspective of individuals facing convictions; it is primarily interested in preserving or enhancing their ability to cope with life in a healthy way, counteracting the negative effects of punishment, and striving toward their social reintegration. When social rehabilitation is seen as individual-centred, its independence from its outcome becomes evident.

Although special deterrence is not the primary or necessary goal of social rehabilitation, this does not mean that social rehabilitation loses sight of the societal impact of rehabilitation or disregards the state interest in guaranteeing public safety. Social rehabilitation endorses the provision of services and programmes that possibly lead an individual to re-engage, both morally and socially, with the community. Such efforts 'should be most likely to augment a person's motivation to live a crime-free life, enrich their skills, or improve their psychological condition'.[92] Hence, 'minimum standards of seriousness' are needed and 'a certain degree of quality and efficacy is inherent in any serious rehabilitative undertaking'.[93]

Thus, although special deterrence is not the ultimate goal of rehabilitation, social rehabilitation is, nevertheless, committed to ensuring that individuals resolve to live a respectable life within the community, and the concept works toward this end. However, social rehabilitation rejects the assumption that crime reduction can be achieved through greater punitiveness,[94] which may result in state abuses. Instead, the concept endorses the view that crime reduction is best achieved through constructively fostering change through empowerment, inclusion, and support. Considering the disastrous effects of punitive justice at reducing recidivism, social rehabilitation is more likely to satisfy the state's interest in public safety when it punishes someone.

[92] Rotman, 'Do Criminal Offenders Have a Constitutional Right to Rehabilitation?' (n 9) 1036.
[93] ibid.
[94] See also M Bagaric and T Alexander, 'The Capacity of Criminal Sanctions to Shape the Behaviour of Offenders: Specific Deterrence Doesn't Work, Rehabilitation Might and the Implications for Sentencing' (2012) 36 *Criminal Law Journal* 159, 159.

E. Social Rehabilitation and Restorative Justice

Social rehabilitation heavily merges with – and, in a sense, resolves the limits of – many aspects of restorative justice. Although discrepancies in its definition and parameters still exist, restorative justice can be described as a normative theory of justice that focuses on repairing the harm caused by criminal behaviour. The theory positions crime as a disruption of social relationships, not only as a breaking of the law.[95] With this relational understanding of crime, restorative justice rejects a punitive approach to offending.[96] Instead, it aims to reconcile the perpetrator with the victim and the community through cooperative processes that involve an active participation of all parties that were affected by the crime, to identify constructive solutions to repair the resulting damages, and to favour the development and cohesion of the community.

Similar to social rehabilitation, restorative justice revolves around the ideas that 'moral character is dynamic'[97] and that individuals can change their behaviour. Hence, restorative justice philosophy rejects challenging wrongdoing with punitiveness and social exclusion, and instead places values like voluntariness, accountability, inclusiveness, and empowerment at the centre of the process of finding constructive solutions to the harm caused by the crime.[98] Espousing the empowerment model of human agency that I discussed previously, restorative justice aims at repairing relationships between the parties affected by crime by encouraging the responsible party to take accountability for his or her behaviour and act to make amends to provide either material or symbolic restitutions to victims and communities. A key distinguishing aspect of restorative processes is 'reintegrative shaming'.[99] Although the concept of 'shaming' has incited several controversies, the strength of this theory is that the wrongfulness of the offence – rather than of the person – needs to be the focus of disapproval. Through disapproval of the action rather than the person, this theory posits that people are more likely to recognise their behaviour as wrong, feel compelled to take ownership and responsibility for it, and be motivated to refrain from future re-offence. Admittedly, it is difficult to accept full responsibility for harming others without a support system in place and a sense that there will be an opportunity to gain acceptance in the community. Therefore, accountability, inclusion and support must go hand in hand.

The philosophy of restorative justice is deeply rooted in the belief that emotions are powerful transformational factors to foster positive human relationships

[95] H Zehr, *Changing Lenses: A New Focus for Crime and Justice* (Scottsdale, Herald Press, 1990).

[96] L Sherman and H Strang, *Restorative Justice: The Evidence* (London, The Smith Institute, 2008) 32.

[97] S Maruna, 'Desistance and Restorative Justice: It's Now or Never' (2016) 4 *Restorative Justice: An International Journal* 289, 295.

[98] D O' Mahony and J Doak, *Reimagining Restorative Justice* (Portland, Bloomsbury, 2017).

[99] J Braithewaite, *Crime, Shame and Reintegration* (New York, Cambridge University Press, 1989).

and can yield positive individual change.[100] The potential of restorative justice processes, such as victim-offender mediation programmes (either direct or indirect) and community conferencing, has been widely attributed to the approach's ability to actively and emotionally engage participants and enable dialogue, reparation, restoration and healing by evoking certain emotional dynamics. While more empirical evidence is needed regarding how exactly these emotional dynamics operate to underpin the transformative mechanisms of restorative justice – also considering the critiques[101] that some scholars have raised against the rhetoric of the restorative movement – the evocation of empathy and adaptive social emotions like remorse and regret, has been heralded as the driving force of restorative justice, as it appeals to the parties' moral values and consciences.

By harnessing the healing and cathartic power of these emotions, restorative justice processes are presumably more likely to direct people to re-engage morally[102] with the people they harmed to develop a sense of the negative consequences of their conduct, to make amends, to repair the harm caused by the crime, and to foster motivation and resolve to improve in the future. Some empirical studies have crucially suggested that these processes have the potential to influence desistance by triggering change as well as by supporting an ongoing desistance process.[103]

Thus, restorative justice processes are framed as 'morally formative experiences'[104] that contribute to the moral and social growth of individuals by encouraging a gateway to prosocial change. As Reisel[105] has interestingly posited, such emotionally draining circumstances provide positive stimulation for the brain areas involved in morality. Moreover, these processes increase chances of neuroplasticity, alter procedural memory, and ultimately facilitate the creation of adaptive patterns of behaviour. If these processes are integrated with rehabilitation and support – for example, emotion regulation training, social skills training, job training, and educational programmes – individuals can actually undergo profound change on both behavioural and neurobiological levels. Therefore, restorative justice principles and processes have high potential to provide the opportunity for personal growth as well as for a more effective and satisfying resolution of criminal matters as well as for beneficial outcomes for individuals in terms of their successful reintegration into the community.

Admittedly, restorative justice may be challenging from a due process perspective (eg, it poses risks for the privilege against self-incrimination, for the right to

[100] M Rossner, *Just Emotions: Rituals of Restorative Justice* (Oxford, Oxford University Press, 2013).

[101] A Acorn, *Compulsory Compassion: A Critique of Restorative Justice* (Vancouver, UBC Press, 2004).

[102] See Maruna (n 97); see also N Harris et al, 'Emotional Dynamics in Restorative Justice Conferences' (2004) 8 *Theoretical Criminology* 191.

[103] See Maruna (n 97).

[104] C Barton, *Restorative Justice: The Empowerment Model* (Sydney, Hawking Press, 2003).

[105] D Reisel, *Rewiring Our Morality* (New York, TED Books, 2014).

silence, or for the right to counsel).[106] Moreover, many concerns have emerged regarding the actual voluntary nature of restorative justice processes when offered as a more lenient alternative to 'regular' criminal process and punishment. It is true that restorative justice presupposes a prior admission of guilt and a conscious decision to take reparative action to make amends and repair the harm done by crime. According to some authors,[107] admitting guilt with the prospect of either avoiding trial or receiving a lesser sentence can manifest a tacit form of coercion. There is a risk that an individual could feel pressured to choose restorative justice and plead guilty as a consequence just to escape harsher sentences or any other negative repercussions than if he or she opted to remain silent and face trial. These practical concerns are founded and reasonable, and I shall address them in the next section.

From a theoretical perspective, restorative justice outcomes including taking personal responsibility for the harm done, making amends, making restitutions and repairing damages are not the ultimate goals of social rehabilitation. However, these outcomes may nevertheless prompt positive change and favour social reintegration. Therefore, restorative justice must be viewed as instrumental to social rehabilitation, that is, as one of the tools that the justice system must offer to the individual to pursue social rehabilitation and that the individual could opt for. Since accountability, apologies, or reparations cannot be imposed, restorative justice should be best conceptualised as one of the many social rehabilitation means that the state must offer individuals as an option for pursuing social rehabilitation and to provide multifaceted solutions for a variety of cases. The processes of restorative justice can be pursued only if all the parties affected by crime consent to them.

IV. Practical Corollaries

The adoption of a system informed by social rehabilitation would imply a broad constellation of tremendous consequences for criminal justice. In such a system, courts and legislators would encourage, rather than discourage, the continuation of family and community relationships. They would assure education, job training, and other rehabilitation opportunities. They would insist that state and federal authorities encourage, rather than withhold, the franchise by including political education in prisons, and they would overturn laws that brand formerly incarcerated people and deny them public benefits, services, and the basic privileges of citizenship. It would be a system that responds to crime and the care of the

[106] See eg E Hanan, 'Decriminalizing Violence: A Critique of Restorative Justice and Proposal for Diversionary Mediation' (2016) 46 *New Mexico Law Review* 123.

[107] eg ibid, 132; ME Reimund, 'The Law and Restorative Justice: Friend or Foe? A Systemic Look at the Legal Issues in Restorative Justice' (2005) 53 *Drake Law Review* 667, 684.

victims, but would also preserve social relationships, respect people's individuality, and restore safety in the community.

If social rehabilitation was pursued as a fundamental principle of punishment, it could lead to, among other consequences, shorter sentences; a wider use of non-custodial sentences and diversion programmes; the provision of trauma-informed responses at any stage of criminal proceedings; incarceration as a last resort; the abolition of life imprisonment without the possibility of parole; the abolition of purely incapacitating sentencing laws, such as three-strike laws; sentencing review mechanisms for early release from prison; a normalisation approach to convicted individuals with serious mental illness; the reform of civil commitment regimes; accountability for ruinous conditions of confinement; the transformation of prison environments and a drastic reduction of solitary confinement; and the elimination of legal barriers to full citizenship for formerly incarcerated people.[108]

Each corollary is important and requires a thorough discussion. Unfortunately, space does not allow me to analyse and discuss each in detail, but I hope to be able to do so in future works. In the next section, I limit the scope of my analysis to the following macro-corollaries: the re-organisation of sentencing goals and criteria, the banning of mandatory life imprisonment without parole, the transformation of incarceration, and the abolition of solitary confinement.

A. Humanising Sentencing

As discussed in chapter two, modern criminal justice predominantly operates through schemes of 'limiting retributivism',[109] whereby desert considerations set upper and occasionally lower limits on sentencing severity, which can then generate a range of acceptable sentencing options. Once desert concerns have set this range (minimum and maximum), other utilitarian considerations, such as incapacitation, rehabilitation, or special deterrence, provide the necessary 'fine-tuning'. If the punishment is within the prescribed range based on desert considerations, non-retributive concerns could guide the method of punishment and the specific punishment without undermining retributive principles. Thus, backward-looking desert considerations are paramount in sentencing, while forward-looking considerations of special deterrence, incapacitation, and rehabilitation are secondary and subordinated to a series of additional evaluations based on the type of offence committed and the personality of the perpetrator, including his or her past criminal record and potential future dangerousness. Notably, sentencing generally pursues rehabilitation as long as it is 'reasonably feasible',[110] that is, when there

[108] It is worth mentioning that some of these changes have been implemented to some extent in some states or are a part of agendas for criminal justice reforms in others.

[109] N Morris, *The Future of Imprisonment* (Chicago, University of Chicago Press, 1974).

[110] See American Law Institute, Model Penal Code: Sentencing § 1.02 (2017).

is a reasonable hope and sufficient evidence that a person has the propensity to reform, and that there are concrete prospects of specific deterrence.

The envisioning of social rehabilitation as an overarching principle of punishment – to be pursued *a priori* and universally and not only when reasonably feasible, with little discretion left to the sentencing authorities – places further limits on the risks of punitiveness resulting from current hybrid systems based on limiting retributivism.[111] The principle would operate at both a systemic and a case level.[112] At a systemic level, this principle would inform decisions on severity and recommended sentences. At a case level, it would assist courts to tailor sentencing according to the effects (including the collateral consequences) of a given penalty for the relevant person and to ensure that considerations of social (re)integration are considered. The basic rule on sentencing would remain, then, the gravity of the offence. However, under such an approach, considerations of gravity would have to be counterbalanced by (governing) considerations of social (re)integration.

Sentencing should be guided by a principle of minimum harm: the appropriate sentence would be one which is expected to achieve the desired purpose (with consideration of the seriousness of the offence) and inflicts the least possible harm in terms of social exclusion and anticipated effects on psychological well-being.[113] The calculus and choice of sentences, then, must also draw on what Richard Frase has named 'ends-benefits proportionality',[114] meaning the burdens of a criminal penalty must not exceed the benefits of that penalty, while consideration also needs to be given to the cost of a criminal penalty. Under the approach I propose, however, the criterion for this evaluation lies in the pursuit of social reintegration. Among the factors that figure within the costs of burdens of a penalty are also the collateral consequences – both direct and indirect –[115] of a given sanction for the relevant person and others (including his or her family). An individual facing conviction remains a member of the society (eg, he or she has a family, he or she possibly has a job or is in search for one, or is pursuing education), and sentencing must ensure that penalties do not frustrate these basic needs of social life. Sentencing determinations should also consider the impact that a given sentence could have on an individual and his or her social life in view of his or her

[111] See also R Frase, *Just Sentencing: Principles and Procedures for a Workable System* (New York, Oxford University Press, 2013) 25 (suggesting an expanded model of limiting retributivism, one that also recognises a 'definite yet asymmetric limits' principle, for which deserts should set upper limits on sanction severity but much more flexible lower limits, or none at all. Accordingly, courts should be given more discretionality in sentencing determinations).

[112] ibid.

[113] See also RA Duff, *Punishment, Communication, and Community* (Oxford, Oxford University Press, 2001).

[114] See Frase (n 111) 25 (suggesting that '[t]wo very important considerations at sentencing are not addressed at all: utilitarian ends-benefits proportionality and social equality').

[115] See also A Kolber, 'The Subjective Experience of Punishment' (2009) 109 *Columbia Law Review* 183 (suggesting that sentencing should also take account of individuals' *vulnerability* to sentences, notably incarceration); R Lippke, 'Punishment Drift: The Spread of Penal Harm and What We Should Do About It' (2017) 11 *Criminal Law and Philosophy* (2017) 645.

conditions, and address protective factors that can buffer the risk of reoffending and foster pathways to desistance.[116] However, social rehabilitation cannot be used as a justification for more severe or lengthier sentences.

Individual and social variables should not only receive a quantitative weight – either mitigating or aggravating – but also, and in more depth, be valued as *qualitative* benchmarks of sentencing to consider in determining the most appropriate options to respond to crime and to address the background and needs of individuals facing conviction. Admittedly, close, holistic attention to these elements can 'allow judges and other actors in the criminal justice system to develop a more nuanced portrait of defendants' as well as 'to develop more creative solutions to criminal matters'.[117]

On the other hand, incapacitation-based considerations could be added to justify the imposition of a custodial sentence only when there is a concrete, imminent and exigent risk that the person may pose a substantial threat to public safety if he or she was left in the community.[118] However, incapacitation should never legitimise predictive judgements of future dangerousness nor form a valid justification for harsher sentences based on the alleged future dangerousness of the individual. As discussed, empirical evidence suggests that courts cannot reliably distinguish the dangerous from the non-dangerous individuals. Given so, the presumption of future change must prevail over a presumption of future threat.

The inclusion of social rehabilitation as a paramount guiding principle of sentencing implies a greater individualisation of sentencing criteria, which should also, and more consistently, consider an individual's motivational, contextual, and social factors that may be linked with the crime. Critically, courts should include an exploration of a defendant's trauma history.[119] That exploration should delve into the trauma's effect on the defendant's behaviour to allow sentencers to view people's action in the context of their own victimisation and to identify sentences that might best address his or her trauma rather than redistribute it.[120] In chapter one, I discussed how trauma is barely and inconsistently considered in sentencing determinations; instead, retributive and – especially – incapacitation-based considerations prevail over the neglected background of a person. In the previous chapter, I provided the normative argument that prolonged, repeated, and unbuffered victimisations and exposure to traumatic events (eg, violence and severe

[116] See also M Gohara, 'Grace Notes: A Case for Making Mitigation the Heart of Noncapital Sentencing' (2013) 41 *American Criminal Law Journal* 41, 69 (suggesting that sentencing should place an 'emphasis on positive factors in the defendant's life, such as educational and employment opportunities, family support, and access to and amenability to rehabilitative services').

[117] K Thomas, 'Beyond Mitigation: Towards a Theory of Allocution' (2007) 75 *Fordham Law Review* 2641, 2645.

[118] *Graham* (n 57) 73 ('Here one cannot dispute that this defendant posed an immediate risk ... but it does not follow that he would be a risk to society for the rest of his life'). See also below.

[119] My argument primarily concerns non-capital cases.

[120] See ch 1.

socio-environmental deprivation) resulting in toxic stress are eligible conditions for a (hypothetical) generic partial excuse, provided that there is a clear and direct link with the offence committed. The defence I proposed presumes that the exigencies of the desperate situations in which people find themselves significantly affect their decision to abide by the law, even if they do not impair it entirely to ground a full excuse.

Trauma considerations in sentencing would be justified by the same normative excusing conditions (ie, either a diminished capacity or a diminished fair opportunity to do otherwise). Such considerations include situations that are relevant to the partial excuse defence but do not technically or fully conform to its requirements. Such considerations would extend to other significant traumas that do not have a direct link with the offence (that is, trauma is not the principal reason for its commission), but they nevertheless contributed[121] to it. As explained, compelling evidence exists that having being a victim of physical or sexual abuse during childhood increases the risk of offending later in adulthood. An increasing number of authors[122] maintains that childhood trauma should qualify as a mitigating factor at sentencing if a connection is drawn between such trauma and adult behaviour.[123] Other types of trauma such as disadvantaged youth, racial discrimination, poverty, or lack of guidance should equally factor into mitigation considerations to the extent that they are salient to the relevant case.[124]

Moreover, and in line with the claims made above, evidence of trauma should also assist sentencing authorities in tailoring the specific form of a sentence, so that, while it addresses crime, it also avoids re-traumatising the relevant person.

[121] See eg *United States v Cockett*, 330 F.3d 706, 714 (6th Cir. 2003) (the 'extent of the departure should reflect the extent to which the reduced mental capacity contributed to the commission of the offense'); *United States v Matney*, 375 F. Supp. 2d 482, 488 (W.D. Va. 2005) ('Diminished capacity need not be the sole cause of the offense to justify a departure, but should comprise … a contributing factor in the commission of the offense') (citation omitted). See also see also *Miller* n 57 (introducing the defendant's 'pathological background' as the contributing reason behind his commission of the crime).

[122] M Bagaric et al, 'Trauma and Sentencing: The Case for Mitigating Penalty for Childhood Physical and Sexual Abuse' (2019) 30 *Stanford Law Review & Policy* 1, 41 ('Childhood trauma unquestionably limits the victims' choices. The key consideration is the extent to which the choices of people who were sexually or physically abused during their youth are limited, and the degree to which this experience inclines them towards committing crimes. It is impossible to quantify the extent to which people who had traumatic upbringings have diminished opportunities. Yet it is clear that, not only are traumatised people's choices restricted, but also that those limitations make them more prone to offending. This reality means that such individuals are less responsible for their crimes than offenders who have not experienced childhood sexual or physical abuse. Thus, a strong argument exists that traumatised individuals should receive a reduced sentence'). See also M Gohara, 'In Defense of the Injured: How Trauma-Informed Criminal Defense Can Reform Sentencing' (2018) 45 *American Criminal Law Journal* 1.

[123] See D Denno, 'How Courts Respond to Childhood Trauma' (2019) 103 *Marquette Law Review* 302 (mostly focusing on capital cases).

[124] See Gohara (n 116) 61–5; see also Bagaric et al (n 122) 11 ('After *Booker*, there is no longer any need to show extreme abuse or neglect to avoid the prohibitions of § 5H1.12, and courts have begun to consider disadvantaged youth or lack of guidance as a youth as a factor for sentencing below the guideline range').

The sentencing discount that people with traumas should receive needs to be sizable enough to reflect their role in the person's behaviour and to address relevant penalties in light of considerations about the gravity of the offence and public safety needs – all of which operate, however, under the governing ultimate goal of social (re)integration. Reducing penalties for traumatised people will not reduce public safety if the objective of social rehabilitation is also pursued.[125]

Under such an approach, incarceration is limited to the most severe cases and when there is no major risk of further grave offences (the principle of 'incarceration as a last resort'). Instead, there should be a greatly expanded use of alternative, non-custodial sanctions, to be possibly served in the community, such as probation programmes that involve community work, as well as diversion programmes such as restitutions, education, and restorative justice. With specific regard to the latter, restorative justice processes and programmes should be offered as either an alternative or an additional (depending on the crime at stake) option for dispute resolution at any stage of the criminal process and for any crime, as long as the parties consent, in full acceptance of due process and procedural safeguards, and in compliance with the principle of proportionality. Communications that emerge during restorative justice encounters or programmes must be kept confidential and can never be used as evidence against the responsible party. If the restorative encounters or programmes succeed, the court must consider this information to either discharge the case or to mitigate the sentence. If the restorative justice encounters or programmes fail, the court cannot use such information to impose a more severe sentence.

One last macro-implication concerns the dynamics and settings of sentencing hearings. While sentencing must guarantee accuracy, proportionality, fairness and equality to the parties involved, more consideration should be given to the voices of the people involved, and opportunities of reconciliation and humanisation should be created whenever possible. Defendants and their respective families should be given more opportunities to speak and tell their stories.[126] Obviously, fact-finders must be impartial and neutral parties, and their primary focus in determining sentences must be the harm suffered by the victims. Yet nothing precludes fact-finders from empathising with the defendants' feelings and faultless suffering. As Judge Jack B Weinstein observed, '[s]entencing … turns on the judge's heart and life experience. It reveals the human face of the law. Without empathy between judge and defendant, sentencing lacks humanity. It becomes a form of robotism.'[127]

[125] See also Gohara (n 116) 48 (arguing that rehabilitation of injured people is essential to preserve public safety).

[126] See C Haney, 'Evolving Standards of Decency: Advancing the Nature and Logic of Capital Mitigation' (2008) 36 *Hofstra Law Review* 835, 882 (suggesting that a 'mitigating counter-narrative' demonstrating that a person's criminal behaviour is 'restricted to a particular context or situation helps jurors avoid making unwarranted inferences about future dangerousness in settings that are not at all similar').

[127] JB Weinstein, 'Does Religion Have a Role in Criminal Sentencing?' (2007) 23 *Touro Law Review* 539, 539 (2014).

The underlying theme here is that proper consideration of emotions and contexts deserves full consideration. Accepting the role of such factors in driving human experience and behaviour might pave the way for a sentencing system that acknowledges the universal and 'diverse frailties of human kind'[128] and offers greater mercy, compassion, empathy and dialogue, reducing the inevitable gap that crime generates among people whenever the circumstances make this possible.

B. Banning Mandatory Life Sentences

The adoption of a social rehabilitation-oriented model of punishment would lead to the categorical and universal ban of mandatory life imprisonment without parole (LWOP). In view of what I have discussed previously in this chapter, such a penalty – which is already the target of harsh criticism in legal scholarship – would lose its *raison d'être* for both empirical and normative reasons. First, the incapacitating rationale of mandatory life sentences is entirely incompatible with the body of empirical evidence regarding adult change. Second, such a penalty runs against the rehabilitative goal of social reintegration as it poses an inflexible barrier to an individual's re-entry into society from the outset.

Regarding the first reason, predictions of future dangerousness that justify the infliction of mandatory life sentences lack any strong empirical support. As I have mentioned more than once throughout this chapter, predicting the life course of an individual based on existing individual and social variables is hardly possible. Such variables are not fixed; they are dynamic, in continuous evolution, and strongly malleable. Thus, presuming that an individual will certainly or most likely fare badly for the entire course of his or her life based on a prognostic judgement is empirically impossible. Therefore, a universal presumption of future change should always prevail over a prediction of inflexible dangerousness.

Regarding the second, and consequential, reason, a model of punishment that hinges upon and aims at inclusion and social reintegration entails that rehabilitative considerations largely trump incapacitation arguments. A severely incapacitating and exclusionary penalty such as LWOP implies the harshest judgement – the rejection of a person from the rest of society. Such a judgement severely violates the dignity of an individual as a rational and autonomous being, for it ultimately denies his or her capacity to pursue change and to self-rehabilitate, regardless of the crime he or she committed. Denying hope for rehabilitation and release at the outset not only implies a severe violation of this aspect of human dignity, but

[128] See D Kahan and M Nussbaum, 'Two Conceptions of Emotions in Criminal Law' (1996) 96 *Columbia Law Review* 269, 370–71 ('We want the law to condemn the crime, including the reprehensible emotional motivations underlying it. We want it to reaffirm the worth of the victim … But we also demand (or should demand) that the law acknowledge "the diverse frailties of the human kind". This requires … taking up a certain attitude toward ourselves – saying, perhaps, we are all weak and subject to deformation, and had we been in that shoes, who knows what we would have done …').

is also indicative of a justice system that assumes *a priori* that human beings are irredeemable and irreparably corrupt by their very nature.

In *Graham*, Justice Kennedy made similar observations when he wrote that:

> a sentence of life imprisonment without parole … cannot be justified by the goal of rehabilitation. The penalty forswears altogether the rehabilitative ideal. By denying the defendant the right to reenter the community, the State makes an irrevocable judgment about that person's value and place in society.[129]

It is of utmost importance to note that the *Graham* opinion was remarkably pointed in support of the European Court of Human Rights (ECtHR) when it abolished life sentences with no possibility of release for *all* persons.[130] Embracing and expanding the words of the Supreme Court in *Graham*, including human dignity, hope for rehabilitation, and hope for release, the ECtHR established that, 'an unreviewable whole life order mean[s] that a prisoner would remain incarcerated until death irrespective of whatever changes … might take place in the course of his or her sentence'.[131] According to the ECtHR, the irrevocable nature of mandatory life sentences is not only incompatible with an idea of punishment that also pursues rehabilitation, but entails a severe violation of human dignity inherent to all persons. As Martufi explained, for the ECtHR, such a sentence

> would be incompatible with human dignity – which forms the very essence of the Convention system – to sentence a person to life imprisonment without at least providing him or her with the chance to someday regain freedom. In referring to the notion of human dignity, the Court's arguments on rehabilitation blend into broader humanitarian considerations as to the condition of life prisoners. More specifically, the Court takes the view that life prisoners cannot be deprived of the right to hope of one day having atoned for the wrongs that they have committed. In doing so, the ECtHR recognizes implicitly 'that hope is an important and constitutive aspect of the human person'.[132]

In 2019, the ECtHR reaffirmed this line of reasoning in *Viola v Italy*,[133] in which it found that the application or the continuation of mandatory life sentences for people involved in Mafia crimes, in addition to murder, abduction, and other serious crimes, is an inhumane and degrading punishment under Article 3 of the European Convention of Human Rights (ECHR). Notably, the ECtHR considered that the lack of cooperation of the relevant individual (which national authorities had qualified as a sign of his dangerousness) could not be viewed as indicative of his lack of rehabilitation or used as a barrier to his social re-entry. The Court

[129] *Graham* (n 57) 74.

[130] *Vinter and Others v the United Kingdom* 66069/09, 130/10, and 3896/10, ECHR. 73 (2013) (citing *Graham*, 560 U.S. at 48).

[131] ibid, 99.

[132] A Martufi, 'The Paths of Offender Rehabilitation and the European Dimension of Punishment: New Challenges for an Old Ideal?' (2019) 25 *Maastricht Journal of European and Comparative Law* 672, 676–7 (citation omitted).

[133] *Viola v Italy* (no. 2) 77633/16 Eur. Ct. H.R. (2019).

observed that there could be situations in which a person cooperates fully but provides no sign of rehabilitation. Thus, using lack of cooperation as a barrier to social re-entry gives 'rise to an irrebuttable presumption of dangerousness', one that deprives an individual 'of any realistic prospect of release'.[134] The Court clarified that even those who commit the worst and most dangerous crimes, such as Mafia-type crimes, cannot be deprived of their hope for rehabilitation and release by imposing a penalty such as a mandatory life sentence. The principle of human dignity mandates that every justice-involved individual deprived of his or her freedom must be given the opportunity to change, self-rehabilitate, and regain his or her freedom someday without any discrimination based on crime type. Even '[t]hose who commit the most abhorrent and egregious of acts and who inflict untold suffering upon others, nevertheless retain their fundamental humanity and carry within themselves the capacity to change'.[135]

As is evident, the two Courts used precisely the same arguments to ban mandatory life sentences. However, the distinguishing element between them lies in the (lack of) recognition of the capacity for adult subjects to change. By recognising that mandatory LWOP must not apply to adolescents because of their capacity to change, the US Supreme Court has endorsed the view that LWOP can legitimately apply to adults precisely because adults are allegedly incapable or less capable of change.[136] On the other hand, as Hanan correctly observed, the ECtHR 'incorporates the idea of change at any age into its standard for reviewing life sentences'.[137] Thus, life sentences must be reviewed based on 'any changes in the life [of the] prisoner [that] are so significant … as to mean that continued detention can no longer be justified on legitimate penological grounds'.[138]

As mentioned previously, if the US Supreme Court acknowledged that adults are also capable of change, and bolstered stronger conceptions of human dignity and hope for rehabilitation, then the arguments it made in *Graham* would naturally and automatically extend to adult justice. As several authors have observed, the slight opening of the Supreme Court to the (neuro)science of change might presage a new approach in the Supreme Court to categorically ban mandatory life sentences for adults. It is, however, difficult to imagine such a change in the immediate future. Nevertheless, it is not implausible that the Court, as it has in the past,[139] might consider and value the growing (neuro)scientific evidence concerning adult change and global standards of decency, dignity, and humanity to review its position and find mandatory LWOP a cruel and unusual punishment.

[134] ibid.
[135] *Vinter* (n 130) 54 (Power-Forde, J, concurring).
[136] *Graham* (n 57) 68–9.
[137] Hanan (n 61) 190.
[138] ibid, 190–1.
[139] *Roper* (n 51).

C. Transforming Incarceration

Incarceration is, by definition, incompatible with social rehabilitation.[140] The idea of incarceration is at odds with the inclusionary and socially reintegrative spirit of social rehabilitation. Given so, under social rehabilitation, incarceration should be a last resort, restricted to the most severe cases, and only used when all other measures are inadequate to respond to public safety needs. Nevertheless, social rehabilitation is never a justification for incarceration; people cannot be incarcerated to be socially rehabilitated. Instead, social rehabilitation 'enters' incarceration as a 'protective shield' against the harmful effects of the latter and guarantees that those who are incarcerated are provided with the means to keep their individual and social skills, maintain or cultivate social relationships and bonds, and continue efforts toward personal growth in view of their return to society. Thus, even when incarceration is the only option available, positive actions toward rehabilitation are essential to avoid harmful and traumatising effects on the mental and social health of incarcerated people and for them to be successfully reintegrated into society upon release.

Therefore, a transformation of the philosophy behind incarceration and the social and physical environment of incarceration facilities is imperative. Such transformation entails, primarily, a replacement of the current 'principle of less eligibility' – according to which a person in prison's standard of life should not exceed that of the poorest members of society – with the 'principle of approximation (or normalcy)' – according to which prison conditions should be, as much as possible, approximate to life on the outside and favour the flourishing of the person in a healthy environment.

Prison administrators are expected, therefore, to work under the principle of approximation, which means that prison life must offer contact with the outside world, relevant education programmes, skills training, trauma-healing programmes, and psychotherapy, vocational training, and social and recreational activities, as well as meaningful paid labour to also help support their families. By meaningful paid labour, I do not mean labour that is paid around two dollars a day.[141] Instead, I mean work that requires some skills that will be a stepping stone to allow incarcerated individuals to pursue employment in a similar field upon release.

Incarcerated individuals must be given the opportunity to form relationships that can continue outside. Such relationships are important to allow people who are incarcerated to keep or repristinate a sense of self-esteem and self-worth during their incarceration in view of their social re-entry. Furthermore, allowing

[140] See also American Law Institute, Model Penal Code: Sentencing § 6.01 (2017). See also *Tapia v United States* 131 S. Ct. 2382 (2011).

[141] See J Kovensky, 'It's Time to Pay Prisoners the Minimum Wage' (2014) *The New Republic*, available at newrepublic.com/article/119083/prison-labor-equal-rights-wages-incarcerated-help-economy.

the 'outside world' to enter facilities is fundamental to combat the 'us versus them' mentality that inevitably accompanies and makes the life of incarcerated people difficult when they return to society. Therefore, and consistent with a growing number of views in the literature,[142] incarceration facilities must also offer restorative justice-based programmes[143] to allow people in prison to accept accountability and to acknowledge the consequences of their behaviour through dialogue and confrontations, including with community members.

People who are incarcerated must not be required to wear uniforms, and they must be addressed respectfully and humanely by prison personnel. In legal systems following a 'dynamic security' model,[144] interpersonal relationships between prison personnel and incarcerated people are a crucial factor in preserving prison and public safety. Frequent socialisation between prison staff and incarcerated individuals creates an atmosphere of mutual trust and respect, which has proven fundamental for ameliorating life in prison and for discouraging institutional incidents.[145] Importantly, such meaningful rehabilitative endeavours should aim to eradicate the risk of violence, avoid the formation of prison subcultures, and overcome racial conflict.

Overall, viewed through the lens of social rehabilitation, incarceration becomes a safe and empowering venue of dialogue, support, cooperation, and accountability. An incarceration system that adheres to this ideal would offer those impacted by it the chance to retain their social identities and to receive social and emotional support in a humane context. The behavioural literature I discussed in chapter four suggested that inclusionary and relationally-based approaches, such as the involvement of positive social engagements and activities, are more likely to aid people in eliminating profound feelings of rejection, exclusion, and humiliation and to stimulate them to act in prosocial ways through training, dialogue, and inclusion. These elements can enhance the skills and accomplishments of incarcerated people, which can serve as internalised and reality-based sources of self-respect and self-esteem, as well as attracting respect and esteem from others and motivating their process of reconstructing their life self-narrative. The importance of developing healthy social relationships during incarceration finds further and critical evidence-based support in the strict tie between the brain and healthy social connections that I have mentioned throughout the chapter.

Another implication for the prison environment under social rehabilitation is the transformation of the physical layout of incarceration facilities. The empirical

[142] eg B Toews, *The Little Book of Restorative Justice for People in Prison: Rebuilding the Web of Relationships* (Intercourse, PA, Good Books, 2006); N Dhami, 'Restorative Justice in Prisons' (2009) 12 *Contemporary Justice Review: Issues in Criminal, Social, and Restorative Justice* 433.

[143] See eg *Insight Prison Project*, available at www.insightprisonproject.org/.

[144] J Benko, 'The Radical Humaneness of Norway's Halden Prison: The Goal of the Norwegian Penal System is to Get Inmates Out of It' *The New York Times* (25 March 2015) available at www.nytimes.com/2015/03/29/magazine/the-radical-humaneness-of-norways-halden-prison.html?_r=0.

[145] ibid.

research reported in chapter four emphasises the fundamental importance of stimulating and enriched environments for physiological brain activity, mental health, and positive sociable tendencies. Environmental deprivation, which is understood as living in scarce or poor environments without significant external stimuli, may have negative repercussions for the structure and function of brain areas that are linked with a variety of cognitive, affective, and social skills associated with morally adaptive behaviour.

Taken together, these insights strongly support the transformation of detention facilities into locations that are as dignified, humane, and approximated to general living conditions as much as possible. These settings should allow the people within them to have as much internal freedom as possible considering their temporary deprivation of liberty and separation from the community. Several scholars and national associations have recommended the transformation of jails and prisons from exclusionary and often precarious facilities into secure yet humane settings, such as residential centres or therapeutic communities, with proper bedding, furniture, and natural light. For instance, the VERA Institute of Justice, a US non-profit organisation for criminal justice, has partnered with a team of architects from the MASS Design Group to launch an experimental project that targets the development of future correctional facilities.[146] Inspired by the 'Norwegian prison model',[147] the project reimagines the physical layout of prison facilities to achieve a design that conveys respect for human dignity and promotes inclusivity, dialogue, and effective rehabilitation. This project would transform 'prisons' into open yet secure spaces wherein the people who reside there can heal and feel empowered to change their own lives. This design for prisons would facilitate personal growth and change, and, ultimately, restore communities.

Such a model promotes the implementation of the previously reported dynamic socio-environmental factors of protection for mental health, psychological well-being, and prosocial attitudes. Thus, while encouraging individual change, a humanised detention environment that favours inclusion, social relationships, dialogue, and dignity could also be instrumental in resolving the excessive violence in institutionalised settings and, eventually, decreasing recidivism rates. Overall, the transformation of correctional facilities into the described centres could be a vital change to not only improve the lives of the people they house, but also to satisfy more fully the public demands for safety and security to ameliorate the workings and outcomes of criminal justice as a whole.

Finally, I share the view that the rehabilitative opportunities offered to incarcerated individuals should be 'made in a social policy context which also guarantees

[146] Vera Institute of Justice, 'Human Dignity and Prison Design' (2019), available at www.vera.org/research/human-dignity-and-prison-design.

[147] See Benko (n 144).

opportunities to those who do not offend'[148] and promotes equality. To offer such life chances to individuals facing conviction alone contravenes principles of social justice. A rehabilitative criminal justice strategy must form part of a broader and solid social policy agenda that recognises everyone's basic needs. As Rotman argued, 'a humanistic public policy regarding crime implies the idea of human perfectibility, which at the level of rehabilitation includes not only the offenders themselves, but also the society that bred them and the institutions and persons involved in their treatment'.[149] Perhaps this is the most difficult, and yet most critical, change of all.

D. Abolishing (or Profoundly Reforming) Solitary Confinement

The suggested transformation of prison environments into humane venues naturally entails that solitary confinement would be abolished, or at the very least, profoundly re-thought. As it currently stands (and is notoriously known), solitary confinement is a correctional measure that prison administrations apply to meet disciplinary, security or safety needs of prisons. On average, solitary confinement entails the nearly total isolation of an individual for 22 or 23 hours per day without any meaningful social contact, in impoverished environments, and indefinite periods of time. Despite its persistence within the incarceration system, solitary confinement is largely viewed as an inhumane practice that severely violates human dignity and exposes confined people to severe risks for their mental and physical health, as well as their own life.[150]

To remain within the scope of my argument, the total incompatibility between solitary confinement and social rehabilitation is crystal clear. As discussed, social rehabilitation promotes as much inclusiveness and positive social engagement as possible while perpetrators serve their prison sentence and works to protect incarcerated individuals from the potential deteriorating effects of incarceration on their mental and physical integrity. Accordingly, the extremely exclusionary and debilitating nature of solitary confinement makes the accomplishment of these aims hardly possible.

In addition to opposing the tenets of social rehabilitation, the potential harms of solitary confinement may seriously compromise an individual's social functioning. Therefore, these harms seriously compromise the rehabilitation

[148] P Raynor, 'Some Observations on Rehabilitation and Justice' (1997) 36 *The Howard Journal* 248, 259.

[149] Rotman (n 18) at 292.

[150] C Wildeman and L Andersen, 'Solitary Confinement Placement and Post-Release Mortality Risk Among Formerly Incarcerated Individuals: A Population-Based Study' (2020) 5 *Lancet Public Health* e107.

and resocialisation process and render it more difficult, if not nearly impossible in some cases. Abundant psychological literature has extensively reported the psycho(patho)logical effects of solitary confinement.[151] Numerous psychological, psychiatric and observational studies have carefully documented the vastity of adverse consequences of living in isolation in deprived environments for mental health, well-being, and behaviour in both healthy and unhealthy populations.[152] Amongst others, socio-environmental deprivation entails maladaptive psychological symptoms that are normally linked with the experience of social pain, which can not only diminish the psychological and physical well-being of the individual but also result in maladaptive action tendencies and dysfunctional behaviours, other than precipitating the risk of developing serious mental conditions. As I discussed in chapter four, the psychological deteriorations following extreme isolation are linked to alterations that occur in the brain. These brain alterations have implications beyond the immediately visible behaviours, and can lead to a wide range of adverse psychological effects, many of which may be long-lasting or even permanent. The longer the period of extreme isolation, the more likely it is that these damages can manifest and grow.

The acknowledgment of the dramatic neurobiological effects of extreme isolation leads us primarily to challenge the constitutionality of solitary confinement under the Eighth Amendment. I have extensively analysed this issue elsewhere,[153] so I will not repeat myself here. Yet, I want to re-state that the neurobiological damages that solitary confinement risks either precipitating or aggravating make it a cruel and unusual punishment *even under the current standards* established by the Supreme Court.[154] Foremost, solitary confinement deprives individuals of social interaction and environmental stimulation, both of which are basic human needs that are essential to physiological brain function and mental health. Second, such deprivation seriously risks damaging the brain, which means that the harms accrued through solitary confinement are physical. Third, the extent and type of the organic damages that solitary confinement risks implying are too excessive (ie, excessively disproportionate) compared to the legitimate needs of discipline, security and safety that may possibly justify its infliction. Considering its disfiguring and excessively disproportionate nature, I have argued that solitary confinement should be viewed as per se a cruel and unusual punishment.

[151] eg P Scharff Smith, 'The Effects of Solitary Confinement on Prison Inmates: A Brief History and Review of the Literature' (2006) 34 *Crime & Justice* 441; C Haney, 'Mental Health Issues in Long-Term Solitary and 'Supermax' Confinement' (2003) 49 *Crime & Delinquency* 124; C Haney, 'The Psychological Effects of Solitary Confinement: A Systematic Critique' (2018) 47 *Crime & Justice* 365.

[152] For a review, see F Coppola, 'The Brain in Solitude: An(other) Eighth Amendment Challenge to Solitary Confinement' (2019) *Journal of Law and the Biosciences* 184, 207–8.

[153] ibid.

[154] *Estelle v Gamble*, 429 U.S. 97 (1976); *Hutto* (n 66); *Rhodes* (66); *Farmer v Brennan*, 511 U.S. 825, 837 (1994).

Moving beyond its constitutional questionability, the current nature and features of solitary confinement would not find any space within a model of punishment inspired to social rehabilitation and would, therefore, be abolished. Regrettably, even within a prison environment informed by the principles of social rehabilitation, a temporary separation of one person from the rest of the incarcerated population might still be warranted in those instances that require an individual's protection or for possible serious incidents, though only when other measures have been tried without satisfactory results. Even in such instances though, the separation regime of an individual from the rest of the population would have to be subject to strict time limits as well as sociability and environmental standards.

In regard to time limits, more empirical research is needed to assess the exact maximum time limit for depriving an individual of constant social contact without causing damages. Nevertheless, given the current paucity of jurisprudence on duration limits for solitary confinement, international guidelines[155] that mandate a maximum of 15 days of separation of a person from the rest of the prison population would apply. With respect to sociability conditions, temporarily separated people should be able to access as much social engagement as possible, including through education and job programmes, rehabilitation and recreation activities, and time with visitors. Finally, the design of 'separation' settings should follow strict environmental standards. In line with the aforementioned argument for transforming incarceration, separation settings should also be designed as spaces that are as secure yet home-like as possible to allow the people who live in them to experience their confinement in the most dignified and humanised conditions.

V. Conclusion

All life events are made of a past and a future. Human actions and the people behind them too. Confining an individual to his or her past wrong and harmful actions while denying his or her chances to construct a better future is a fundamental negation of his or her humanity. A justice system that truly respects the dignity of individuals as humans should be more sensitive to their emotional and social life and work to address the frailties that too often hide profound traumas. Such a system should also value the uniquely human capacity for change and empower individuals to build such a change to overcome their past and get on with their lives. Hence, punishment should not mark the diminution, the disappearance or the civil death of the individual because of a mistake. Rather, it should seek to prompt the personal growth, self-discovery, or even the re-birth of the individual *despite that mistake*.

[155] UN General Assembly, 'Standard Minimum Rules for the Treatment of Prisoners', Res. 70/175 (Dec. 17, 2015), Rule 44.

I am a firm believer that criminal justice must respond to crime with certainty, reasonableness and proportionality. Yet, I also believe that justice must also and more fundamentally preserve the person, protect his or her emotional life, and respect his or her dignity and social identity. Criminal justice must value the multifaceted and dynamic nature of persons in order to allow them to retain the humanity they carry within themselves. This entails providing the people impacted by the criminal justice system with conditions and opportunities that allow them to keep or (re)discover their sense of self-worth and belongingness, value their positive contribution to society, and either maintain or attract respect and esteem from others. This idea of justice does seek to promote fairness and public safety. However, it does not hide itself behind the utopic presumption that fairness and safety can be obtained through suffering, exclusion, and deprivation. A justice system that disregards and disparages the humanity of people forsakes its function of guidance and social protection, and simply becomes an instrument of blinding grief and vindication. Thus far, such a justice has proven inhumane and largely ineffective. Most importantly, it has heavily disregarded the unique quintessence of people as dynamic emotional and social beings. As Bryan Stevenson said, '*each of us is much more than the worst thing we've ever done*'.[156]

[156] B Stevenson, *Just Mercy: A Story of Justice and Redemption* (New York, Spiegel & Grau, 2015) 17.

Epilogue

During my lessons at Edgecombe, I asked the students to write a short essay on what they would like to change about themselves and what steps they would have to take to do so. I read the essays at the end of the course. All were inspirational, but one in particular captured my attention. This Edgecombe student, A, wrote that her personal change project was to stop giving up on herself. She explained that she tended to quit on commitments quite easily, to drop projects or jobs any time life confronted her with an obstacle because she felt she was not resilient enough to continue them. She also admitted that she wanted to drop the course after the first class; but she did not, she said, because she was given a valid opportunity not to give up. It took a lot of self-determination, effort, constant commitment, and self-reminders to continue. One factor that significantly supported her change was the 'positive people in my corner', that is, people who affirmed her self-worth and supported her to complete the course. She did not miss any classes.

On 28 January, the John Jay College of Criminal Justice hosted the graduation ceremony of the *Inside Criminal Justice* course. The students had the opportunity to present, in groups, their policy proposals and to suggest reforms in criminal justice in order to receive their diplomas. The proposals were all impressive. Observing the synergy and harmony among the students, I realised that a change had really happened and that the goal of the course had been achieved: they were seeing each other as humans.

The course I had the privilege to teach at Edgecombe, and more broadly the *Inside Criminal Justice* programme, is a special gem and a strong signal of change within the slow and difficult process of criminal justice reform that is taking place in many states across the country. Countless initiatives, programmes, and projects have been undertaken to support and inform reforms to diminish punitiveness, encourage inclusion, contrast discrimination and stigma, and increase opportunities for rehabilitation. Ranging from trauma-informed prosecution to collaborative education programmes, all these initiatives have the ultimate goal of reducing mass incarceration and keeping criminal justice up to date with the realities and needs of the people impacted. Yet more than once, I have heard well-intentioned legal professionals saying that they wish they could do more but are restricted because 'the law does not allow us to do so'.

Every legal scholar knows that the law is difficult to evolve, and legal traditions stubbornly refuse to die. Nevertheless, the time is ripe for change. I believe that legal scholarship bears a huge responsibility in supporting this change and ensuring that the law keeps pace with the times and with changing sensitivities. This book provides a small scholarly contribution to endorse this change. Notably, the general rethinking of the paradigms of culpability and punishment that this book argued for represents only an initial step toward incorporating growing calls for change within a unitary normative framework. Admittedly, many aspects have been left unexplored, while others call for further analysis. I intend to address these aspects in future works, including future editions of this book.

This book proposed changes to the current paradigms of culpability and punishment that go beyond abstract normative constructs and look, more closely, to the people behind these constructs and whose lives depend on them. I believe that criminal law's complex guidance of human behaviour cannot leave people behind, nor can it ignore social reality. As I have argued, reframing the paradigms of culpability and punishment, so that they take account of people's emotional and social dimensions, implies neither a denial of people's criminal liability nor a reduction of the legal and social gravity of certain behaviours. Instead, such a reframing implies viewing culpability and punishment through a broader and more reality-based lens, one that assigns a heavier normative weight to the emotional, motivational, and social aspects of human decisions and behaviour. People are more than abstract mental states, they are more than a mental capacity, they are more than their actions. In Stephanos Bibas's words, 'crime has a human face, and that face deserves standing and a say in the matter'.[1]

In this book, I have tried to convey this message through arguments based on empirical evidence, notably emanating from the science of the brain. For a long time, a popular claim that loomed large in neurolaw discussions was that neuroscience would eventually lead to the death of the person in criminal law. By suggesting that the mind is just the shadow of the brain, neuroscience would eventually lead to the dismissal of ideas of responsibility, free will, and punishment as actions and mental states turn out to be just the product of automatic brain mechanisms over which people have no control. I have never found this claim compelling; I have always thought of the contribution of neuroscience to criminal law in less invasive but more powerful terms.

Over the years, I have worked on the hypothesis that neuroscience could be used as an important tool to support the return of the person in criminal law. Across my works, including in this book, I have endorsed the idea that, even if our actions are governed by brain mechanisms, we remain agents of them. However, importantly, neuroscience suggests that the way in which human agency operates and manifests, especially in moral and social contexts, entails an extensive recruitment of our emotions and is inextricably bound to our social contexts and histories. Criminal law's acknowledgement of these factors in its conception of 'the person' does not lead to the claim that people are not responsible for their actions, nor that they should not be held accountable for them. Instead, such an acknowledgement leads to the far more modest claim that these ineradicable aspects of

[1] S Bibas, *The Machinery of Criminal Justice* (New York, Oxford University Press, 2012) 85.

human agency should factor into analyses of culpability and punishment and, possibly, ground these factors in a more realistic narrative of human behaviour – a narrative that recognises, to a larger extent, the complex dynamics behind offending behaviour and shifts away from moralistic and intuitive notions of badness and evil. Thus, I suggest that criminal law theory and doctrine should be more sensitive and receptive to this body of empirical knowledge to value certain aspects of personhood and human agency that are currently disregarded, but without implying a drastic revolution or dismissal of basic normative concepts.

(Neuro)science cannot revolutionise centuries-old legal doctrine or ideas of culpability and punishment. On its own, without any ideological aim or normative justification, it cannot affect normative practices. In this book, I have engaged with certain ideological aims and normative justifications to suggest that (neuro)science can guide criminal law to humanise its subjects. Humanising does not mean to excuse or dismiss state responses to crime. Humanising means to acknowledge the multidimensionality of individuals and attribute universal human capacities to them, including the capacities to think critically about one's own behaviour, to be accountable, to process and elaborate healthily the social emotions involved when hurting someone, to act to get one's life back on track, and to improve in the future. Humanising means valuing the importance of social relationships and positive environments to allow people to keep their sense of self-worth that lies at the core of their dignity. Essentially, humanising refers to seeing the human dimension of the other, including his or her fallibility, and, simultaneously, valuing his or her full social identity and his or her power to change the course of his or her life. A humanising law and justice system that considers the importance of the emotional and social life of the people within it and provides a second chance, or often a first chance, is vital for addressing crime adequately and fairly. Most importantly, such a system is key for preserving the dignity of justice-involved people as full human agents.

As I write these conclusions, the world is slowly recovering from months of fighting against an invisible enemy, and likely the battle is not yet won. In the arc of a few weeks, people found themselves isolated, quarantined, distanced, and partly deprived of their individual and social freedoms. Many people were stuck, far from home, in distant parts of the world and away from their loved ones, while many others have lost their jobs, and others have quit their education. Too many people have lost their life as they know it, many have been alone, and many have died without the possibility of saying goodbye to their families. Habits have changed. In some countries, the law has changed, and people's morals have changed accordingly. Empirical studies have begun to point out the severe risks to physical and mental health due to isolation and social distancing measures. Furthermore, such studies have highlighted the adverse consequences for behaviour, including greater social avoidance, alienation, and aggressiveness. The 'power of the situation' has inevitably influenced our way of perceiving and facing life.

In this pandemic climate of great confusion and uncertainty, we have all been confronted with a fundamental truth: social relations are vital, and social deprivation can have devastating effects on our life. Many people have compared this condition to prison life. I find this comparison bizarre. If people outside become sick, they can access proper treatment; people in prison cannot.[2] Luckily, most people outside can communicate with or even see their relatives and friends, either by using the phone or via social networks; people in prison cannot. Many people outside can self-quarantine in their safe and comfortable homes, surrounded by their own belongings; people in prison cannot. Let us imagine if we were also deprived of all or most of these aspects. Let us imagine living our life with such deprivations for years. How would it feel?

Giorgio Agamben[3] explained that the ancient Greeks used two words to define 'life': *zoé* to refer to natural, biological life, or 'bare life', which belongs to humans, animals, and plants; and *biós* to describe life that has meaning, which comprises social relations, values, rights, inclusion, and participation in political and social communities. A human being becomes a person only when *zoé* turns into *biós*. When a human being is deprived of their *biós*, they are deprived of their humanity and dignity as social and political beings. Thus, the word *biós* specifically refers to human social and political life.

A person who is blamed and punished is condemned to live excluded from society and largely denied his or her civil, political, and moral status. Such exclusion potentially continues even after such person has served his or her sentence. Through the infliction of blame and punishment, or the assignment of the permanent label 'ex-convict', who cannot vote, who struggles to find a job, receive education, or is not entitled to a driving licence, an individual is prevented from manifesting his or her civil and social qualities. While he or she retains natural qualities as a living being, he or she is deprived of the qualities that make him or her a human. In other words, this person is largely deprived of his or her *biós* and largely left only with *zoé*. True, he or she made a mistake, perhaps a major one, but is this enough to allow criminal justice to deprive or diminish his or her opportunity to live as a full human, as a person? No, it is not.

The criminal law and justice system of a democratic society must ensure that *biós* is never reduced to *zoé*. To avoid this outcome, the system must value the people it impacts, acknowledge their frailties, empathise with their needs, value their strengths and social identities, ensure that their social rights are fully preserved, and combat stigma and inequality. When life is so conceived and treated, an individual can be said to be considered a person. Otherwise, when life is reduced to pure *zoé*, the only alternative is its end.

[2] To be sure, federal and state prisons have subjected upward of 300,000 people to solitary confinement in response to COVID-19. Before COVID-19, there were 60,000 people in solitary confinement. See Report by Unlock the Box, Solitary Watch, and The Raben Group, 'Solitary Confinement is Never the Answer' (June 2020), available at static1.squarespace.com/static/5a9446a89d5abbfa67013da7/t/5ee7c4f1860e0d57d0ce8195/1592247570889/June2020Report.pdf.

[3] G Agamben, *Homo Sacer: Sovereign Power and Bare Life* (Stanford, Stanford University Press, 1989).

BIBLIOGRAPHY

Acorn, AE, *Compulsory Compassion: A Critique of Restorative Justice* (Vancouver, UBC Press, 2004).

Adolphs, R, 'How Should Neuroscience Study Emotions? By Distinguishing Emotion States, Concepts, and Experiences' (2017) 12 *Social Cognitive and Affective Neuroscience* 24.

Agamben, G, *Homo Sacer: Sovereign Power and Bare Life* (Stanford, Stanford University Press, 1998).

Aiyer, SM, Heinze, JE, Miller, AL, Stoddard, SA and Zimmerman, MA, 'Exposure to Violence Predicting Cortisol Response During Adolescence and Early Adulthood: Understanding Moderating Factors' (2014) 43(7) *Journal of Youth Adolescence* 1066.

Alexander, M, *The New Jim Crow: Mass Incarceration in the Age of Colorblindness* (New York, Penguin Books, 2010).

Allen, FA, 'The Decline of the Rehabilitative Ideal in American Criminal Justice' (1978) 27 *Cleveland State Law Review* 147.

Alper, M, Durose, MR and Markman, J, '2018 Update on Prisoner Recidivism: A 9-Year Follow-up Period (2005-2014)' (Washington DC, U.S. Department of Justice, 2018).

American Psychiatric Association, 'APA Statement on the Insanity Defense' (1983) 140(6) *American Journal of Psychiatry* 681.

Ardino, V, 'Offending Behaviour: The Role of Trauma and PTSD' (2012) 3 *European Journal of Psychotraumatology* 18968.

Arenella, P, 'Character, Choice and Moral Agency: The Relevance of Character to Our Moral Culpability Judgments', (1990) 7(2) *Social Philosophy and Policy* 59.

—— 'Convicting the Morally Blameless: Reassessing the Relationship Between Legal and Moral Accountability' (1992) 39 *UCLA Law Review* 1511.

Aristotle, 'Rhetoric (Book II), Chapter 1', in WR Roberts (trans), *The Rhetoric and the Poetics of Aristotle* (New York, The Modern Library, 1990).

Ashworth, A, *Principles of Criminal Law*, 3rd edn (New York, Oxford University Press, 1999).

Ashworth, A *Principles of Criminal Law* (Oxford, Oxford University Press, 1991).

Ashworth, A, Roberts, JV and Von Hirsch, A (eds), *Principled Sentencing: Readings on Theory and Policy*, 3rd edn (Portland, Hart Publishing, 2009).

Audi, R, 'Acting for Reasons' (1986) 95(4) *The Philosophical Review* 511.

Auerhahn, K, 'Selective Incapacitation and the Problem of Prediction' (2006) 37 *Criminology* 703.

Bagaric, M, 'Rich Offender, 'Poor Offender: Why It (Sometimes) Matters in Sentencing' (2015) 33 *Law and Inequality: A Journal of Theory and Practice* 1.

Bagaric, M and Alexander, T, 'The Capacity of Criminal Sanctions to Shape the Behaviour of Offenders: Specific Deterrence Doesn't Work, Rehabilitation Might and the Implications for Sentencing' (2012) 36(3) *Criminal Law Journal* 159.

Bagaric, M and Amarasekara, K, 'The Errors of Retributivism' (2000) 24 *Melbourne University Law Review* 124.

Bagaric, M, Wolf, G and Isham, P, 'Trauma and Sentencing: The Case for Mitigating Penalty for Childhood Physical and Sexual Abuse' (2019) 30 *Stanford Law & Policy Review* 1.

Bandes, SA, 'The Heart has Its Reasons: Examining the Strange Persistence of the American Death Penalty' in PH Robinson, S Garvey and KK Ferzan (eds), *Criminal Law Conversations* (New York, Oxford University Press, 2009) 635.

—— 'Remorse and Criminal Justice' (2016) 8 *Emotion Review* 14.

Bandura, A, 'Self-Efficacy' in VS Ramachandran (ed), *Encyclopedia of Human Behavior, Vol. 4* (New York, Academic Press, 1994) 71.

—— 'Moral Disengagement in the Perpetration of Inhumanities' (1999) 3(3) *Personality and Social Psychology Review* 193.
—— 'Selective Moral Disengagement in the Exercise of Moral Agency' (2002) 31(2) *Journal of Moral Education* 101.
—— 'Toward a Psychology of Human Agency' (2006) 1(2) *Perspectives on Psychological Science* 164.
Bandura, A, Freeman, WH and Lightsey, R, *Self-efficacy: The Exercise of Control* (New York, Springer Publishing, 1999).
Banks, SJ, Eddy, KT, Angstadt, M, Nathan, PJ and Phan, KL, 'Amygdala-Frontal Connectivity during Emotion Regulation' (2007) 2(4) *Social Cognitive and Affective Neuroscience* 303.
Barkow, RE, *Prisoners of Politics: Breaking the Cycle of Mass Incarceration* (Cambridge, Harvard University Press, 2019).
Barnes, HE, 'Historical Origin of the Prison System in America' (1921) 12 *Journal of the American Institute of Criminal Law and Criminology* 35.
Barrett, LF, 'Solving the Emotion Paradox: Categorization and the Experience of Emotion' (2006) 10 *Personality and Social Psychology Review* 20.
—— 'Psychological Construction: The Darwinian Approach to the Science of Emotion' (2013) 5(4) *Emotion Review* 379.
—— 'The Theory of Constructed Emotion: An Active Inference Account of Interoception and Categorization' (2017) 12 *Social Cognitive and Affective Neuroscience* 1.
—— *How Emotions are Made: The Secret Life of the Brain* (Boston, Houghton Mifflin Harcourt, 2017).
Barrett, LF and Russell, JA, 'The Structure of Current Affect: Controversies and Emerging Consensus' (1999) 8 *Current Directions in Psychological Science* 10.
Barrett, LF and Salovey, P (eds), *The Wisdom in Feeling: Psychological Processes in Emotional Intelligence* (New York, The Guilford Press, 2002).
Barton, CKB, *Restorative Justice: The Empowerment Model* (Sydney, Hawkins Press, 2003).
Baskin-Sommers, AR and Fonteneau, K, 'Correctional Change Through Neuroscience' (2016) 85 *Fordham Law Review* 423.
Bastian, B, Denson, TF and Haslam, N, 'The Roles of Dehumanization and Moral Outrage in Retributive Justice' (2013) 8(4) *PLoS One* e61842.
Bastian, B, Laham, SM, Wilson, S, Haslam, N and Koval, P, 'Blaming, Praising, and Protecting Our Humanity: The Implications of Everyday Dehumanization for Judgments of Moral Status' (2011) 50(3) *British Journal of Social Psychology* 469.
Bastin, C, Harrison, BJ, Davey, CG, Moll, J and Whittle, S, 'Feelings of Shame, Embarrassment, and Guilt and their Neural Correlates: A Systematic Review' (2016) 71 *Neuroscience and Biobehavioral Reviews* 455.
Baumeister, RF and Leary, MR, 'The Need to Belong: Desire for Interpersonal Attachments as a Fundamental Human Motivation' (1995) 117(3) *Psychological Bulletin* 497.
Baumeister, RF, DeWall, CN, Ciarocco, NJ and Twenge, JM, 'Social Exclusion Impairs Self-Regulation' (2005) 88(4) *Journal of Personality and Social Psychology* 589.
Baumeister, RF, Heatherton, TF and Tice, DM, *Losing Control: How and Why People Fail at Self-regulation* (San Diego, Academic Press, 1994).
Baumeister, RF, Stillwell, AM and Heatherton, TF, 'Guilt: An Interpersonal Approach' (1994) 115 *Psychological Bulletin* 243.
Bayles, MD, 'Character, Purpose, and Criminal Responsibility' (1982) 1 *Law and Philosophy* 1.
Bazelon, DL, 'The Morality of the Criminal Law: A Rejoinder to Professor Morse' (1975) 49 *California Law Review* 1269.
Bazemore, G, 'After Shaming, Whither Reintegration: Restorative Justice and Relational Rehabilitation' in G Bazemore and L Walgrave (eds), *Restorative Juvenile Justice: Repairing the Harm of Youth Crime* (Monsey, Criminal Justice Press, 1999).
Beccaria, C, *An Essay on Crimes and Punishment by Marquis Beccaria of Milan with a Commentary by M. de Voltaire. A New Edition Corrected* (Albany, WC Little and Co, 1872).
Bechara, A, Tranel, D and Damasio, H, 'Characterization of the Decision-Making Deficit of Patients with Ventromedial Prefrontal Cortex Lesions' (2000) 123(11) *Brain* 2189.

Beer, JS, 'Neural Systems for Self-conscious Emotions and Their Underlying Appraisals' in J Tracy, R Robins and J Tagney (eds), *The Self-conscious Emotions: Theory and Research* (New York, Guilford Press, 2007) 53.

Beer, JS, Heerey, EA, Keltner, D, Scabini, D and Knight, RT, 'The Regulatory Function of Self-Conscious Emotion: Insights from Patients with Orbitofrontal Damage' (2003) 85 *Journal of Personality and Social Psychology* 594.

Benko, J, 'The Radical Humaneness of Norway's Halden Prison: The Goal of the Norwegian Penal System is to Get Inmates Out of It' (2018) 10 *The New York Times.*

Bentham, J, *An Introduction to the Principles of Morals and Legislation* (Kitchener, Batoche Books, 2000).

Berlin, I, *Four Essays on Liberty* (Oxford, Oxford University Press, 1969).

Bersani, BE and Doherty, EE, 'Desistance from Offending in the Twenty-First Century' (2018) 1 *Annual Review of Criminology* 311.

Bessler, J, *The Birth of American Law: An Italian Philosopher and the American Revolution* (Durham, Carolina Academic Press, 2014).

Betsey, CL, 'Income and Wealth Transfer Effects of Discrimination in Sentencing' (2005) 32(3-4) *The Review of Black Political Economy* 111.

Beyleveld, B, and Brownsword, R, *Human Dignity in Bioethics and Biolaw* (New York, Oxford University Press, 2001).

Bibas, S, *The Machinery of Criminal Justice* (New York, Oxford University Press, 2012).

Binder, G and Notterman, B, 'Penal Incapacitation: A Situationist Critique' (2017) 54 *American Criminal Law Review* 1.

Blackstone, W, *Commentaries on the Laws of England: In Four Books; With an Analysis of the Work, Vol. 2* (New York, William Dean Publisher, 1853).

Blair, RJR 'A Cognitive Developmental Approach to Morality: Investigating the Psychopath' (1995) 57 *Cognition* 1.

—— 'The Amygdala and Ventromedial Prefrontal Cortex in Morality and Psychopathy' (2007) 11(9) *Trends in Cognitive Sciences* 387.

—— 'Emotion-Based Learning Systems and the Development of Morality' (2017) 167 *Cognition* 38.

Blair, RJR and Fowler, K, 'Moral Emotions and Moral Reasoning from the Perspective of Affective Cognitive Neuroscience: A Selective Review' (2008) 2(3) *International Journal of Developmental Science* 303.

Bonanno, GA, 'Loss, Trauma, and Human Resilience: Have We Underestimated the Human Capacity to Thrive After Extremely Aversive Events?' (2004) 59 *American Psychology* 20.

Bonnie, RJ, Jeffries, JC and Low, PW, *A Case Study in the Insanity Defense: The Trial of John W. Hinckley, Jr.*, 3rd edn (New York, Foundation Press, 2008).

Bowlby, J, Figlio, K and Young, RM, 'An Interview with John Bowlby on the Origins and Reception of His Work' (1986) 1(6) *Free Associations* 36.

Bradley, GV, 'Retribution: The Central Aim of Punishment' (2003) 27 *Harvard Journal of Law and Public Policy* 19.

Braithwaite, J, *Crime, Shame and Reintegration* (New York, Cambridge University Press, 1989).

Bremner, JD, 'Traumatic Stress: Effects on the Brain' (2006) 8(4) *Dialogues in Clinical Neuroscience* 445.

Bremner, JD, Elzinga, B, Schmahl, C and Vermetten, E, 'Structural and Functional Plasticity of the Human Brain in Posttraumatic Stress Disorder' (2007) 167 *Progress in Brain Research* 171.

Briere, J and Scott, C, 'Complex Trauma in Adolescents and Adults: Effects and Treatment' (2015) 38(3) *Psychiatric Clinics* 515.

Brink, DO, 'Situationism, Responsibility, and Fair Opportunity' (2013) 30(1-2) *Social Philosophy and Policy* 121.

—— 'The Nature and Significance of Criminal Culpability' (2019) 13 *Criminal Law and Philosophy* 347.

Brink, DO and Nelkin, D, 'Fairness and the Architecture of Responsibility' in D Shoemaker (ed) *Oxford Studies in Agency and Responsibility, Vol. 1* (New York, Oxford University Press, 2013) 284.

Bronfenbrenner, U, *The Ecology of Human Development* (Cambridge, Harvard University Press 1979).

Brown, B, *I Thought It Was Just Me (But It Isn't): Making the Journey from 'What Will People Think?' to 'I Am Enough'* (New York, Gotham Books, 2008).
Brown, DK, 'Penal Modernism in Theory and Practice' (2014) 1 *Critical Analysis of Law: an International and Interdisciplinary Law Review* 182.
Buckholtz, J, Reyna, VF and Slobogin, C, 'A Neuro-Legal Lingua Franca: Bridging Law and Neuroscience on the Issue of Self-Control' (2016) 5 *Mental Health Law & Policy Journal* 1.
Burke, AS, 'Rational Actors, Self-Defense, and Duress: Making Sense, Not Syndromes, Out of the Battered Woman' (2002) 81 *North Carolina Law Review* 211.
Burnett, R and Maruna, S, 'The Kindness of Prisoners: Strengths-Based Resettlement in Theory and in Action' (2006) 6 *Criminology and Criminal Justice* 83.
Burns, JM and Swerdlow, RH, 'Right Orbitofrontal Tumor with Pedophilia Symptom and Constructional Apraxia Sign' (2003) 60(3) *Archives of Neurology* 437.
Cacioppo, S, Capitanio, JP and Cacioppo, JT, 'Toward a Neurology of Loneliness' (2014) 140(6) *Psychological Bulletin* 1464.
Cannon, WB, 'The James-Lange Theory of Emotions: A Critical Examination and an Alternative Theory' (1927) 39 *The American Journal of Psychology* 106.
Canton, R, *Why Punish?: An Introduction to the Philosophy of Punishment* (London, Palgrave McMillan, 2018).
Caruso, G, 'Skepticism Against Moral Responsibility' in EN Zalta (ed), *Stanford Encyclopedia of Philosophy* (Stanford, 2018).
Castillo-Gómez, E, Pérez-Rando, M, Bellés, M, Gilabert-Juan, J, Llorens, JV, Carceller, H, Bueno-Fernández, C, García-Mompó, C, Ripoll-Martínez, B, Curto, Y and Sebastiá-Ortega, N, 'Early Social Isolation Stress and Perinatal NMDA Receptor Antagonist Treatment Induce Changes in the Structure and Neurochemistry of Inhibitory Neurons of the Adult Amygdala and Prefrontal Cortex' (2017) 4 *eNeuro* 34.
Chen, X, Zheng, T, Han, L, Chang, Y and Luo, Y, 'The Neural Dynamics Underlying the Interpersonal Effects of Emotional Expression on Decision Making' (2017) 7 *Scientific Reports* 46651.
Chesney-Lind, M and Mauer, M (eds), *Invisible Punishment: The Collateral Consequences of Mass Imprisonment* (New York, The New Press, 2003).
Chester, DS, Eisenberger, NI, Pond Jr, RS, Richman, SB, Bushman, BJ and DeWall, CN, 'The Interactive Effect of Social Pain and Executive Functioning on Aggression: An fMRI Experiment' (2014) 9(5) *Social Cognitive and Affective Neuroscience* 699.
Christopher, RL, 'Deterring Retributivism: The Injustice of 'Just' Punishment' (2001) 96 *Northwestern University Law Review* 843.
Clark, L, Bechara, A, Damasio, H, Aitken, MRF, Sahakian, BJ and Robbins, TW, 'Differential Effects of Insular and Ventromedial Prefrontal Cortex Lesions on Risky Decision-Making' (2008) 131(5) *Brain* 1311.
Clarke, R and Capes, J, 'Incompatibilist (Nondeterministic) Theories of Free Will' in EN Zalta (ed), *Stanford Encyclopedia of Philosophy* (Stanford, 2017).
Clore, GL, 'Why Emotions Are Felt' in PE Ekman and RJ Davidson (eds), *The Nature of Emotion: Fundamental Questions* (New York, Oxford University Press, 1994) 103.
Clore, GL and Palmer, J, 'Affective Guidance of Intelligent Agents: How Emotion Controls Cognition' (2009) 10 *Cognitive Systems Research* 21.
Cohen, S and Willis, TA, 'Stress, Support and the Buffering Hypothesis' (1985) 98(2) *Psychological Bulletin* 310.
Connolly, T and Zeelenberg, M, 'Regret in Decision Making' (2002) 11(6) *Current Directions in Psychological Science* 212.
Coppola, F, 'Valuing Emotions in Punishment: An Argument for Social Rehabilitation with the Aid of Social and Affective Neuroscience' (2018) *Neuroethics* 1.
—— 'The Brain in Solitude: An(other) Eighth Amendment Challenge to Solitary Confinement' (2019) 6 *Journal of Law and the Biosciences* 184.
Coricelli, G, Critchley, HD, Joffily, M, O'Doherty, JP, Sirigu, A and Dolan, RJ, 'Regret and its Avoidance: A Neuroimaging Study of Choice Behavior' (2005) 8 *Nature Neuroscience* 1255.

Coricelli, G, Dolan, RJ and Sirigu, A, 'Brain, Emotion, and Decision Making: The Paradigmatic Example of Regret' (2005) 11 *Trends in Cognitive Sciences* 258.

Corrado, M, 'Automatism and the Theory of Action' (1990) 39 *Emory Journal of Law* 1191.

Cotton, M, 'Back with a Vengeance: The Resilience of Retribution as an Articulated Purpose of Criminal Punishment' (2000) 37 *American Criminal Law Review* 1313.

Cottrol, RJ, 'Hard Choices and Shifted Burdens: American Crime and American Justice at the End of the Century' (1996) 65 *George Washington Law Review* 506.

Cozolino, L, *The Neuroscience of Human Relationships: Attachment and the Developing Social Brain*, 2nd edn (New York, WW Norton & Company, 2014).

Craig, AD, 'How Do You Feel–Now? The Anterior Insula and Human Awareness' (2009) 10 *Nature Reviews Neuroscience* 59.

Cullen, FT, 'Rehabilitation: Beyond Nothing Works, Crime and Justice' (2013) 42 *Crime and Justice in America 1975–2025* 299.

Cullen, FT and Gilbert, KE, *Reaffirming Rehabilitation*, 30th Anniversary edn (Waltham, Anderson Publishing, 2013).

Cunningham, WA, Johnsen, IR and Waggoner, AS, 'Orbitofrontal Cortex Provides Cross-Modal Valuation of Self-Generated Stimuli' (2011) 6(3) *Social Cognitive and Affective Neuroscience* 286.

Damasio, AR, *Descartes' Error: Emotion, Reason, and the Human Brain* (New York, Avon Books, 1994).

—— *The Feeling of What Happens: Body and Emotion in the Making of Consciousness* (San Diego, Houghton Mifflin Harcourt, 1999).

Damasio, H, 'Disorders of Social Conduct Following Damage to Prefrontal Cortices' in JP Changeux, AR Damasio and W Singer (eds), *Neurobiology of Human Values* (Heidelberg, Springer, 2005) 37.

Danese, A and McEwen, BS, 'Adverse Childhood Experiences, Allostasis, Allostatic Load, and Age-Related Disease' (2012) 106 *Physiology & Behavior* 29.

Davidson, D, 'Actions, Reasons, and Causes' (1963) 60(23) *The Journal of Philosophy* 685.

Davidson, RJ, 'Cognitive Neuroscience Needs Affective Neuroscience (and Vice Versa)' (2000) 42 *Brain and Cognition* 89.

Davidson, RJ and McEwen, BS, 'Social Influences on Neuroplasticity: Stress and Interventions to Promote Well-being' (2012) 15(5) *Nature Neuroscience* 689.

Davidson, RJ, Jackson, DC and Kalin, NH, 'Emotion, Plasticity, Context, and Regulation Perspectives from Affective Neuroscience' (2000) 126(6) *Psychological Bulletin* 890.

Davis, MH, 'Measuring Individual Differences in Empathy: Evidence for a Multidimensional Approach' (1983) 44(1) *Journal of Personality and Social Psychology* 113.

De Caro, M, 'Utilitarianism and Retributivism in Cesare Beccaria' (2016) 2 *The Italian Law Journal* 1.

Decety, J and Cowell, JM, 'Friends or Foes: Is Empathy Necessary for Moral Behavior?' (2014) 9(5) *Perspectives on Psychological Science* 525.

Decety, J and Cowell, JM, 'Empathy, Justice, and Moral Behavior' (2015) 6(3) *AJOB Neuroscience* 3.

Delgado, R, '"Rotten Social Background": Should the Criminal Law Recognize a Defense of Severe Environmental Deprivation?' (1985) 3 *Law and Inequality* 9.

Denno, DW, 'How Courts in Criminal Cases Respond to Childhood Trauma' (2019) 103 *Marquette Law Review* 301.

Dershowitz, AM, *Fair and Certain Punishment: Report of the Twentieth Century Fund Task Force on Criminal Sentencing* (New York, McGraw-Hill, 1976).

Desbordes, G, Negi, LT, Pace, TW, Wallace, BA, Raison, CL and Schwartz, EL, 'Effects of Mindful-Attention and Compassion Meditation Training on Amygdala Response to Emotional Stimuli in an Ordinary, Non-Meditative State' (2012) 6 *Frontiers in Human Neuroscience* 292.

Devlin, P, 'Mental Abnormality and the Criminal Law' in R MacDonald (ed), *Changing Legal Objectives* (Toronto, University of Toronto Press, 1963) 71.

Dhami, MK, Mantle, G and Fox, D, 'Restorative Justice in Prisons' (2009) 12(4) *Contemporary Justice Review* 433.

Djordjevic, J, Djordjevic, A, Adzic, M and Radojcic, MB, 'Effects of Chronic Social Isolation on Wistar Rat Behavior and Brain Plasticity Markers' (2012) 66(2) *Neuropsychobiology* 112.

Dolinko, D, 'Retributivism, Consequentialism, and the Intrinsic Goodness of Punishment' (1997) 16(5) *Law and Philosophy* 507.

Doll, A, Hölzel, BK, Bratec, SM, Boucard, CC, Xie, X, Wohlschläger, AM and Sorg, C, 'Mindful Attention to Breath Regulates Emotions via Increased Amygdala-Prefrontal Cortex Connectivity' (2016) 134 *Neuroimage* 305.

Doris, JM, *Talking to Our Selves: Reflection, Ignorance, and Agency*' (Oxford, Oxford University Press, 2015).

Dressler, J, 'Exegesis of the Law of Duress: Justifying the Excuse and Searching for Its Proper Limits' (1988) 62 *Southern California Law Review* 1331.

—— *Understanding Criminal Law*, 4th edn (New York, LexisNexis, 2006).

Dripps, DA, 'Fundamental Retribution Error: Criminal Justice and the Social Psychology of Blame' (2003) 56 *Vanderbilt Law Review* 1383.

Dubber, MD, 'Penal Panopticon: The Idea of a Modern Model Penal Code' (2000) 4 *Buffalo Criminal Law Review* 53.

—— 'Criminal Justice Process and War on Crime' in C Sumner (ed), *The Blackwell Companion to Criminology* (Oxford, Blackwell Publishing, 2004) 49.

—— 'The American Law Institute's Model Penal Code and European Criminal Law' in A Klip (ed), *Substantive Criminal Law of the European Union* (Antwerpen, Maklu, 2011).

—— 'The Model Penal Code, Legal Process, and the Alegitimacy of American Penalty' in MD Dubber (ed), *Foundational Texts in Modern Criminal Law* (New York, Oxford University Press, 2014).

—— *An Introduction to the Model Penal Code*, 2nd edn (New York, Oxford University Press, 2015).

—— *The Dual Penal State: The Crisis of Criminal Law in Comparative-Historical Perspective* (New York, Oxford University Press, 2018).

Duff, A, 'Psychopathy and Moral Understanding' (1977) 14(3) *American Philosophical Quarterly* 189.

—— 'Theories of Criminal Law' in EN Zalta (ed), *Stanford Encyclopedia of Philosophy* (Stanford, 2009).

Duff, RA, *Punishment, Communication, and Community* (Oxford, Oxford University Press, 2001).

Duff, RA, 'Choice, Character, and Criminal Liability' (1993) 12 *Law and Philosophy* 345.

—— 'Penal Communications: Recent Work in the Philosophy of Punishment' (1996) 20 *Crime and Justice* 1.

—— 'Who is Responsible, For What, To Whom?' (2004) 2 *Ohio State Journal of Criminal Law* 441.

—— 'Blame, Moral Standing, and the Legitimacy of Criminal Trial' (2010) 23 *Ratio* 123.

—— 'Criminal Responsibility and the Emotions: If Fear and Anger Can Exculpate, Why Not Compassion?' (2015) 58(2) *Inquiry* 189.

Durose, M, Cooper, AD and Snyder, H, 'Recidivism of Prisoners Released in 30 states in 2005: Patterns from 2005 to 2010', U.S. Department of Justice' (Washington, DC: U.S. Department of Justice, 2014).

Ehring, T, 'Editorial for Special Issue Emotion Regulation and Psychopathology' (2013) 4(5) *Journal of Experimental Psychopathology* 448.

Eisenberg, N and Strayer, J, 'Critical Issues in the Study of Empathy' in N Eisenberg and J Strayer (eds), *Cambridge Studies in Social and Emotional Development. Empathy and Its Development* (Cambridge, Cambridge University Press, 1987) 3.

Eisenberger, NI, 'Why Rejection Hurts: What Social Neuroscience Has Revealed About the Brain's Response to Social Rejection' in J Decety, and J Cacioppo (eds), *The Oxford Handbook of Social Neuroscience* (New York, Oxford University Press, 2011) 586.

—— 'The Neural Bases of Social Pain: Evidence for Shared Representations with Physical Pain' (2012) 74(2) *Psychosomatic Medicine* 126.

—— 'The Pain of Social Disconnection: Examining the Shared Neural Underpinnings of Physical and Social Pain' (2012) 13(6) *Nature Reviews Neuroscience* 421.

Eisenberger, NI, Gable, SL and Lieberman, MD, 'Functional Magnetic Resonance Imaging Responses Relate to Differences in Real-World Social Experience' (2007) 7(4) *Emotion* 745.

Eisenberger, NI, Way, BM, Taylor, SE, Welch, WT and Lieberman, MD, 'Understanding Genetic Risk for Aggression: Clues from the Brain's Response to Social Exclusion' (2007) 61(9) *Biological Psychiatry* 1100.

Eisler, R and Levine, DS, 'Nurture, Nature, and Caring: We Are Not Prisoners of Our Genes' (2002) 3 *Brain and Mind* 9.

Elison, J, Garofalo, C and Velotti, P, 'Shame and Aggression: Theoretical Considerations' (2014) 19(4) *Aggression and Violent Behavior* 447.

Espinoza, FA, Vergara, VM, Reyes, D, Anderson, NE, Harenski, CL, Decety, J, Rachakonda, S, Damaraju, E, Rashid, B, Miller, RL and Koenigs, M, 'Aberrant Functional Network Connectivity in Psychopathy from a Large (N=985) Forensic Sample' (2018) 39(6) *Human Brain Mapping* 2624.

Evans, GW, Brooks-Gunn, J and Klebanov, PK, 'Stressing Out the Poor: Chronic Physiological Stress and the Income-Achievement Gap' (2011) *Pathways* 16.

Farmer, L, 'Penal Modernism: An American Tragedy' (2014) 1 *Critical Analysis of Law: an International and Interdisciplinary Law Review* 189.

—— *Making the Modern Criminal Law: Criminalization and Civil Order* (Oxford, Oxford University Press, 2016).

Fehr, B and Russel, JA, 'Concept of Emotion Viewed from a Prototype Perspective' (1984) 113(3) *Journal of Experimental Psychology: General* 464.

Feinberg, J, *Social Philosophy* (Englewood Cliffs, Prentice-Hall, 1973).

FeldmanHall, O, Dalgleish, T, Evans, D and Mobbs, D, 'Empathic Concern Drives Costly Altruism' (2015) 105 *Neuroimage* 347.

Ferzan, KK, 'Holistic Culpability' (2006) 28 *Cardozo Law Review* 2523.

Fingarette, H, *The Meaning of Criminal Insanity* (Berkeley, University of California Press, 1972).

Finkel, NJ, *Commonsense Justice: Jurors' Notions of the Law* (Cambridge, Harvard University Press, 1995).

Finkel, NJ and Parrot, WG, *Emotions and Culpability: How the Law Is at Odds with Psychology, Jurors, and Itself* (Washington DC, American Psychological Association Press, 2006).

Fischer, JM and Ravizza, M, *Responsibility and Control: A Theory of Moral Responsibility* (New York, Cambridge University Press, 1998).

Flanders, C, 'The Supreme Court and the Rehabilitative Ideal' (2014) 49 *Georgia Law Review* 383.

Fletcher, GP, *Rethinking Criminal Law* (Boston, Little Brown and Co., 1988).

Fletcher, GP, *Rethinking Criminal Law* (New York, Oxford University Press, 2000).

Fondacaro, MR and O'Toole, MJ, 'American Punitiveness and Mass Incarceration: Psychological Perspectives on Retributive and Consequentialist Responses to Crime' (2015) 18(4) *New Criminal Law Review* 477.

Fondacaro, MR, 'Toward an Ecological Jurisprudence Rooted in Concepts of Justice and Empirical Research' (2000) 69 *UMCK Law Review* 179.

Fone, K and Porkess, MV, 'Behavioural and Neurochemical Effects of Post-Weaning Social Isolation in Rodents – Relevance to Developmental Neuropsychiatric Disorders' (2008) 32(6) *Neuroscience & Biobehavioral Review* 1087.

Fontaine, RG, 'Adequate (Non)Provocation and Heat of Passion as Excuse, Not Justification' (2009) 43 *University of Michigan Journal of Law Reform* 27.

—— *The Mind of the Criminal: The Role of Developmental Social Cognition in Criminal Defense Law* (New York, Cambridge University Press, 2012).

Foucault, M, *Discipline and Punish: The Birth of the Prison* (A Sheridan tr, New York, Vintage Books, 2012).

Franke, H, 'The Rise and Decline of Solitary Confinement: Socio-Historical Explanations of Long-Term Penal Changes' (1992) 32(2) *The British Journal of Criminology* 125.

Frase, RS, 'Limiting Retributivism: The Consensus Model of Criminal Punishment' in M Tonry (ed), *The Future of Imprisonment* (New York, Oxford University Press, 2004).

—— 'What's Different (Enough) in Eighth Amendment Law' (2013) 11 *Ohio State Journal of Criminal Law* 9.

—— *Just Sentencing: Principles and Procedures for a Workable System* (New York, Oxford University Press, 2013).

Frijda, NH, 'Emotion, Cognitive Structure and Action Tendency' (1987) 1(2) *Cognition and Emotion* 115.

—— 'Emotions are Functional, Most of the Time' in PE Ekman and RJ Davidson (eds), *Series in Affective Science. The Nature of Emotion: Fundamental Questions* (New York, Oxford University Press, 1994) 112.
—— 'Emotions and Action' in ASR Manstead, NH Frijda and A Fischer (eds), *Feelings and Emotions: the Amsterdam Symposium* (Cambridge, Cambridge University Press, 2004) 158.
Garbarino, J, 'Foreword: Pathways from Childhood Trauma to Adolescent Violence and Delinquency' (2002) 6 *Journal of Aggression, Maltreatment, and Trauma* xxv.
Garbarino, J, Bradshaw, CP and Vorrasi, JA, 'Mitigating the Effects of Gun Violence on Children and Youth' (2002) 12 *The Future of Children* 73.
Gardner, M, 'Youthful Offenders and the Eighth Amendment Right to Rehabilitation: Limitations on the Punishment of Juveniles' (2015) 83 *Tennessee Law Review* 455.
Garland, D (ed), *Mass Imprisonment: Social Causes and Consequences* (London, SAGE Publications, 2001).
—— *The Culture of Control: Crime and Social Order in Contemporary Society* (New York, Oxford University Press, 2001).
Gerber, RJ, 'Is the Insanity Test Insane?' (1975) 20 *American Journal of Jurisprudence* 111.
—— *The Insanity Defense* (Port Washington, Associated Faculty Press, 1984).
Gilbert, F and Focquaert, F, 'Rethinking Responsibility in Offenders with Acquired Paedophilia: Punishment or Treatment?' (2015) 38 *International Journal of Law and Psychiatry* 51.
Gilead, M, Katzir, M, Eyal, T and Liberman, N, 'Neural Correlates of Processing "Self-conscious" vs. "Basic" Emotions' (2016) 81 *Neuropsychologia* 207.
Gilligan, J, 'Punishment and Violence: Is the Criminal Law Based on a Huge Mistake?' (2000) 67 *Social Research* 745.
Gilman, ME, 'The Poverty Defense' (2012) 47 *University of Richmond Law Review* 495.
Giner-Sorolla, R, Leidner, B and Castano, E, 'Dehumanization, Demonization, and Morality Shifting: Paths to Moral Certainty in Extremist Violence' in MA Hogg and DL Blaylock (eds), *Extremism and the Psychology of Uncertainty* (Boston, Wiley-Blackwell, 2012) 165.
Giordano, PC, Schroeder, RD and Cernkovich, SA, 'Emotions and Crime over the Life Course: A Neo-Meadian Perspective on Criminal Continuity and Change' (2007) 112(6) *American Journal of Sociology* 1603.
Gleichgerrcht, E and Young, L, 'Low Levels of Empathic Concern Predict Utilitarian Moral Judgment' (2013) 8(4) PLoS One e60418.
Gohara, MS, 'Grace Notes: a Case for Making Mitigation the Heart of Noncapital Sentencing' (2013) 41 *American Journal of Criminal Law* 41.
—— 'In Defense of the Injured: How Trauma-Informed Criminal Defense Can Reform Sentencing' (2018) 45 *American Journal of Criminal Law* 1.
Goldie, P, 'One's Remembered Past: Narrative Thinking, Emotion, and the External Perspective' (2003) 32(3) *Philosophical Papers* 301.
Goldin, PR and Gross, JJ, 'Effects of Mindfulness-Based Stress Reduction (MBSR) on Emotion Regulation in Social Anxiety Disorder' (2010) 10 *Emotion* 83.
Goldstein, AS, *The Insanity Defense* (London, Yale University Press, 1967).
Goleman, D, *Emotional Intelligence: Why It Can Matter More than IQ* (New Delhi, Bloomsbury Publishing, 1996).
Gottschalk, M, 'Sentenced to Life: Penal Reform and the Most Severe Sanctions' (2013) 9 *Annual Review of Law and Social Science* 353.
Gray, D, 'Punishment as Suffering' (2010) 63 *Vanderbilt Law Review* 1619.
Green, TA, *Freedom and Criminal Responsibility in American Legal Thought* (New York, Cambridge University Press, 2014).
Greenaway, KH, Kalokerinos, EK and Williams, LA, 'Context is Everything (in Emotion Research)' (2018) 12(6) *Social and Personality Psychology Compass* e12393.
Greenspan, P, 'Practical Reasoning and Emotion' in AR Mele and P Rawling (eds), *The Oxford Handbook of Rationality* (New York, Oxford University Press, 2004) 206.

Grey, BJ, 'Neuroscience, PTSD, and Sentencing Mitigation' (2012) 34 *Cardozo Law Review* 53.
Gross, JJ, 'Emotion and Emotion Regulation' (1999) in LA Pervin and OP John (eds), *Handbook of Personality: Theory and Research*, 2nd edn (New York, Elsevier, 1999) 525.
—— 'Emotion Regulation: Current Status and Future Prospects' (2015) 26 *Psychological Inquiry* 1.
Hall, J, 'Responsibility and Law: In Defense of the McNaghten Rules' (1956) 42 *American Bar Association Journal* 917.
—— *General Principles of Criminal Law*, 2nd edn (Clark, The Lawbook Exchange Ltd., 2005).
Hampton, AN, Adolphs, R, Tyszka, JM and O'Doherty, JP, 'Contributions of the Amygdala to Reward Expectancy and Choice Signals in Human Prefrontal Cortex' (2007) 55(4) *Neuron* 545.
Hanan, ME, 'Decriminalizing Violence: A Critique of Restorative Justice and Proposal for Diversionary Mediation' (2016) 46 *New Mexico Law Review* 123.
—— 'Incapacitating Errors: Sentencing and the Science of Change' (2019) 97 *Denver Law Review* 151.
Haney, C, 'Criminal Justice and the Nineteenth-Century Paradigm: The Triumph of Psychological Individualism in the "Formative Era"' (1982) 6(3–4) *Law and Human Behavior* 191.
—— 'Mental Health Issues in Long-Term Solitary and "Supermax" Confinement' (2003) 49 *Crime & Delinquency* 124.
—— 'Evolving Standards of Decency: Advancing the Nature and Logic of Capital Mitigation' (2007) 36 *Hofstra Law Review* 835.
—— 'The Psychological Effects of Solitary Confinement: A Systematic Critique', (2018) 47 *Crime and Justice* 365.
Haney, C, Banks, C and Zimbardo, P, 'Interpersonal Dynamics in A Simulated Prison' (1972) 1 *International Journal of Criminology and Penology* 69.
—— 'The Contextual Revolution in Psychology and the Question of Prison Effects' in A Liebling and S Maruna (eds), *The Effects of Imprisonment* (New York, Routledge, 2005) 66.
Harcourt, BE, *The Illusion of Free Markets: Punishment and the Myth of Natural Order* (Cambridge, Harvard University Press, 2011).
—— 'Beccaria's 'On Crimes and Punishments': A Mirror on the History of the Foundations of Modern Criminal Law' in M Dubber (ed), *Foundational Texts in Modern Criminal Law* (Oxford, Oxford University Press, 2014) 39.
Hare, RD, *The Hare Psychopathy Checklist-Revised* (Toronto, Multi-Health Systems, 1991).
Harris, N, 'Reassessing the Dimensionality of the Moral Emotions' (2003) 94(4) *British Journal of Psychology* 457.
Harris, N, Walgrave, L and Braithwaite, J, 'Emotional Dynamics in Restorative Conferences' (2004) 8(2) *Theoretical Criminology* 191.
Hart, HLA, *Punishment and Responsibility: Essays in the Philosophy of Law* (Oxford, Oxford University Press, 1968).
Haslam, N, 'Dehumanization: An Integrative Review' (2006) 10(3) *Personality and Social Psychology Review* 252.
Healy, D, 'Changing Fate? Agency and the Desistance Process' (2013) 17(4) *Theoretical Criminology* 557.
Hegel, GWF, *Elements of the Philosophy of Right: Abstract Right*, A Wood (ed), (Cambridge, Cambridge University Press, 1991).
Helion, C and Ochsner, KN, 'The Role of Emotion Regulation in Moral Judgments' (2018) 11(3) *Neuroethics* 297.
Helion, C, Krueger, SM and Ochsner, KN, 'Emotion Regulation Across the Life Span' in M D'Esposito and JH Grafman (eds), *Handbook of Clinical Neurology Vol. 163: The Frontal Lobes* (New York, Elsevier, 2019) 257.
Hirstein, W, Sifferd, KL and Fagan, TK, *Responsible Brains: Neuroscience, Law, and Human Culpability* (Cambridge, MIT Press, 2018).
Hofmann, W, Schmeichel, BJ and Baddeley, AD, 'Executive Functions and Self-Regulation' (2012) 16(3) *Trends in Cognitive Sciences* 174.

Hölzel, BK, Carmody, J, Vangel, M, Congleton, C, Yerramsetti, SM, Gard, T and Lazar, SW, 'Mindfulness Practice Leads to Increases in Regional Brain Gray Matter Density' (2011) 191 *Psychiatric Research: Neuroimaging* 36.

Horberg, EJ, Oveis, C and Keltner, D, 'Emotions as Moral Amplifiers: An Appraisal Tendency Approach to the Influences of Distinct Emotions upon Moral Judgment' (2011) 3 *Emotion Review* 237.

Hu, C and Jiang, X, 'An Emotion Regulation Role of Ventromedial Prefrontal Cortex in Moral Judgment' (2014) 8 *Frontiers in Human Neuroscience* 873.

Husak, DN, *The Philosophy of Criminal Law: Selected Essays*, (Oxford, Oxford University Press, 2010).

—— 'Broad Culpability and the Retributivist Dream' (2011) 9 *Ohio State Journal of Criminal Law* 449.

Ieraci, A, Mallei, A and Popoli, M, 'Social Isolation Stress Induces Anxious-Depressive-Like Behavior and Alterations of Neuroplasticity-Related Genes in Adult Male Mice' (2016) 2016 *Neural Plasticity*.

Inwood, E and Ferrari, M, 'Mechanisms of Change in the Relationship Between Self-Compassion, Emotion Regulation, and Mental Health: A Systematic Review' (2018) 10(2) *Applied Psychology: Health and Well-Being* 215.

Izard, CE, 'The Many Meanings/Aspects of Emotion: Definitions, Functions, Activation, and Regulation' (2010) 2(4) *Emotion Review* 363.

James, W, 'What is an Emotion?' (1884) 9 *Mind* 188.

Janofsky, JS, Hanson, A, Candilis, PJ, Myers, WC, Zonana, H, Irving, B, Giorgi-Guarnieri, D, Janofsky, J, Keram, E, Lawsky, S and Merideth, P, 'AAPL Practice Guideline for Forensic Psychiatric Evaluation of Defendants Raising the Insanity Defense' (2014) 42 *Journal of the American Academy of Psychiatry and the Law* S3.

Johnston, EL, 'Reconceptualizing Criminal Justice Reform for Offenders with Serious Mental Illness' (2019) 71 *Florida Law Review* 515.

Johnston, EL and Olson, L, *The Feeling Brain: The Biology and Psychology of Emotions* (New York, WW Norton & Company, 2015).

Jouet, M, *Exceptional America: What Divides Americans from the World and from Each Other* (Oakland, University of California Press, 2017).

—— 'Mass Incarceration Paradigm Shift: Convergence in an Age of Divergence' (2019) 109 *Journal of Criminal Law and Criminology* 703.

Justice Kennedy, A, 'Speech Delivered at the American Bar Association Annual Meeting' (2003) 16 *Federal Sentencing Reporter* 126.

Kadish, SH, 'Codifiers of the Criminal Law: Wechsler's Predecessors' (1978) 78(5) *Columbia Law Review* 1098.

—— 'Excusing Crime' (1987) 75 *California Law Review* 257.

—— 'Fifty Years of Criminal Law: An Opinionated Review' (1999) 87 *California Law Review* 943.

Kahan, DM and Nussbaum, MC, 'Two Conceptions of Emotion in Criminal Law' (1996) 96(2) *Columbia Law Review* 269.

Kandel, ER, *The Disordered Mind: What Unusual Brains Tell Us About Ourselves* (New York, Farrar, Straus and Giroux, 2018).

Kant, I (Ladd, J transl), *The Metaphysics of Morals: The Metaphysical Elements of Justice* (Indianapolis, Bobbs-Merrill, 1965).

Kant, I (Wood A ed and transl), *Groundwork of the Metaphysics of Morals* (New York, Yale University Press, 2002).

Kaye, A, 'The Secret Politics of the Compatibilist Criminal Law' (2006) 55 *Kansas Law Review* 365.

Keller, LB, Oswald, ME, Stucki, I and Gollwitzer, M, 'A Closer Look at An Eye for An Eye: Laypersons' Punishment Decisions are Primarily Driven by Retributive Motives' (2010) 23(2–3) *Social Justice Research* 99.

Kelman, HG, 'Violence Without Moral Restraint: Reflections on the Dehumanization of Victims and Victimizers' (1973) 29(4) *Journal of Social Issues* 25.

—— 'Violence Without Restraint: Reflections on the Dehumanization of Victims and Victimizers' in GM Kren and LH Rappoport (eds), *Varieties of Psychohistory* (New York, Springer, 1976) 282.

Kim, P, Evans, GW, Angstadt, M, Ho, SS, Sripada, CS, Swain, JE, Liberzon, I and Phan, KL, 'Effects of Childhood Poverty and Chronic Stress on Emotion Regulatory Brain Function in Adulthood' (2013) 110(46) *Proceedings of the National Academy of Sciences* 18442.

Kleinginna, PR and Kleinginna, AM, 'A Categorized List of Emotion Definitions, with Suggestions for a Consensual Definition' (1981) 5(4) *Motivation and Emotion* 345.

Klimecki, OM, Leiberg, S, Lamm, C and Singer, T, 'Functional Neural Plasticity and Associated Changes in Positive Affect after Compassion Training' (2013) 23(7) *Cerebral Cortex* 1552.

Koenigs, M, Young, L, Adolphs, R, Tranel, D, Cushman, F, Hauser, M and Damasio, A, 'Damage to the Prefrontal Cortex Increases Utilitarian Moral Judgments' (2007) 446(7138) *Nature* 908.

Kohlberg, L, *The Psychology of Moral Development: Essays on Moral Development (Vol. 2)* (San Francisco, Harper & Row, 1984).

Kolber, AJ, 'The Subjective Experience of Punishment' (2009) 109 *Columbia Law Review* 182.

Korponay, C and Koenigs, M, 'The Neurobiology of Antisocial and Amoral Behavior: Insights from Brain Science and Implications for Law' in S Moratti and D Patterson (eds), *Legal Insanity and the Brain: Science, Law and European Courts* (Oxford, Hart Publishing, 2016) 10.

Korsgaard, CM, *The Constitution of Agency: Essays on Practical Reason and Moral Psychology* (New York, Oxford University Press, 2008) 212.

—— 'The Activity of Reason' (2009) 83(2) *Proceedings and Addresses of the American Philosophical Association* 23.

Kovensky, J, 'It's Time to Pay Prisoners the Minimum Wage' (2014) *The New Republic*.

Kramer, H, Sprenger, J (Summers, M transl), *Malleus Maleficarum (The Hammer of the Witches)* (New York, Dover Publications, 1971).

Kringelbach, ML, 'The Human Orbitofrontal Cortex: Linking Reward to Hedonic Experience' (2005) 6(9) *Nature Reviews Neuroscience* 691.

Kristof, Z, Kresznerits, S, Olah, M, Gyollai, A, Lukacs-Miszler, K, Halmai, T, Fountoulakis, KN, Tenyi, T, Dome, P and Gonda, X, 'Mentalization and Empathy as Predictors of Violence in Schizophrenic Patients: Comparison with Nonviolent Schizophrenic Patients, Violent Controls and Nonviolent Controls' (2018) 268 *Psychiatric Research* 198.

Kuh, RH, 'The Insanity Defense: An Effort to Combine Law and Reason' (1962) 110(6) *University of Pennsylvania Law Review* 771.

Lacey, N, *State Punishment: Political Principles and Community Values* (London, Routledge, 1988).

—— 'The Resurgence of Character: Criminal Responsibility in the Context of Criminalisation' in A Duff and S Green (eds), *Philosophical Foundations of Criminal Law* (Oxford, Oxford University Press, 2011) 151.

—— 'Socializing the Subject of Criminal Law: Criminal Responsibility and the Purposes of Criminalization' (2016) 99 *Marquette Law Review* 541.

—— *In Search of Criminal Responsibility: Ideas, Interests, and Institutions* (Oxford, Oxford University Press, 2016).

Lambert, EW, 'A Way Out of the Rotten Social Background Stalemate: 'Scarcity' and Stephen Morse's Proposed Generic Partial Excuse' (2018) 21 *University of Pennsylvania Journal of Law and Social Change* 297.

Laub, JH and Sampson, RJ, *Shared Beginnings, Divergent Lives: Delinquent Boys to Age 70* (Cambridge, Harvard University Press, 2006).

Laws, B, 'The Return of the Suppressed: Exploring How Emotional Suppression Reappears as Violence and Pain among Male and Female Prisoners' (2019) 21(5) *Punishment and Society* 560.

Lazarus, RS, Kanner, AD and Folkman, S, 'Emotion: A Cognitive-Phenomenological Analysis' in R Plutchik and H Kellerman (eds), *Theories of Emotion, Vol. I* (New York, Academic Press, 1980) 189.

Lazuras, L, Ypsilanti, A, Powell, P and Overton, P, 'The Roles of Impulsivity, Self-Regulation, and Emotion Regulation in the Experience of Self-Disgust' (2019) 43 *Motivation & Emotion* 145.

Leary, MR, Twenge, JM and Quinlivan, E, 'Interpersonal Rejection as a Determinant of Anger and Aggression' (2006) 10(2) *Personality and Social Psychology Review* 111.

LeDoux, JE, 'Feelings: What are They and How Does the Brain Make Them?' (2015) 144 *Daedalus, Journal of the American Academy of Arts and Science* 96.

LeDoux, JE and Brown, R, 'A Higher-Order Theory of Emotional Consciousness' (2017) 114(10) *Proceedings of the National Academy of Sciences* E2016.

Lee, Y, 'The Constitutional Right Against Excessive Punishment' (2005) 91 *Vanderbilt Law Review* 677.

Leonard, G, 'Towards a Legal History of American Criminal Theory: Culture and Doctrine from Blackstone to the Model Penal Code' (2003) 6(2) *Buffalo Criminal Law Review* 691.

Lerner, JS, Han, S and Keltner, D, 'Feelings and Consumer Decision Making: Extending the Appraisal-Tendency Framework' (2007) 17(3) *Journal of Consumer Psychology* 181.

Lerner, JS, Li, Y, Valdesolo, P and Kassam, KS 'Emotion and Decision-making' (2015) 66 *Annual Review of Psychology* 33.

Levitt, A, 'Some Societal Aspects of the Criminal Law' (1922) 13 *Journal of the American Institute of Criminal Law and Criminology* 90.

Levy, N 'The Responsibility of the Psychopath Revisited' (2007) 14(2) *Philosophy, Psychiatry & Psychology* 129.

Lewis, MD and Todd, RM, 'The Self-Regulating Brain: Cortical-Subcortical Feedback and the Development of Intelligent Action' (2007) 22(4) *Cognitive Development* 406.

Lewis, S, 'Rehabilitation: Headline or Footnote in the New Penal Policy?' (2005) 52(2) *Probation Journal* 119.

Lieberman, MD, *Social: Why Our Brains Are Wired to Connect* (New York, Crown Publishing, 2013).

Link, TC and Oser, CB, 'The Role of Stressful Life Events and Cultural Factors on Criminal Thinking among African American Women Involved in the Criminal Justice System' (2018) 45 *Criminal Justice and Behavior* 8.

Lippke, RL, 'Retribution and Incarceration' (2003) 17 *Public Affairs Quarterly* 29.

—— 'Diminished Opportunities, Diminished Capacities: Social Deprivation and Punishment' (2003) 29(3) *Social Theory and Practice* 459.

—— *Rethinking Imprisonment* (New York, Oxford University Press, 2007).

—— 'Punishment Drift: The Spread of Penal Harm and What We Should Do About It' (2017) 11(4) *Criminal Law and Philosophy* 645.

Liu, J, Dietz, K, DeLoyht, JM, Pedre, X, Kelkar, D, Kaur, J, Vialou, V, Lobo, MK, Dietz, DM, Nestler, EJ and Dupree, J, 'Impaired Adult Myelination in the Prefrontal Cortex of Socially Isolated Mice' (2012) 15(12) *Nature Neuroscience* 1621.

Loewenstein, G and Lerner, JS, 'The Role of Affect in Decision Making' in RJ Davidson, KR Scherer, and HH Goldsmith (eds), *Series in Affective Science. Handbook of Affective Sciences* (New York, Oxford University Press, 2003) 619.

Lupien, SJ, McEwen, BS, Gunnar, MR and Heim, C, 'Effects of Stress Throughout the Lifespan on the Brain, Behaviour and Cognition' (2009) 10(6) *Nature Reviews Neuroscience* 434.

Lutz, A, Brefczynski-Lewis, J, Johnstone, T and Davidson, RJ, 'Regulation of the Neural Circuitry of Emotion by Compassion Meditation: Effects of Meditative Expertise' (2008) 3(3) *PLoS One* e1897.

Lynch, G, 'Revising the Model Penal Code: Keeping It Real' (2003) 1 *Ohio State Journal of Criminal Law* 219.

MacLean, PD, 'Psychosomatic Disease and the Emotional Brain: Recent Developments Bearing on the Papez Theory of Emotion' (1949) 11(6) *Psychosomatic Medicine* 338.

Makinodan, M, Rosen, KM, Ito, S and Corfas, G, 'A Critical Period for Social Experience–Dependent Oligodendrocyte Maturation and Myelination' (2012) 337(6100) *Science* 1357.

Mansfield, HC and Winthrop, D (eds and transl), *Alexis de Tocqueville, Democracy in America* (Chicago, The University of Chicago Press, 2000).

Marazziti, D, Baroni, S, Landi, P, Ceresoli, D and Dell'Osso, L, 'The Neurobiology of Moral Sense: Facts or Hypotheses?' (2013) 12(1) *Annals of General Psychiatry* 6.

Marinova, Z and Maercker, A, 'Biological Correlates of Complex Posttraumatic Stress Disorder – State of Research and Future Directions' (2015) 6 *European Journal of Psychotraumatology* 25913.

Martinson, R, 'What Works? – Questions and Answers About Prison Reform' (Spring 1974) 35 *The Public Interest* 22.

—— 'New Findings, New Views: A Note of Caution Regarding Sentencing Reform' (1978) 7 *Hofstra Law Review* 243.

Martufi, A, 'The Paths of Offender Rehabilitation and the European Dimension of Punishment: New Challenges for an Old Ideal?' (2018) 25(6) *Maastricht Journal of European and Comparative Law* 672.

Maruna, S, 'Desistance and Restorative Justice: It's Now or Never' (2016) 4 *Restorative Justice: An International Journal* 289.

Maruna, S and LeBel, TP, 'The Desistance Paradigm in Correctional Practice: From Programmes to Lives' in F McNeill, P Raynor and C Trotter (eds), *Offender Supervision: New Directions in Theory, Research and Practice* (Cullompton, Willan Publishing, 2010) 65.

Matsuda, KN, Melde, C, Taylor, TJ, Freng, A and Esbensen, FA, 'Gang Membership and Adherence to the "Code of the Street"' (2013) 30(3) *Justice Quarterly* 440.

McCrory, E, De Brito, SA and Viding, E, 'Research Review: The Neurobiology and Genetics of Maltreatment and Adversity' (2010) 51(10) *Journal of Child Psychology and Psychiatry* 1079.

McNeill, F, 'Four Forms of 'Offender' Rehabilitation: Towards an Interdisciplinary Perspective' (2012) 17 *Legal and Criminological Psychology* 18.

—— 'Punishment as Rehabilitation' in G Bruinsma and D Weisburd (eds), *Encyclopedia of Criminology and Criminal Justice* (New York, Springer, 2014) 4195.

Melde, C and Esbensen, FA, 'Gang Membership as a Turning Point in the Life Course' (2011) 49(2) *Criminology* 513.

Mendez, MF, Anderson, E and Shapira, JS, 'An Investigation of Moral Judgement in Frontotemporal Dementia' (2005) 18(4) *Cognitive and Behavioral Neurology* 193.

Mendez, M, 'The Neurobiology of Moral Behavior: Review and Neuropsychiatric Implications' (2009) 14(11) *CNS Spectrums* 608.

Metcalfe, J and Mischel, W, 'A Hot/Cool System Analysis of Delay of Gratification: Dynamics of Willpower' (1999) 106 *Psychological Review* 3.

Michael, J and Wechsler, H, 'A Rationale of the Law of Homicide II' (1937) 37(8) *Columbia Law Review* 1261.

Miller, EM, Rodriguez, C, Kim, B and McClure, SM, 'Delay Discounting: A Two-Systems Perspective' in JJ Gross (ed) *Handbook of Emotion Regulation*, 2nd edn (New York, Guilford Press, 1995) 93.

Misheva, V, Webbink, D and Martin, NG, 'The Effect of Child Maltreatment on Illegal and Problematic Behaviour: New Evidence on the "Cycle of Violence" Using Twins Data' (2017) 30 *Journal of Population Economics* 1035.

Moe, AM, 'Blurring the Boundaries: Women's Criminality in the Context of Abuse' (2004) 32(3–4) *Women's Studies Quarterly* 116.

Moore, MS, 'The Relevance of Philosophy to Law and Psychiatry' (1983) 6(2) *International Journal of Law and Psychiatry* 177.

—— *Law and Psychiatry: Rethinking the Relationship* (New York, Cambridge University Press, 1984).

—— 'Choice, Character, and Excuse' in EF Paul, FD Miller and J Paul (eds), *Crime, Culpability, and Remedy* (Oxford, Blackwell, 1990).

—— *Act and Crime: The Philosophy of Action and Its Implications for Criminal Law* (New York, Oxford University Press, 1993).

—— *Placing Blame: A Theory of the Criminal Law* (New York, Oxford University Press, 1997).

—— 'Stephen Morse on the Fundamental Psycho-Legal Error' (2016) 10 *Criminal Law and Philosophy* 45.

—— 'The Neuroscience of Volitional Excuse' in DM Patterson (ed), *Philosophical Foundations of Law and Neuroscience: State of the Art* (New York, Oxford University Press, 2016) 179.

—— *Law and Psychiatry: Rethinking the Relationship* (New York, Cambridge University Press, 1984).

Moors, A, Ellsworth, PC, Scherer, KR and Frijda, NH, 'Appraisal Theories of Emotion: State of the Art and Future Development' (2013) 5(2) *Emotion Review* 119.

Morris, A, 'Criminal Insanity' (1967) 43 *Washington Law Review* 583.

Morris, H, 'Persons and Punishment' (1968) 52 *The Monist* 475.

Morris, N, *The Future of Imprisonment* (Chicago, University of Chicago Press, 1974).

Morse, SJ, 'The Twilight of Welfare Criminology: A Reply to Judge Bazelon' (1975) 49 *Southern California Law Review* 1247.

—— 'Undiminished Confusion in Diminished Capacity' (1984) 75 *Journal of Criminal Law and Criminology* 1.

—— 'Excusing the Crazy: The Insanity Defense Reconsidered' (1985) 58 *Southern California Law Review* 777.
—— 'Culpability and Control' (1993) 142 *University of Pennsylvania Law Review* 1587.
—— 'Excusing and the New Excuse Defenses: A Legal and Conceptual Review' (1998) 23 *Crime and Justice* 329.
—— 'Deprivation and Desert' in WC Heffernan and J Kleinig (eds), *From Social Justice to Criminal Justice: Poverty and the Administration of Criminal Law* (New York, Oxford University Press, 2000) 114.
—— 'Rationality and Responsibility' (2000) 74 *Southern California Law Review* 251.
—— 'Diminished Capacity' in J Dressler (ed) *Encyclopedia of Crime and Justice, Vol. 2* (New York, Macmillan Reference USA, 2002).
—— 'Diminished Rationality, Diminished Responsibility' (2003) 1 *Ohio State Journal of Criminal Law* 289.
—— 'New Neuroscience, Old Problems: Legal Implications of Brain Science' (2004) 6(4) *Cerebrum: the Dana Forum of Brain Science* 81.
—— 'The Non-problem of Free Will in Forensic Psychiatry and Psychology' (2007) 25(2) *Behavioral Sciences and the Law* 203.
—— 'Determinism and the Death of Folk Psychology: Two Challenges to Responsibility from Neuroscience' (2008) 9 *Minnesota Journal of Law Science and Technology* 1.
—— 'Insanity Defense Reform Act (IDRA)' in BL Cutler (ed), *Encyclopedia of Psychology and Law* (Thousand Oaks, SAGE Publications, 2008) 373.
—— 'Avoiding Irrational Neurolaw Exuberance: A Plea for Neuromodesty' (2011) 62 *Mercer Law Review* 837.
—— 'Severe Environmental Deprivation (aka RSB): A Tragedy, Not a Defense' (2011) 2 *Alabama Civil Rights and Civil Liberties Law Review* 147.
—— 'Commentary: Reflections on Remorse' (2014) 42 *Journal of the American Academy of Psychiatry and the Law* 15.
—— 'Legal Insanity in the Age of Neuroscience' in DM Patterson and S Moratti (eds), *Legal Insanity and the Brain* (Oxford, Hart Publishing, 2014) 260.
Mousourakis, G, 'Character, Choice, and Criminal Responsibility' (1998) 39 *Le Cahiers De Droit* 51.
Mumtaz, F, Khan, MI, Zubair, M and Dehpour, AR, 'Neurobiology and Consequences of Social Isolation Stress in Animal Model – A Comprehensive Review' (2018) 105 *Biomedicine and Pharmacotherapy* 1205.
Murphy, CM, Stosny, S and Morrel, TM, 'Change in Self-Esteem and Physical Aggression during Treatment for Partner Violent Men' (2005) 20(4) *Journal of Family Violence* 201.
Murphy, JG, *Retribution, Justice and Therapy* (Dordrecht, D. Reidel Pub, 1979).
—— 'Retribution' in E Luna (ed), *Reforming Criminal Justice, Vol. 4: Punishment, Incarceration and Release* (Phoenix, Arizona State University, 2017).
Muscatell, KA, Addis, DR and Kensinger, EA, 'Self-Involvement Modulates the Effective Connectivity of the Autobiographical Memory Network' (2010) 5 *Social Cognitive and Affective Neuroscience* 68.
Mustard, D, 'Racial, Ethnic, and Gender Disparities in Sentencing: Evidence from the U.S. Federal Courts' (2001) 44 *The Journal of Law and Economics* 285.
Naqvi, N, Shiv, B and Bechara, A, 'The Role of Emotion in Decision Making: A Cognitive Neuroscience Perspective' (2006) 15(5) *Current Directions in Psychological Science* 260.
Neal, S, Kent, M, Bardi, M and Lambert, KG, 'Enriched Environment Exposure Enhances Social Interactions and Oxytocin Responsiveness in Male Long-Evans Rats' (2018) 12 *Frontiers in Behavioral Neuroscience* 198.
Nee, C and Vernham, Z, 'Expertise and Its Contribution to the Notion of Protective Factors in Offender Rehabilitation and Desistance' (2017) 32 *Aggression and Violent Behavior* 37.
Neff, KD, Kirkpatrick, KL and Rude, SS, 'Self-Compassion and Adaptive Psychological Functioning' (2007) 41 *Journal of Research in Personality* 139.
Nelkin, DK, 'Freedom, Responsibility, and the Challenge of Situationism' (2005) 29 *Midwest Studies in Philosophy* 181.

Nicolle, A, Bach, DR, Frith, C and Dolan, RJ, 'Amygdala Involvement in Self-blame Regret' (2011) 6(2) *Social Neuroscience* 178.

Nilsen, ES, 'Decency, Dignity, and Desert: Restoring Ideals of Humane Punishment to Constitutional Discourse' (2007) 41 *University of California Davis Law Review* 111.

Norrie, A, *Crime, Reason, and History: A Critical Introduction to Criminal Law* (Cambridge, Cambridge University Press, 1993).

—— 'The Limits of Justice: Finding Fault in the Criminal Law' (1996) 59 *The Modern Law Review* 540.

—— 'Practical Reasoning and Criminal Responsibility: A Jurisprudential Approach' in DB Cornish and RV Clarke, *The Reasoning Criminal: Choice Perspectives on Offending* (New Brunswick, Transaction Publishers, 2014) 217.

Norris, DN, 'Reports to the Membership' (2008) 165(9) *American Journal of Psychiatry* 1214.

Nourse, VF, 'Hearts and Minds: Understanding the New Culpability' (2002) 6 *Buffalo Criminal Law Review* 361.

Nussbaum, MC, *Women and Human Development: the Capabilities Approach, Vol 3* (New York, Cambridge University Press, 2000).

O'Hare, MR, *The History of the Pleas to the Crow, Vol.1* (In the Savoy, 1736).

O'Hear, MM, 'Not Just Kids Stuff – Extending Graham and Miller to Adults' (2013) 78 *Missouri Law Review* 1087.

O'Mahony, D and Doak, J, *Reimagining Restorative Justice: Agency and Accountability in the Criminal Process* (Portland, Bloomsbury Publishing, 2017).

Ochsner, KN and Gross, JJ, 'The Neural Bases of Emotion and Emotion Regulation: A Valuation Perspective' in JJ Gross and R Thompson (eds), *The Handbook of Emotion Regulation*, 2nd edn (New York, Guilford Press, 2014) 23.

Ochsner, KN, Silvers, JA and Buhle, JT, 'Functional Imaging Studies of Emotion Regulation: A Synthetic Review and Evolving Model of the Cognitive Control of Emotion' (2012) 1251 *Annals of the New York Academy of Sciences* E1.

Ogloff, JRP, 'A Comparison of Insanity Defense Standards on Juror Decision Making' (1991) 15(5) *Law and Human Behavior* 509.

Osofsky, MJ, Bandura, A and Zimbardo, PG, 'The Role of Moral Disengagement in the Execution Process' (2005) 29(4) *Law and Human Behavior* 371.

Oveis, C, Horberg, EJ and Keltner, D, 'Compassion, Pride, and Social Intuitions of Self-Other Similarity' (2010) 98(4) *Journal of Personality and Social Psychology* 618.

Papez, JW, 'A Proposed Mechanism of Emotion' (1937) 38(4) *Archives of Neurology and Psychiatry* 725.

Parry, J, *Criminal Mental Health and Disability Law, Evidence, and Testimony: A Comprehensive Reference Manual for Lawyers, Judges, and Criminal Justice Professionals* (Chicago, American Bar Association, 2009).

Pascual, L, Gallardo-Pujol, D and Rodrigues, P, 'How Does Morality Work in the Brain? A Functional and Structural Perspective of Moral Behavior' (2013) 7 *Frontiers in Integrative Neuroscience* 65.

Paternoster, R and Bushway, S, 'Desistance and the "Feared Self": Toward an Identity Theory of Crime Desistance' (2009) 99 *Journal of Criminal Law and Criminology* 1103.

Patil, I and Silani, G, 'Reduced Empathic Concern Leads to Utilitarian Moral Judgments in Trait Alexithymia' (2014) 5 *Frontiers in Psychology* 501.

Penney, S, 'Impulse Control and Criminal Responsibility: Lessons from Neuroscience' (2012) 35(2) *International Journal of Law and Psychiatry* 99.

Pereboom, D, *Living Without Free Will* (Cambridge, Cambridge University Press, 2006).

Perelman, AM, Miller, SL, Clements, CB, Rodriguez, A, Allen, K and Cavanaugh, R, 'Meditation in a Deep South Prison: A Longitudinal Study of the Effects of Vipassana' (2012) 51(3) *Journal of Offender Rehabilitation* 176.

Perry, D, Hendler, T and Shamay-Tsoory, SG, 'Projecting Memories: The Role of the Hippocampus in Emotional Mentalizing' (2011) 54(2) *Neuroimage* 1669.

Pessoa, L, 'On the Relationship Between Emotion and Cognition' (2008) 9(2) *Nature Reviews Neuroscience* 148.

Pfaff, J, *Locked In: The True Causes of Mass Incarceration and How to Achieve Real Reform* (New York, Basic Books, 2017).

Phelps, EA, Lempert, KM and Sokol-Hessner, P, 'Emotion and Decision Making: Multiple Modulatory Neural Circuits' (2014) 37 *Annual Review of Neuroscience* 263.

Phelps, MS, 'The Paradox of Probation: Community Supervision in the Age of Mass Incarceration' (2013) 35(1–2) *Law & Policy* 51.

Piaget, J, *The Moral Judgment in the Child* (Harcourt, Brace & Company, 1932).

Pifferi, M, *Rethinking Punishment, A Comparative History of Criminology and Penology in the Nineteenth and Twentieth Centuries* (New York, Oxford University Press, 2016).

Pillsbury, SH, *Judging Evil: Rethinking the Law of Murder and Manslaughter* (New York, New York University Press, 1998).

—— 'Emotion and Criminal Punishment: in Principle and in Practice' (2016) *Emotion Researcher*.

Piquero, AR, 'Youth Matters: The Meaning of Miller for Theory, Research, and Policy Regarding Developmental/Life-Course Criminology' (2013) 39 *New England Journal on Criminal and Civil Confinement* 347.

Piquero, AR and Blumstein, A, 'Does Incapacitation Reduce Crime?' (2007) 23(4) *Journal of Quantitative Criminology* 267.

Ploch, A, 'Why Dignity Matters: Dignity and the Right (or Not) to Rehabilitation from International and National Perspectives' (2011) 44 *New York University Journal of International Law and Politics* 887.

Porcelli, AJ and Delgado, MR, 'Acute Stress Modulates Risk Taking in Financial Decision Making' (2009) 20(3) *Psychological Science* 278.

Pound, R, 'Do We Need a Philosophy of Law?' (1905) 5 *Columbia Law Review* 339.

—— *Introduction to Sayre's Cases on Criminal Law* (Eagan, MN: Lawyers Co-Operative, 1927).

—— *The Formative Era of American Criminal Law* (Boston, Little, Brown & Co., 1938).

Power, JD and Schlaggar, BL, 'Neural Plasticity Across the Lifespan' (2017) 6 *Wiley Interdisciplinary Reviews: Developmental Biology* e216.

Powers, JP and LaBar, KS, 'Regulating Emotion Through Distancing: A Taxonomy, Neurocognitive Model, and Supporting Meta-Analysis' (2019) 96 *Neuroscience and Biobehavioral Reviews* 155.

Preckel, K, Kanske, P and Singer, T, 'On the Interaction of Social Affect and Cognition: Empathy, Compassion, and Theory of Mind' (2018) 19 *Current Opinion in Behavioral Sciences* 1.

Primoratz, I, *Justifying Legal Punishment* (London, Humanities Press, 1989).

Prochaska, JO, DiClemente, CC and Norcross, JC, 'In Search of How People Change: Applications to Addictive Behaviors' (1992) 47 *American Psychologist* 1102.

Prochaska, JO, Redding, CA and Evers, KE, 'The Transtheoretical Model and Stages of Change' in K Glanz, BK Rimer and FM Lewis (eds), *Health Behavior and Health Education: Theory, Research, and Practice*, 3rd edn (San Francisco, Jossey-Bass Inc., 2002).

Prochaska, JO, Velicer, WF, DiClemente, CC and Fava, J, 'Measuring Processes of Change: Applications to the Cessation of Smoking' (1988) 56(4) *Journal of Consulting and Clinical Psychology* 520.

Quigley, B and Godchaux, S, 'Prisoner Human Rights Advocacy' (2014) 16 *Loyola Journal of Public Interest Law* 359.

Raider, L, 'Toward a New Test for the Insanity Defense: Incorporating the Discoveries of Neuroscience into Moral and Legal Theories' (1998) 46 *UCLA Law Review* 289.

Raine, A and Yang, Y, 'Neural Foundations to Moral Reasoning and Antisocial Behavior' (2006) 1(3) *Social Cognitive and Affective Neuroscience* 203.

Rawls, J, '*Two Concepts of Rules*' (1955) 64 *The Philosophical Review* 3.

Raynor, P, 'Some Observations on Rehabilitation and Justice' (1997) 36(3) *The Howard Journal of Criminal Justice* 248.

Raz, J, *Engaging Reason: On the Theory of Value and Action* (Oxford, Oxford University Press, 1999).

Reimund, ME, 'The Law and Restorative Justice: Friend or Foe? A Systemic Look at the Legal Issues in Restorative Justice' (2004) 53 *Drake Law Review* 667.

Reisel, D, *Rewiring Our Morality* (New York, TED Conferences, 2014).

Reitz, KR, 'Sentencing Guidelines' in J Dressler (ed), *Encyclopedia of Crime and Justice, Vol. 2* (New York, MacMillan Reference, 2002) 1429.
—— *American Exceptionalism in Crime and Punishment* (New York, Oxford University Press, 2017).
Rimé, B, 'Interpersonal Emotion Regulation' in JJ Gross and RA Thompson (ed), *Handbook of Emotion Regulation* (New York, The Guilford Press, 2007) 466.
Ristroph, A, 'Desert, Democracy and Sentencing Reform' (2005) 96 *Journal of Criminal Law and Criminology* 1293.
—— 'Desert, Democracy, and Sentencing Reform' (2005) 96 *Journal of Criminal Law and Criminology* 1293.
—— 'Proportionality as a Principle of Limited Government' (2005) 55 *Duke Law Journal* 263.
—— 'How (Not) To Think Like a Punisher' (2009) 61 *Florida Law Review* 727.
—— 'Respect and Resistance in Punishment Theory' (2009) 97(2) *California Law Review* 601.
—— 'Hope, Imprisonment, and the Constitution' (2010) 23 *Federal Sentencing Reporter* 75.
Roberton, T, Daffern, M and Bucks, RS, 'Emotion Regulation and Aggression' (2012) 17 *Aggression and Violent Behavior* 72.
Robinson, G and McNeill, F, 'Exploring the Dynamics of Compliance with Community Penalties' (2008) 12(4) *Theoretical Criminology* 431.
Robinson, PH, 'Criminal Law Defenses: A Systematic Analysis' (1982) 82(2) *Columbia Law Review* 199.
—— 'Mens Rea' in J Dressler (ed), *Encyclopedia of Crime and Justice, Vol. 2* (New York, Macmillan Reference USA, 2002) 995.
—— 'Abnormal Mental State Mitigations of Murder – The U.S. Perspective' in A Reed and M Bohlander (eds), *Loss of Control and Diminished Responsibility: Domestic, Comparative and International Perspectives* (New York, Ashgate Publishing, 2011) 291.
Robinson, PH and Williams, TS, 'Mapping American Criminal Law: Variations Across the Fifty States: Ch. 14 Insanity Defense' (2017) *Faculty Scholarship at University of Pennsylvania Law* 1718.
Rolls, ET, *The Brain and Emotion* (New York, Oxford University Press, 1999).
Rosenzweig, MR and Bennett, EL, 'Cerebral Changes in Rats Exposed Individually to an Enriched Environment' (1972) 80(2) *Journal of Comparative and Physiological Psychology* 304.
Rossner, M, *Just Emotions: Rituals of Restorative Justice* (Oxford, Oxford University Press, 2013).
Rotman, E, 'Do Criminal Offenders Have a Constitutional Right to Rehabilitation?' (1986) 77 *Journal of Criminal Law and Criminology* 1023.
—— *Beyond Punishment: A New View on the Rehabilitation of Criminal Offenders*, (Westport, Greenwood Press, 1990).
—— 'Beyond Punishment' in A Duff and D Garland (eds), *A Reader on Punishment* (Oxford, Oxford University Press, 1994) 281.
Rubin, E, 'Just Say No to Retribution' (2003) 7 *Buffalo Criminal Law Review* 17.
Sabini, J and Silver, M, 'In Defense of Shame: Shame in the Context of Guilt and Embarrassment' (1997) 27(1) *Journal for the Theory of Social Behavior* 1.
Sale, A, Berardi, N and Maffei, L, Environment and Brain Plasticity: Towards an Endogenous Pharmacotherapy' (2014) 94 *Physiological Reviews* 189.
Sander, D, 'Models of Emotion: The Affective Neuroscience Approach' in J Armony and P Vuilleumier (eds), *The Cambridge Handbook of Human Affective Neuroscience* (New York, Cambridge University Press, 2013) 5.
Saver, JL and Damasio, AR, 'Preserved Access and Processing of Social Knowledge in a Patient with Acquired Sociopathy Due to Ventromedial Frontal Damage' (1991) 29(12) *Neuropsychologia* 1241.
Schachter, S and Singer, J, 'Cognitive, Social, and Physiological Determinants of Emotional State' (1962) 69(5) *Psychological Review* 379.
Scheff, TJ and Retzinger, SM, *Emotions and Violence: Shame and Rage in Destructive Conflicts* (Lincoln, iUniverse Inc, 1991).
Schipper, M and Petermann, F, 'Relating Empathy and Emotion Regulation: Do Deficits in Empathy Trigger Emotion Dysregulation?' (2013) 8(1) *Social Neuroscience* 101.
Schneider, B and Koenigs, M, 'Human Lesion Studies of Ventromedial Prefrontal Cortex' (2017) 107 *Neuropsychologia* 84.

Schopp, RF, *Automatism, Insanity, and the Psychology of Criminal Responsibility: A Philosophical Inquiry* (New York, Cambridge University Press, 1991).

Schore, AN, 'Early Relational Trauma, Disorganized Attachment, and the Development of a Predisposition to Violence', in D Siegel and M Solomon (eds), *Healing trauma: Attachment, Mind, Body, and Brain* (New York, WW Norton & Company, 2003) 107.

Schwartz, N, 'Emotion, Cognition, and Decision Making' (2000) 14(4) *Cognition and Emotion* 433.

Schwartz, N and Clore, GL, 'How Do I Feel about It? The Informative Function of Mood' in K Fiedler and JP Forgas (eds), *Affect, Cognition, and Social Behavior* (Toronto, Hogrefe & Huber Publishers, 1988) 44.

Schwartz, N, Van Lange, PA, Kruglanski, A and Higgins, ET, 'Feeling as Information' in PA Van Lange, AW Kruglanski and ET Higgins (eds), *Handbook of Theories of Social Psychology, Vol. 2* (Thousand Oaks, SAGE Publications, 2011) 562.

Scott, E, Duell, N and Steinberg, L, 'Brain Development, Social Context, and Justice Policy' (2018) 57 *Washington University Journal of Law and Policy* 13.

Sentencing Reform Act of 1983: Report of the Committee on the Judiciary United States Senate, (Washington, US Government Printing Office, 1983).

Seppala, E, Rossomando, T and Doty, JR, 'Social Connection and Compassion: Important Predictors of Health and Well-Being' (2013) 80(2) *Social Research: An International Quarterly* 411.

Shalev, S, 'Solitary Confinement and Supermax Prisons: A Human Rights and Ethical Analysis' (2011) 11(2–3) *Journal of Forensic Psychology Practice* 151.

Shannon, BD, 'The Time is Right to Revise the Texas Insanity Defense: An Essay' (2006) 39 *Texas Tech Law Review* 67.

Sherman, LW, 'Defiance, Deterrence, and Irrelevance: A Theory of the Criminal Sanction' (1993) 30(4) *Journal of Research in Crime and Delinquency* 445.

Sherman, LW and Strang, H, *Restorative Justice: The Evidence* (London, The Smith Institute, 2007).

Shih, M, Wang, E, Trahan Bucher, A and Stotzer, R, 'Perspective Taking: Reducing Prejudice Towards General Outgroups and Specific Individuals' (2009) 12(5) *Group Processes & Intergroup Relations* 565.

Shoemaker, DW, 'Caring, Identification, and Agency' (2003) 114 *Ethics* 88.

Shultziner, D and Rabinovici, I, 'Human Dignity, Self-Worth and Humiliation: A Comparative Legal–Psychological Approach' (2012) 18 *Psychology, Public Policy, and Law* 105.

Siegel, DJ, *The Developing Mind: How Relationships and the Brain Interact to Shape Who We Are* (New York, Guildford Press, 2020).

Simon, HA, *Models of Man: Social and Rational. Mathematical Essays on Rational Behavior in Social Settings* (New York, Wiley, 1957).

—— *Reason in Human Affairs* (Stanford, Stanford University Press, 1983).

Simon, J, 'Dignity and Risk: The Long Road from Graham v. Florida to Abolition of Life Without Parole' in CJ Ogletree and A Sarat (eds), *Life Without Parole: America's New Death Penalty?* (New York, NYU Press, 2012) 282.

Simon, RJ and Aaronson, DE, *The Insanity Defense: A Critical Assessment of Law and Policy in the Post-Hinckley Era* (New York, Praeger Publishers, 1988).

Singer, T and Klimecki, OM, 'Empathy and Compassion' (2014) 24(18) *Current Biology* R875.

Sinnott-Armstrong, W and Levy, K, 'Insanity Defenses' in J Deigh and D Dolinko (eds), *The Oxford Handbook of Philosophy of Criminal Law* (New York, Oxford University Press, 2011) 299.

Slovenko, R, 'Psychiatry, Criminal Law, and the Role of the Psychiatrist' (1963) *Duke Law Journal* 395.

—— *Psychiatry in Law/Law in Psychiatry*, 2nd edn (New York, Routledge, 2009).

Smith, CA and Thornberry, TP, 'The Relationship Between Childhood Maltreatment and Adolescent Involvement in Delinquency' (1995) 33(4) *Criminology* 451.

Smith, CA and Lazarus, RS, 'Emotion and Adaptation' in LA Pervin (ed), *Handbook of Personality: Theory and Research* (New York, Guilford Press, 1990) 609.

Smith, PS, 'The Effects of Solitary Confinement on Prison Inmates: A Brief History and Review of the Literature' (2006) 34 *Crime and Justice* 441.

Snowden, JS, 'Empathy in Frontotemporal Dementia' (2018) 31(2) *Cognitive and Behavioral Neurology* 111.

Sobeloff, SE, 'Insanity and the Criminal Law: From McNaghten to Durham, and Beyond' (1955) 41 *American Bar Association Journal* 793.

Solomon, RC, *Not Passion's Slave: Emotions and Choice* (New York, Oxford University Press, 2003).

Spain, E, *The Role of Emotions in Criminal Law Defences: Duress, Necessity and Lesser Evils* (Cambridge, Cambridge University Press, 2011).

Starcke, K, Wolf, OT, Markowitsch, HJ and Brand, M, 'Anticipatory Stress Influences Decision Making under Explicit Risk Conditions' (2008) 122(2) *Behavioral Neuroscience* 1352.

Steiker, CS and Steiker, JM, 'Graham Lets the Sun Shine In: The Supreme Court Opens a Window Between Two Formerly Walled-off Approaches to Eighth Amendment Proportionality Challenges' (2010) 23 *Federal Sentencing Reporter* 79.

Steiner, B and Cain, CM, 'The Relationship Between Inmate Misconduct, Institutional Violence, and Administrative Segregation: A Systematic Review of the Evidence' in M Garcia, CM Cain, F Cohen, H Foster, NA Frost, R Kapoor and RM Labrecque, *Restrictive Housing in the U.S.: Issues, Challenges, and Future Directions* (Washington DC, National Institute of Justice, 2016) 165.

Stevens, FL, Hurley, RA and Taber, KH, 'Anterior Cingulate Cortex: Unique Role in Cognition and Emotion' (2011) 23(2) *Journal of Neuropsychiatry and Clinical Neurosciences* 121.

Stevenson, B, *Just Mercy: A Story of Justice and Redemption* (New York, Spiegel & Grau, 2015).

Stosny, S, *Treating Attachment Abuse: A Compassionate Approach* (New York, Springer Publishing Co., 1995).

Stuewig, J, Tangney, JP, Heigel, C, Harty, L and McCloskey, L, 'Shaming, Blaming, and Maiming: Functional Links Among the Moral Emotions, Externalization of Blame, and Aggression' (2010) 44(1) *Journal of Research in Personality* 91.

Tadros, V, 'The Characters of Excuse' (2001) 21(3) *Oxford Journal of Legal Studies* 495.

Tangney, JP, Stuewig, J and Hafez, L, 'Shame, Guilt and Remorse: Implications for Offender Populations' (2011) 22(5) *Journal of Forensic Psychiatry and Psychology* 706.

Tangney, JP, Stuewig, J and Mashek, DJ, 'Moral Emotions and Moral Behavior' (2007) 58 *Annual Review of Psychology* 345.

Telzer, EH, Van Hoorn, J, Rogers, CR and Do, KT, 'Social Influence on Positive Youth Development: A Developmental Neuroscience Perspective' (2018) 54 *Advances in Child Development and Behavior* 215.

Teper, R, Zhong, CB and Inzlicht, M, 'How Emotions Shape Moral Behavior: Some Answers (and Questions) for the Field of Moral Psychology' (2015) 9(1) *Social & Personality Psychology Compass* 1.

The Associated Press, 'Hinckley Acquittal Brings Moves to Change Insanity Defense' (1982) *The New York Times* D21.

The Sentencing Project, 'Report of The Sentencing Project to the United Nations Special Rapporteur on Contemporary Forms of Racism, Racial Discrimination, Xenophobia, and Related Intolerance Regarding Racial Disparities in the United States Criminal Justice System' (March 2018).

Thoits, PA, 'Social Support as Coping Assistance' (1986) 54(4) *Journal of Consulting and Clinical Psychology* 416.

Thomas, KA, 'Beyond Mitigation: Towards a Theory of Allocution' (2006) 75 *Fordham Law Review* 2641.

Thomson, JJ, 'Killing, Letting Die, and the Trolley Problem' (1976) 59(2) *The Monist* 204.

Toews, B, *The Little Book of Restorative Justice for People in Prison: Rebuilding the Web of Relationships* (Intercourse, Good Books, 2006).

Tonry, M, 'Can Twenty-First Century Punishment Policies Be Justified in Principle?' in M Tonry (ed), *Retributivism Has a Past: Has it a Future?* (New York, Oxford University Press, 2011).

—— 'Remodeling American Sentencing: A Ten-Step Blueprint for Moving Past Mass Incarceration' (2014) 13(4) *Criminology and Public Policy* 503.

—— 'Can Desert be Just in an Unjust World?' in A Simester, A du Bois-Pedain, U Neuman (eds), *Liberal Criminal Theory: Essays for Andreas von Hirsch* (Portland, Hart Publishing, 2014).

Tracy, JL, Robins, RW and Tangney, JP 'The Self in Self-conscious Emotions: A Cognitive Appraisal Approach' in JL Tracy, RW Robins and JP Tangney (eds), *The Self-Conscious Emotions: Theory and Research* (New York, Guilford Press, 2007) 3.

Twenge, JM and Baumeister, RF, 'Social Exclusion Increases Aggression and Self-Defeating Behavior while Reducing Intelligent Thought and Prosocial Behavior' in D Abrams, MA Hogg and J Marques (eds), *Social Psychology of Inclusion and Exclusion* (New York, Psychology Press, 2004) 27.

Twenge, JM, Baumeister, RF, DeWall, CN, Ciarocco, NJ and Bartels, JM, 'Social Exclusion Decreases Prosocial Behavior' (2007) 92 *Journal of Personality and Social Psychology* 56.

Umbach, R, Raine, A and Leonard, NR, 'Cognitive Decline as a Result of Incarceration and the Effects of a CBT/MT Intervention: A Cluster-Randomized Controlled Trial' (2018) 45 *Criminal Justice and Behavior* 31.

U.S. Department of Justice, 'Prisoners in 2018' (NCJ 253516) (April 2020).

U.S. Department of Justice, 'Jail Inmates in 2018' (NCJ 253044) (March 2020).

Valk, SL, Bernhardt, BC, Trautwein, FM, Böckler, A, Kanske, P, Guizard, N, Collins, DL and Singer, T, 'Structural Plasticity of the Social Brain: Differential Change after Socio-Affective and Cognitive Mental Training' (2017) 3(10) *Science Advances* e1700489.

Van den Stock, J and Kumfor, F, 'Behavioural Variant Frontotemporal Dementia: At the Interface of Interoception, Emotion and Social Cognition?' (2019) 115 *Cortex* 335.

Van der Kolk, BA, *The Body Keeps the Score: Brain, Mind, and Body in the Healing of Trauma* (New York, Penguin Books, 2014) 170.

Van der Kolk, BA and Rita, E, 'Childhood Abuse and Neglect and Loss of Self-regulation' (1994) 58(2) *Bulletin of the Menninger Clinic* 145.

Vasiljevic, M and Viki, GT, 'Dehumanization, Moral Disengagement and Public Attitudes to Crime and Punishment' in PG Bain, J Vaes and JP Leyens (eds), *Humanness and Dehumanization* (New York, Psychology Press, 2013) 137.

Vaughan, B, 'The Internal Narrative of Desistance' (2007) 47(3) *The British Journal of Criminology* 390.

Velotti, P, Garofalo, C, Bottazzi, F and Caretti, V, 'Faces of Shame: Implications for Self-Esteem, Emotion Regulation, Aggression, and Well-Being' (2017) 151(2) *The Journal of Psychology* 171.

Von Hirsch, A, *Doing Justice: The Choice of Punishments, Report of the Committee for the Study of Incarceration* (New York, Hill and Wang, 1976).

Wagner, DD and Heartherton, TF, 'Giving in to Temptation: The Emerging Cognitive Neuroscience of Self-Regulatory Failure' in KD Vohs and RF Baumeister (eds), *Handbook of Self-Regulation: Research, Theory and Applications*, 2nd edn (New York, Guilford Press, 2011) 41.

Walker, AE, 'American Oresteia: Herbert Wechsler, the Model Penal Code, and the Uses of Revenge' (2009) *Wisconsin Law Review* 1017.

Wall, AE and Barth, RP, 'Aggressive and Delinquent Behavior of Maltreated Adolescents: Risk Factors and Gender Differences' (2005) 8 *Stress, Trauma, & Crisis* 1.

Ward, BH, 'Sentencing Without Remorse' (2006) 38 Loyola University Chicago Law Journal 131.

Wayland, K, 'The Importance of Recognizing Trauma Throughout Capital Mitigation Investigations and Presentations' (2008) 36 *Hofstra Law Review* 923.

Weaver, B, *Offending and Desistance: The Importance of Social Relations* (New York, Routledge, 2015).

Wechsler, H and Michael, J, 'A Rationale of the Law of Homicide I' (1937) 37(5) *Columbia Law Review* 701.

Weinstein, JB, *Does Religion Have a Role in Criminal Sentencing?'* (2007) 23 *Touro Law Review* 539.

Weisberg, R, 'Barrock Lecture: Reality-Challenged Philosophies of Punishment' (2011) 95 *Marquette Law Review* 1203.

Wendell Holmes, O, *The Common Law* (Boston, Little, Brown & Company, 1881).

Wermink, H, Apel, B, Blokland, AAJ and Nieuwbeerta, P, 'Crime Preventive Effects of Incapacitation' in G Bruinsma and D Weisburd (eds), *Encyclopedia of Criminology and Criminal Justice* (New York, Springer, 2014) 731.

Westen, P, 'An Attitudinal Theory of Excuse' (2006) 25(3) *Law and Philosophy* 289.

Whitman JQ, *Harsh Justice: Criminal Punishment and the Widening Divide Between America and Europe* (New York, Oxford University Press, 2003).

—— 'A Plea Against Retributivism' (2003) 7 *Buffalo Criminal Law Review* 85.
—— 'What Happened to Tocqueville's America?' (2007) 74(2) *Social Research: an International Quarterly* 251.
—— 'The Case for Penal Modernism: Beyond Utility and Desert' (2014) 1(2) *Critical Analysis of Law: An International and Interdisciplinary Law Review* 143.
Widom, CS, 'Does Violence Beget Violence? A Critical Examination of the Literature' (1989) 106 *Psychological Bulletin* 3.
Wildeman, C and Andersen, L, 'Solitary Confinement Placement and Post-Release Mortality Risk Among Formerly Incarcerated Individuals: A Population-Based Study' (2020) 5(2) *Lancet Public Health* e107.
Wilkström, POH and Treiber, K, 'The Role of Self-control in Crime Causation: Beyond Gottfredson and Hirschi's general theory of crime' (2007) 4(2) *European Journal of Criminology* 237.
Williams, JEH, 'Defect of Reason from Disease of the Mind' (1957) 20 *Modern Law Review* 55.
Wilson, JQ, 'What Works?" Revisited: New Findings on Criminal Rehabilitation' (1980) 61 *The Public Interest* 3.
Wilson-Mendenhall, CD, Barrett, LF and Barsalou, LW, 'Situating Emotional Experience' (2013) 7 *Frontiers in Human Neuroscience* 764.
Wolf, S, *Freedom Within Reason* (New York, Oxford University Press, 1990).
Wolitz, D, 'Herbert Wechsler, Legal Process, and the Jurisprudential Roots of the Model Penal Code' (2015) 51 *Tulsa Law Review* 633.
Woo, CW, Koban, L, Kross, E, Lindquist, MA, Banich, MT, Ruzic, L, Andrews-Hanna, JR and Wager, TD, 'Separate Neural Representations for Physical Pain and Social Rejection' (2014) 5 *Nature Communications* 1.
Wright, RG, 'The Progressive Logic of Criminal Responsibility and the Circumstances of the Most Deprived' (1993) 43 *Catholic University Law Review* 459.
Yates, JF, 'Emotion Appraisal Tendencies and Carryover: How, Why, and … Therefore?' (2007) 17(3) *Journal of Consumer Psychology* 179.
Young, L and Koenigs, M, 'Investigating Emotion in Moral Cognition: A Review of Evidence from Functional Neuroimaging and Neuropsychology' (2007) 84(1) *British Medical Bulletin* 69.
Young, L, Bechara, A, Tranel, D, Damasio, H, Hauser, M and Damasio, A, 'Damage to Ventromedial Prefrontal Cortex Impairs Judgment of Harmful Intent' (2010) 65(6) *Neuron* 845.
Zaibert, L, 'The Instrument of Abolition, or Why Retributivism is the Only Real Justification of Punishment' (2013) 32 *Law and Philosophy* 33.
Zaki, J and Ochsner, KN, 'The Neuroscience of Empathy: Progress, Pitfalls and Promise' (2012) 15(5) *Nature Neuroscience* 675.
Zaki, J, 'Empathy Is a Moral Force' in K Gray and J Graham (eds), *Atlas of Moral Psychology* (New York, The Guilford Press, 2018) 49.
Zeelenberg, M, Nelissen, RM, Breugelmans, SM and Pieters, R, 'On Emotion Specificity in Decision Making: Why Feeling Is for Doing' (2008) 3 *Judgment and Decision Making* 18.
Zehr, H, *Changing Lenses: A New Focus for Crime and Justice* (Scottsdale, Herald Press, 1990).
—— *Changing Lenses: Restorative Justice for Our Times*, 25th Anniversary edn (Harrisonburg, Herald Press, 2015).
Zimring, FE and Hawkins, G, *Incapacitation: Penal Confinement and the Restraint of Crime* (New York, Oxford University Press, 1995).

INDEX

www.ingramcontent.com/pod-product-compliance
Ingram Content Group UK Ltd.
Pitfield, Milton Keynes, MK11 3LW, UK
UKHW022222151225
9585UKWH00003B/116

9 781509 934294